The *Mysterium* Lectures

Marie-Louise von Franz, Honorary Patron

**Studies in Jungian Psychology
by Jungian Analysts**

Daryl Sharp, General Editor

THE MYSTERIUM LECTURES

A Journey through C.G. Jung's
Mysterium Coniunctionis

EDWARD F. EDINGER

Transcribed and Edited by Joan Dexter Blackmer

Canadian Cataloguing in Publication Data

Edinger, Edward F. (Edward Ferdinand),
     The Mysterium lectures: a journey through C.G. Jung's
     Mysterium coniunctionis

(Studies in Jungian psychology by Jungian analysts; 66)

Lectures originally presented to the C.G. Jung Society of Los Angeles.

Includes bibliographical references and index.

ISBN 9780919123663

1. Jung, C.G. (Carl Gustav), 1875-1961.
Mysterium coniunctionis.   2. Alchemy.
3. Individuation (Psychology).
I. Blackmer, Joan. II. Title. III. Series.

QD26.E35 1995   150.19'54   C94-931717-9

INNER CITY BOOKS
21 Milroy Crescent Toronto, ON M1C 4B6
416-927-0355
www.innercitybooks.net / sales@innercitybooks.net

Honorary Patron: Marie-Louise von Franz.
Publisher and General Editor: Daryl Sharp.
Senior Editor: Victoria Cowan.

INNER CITY BOOKS was founded in 1980 to promote the
understanding and practical application of the work of C.G. Jung.

Cover: "Resurrection of the United Eternal Body," colorized woodcut
from the Frankfurt first edition of *Rosarium philosophorum* (1550).

Index by Daryl Sharp

Printed and bound in Canada by Rapido Livres Books
Reprinted 2021

Contents

Illustrations and Credits

CW refers to C.G. Jung, *The Collected Works:*
  CW 9ii = *Aion*
  CW 12 = *Psychology and Alchemy*
  CW 13 = *Alchemical Studies*
  CW 14 = *Mysterium Coniunctionis*
  CW 16 = *The Practice of Psychotherapy.*

Editor's Foreword

Mysterium Coniunctionis has been an object of fascination for me from the very start of my acquaintance with Jung's work almost twenty-five years ago. For many years I read at it and struggled unsuccessfully to grasp its heavily veiled meaning. Its images and phrases kept coming back to me as apt symbols of my experience, but always clothed in the riddles that symbols present—riddles that defied solution.

Thus, it was with considerable excitement that I learned of Edward Edinger's long seminar on *Mysterium Coniunctionis* presented during 1986-87 at the Jung Institute of Los Angeles. Eagerly I ordered the audio tapes.

With *Mysterium* in one hand, Edinger's voice in my ears and dictionaries at my elbow, I set out yet one more time to study the volume which had for so long both pulled me to it and kept me standing before its beautiful but locked gates. Here at last was someone who held keys to the gates and could provide an Ariadne's thread through the labyrinth. Lit by the lantern of Edinger's keen intelligence and long experience, the treasures heaped up by Jung's prodigious efforts in the gold mines of alchemy became more visible.

It was not long before I wanted to see a text of the lectures, so I set about transcribing the tapes. The material was proving to be of great practical value so I suggested to Edinger that it be put into written form for others who cared about Jung and who were as flummoxed as I by the complexities of *Mysterium.* He encouraged me to give it a try.

As the work proceeded, from across a continent Edinger patiently answered hundreds of queries ranging from the picayune to the cosmic; slowly *The Mysterium Lectures* found form. It was good news indeed when Inner City Books agreed to take on the task of publication.

In editing the transcript I have tried to keep the informal tone and personal immediacy of the original.* To aid those reading these lectures side by side with *Mysterium Coniunctionis,* I have cited the paragraphs in *Mysterium* that are relevant to Edinger's amplifications and reflections. We have included the illustrations mentioned in the seminar and have added others.

Jung is the great pioneer of the coming aeon. Through his Herculean labors in the alchemical mines he extracts a treasury of magnificent psychological material. Edinger mediates Jung's vast discoveries by connecting them to individual experience and everyday reality. He goes through *Mysterium* paragraph by paragraph,

---

* For those interested in listening to Edinger's presentation, the audio tapes are available from the C.G. Jung Bookstore in Los Angeles.

dissecting and amplifying the compact clusters of imagery so they become comprehensible, and shows us how to approach for ourselves others he must leave unexamined.

Edinger shares the practical tools he has fashioned over his many years of experience with the art and craft of psychotherapy. Throughout his vivid illumination of *Mysterium* he weaves what amounts to a working description of the anatomy of the psyche, a laboratory manual of developmental psychology and generous instruction in clinical practice. To my mind, he has rendered a service of the greatest importance.

I would like to acknowledge others, women in particular, who labored to give earthly reality to *Mysterium Coniunctionis*. Marie-Louise von Franz worked at Jung's side for many years in mining the alchemical gold. Barbara Hannah, who introduced me to *Mysterium* and who loved it and lived it, was the first to translate the book from German into English. And I would also like to thank my friend Una Thomas, faithful recorder of von Franz's many lectures. It was her example that gave me the idea of transcribing Edinger's lectures.

Now *The Mysterium Lectures* are launched. May they prove to be a useful guide to that great city of the psyche that is Jung's *Mysterium Coniunctionis*.

Joan Dexter Blackmer
Wilmot Flat, NH

Author's Note

I want to thank warmly my friend and colleague Joan Blackmer for her *opus amoris*. Her talents and devotion have enabled her to fulfill a task that I feared would never find a hand, head and heart adequate for its completion. Also I thank Daryl Sharp, publisher of Inner City Books, for his energy and initiative in bringing Jungian psychology to the world, and in particular for his willingness to commit himself to a project of this magnitude.

May our mutual efforts bring greater understanding of Jung at a depth from which he wants to be known.

Edward F. Edinger
Los Angeles

C.G. Jung in 1947, at the age of 72.

1
Introduction and Paragraphs 1-12

I want to welcome you all to a very sizable enterprise. It's quite a difficult project to make our way through this entire book. *Mysterium Coniunctionis* is really the *summa* of Jungian psychology, and I think it's safe to say that if you can achieve a really living and working relationship to this book, you then achieve simultaneously a living, working relationship to the autonomous psyche.

I must warn you there will be difficulties. It is likely that you will all fall into confusion at one time or another in the course of the year—probably more than once. This is absolutely inevitable because *Mysterium* is like the psyche itself. It's oceanic and to take it seriously means to run the risk of drowning.

In my opinion, this book will be a major object of study for centuries, so of course we're not going to master it in one brief course. But what I think is possible is that some of you will at least be able to make a connection to it that can then blossom into a lifetime relationship. My hope is that as you pour effort into it, and as each period of confusion is mastered, love for this magnificent work will progressively grow on you.

What makes *Mysterium* so exasperating is that every paragraph, every sentence, confronts us with material with which we are unfamiliar, and that's very hard on one's vanity. As well, you'll notice immediately the frequent use of Greek and Latin terms. Jung uses them freely and he does it on purpose—there's real method to all this. But it's particularly difficult for those of us with an American education because for us the classical languages have pretty much gone by the board. In my day Latin was still a requirement in high school, but you forgot it just as soon as you got out, and I don't think even that exists any more. And of course as far as Greek is concerned, forget it! Greek hasn't been around in American education since the turn of the century.

Nevertheless I hope you do try to pay attention to these foreign terms because they constellate unconscious reverberations. More than fifty percent of English words have Latin or Greek derivations. Latin and Greek make up the unconscious of our language and to be aware of that opens up the unconscious dimension of the psyche. So even though the majority of the Latin terms are translated in the text, I suggest you have a Latin dictionary at your elbow.

Now Greek is a somewhat more difficult problem but for the enterprising I would suggest that you can at least transliterate the Greek words. You can master the Greek alphabet in an hour or two, and with that knowledge at your disposal you can then transliterate the Greek terms—there's much less Greek than Latin. This then will open up meanings that would otherwise be invisible.

For example, in footnote 23 to paragraph 5 we find the statement: "A similar ancient idea seems to be that of the ηλιακη τραπεζα (solar table) in the Orphic mysteries." Transliterated, that becomes h-e-l-i-a-k-e t-r-a-p-e-z-a. Once you write that down, you can begin to make associations to those Greek words from their English derivatives. *Heliake* reminds us of the word helium, the gas that was discovered in the sun, or the heliotrope plant, or the sun god Helios; so we immediately know what that means. *Trapeza* reminds us of the geometrical figure of the trapezoid, the four-sided thing, and we learn that *trapeza* was the Greek word for table. Little insights of this sort strike sparks, and if you get a number of those sparks they create a glow; the overall glow is a psychological effect of having mastered some of the material.

This book can't be read the way one reads an ordinary book—it has to be worked on the way one works on a dream. Initially, almost every sentence will present you with something that is more or less unfamiliar, and that adds up to a whole series of defeats for the ego. But if you can disidentify from the ego sufficiently, then that may enable you to keep going.

The language of *Mysterium* is not exactly the language of the unconscious as it appears in myth and dreams and fairy tales. This is not a fairy tale or myth or dream but its content, its subject matter, is the content of the unconscious, and specifically the collective or objective unconscious. These contents are communicated and mediated for us through the consciousness of Jung. Although he's talking about the objective, factual contents of the psyche, he is transmitting them through what I can only call a magisterial consciousness.

It's important at the outset to understand that Jung's method of approach is rigorously empirical. He lays before us, with utter objectivity, the facts of the psyche. These are not the facts of the personal psyche—the facts of the personal psyche are all different because each individual has his or her own life story. Jung presents the facts of the objective psyche, the transpersonal psyche. And specifically they are the facts that manifest themselves in alchemy. He explains his rationale in a passage in *Alchemical Studies:*

> It is often impossible to establish [the] full range of meaning [of an archetypal image] from the associative material of a single individual. . . . [Hence] the necessity of comparative research into symbols. . . . For this purpose the investigator must turn back to those periods in human history when symbol formation still went on unimpeded, that is, when there was still no epistemological criticism of the formation of images, and when, in consequence, facts that in themselves were unknown could be expressed in definite visual form. The period of this kind closest to us is that of medieval natural philosophy . . . . Here, as in a reservoir, were collected the most enduring and the most important mythologems of the ancient world.[1]

---

[1] "The Philosophical Tree," CW 13, par. 353. [CW refers throughout to C.G. Jung, *The Collected Works]*

Now "medieval natural philosophy"—that's alchemy. He says we "must turn back to those periods in human history when symbol formation still went on unimpeded, that is, when there was still no epistemological criticism of the formation of images." This means one could fantasize at liberty, and describe, using the categories of one's own fantasy, the phenomena of the outer world as seen in the test tube or the retort. One can't do that anymore in modern science because there is, to use the fancy term, "epistemological criticism." When a distinction is made between the subjective source of data and the objective source of data, that's epistemological criticism.

But the alchemists lacked that, so their fantasy flowed freely into their descriptions. And as the result we have this marvelous panorama of the objective psyche unfolded before our eyes. It's that vast literature of alchemy, extending over many centuries, which Jung has mastered in an absolutely astonishing tour de force. He has condensed, extracted and abstracted, and presented it all between these two covers. It's just an astonishing accomplishment.

Jung says that this method of comparative research into the history of symbols is similar to the relation "between comparative anatomy and human anatomy."[2] Comparative anatomy studies the anatomical structure of various specimens in the course of the evolutionary process; when we do comparative symbol research we're doing something analogous to the anatomy of the psyche. The anatomy of the psyche consists of images, and that's what this book is about. Here is another passage, from Jung's essay, "Spirit and Life":

> The psyche consists essentially of images. It is a series of images in the truest sense . . . a structure that is throughout full of meaning and purpose; it is a "picturing" of vital activities. . . .
>
> Mind and body are . . . the expression of a single entity. . . . This living being appears outwardly as the material body, but inwardly as a series of images of the vital activities taking place within it.[3]

Now these images are not random; they are highly organized and interconnected. Although the variations of individual images can be almost infinite, nonetheless psychic images all derive from a quite limited number of uniform recurrent patterns. These are what we call the archetypes. If we're not to get lost in the particulars of our own unconscious imagery, or in the unconscious imagery of others, we really need to have a thorough knowledge of these psychic uniformities. Only with that knowledge can we recognize them when they occur in a particular manifestation.

This is not so easy, because to learn about these uniformities of imagery we have to take images seriously, and that goes against a major individual and col-

---

[2] Ibid., note 4.
[3] *The Structure and Dynamics of the Psyche,* CW 8, pars. 618f.

lective predisposition to the contrary. We've all learned from our collective education to depreciate images, to concentrate rather on ideas, conceptual formations, and to assume that the psyche and the ego are equivalent. This has the effect of blinding us to the reality of the psyche as an autonomous, objective entity. And I would remind you that the reality of the psyche has just been discovered! It was just discovered yesterday, and nobody knows it yet. The discovery of the reality of the psyche and taking images seriously belong to the same phenomenon—they go together.

You see, rationalistic consciousness is so identified with the psyche that it can't perceive the objective reality of psychic imagery. From that point of view, images are nothing but a derivative of consciousness. We all participate in this rationalistic consciousness, so let's not project it onto others. It's a problem for every one of us, and it makes the study of the anatomy of psychic images exceedingly difficult. It's hard for us to perceive mere images as substantial psychic entities, but that's exactly what they are, and that's the way Jung treats them in *Mysterium.* The images he talks about have for him the same degree of reality as any other biological specimen—a giraffe or a hippopotamus or a turtle.

It may be helpful, in terms of the attitude necessary to venture into this book, to consider three different kinds of thinking. In *Symbols of Transformation,* Jung discusses two kinds of thinking.[4] One is directional or purposeful thinking; it is linear and willed by the ego. The second kind is fantasy thinking—the thinking of the unconscious—in which the ego lies back and goes to sleep, so to speak, and lets the unconscious follow whatever associative process it wishes. It's day-dream thinking, and it's effortless; it doesn't use any conscious libido, whereas directed thinking is hard work.

But there is a third kind of thinking. It's what I would call network or cluster thinking, and it's really a union of fantasy thinking and directed thinking. Network thinking is neither linear nor meandering and associational. It's purposeful, but it is also concerned with elaborating a network of expanded meanings deriving from a central image. It is thinking that is oriented around a center, and moves radially to and from that center, circumambulating it. It goes back and forth, returning to the central image again and again, building up a rich associative cluster of interconnecting images—something like a spider web. The result of such thinking is a rich tapestry of elaboration around a central image.[5] This is what *Mysterium* is. And if you take it as a whole, the net result is an exceedingly rich picture of the anatomy of individuation, with all its interconnecting images dissected out for us.

---

[4] CW 5, pars. 4ff.

[5] For examples of such clusters, see the diagrams preceding each chapter in Edinger, *Anatomy of the Psyche: Alchemical Symbolism in Psychotherapy;* also below, p. 140.

Mysterium is quite strictly a descriptive book. It describes the anatomy of the psyche. It is a book of facts, not theories, and it is difficult for us in the same way that an anatomy book is difficult. In the first semester of medical school the hardest time I had was with anatomy. I was suddenly confronted with this sea of facts, each of which had a strange, unfamiliar name. Not being familiar with any of them, one can be inundated, and that was the way I felt until I got my bearings. I recognized something of the same feeling when I first started to deal with *Mysterium.*

In order to grasp the facts of anatomy one has to experience them. Go into the dissecting room and start working on a cadaver; then the facts in the anatomy book take on meaning because you can relate them to something you can actually see. Psychologically we get this same experience from analysis—primarily from our own analysis, our own self-dissection, so to speak. Secondarily, we get it from analytic work with others. So analysis is where we dissect the psyche and lay bare its structure.

I would suggest you keep constantly in mind that *Mysterium* is a book describing images. The operative word, the key word to this book, is "images." To keep your bearings, you should pay attention to the major images in each assignment. Ask yourself, "What images are we dealing with here?" In some cases it can be very helpful to draw a chart of the network of interconnecting images Jung chooses for elaboration. I also advise you to read the assigned paragraphs twice: once before the lecture and then again after.

Here is my list of the chief images in the first assignment:

1. The opposites: arranged as pairs, and as quaternities.
2. The solar table.
3. Ostanes caught in Heimarmene.
4. The crown.
5. The Pelican or magical Septenary.
6. The Ecclesia spiritualis.
7. Mercurius as peacemaker, and Mercurius as the Original Man scattered throughout the world.

Seven major images. Now if one boils an assignment down to that, it becomes manageable, and then subsidiary images and associations can be subsumed under the main categories. That's what I'm going to try to do tonight and hereafter— I'm going to take each assignment and boil it down to a small list of its major images and then talk about each of them. My hope will be to render them sufficiently vivid so that they'll stick in your memory. The way one remembers something is to nail it down by meaningful associative connections; when you can find such connections, it will stay in consciousness. If you can't find such connections, whatever you're trying to remember drops back into the unconscious as soon as you look away.

l. The Opposites

Jung starts *Mysterium* with a blockbuster of a sentence:

> The factors which come together in the coniunctio are conceived as opposites, either
> confronting one another in enmity or attracting one another in love.

That epitomizes the whole book, and it tells us what the basic subject of the
book is going to be: it's going to be about the opposites. It also tells us that the
opposites do two different things: they come together in love and they fight in
enmity. They are the dynamo of the coniunctio. And I remind you of the title of
the book—the Mystery of the Coniunctio. So whenever one encounters a dream
that involves an attraction or an enmity between two figures one knows that it's
at least an echo of the central symbolism of the coniunctio. Once one has become
thoroughly familiar with such imagery, one will see in unconscious material what
was previously completely invisible.

The objective, transpersonal psyche is shining through unconscious material
constantly, but if we are totally preoccupied with the personal dimension we'll
only be able to see the personal aspects of the material. Almost all dreams are full
of personal aspects of course, but in a great many the objective psyche shines
through too. You can't point it out to the analysand, however, if you don't see it
yourself. That's one of the great values of studying this material—you learn how
to see the imagery of the objective psyche.

In the next few paragraphs, Jung points out that these opposites have a tendency to arrange themselves in pairs or in quaternities. So here we have some
images to look out for in dream material—things showing up in twos or in fours.
In paragraph 2 he gives more particular examples. He speaks, for instance, of the
fact that often the pairs manifest as royalty—king and queen, emperor and em-
press—and an example of that is in the *Rosarium* pictures Jung analyzes in "The
Psychology of the Transference."[6] We also find the so-called theriomorphic
pairs—the animal forms. These usually express themselves as a pair of animals in
conflict, and Jung cites several examples of such images in various alchemical
pictures, though he doesn't bother to reproduce them; you have to track them
down yourself. I've done that and I'll go through a few.

For instance, two fishes in the sea, swimming in opposite directions (figure 1-
1); male and female lions (figure 1-2); a wolf and dog fighting (figure 1-3); an
eagle in the sky connected by a chain to an earth animal (figure 1-4). Two of these
pictures are from *The Book of Lambspring* which Jung alludes to in paragraph 3.
He also mentions the images of stag and unicorn meeting in the forest, winged
and wingless birds or dragons, and fledged and unfledged birds.

---

[6] See *The Practice of Psychotherapy,* CW 16, pars. 402ff; also Edinger, *The Mystery of the
Coniunctio: Alchemical Image of Individuation,* part 2.

Figure 1-1. Two fishes in the sea.

Figure 1-2. Male and female lions.

Figure 1-3. Wolf and dog fighting.

Figure 1-4. Eagle chained to earth animal.

In paragraph 4 Jung explains the psychological meaning of royal pairings or animal pairings:

> The elevation of the human figure to a king or a divinity, and on the other hand its representation in subhuman, theriomorphic form, are indications of the *transconscious character* of the pairs of opposites.

This is a very important point. The fact that the pairs of opposites are represented on the one hand as royalty—something more than ordinary human life—or on the other hand as animals—something below human life—indicates the *"transconscious character* of the pairs of opposites."

> They do not belong to the ego-personality but are supraordinate to it. . . . The pairs of opposites constitute the phenomenology of the paradoxical *self,* man's totality.

For instance, you have a dream of two animals locked in mortal combat—not such an unusual dream incidentally—and you immediately have an association to that image: "Yes, that's a picture of the conflict I have regarding such and such." With this comment of Jung's in mind, you should then understand that the dream refers to the *transconscious character* of the pair of opposites that are locked in conflict *in you.*

Do not identify with them personally; it doesn't mean the conflict will be banished. But if you really get what that means—not so easy when the conflict is raging inside you—if you manage to do it, it changes the whole situation drastically and changes your relation to the conflict.

By disidentifying from it, a psychological situation is set up in which a third reconciling possibility can emerge—and often does. It cannot emerge, it doesn't have any room to emerge, until the ego has ceased to identify with the conflict.

2. The Solar Table

In paragraph 5, Jung speaks of the fact that not only do the opposites arrange themselves in pairs, they also arrange themselves in quaternities. As an example, he mentions this interesting picture in Stolcenberg's *Viridarium chymicum* (figure 1-5). It is a picture of a round table with four feminine figures sitting at it, each with the head of the sun.

Those four figures represent the sun as it is placed in the circle of the Zodiac in the four seasons of the year. One represents spring, one summer, one fall, one winter. Placed on the table in front of each of the four figures is the astrological sign corresponding to the season each figure refers to: the ram for Aries, the crab for Cancer, the balance for Libra and the goat for Capricorn. And Jung tells us:

> The goddesses represent the four seasons of the sun . . . and at the same time the four degrees of heating, as well as the four elements "combined" around the circular table.

Figure 1-5. The sun as the four seasons.

This is a very interesting image that grows on you as you reflect on it. If, for instance, we think of it as a photograph of the sun in its four stations of the yearly cycle, we must ask who could have taken that photograph? It would have to be a quadruple time-lapse photograph, wouldn't it? In other words, that picture has to be taken from a position outside of time. Now time and space are categories of consciousness—they do not apply to the unconscious. This picture is thus a reminder of the statement Jung made about the *"transconscious character* of the pairs of opposites." It is an illustration of the fact that the opposites are transconscious; here they are pictured in a setting that is transtemporal, beyond the categories of space and time.

Every now and then we get images of this same character in dreams; often the reference is subtle and if you're not alert to it, it can slip right by you. But if you're familiar with this type of imagery, you'll catch it and I can assure you that the unconscious loves to be seen and to be recognized. When you get it and are able to say, "Oh, this belongs to the transconscious nature of the opposites!", that insight is very apt to be followed up by a response from the unconscious that says, "Right on!"

3. Ostanes Caught in Heimarmene

Continuing his elaboration, Jung then gives us another example of essentially the same image, embedded in a text that's a little obscure. It takes some work to extract it, so let me read the text from paragraph 5.

> Ostanes said, Save me, O my God, for I stand between two exalted brilliancies known for their wickedness, and between two dim lights; each of them has reached me and I know not how to save myself from them. And it was said to me, Go up to Agathodaimon the Great and ask aid of him, and know that there is in thee somewhat of his nature, which will never be corrupted. . . . And when I ascended into the air he said to me, Take the child of the bird which is mixed with redness and spread for the gold its bed which comes forth from the glass, and place it in its vessel whence it has no power to come out except when thou desirest, and leave it until its moistness has departed.

Now when Jung reads that, he sees this image:

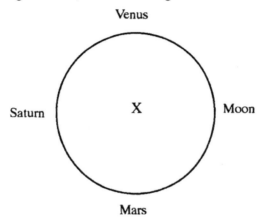

We wouldn't see that immediately, but he does try to spell it out for us. He tells us that the "two exalted brilliancies" and the "two dim lights" refer to Mars and Saturn on the one hand, and to the moon and Venus on the other.

This diagram is at the same time a picture of Ostanes caught in Heimarmene. Ostanes is the X at the center, caught between Mars on the bottom and Venus on the top, and between the moon on the right and Saturn on the left. The ruling houses of each of those planets are the same Zodiac signs that showed up in our previous solar table picture. So Ostanes, because of some peculiar business, has gotten caught in the middle of the solar table and he's in trouble. He's saying, "Save me! I'm in trouble because each of them has reached me." "Heimarmene" is the ancient term for the compulsion of the stars and Jung tells us that Ostanes, because of what he's complaining about, must be subject to Heimarmene.

The fact that Ostanes is standing between these two pairs of opposites indicates he's occupying the center of the solar table. He's identified with the center of the mandala, and this corresponds to identification with the Self—an exceedingly dangerous position to be in. Identification with the Self is accompanied by fragmentation and dismemberment, so no wonder he's calling for help. The ego is tossed about, possessed by first one and then another of the various opposites— that's Heimarmene.

But the text informs Ostanes how to get out of identification with the Self: he must acknowledge his need and consult Agathodaimon. "Agathodaimon" means the good spirit, the good daimon. So by acknowledging his need, and by consulting a source of wisdom greater than his own, he relinquishes the central position. He hands it over to Agathodaimon, you might say. Ultimately he hands it over to what's called "the child of the bird," a symbolic term for the Philosophers' Stone. Since Ostanes is an alchemist, it's the Philosophers' Stone he supposedly is in the process of creating. But when you're trying to work on such a project the danger is that you'll fall into your own creation and become identified with the Philosophers' Stone yourself. Then you get into Ostanes' difficulty.

4. The Crown

Ostanes gets out of his dilemma and the text continues in paragraph 6. This is Hermes speaking:

> I cause to come out to thee the spirits of thy brethren [the planets], O Sun, and I make them for thee a crown the like of which was never seen; and I cause thee and them to be within me, and I will make thy kingdom vigorous.

So when Ostanes gets disidentified from the Self, the sevenfold crown can be synthesized. Jung writes:

> The crown signifies the kingly totality; it stands for unity and is not subject to Heimarmene. This reminds us of the seven- or twelve-rayed crown of light which the Agathodaimon serpent wears on Gnostic gems [figure 1-6].

Figure 1-6
Gnostic gem
and amulet.

This tells us that the crown, synthesized or created when Ostanes becomes disidentified from the Self, amounts to a synthesis of the mandala or totality as an objective entity, rather than one that is subjectively identified with.

Jung uses another very interesting image in paragraph 7, another double quaternity, to illustrate how the opposites unite themselves (figure 1-7). He extracts the mandala image from this quoted passage:

> In it [the Indian Ocean] are images of heaven and earth, of summer, autumn, winter, and spring, male and female. If thou callest this spiritual, what thou doest is probable; if corporeal, thou sayest the truth; if heavenly, thou liest not; if earthly, thou hast well spoken.

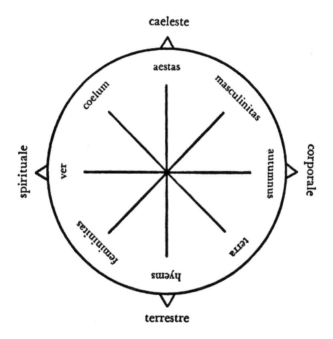

Figure 1-7. Double quaternity.

This gives us a glimpse into Jung's marvelous visual power, his image-making capacity. I don't think many of us would have extracted this figure from that text, but if we follow it up, we'll see heaven, earth, summer, autumn, winter, spring—yes, it all fits, it's all there. He put it in Latin, but he's being true to the original Latin text—he's not prettying it up. It's a good example of the kind of capacity we need to develop if we're going to extract vivid imagery from the rather loosely presented material we encounter all the time.

5. The Pelican or Magical Septenary

I want to go on to the image in paragraph 8, "the true philosophical Pelican" (figure 1-8). It is composed of the central circle A which has four radiations from it: B, C, D, E. And then further distinctions of upper semicircle F, lower semicircle G.

Now this is another variation of the solar table—we're still on that same image. It's part of a network of images elaborating the basic uniformity of the quaternity of which the solar table is one example. We're told that A represents the center and original unity of the circle; F and G, its upper and lower parts created by the line BD; and the points BCDE are the four points created when the line CE is added to line BD.

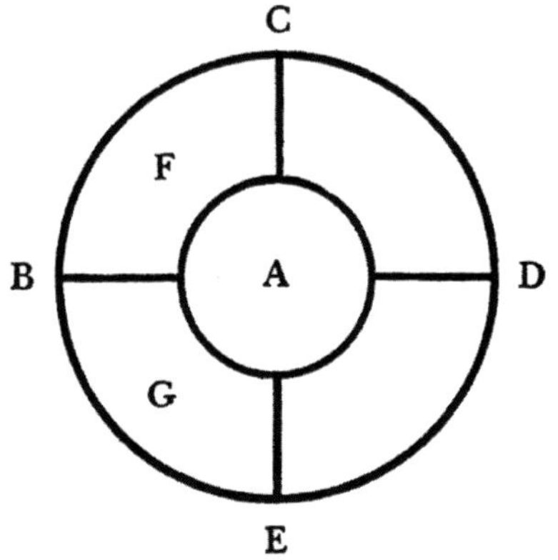

Figure 1-8.
The true philosophical
Pelican.

If you reflect on this, you realize that it's made in a sequence of three operations. Initially, there's one entity, a circle with a center. And one horizontal line is drawn that cuts it into two—above and below. Then a second line vertically which divides it into four. That gives us a sequence of one, two, four. Now you add those together, 1 + 2 + 4, and you get 7, the so-called magical Septenary. That 7 corresponds to the seven planets of the ancient cosmology and it corresponds to the seven-rayed crown we've been speaking about.

Another amplification to this sequence of 1, 2, 4, is to be found in the crucial dream of a patient that Gerhard Adler discusses in *The Living Symbol.*[7] An absolutely central dream in that very extensive dream series is that of a symbolic entity, a *labarum*[8] that had superimposed on it the numbers 1, 2, 4 (figure 1-9). The

---

[7] Chap. 3, "The Dream of the Rod," pp. 26ff.

[8] "The labarum is the standard which was given to the Emperor Constantine in a vision . . . with the words "In hoc signo vinces" ('In this sign you will conquer'). It was composed of a long lance with a short transverse bar near its end (thus forming a cross) and it carried on its point the monogram of Christ." (Ibid. p. 28)

Pelican image would be a parallel to that dream.

Incidentally, I recommend Adler's book; it's a marvelous and extensive Jungian case history. We have almost no comprehensive Jungian case histories available and this is a wonderful one.

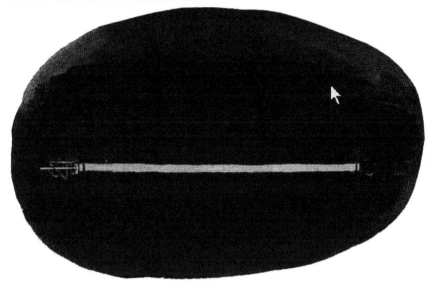

Figure 1-9. The rod/labarum.

6. Mercurius as Peacemaker

Back to our picture of the Pelican. Jung tells us that the center, A, which is the source of the other letters, is equated with Mercurius. In paragraph 9 he says: "This little inner circle corresponds to the Mercurial Fountain in the *Rosarium.*" That's the first picture in the sequence Jung discusses in "The Psychology of the Transference."[9] The central point A symbolizes the spirit Mercurius which is "a peacemaker, the mediator between the warring elements and producer of unity." BCDE are opposites that have come out of A, and they will be in a state of enmity unless a mediator can be found to reconcile them.

This image is so deceptively simple that we might not take it very seriously, but I urge you to do so. The unconscious talks this way, and in your dream work you are very apt to encounter analogous images; if you remember this image it will give you your bearings when working on such a dream.

The basic idea is that first there's a point (and the symbolism of the point will

[9] See *The Practice of Psychotherapy,* CW 16, p. 205; also Edinger, *Mystery of the Coniunctio,* p. 41.

be prominent in later material).[10] Pairs of opposites emanate out of that point: left and right, above and below, inner and outer. Then, to the extent that those emanated opposites lose connection with their source, they are at war with each other, they're in the state of the war of the elements. And only to the extent that they can reconnect with their source are they then mediated and reconciled. The central point which is both their source on the one hand, and their reconciling mediator on the other, is Mercurius.

Jung goes on to speak a bit more about Mercurius but he doesn't say much because, although the symbolism of Mercurius is immensely important in alchemy, he has already treated it extensively in his essay "The Spirit Mercurius."[11] That essay is a kind of appendage to *Mysterium;* there he does justice to the symbolism of Mercurius whereas here he just alludes to it briefly.

7. The Ecclesia Spiritualis

In paragraphs 10 and 11, Jung presents some texts indicating that the spirit Mercurius and the individuals who have made a living connection with that spirit make up an Ecclesia spiritualis. This is a spiritual church, not a concrete, external collective Church. It is a psychological, spiritual church that unites individuals who have had their own deep experience of the autonomous spirit Mercurius. This image of the Ecclesia spiritualis is a very profound and important one.

Jung also brings up a text that compares the reconciling, mediating function of Mercurius with the blood of Christ, as described by the apostle Paul in Ephesians. The passage is quoted in paragraph 10: the blood of Christ is described as the agency by which those "who once were far off have been brought near"; thus he (Christ) "might create in himself one new man in place of two."[12]

---

10 See below, pp. 57ff.

11 See *Alchemical Studies,* CW 13, espec. section 4, pars. 259ff.

12 Eph. 2: 13ff, Revised Standard Version.

2

Paragraphs 13-30

For tonight, I've chosen seven major images to talk around in some detail:

1. The orphan.
2. The widow. Several subsidiary images appear under this heading: the virgin, the whore, the feeble old woman, the virago (female warrior), and the mythological images of Isis and Medea. They all belong to the widow image.
3. The image of the death coniunctio.
4. The Kabbalistic image of the marriage of Malchuth and Tifereth.
5. Luna, the moon.
6. Wounding.
7. Kenosis or emptying.

l. The Orphan

Jung tells us in paragraph 13 that the term "orphan" was a synonym for the Philosophers' Stone. In other words, it's an image of the Self. This reminds me of the inscription Jung carved on the Bollingen stone (figure 2-1). One side of the stone has the image of the eye; another side has this inscription, which Jung says he put together as a composite of various alchemical quotations:

Figure 2-1.
The Bollingen
stone.

I am an orphan, alone; nevertheless I am found everywhere. I am one, but opposed to myself. I am youth and old man at one and the same time. I have known neither father nor mother, because I have had to be fetched out of the deep like a fish, or fell like a white stone from heaven. In woods and mountains I roam, but I am hidden in the innermost soul of man. I am mortal for everyone, yet I am not touched by the cycle of aeons.[13]

This tells us that the experience referred to by the image of the orphan is a part of individuation. The experience of being abandoned, of losing the support of all parental figures and sources of external security—these all belong to the image of the orphan. It's a necessary experience, because you cannot discover the inner source of security upon which your existence rests until you have been deprived of all external supports.

I was once brought a remarkable dream which included this image.[14] It was dreamt by a woman who had to endure a particularly large number of frustrations that most people are spared—biological satisfactions denied her by life—and this was very hard for her to come to terms with. At one time she dreamt that her doorbell rang; she went to the door and opened it, and there on the doorstep was a foundling. The peculiar nature of this foundling was that it was still attached to an umbilical cord and the umbilical cord went up into heaven. That would be an example of the orphan archetype. It "had to be fetched out of the deep like a fish, or fell like a white stone from heaven."

2. The Widow

Etymologically, the word widow derives from the Latin *vidua,* which stems from a lost cognate verb, *videre,* meaning "to part." This is similar to the symbolism of the orphan image. We must be parted from what we depend on, or from what we are in a state of *participation mystique* with, if we are going to become conscious of our indivisible nature. The word individual means indivisible. An individual is one who cannot be divided into smaller parts.

As the alchemists say, the Philosophers' Stone is the "son of the widow." That would mean then that the experience of the Self—individuation—is the son of the experience of widowhood, psychological widowhood in the broadest sense. And the widow was considered to be an image of the prima materia. The widow is the prima materia and the son to whom she gives birth is the Philosophers' Stone. Similar images are the feeble old woman, Mother Alchemy and the old woman who is dropsical in her lower limbs.

In the early phase of my own analysis I had a dream that brought up this image. In the dream I'm exploring a deep underground room with stone walls, and there

---

13 *Memories, Dreams, Reflections,* p. 227.
14 See Edinger, *Ego and Archetype,* p. 270.

I encounter a feeble, senile old woman with withered paralyzed legs. This is an example of the feeble old woman or the woman with dropsy. Why paralyzed legs, or why dropsical legs? Well, one way of seeing it is that paralysis of the legs roots one to the spot. It's almost as though the lower extremities merge with the earth. This would correspond to the experience of discovering that one doesn't have the capacity to stand on one's own feet. Through those experiences one discovers what the source of support is when one can't stand on one's own—when the ego can't provide the necessary support.

Another way of seeing the dropsical lower limbs is that the old woman, in her lower extremities, merges with water; she is something like a mermaid. Just as a mermaid loses its human form and turns, in its lower extremities, into a fish, so the dropsical old woman merges with the element of water, so to speak. In her lower extremities she becomes the unconscious itself.

In his discussion of the various aspects of the widow figure, Jung talks about the Egyptian goddess Isis, the Black One, the teacher of alchemy, which as you know began in Egypt. Isis was considered both a healer and a poisoner. On the one hand she reconstituted the dismembered pieces of Osiris, which demonstrates her healing capacity. But there is also the myth of Isis and Ra, according to which Isis put on Ra's path a poisonous worm that bit him and forced him to retire on the heavenly cow. Later she healed him again. These are further images of the unconscious—the unconscious as prima materia which, on the one hand, can poison the ego or the contrasexual figure, and, on the other, can heal and transform it.

The image of Medea is another example. In effect, Medea became a widow because her husband, Jason, abandoned her; in her rage and resentment at being abandoned, she killed her children.

A case comes to mind in which this particular archetype manifested itself. It involved a woman who was divorced but was not at all reconciled to the separation, even though she had instigated it. That doesn't make any difference, you know; the unconscious doesn't operate rationally at all. So although she initiated the divorce, she was harboring terrible rage at her husband for abandoning her. She maintained the fantasy that they were going to get back together again, even though the husband had remarried. Somehow that didn't matter—the new wife wasn't right for him anyway.

After a certain period of time, her son began to have a series of rather ominous car accidents, and she had the vague sense that she might have something to do with that. One day we were talking about a dream she'd had, a dream of a woman who killed her child, and I said, "That reminds me of Medea." Then all of a sudden I had the insight, "That's what's happening with you and your son who is having these car accidents—Medea is living itself out here! You're living out the Medea myth!"

That had the effect of a thunderbolt. When an interpretation both hits the mark and comes at the right time, when those two come right together, it is as though search lights go on, bells go off. That was what happened in this case; the whole issue erupted into view. Then of course everything can change. When consciousness enters the picture the myth isn't going to live itself out inexorably anymore because a conscious ego has something to say about it. So that was an example of the prima materia as Medea, manifesting itself in a specific analytic situation.

3. The Death Coniunctio

Jung brings this up in paragraph 14, referring to the marriage of Mother Beya and her son Gabritius. He quotes a text of Michael Maier:

> "But this marriage, which was begun with the expression of great joyfulness, ended in the bitterness of mourning," says Maier, adding the verses:
>
>> Within the flower itself there grows the gnawing canker:
>> Where honey is, there gall, where swelling breast, the chancre.
>
> For, "when the son sleeps with the mother, she kills him with the stroke of a viper."

This is followed, in paragraph 15, by another text with the same theme. As I am reading this, try to visualize a particular image for it. As I said last time, that's the way to understand these difficult passages—you have to visualize the image. After you visualize it, I'll show you how the alchemists visualized this particular quotation.

> Nevertheless the Philosophers have put to death the woman who slays her husbands, for the body of that woman is full of weapons and poison. Let a grave be dug for that dragon, and let that woman be buried with him, he being chained fast to that woman; and the more he winds and coils himself about her, the more will he be cut to pieces by the female weapons which are fashioned in the body of the woman. And when he sees that he is mingled with the limbs of the woman, he will be certain of death, and will be changed wholly into blood. But when the Philosophers see him changed into blood, they leave him a few days in the sun, until his softness is consumed, and the blood dries, and they find that poison. What then appears, is the hidden wind.

Concerning this text, Jung comments: "The coniunctio can therefore take more gruesome forms than the relatively harmless one depicted in the *Rosarium.*" Well, it's not all that harmless, because the two partners *die*—that's not so harmless! Just the first two or three pictures look harmless.[15] Now this isn't a crystal clear image by any means. You see, these texts are like dreams—the images are fluid, they flow into one another.

The question comes up, who is this dragon or serpent that's to be chained fast

---

[15] See "The Psychology of the Transference," *The Practice of Psychotherapy,* CW 16; also Edinger, *Mystery of the Coniunctio,* part 2.

to the woman? Apparently he's the husband who had already been slain by the woman. The sequence of the text would suggest that, as the husband begins to lie with the woman, he turns into a dragon or serpent. To put it another way, as they lie together the dragon aspect of the instinctual relationship is constellated —in other words, lust. The ensuing coniunctio, then, amounts to a dismemberment of the dragon, a dismemberment of primitive desirousness.

Here's the illustration (figure 2-2), a picture of a woman in a grave, encoiled by a great serpent. Under it is a quotation:

> Have a deep grave dug for the poisonous dragon with which the woman should be tightly intertwined. While it rejoices in the marriage bed, she dies; and have the dragon buried together with her. In doing so, its body is abandoned to death, and is embued with blood. Now this is the true path of your art.[16]

We have to keep reminding ourselves that all these texts are talking about the chemical process going on in the retort. They are so dramatic and vivid in their imagery that we're apt to start taking them concretely rather than chemically.

Figure 2-2. Woman in a grave, encoiled by serpent.

[16] Michael Maier, *Atalanta fugiens.* emblem no. 50.

In *Anatomy of the Psyche* I speak of this as an image of the lesser coniunctio.[17] It's a picture of what happens when the immature aspect of the ego embraces the unconscious: it undergoes death or dissolution. For the immature ego, it is very dangerous to have any dealings with the unconscious. (What we're talking about here is the psychological basis of the incest taboo.) The "dismem-berment" that the alchemical texts speak of could correspond to a psychosis or some other fatal psychic event.

This is illustrated frequently in the phenomenology of erotic love. We have a good example of it in Goethe's early novel, *The Sorrows of Young Werther,* which made young Goethe's reputation as a writer. Published in 1774, it was a bestseller and a literary sensation across Europe. The basic plot of the book is that Werther, a passionate, idealistic young man, falls hopelessly in love with Charlotte. But Charlotte marries another man and Werther shoots himself. This book started an epidemic of suicides across Europe. Werther, in falling in love (that term, "fall," is very appropriate psychologically—it really is a fall), thinks he's embracing a desirable and beautiful young woman. Actually he's embracing a deadly serpent, and that serpent kills him. He's possessed by the image of the coniunctio, but it's the lesser coniunctio, the deadly version. Werther personifies a young man in whom the masculine principle is not sufficiently crystallized, coagulated, not strong enough to endure an encounter with its opposite. Therefore it perishes in the attempted coniunctio. This all belongs to the symbolism of incest, which is absolutely basic to coniunctio imagery.

Freud was the discoverer of the incest archetype. He called it the Oedipus complex and interpreted it personalistically and concretely. Jung took that motif and understood it both subjectively and transpersonally. From the subjective standpoint, incest refers to the ego's having intimate connections with its own origin—it's psychological mother—the unconscious. Incest is such a violently forbidden issue because in the psychological evolutionary process it took im-mense efforts for the human ego to separate itself from the unconscious—its mother—in order to stand as a more or less conscious entity, responsible and separate. The backward pull to regress to one's origins, to lose that hard-won position, must have been very powerful in the past and therefore had to be coun-tered by a very strict incest taboo. I'm speaking now of psychological incest which means one is forbidden to have dealings with the unconscious.

We saw a good example of that in our study of the Ten Commandments in the Old Testament. Images were forbidden by the Second Commandment. That is an example of the incest taboo in operation because images would open the door to the unconscious.[18] This means of course that the synthetic approach and the

---

[17] *Anatomy,* pp. 212f.
[18] See Edinger, *The Bible and the Psyche*, p. 61.

archetypal approach to dream interpretation, which open the door to the unconscious, also smack of incest and are by no means appropriate for everybody. The personalistic and reductive modes of explanation, which to a large extent honor the incest taboo, are the appropriate ones for the immature ego.

4. Malchuth and Tifereth

In talking about the symbolism of the widow in paragraph 18, Jung says that Malchuth, the tenth figure of the Sefirotic Tree, was called a widow. Now what is the Sefirotic Tree? There will be another occasion later to talk a bit about the Kabbalistic symbolism of the Sefirotic Tree, but in order to know what Jung is talking about here, I thought a few remarks about it would be useful.

According to Kabbalistic symbolism, the Sefirotic Tree is an image of the tenfold emanation of the Godhead (figure 2-3). It's an image of God unfolded into ten aspects, so to speak; it was thought of as an upside-down tree with its roots in heaven and its branches down on earth.

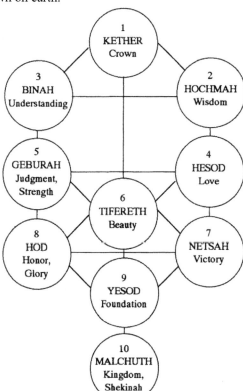

Figure 2-3.
The Sefirotic Tree.

Without going into all ten of those aspects of the Godhead, let's just talk about four, the so-called central pillar, numbers 1, 6, 9 and 10. Number 1 at the top is called Kether or Crown—that's up in heaven. Number 6, Tifereth, is an image of the king; number 9, Yesod, is an image of his phallus; and number 10, Malchuth, is an image of the widow or the moon, the lowest manifestation of the Deity, of a feminine nature and right next to earth. We have here not only an image of an upside-down tree but also an image of a person: a masculine person in the upper three entities, and a feminine person in the lowest entity.

According to Kabbalistic mythology, Tifereth, the upper masculine person, and Malchuth, the lowest feminine person, have been separated and therefore Malchuth is a widow. That's why the world is in such an unsatisfactory state. The Godhead is in a state of division—it's not at one with itself—its feminine nature is in a state of widowhood. The idea was that when the Messiah comes, Tifereth and Malchuth will be reunited, and that meeting will restore God to his original unity. So here is a coniunctio symbol, and Jung connects it with the alchemical image of the widow, the prima materia. The connections continue.

5. The Moon

In paragraph 19, we learn that Malchuth is also called the moon; so the moon comes into the widow symbolism of alchemy. I'm not going to talk very much about moon symbolism tonight, because farther along we have a large section on Luna, but I will say a bit.

In order to understand some of the symbolic aspects of the moon, it is necessary to have in mind the ancient image of the structure of the universe, the Ptolemaic notions of the universe. According to those ancient notions, the earth was the center of the universe and it was surrounded by seven planetary spheres, concentrically arranged (figure 2-4). These housed the sun, moon and the five visible planets.

Now I must remind you that I'm not talking about astronomy. I'm talking about psychology. This is the structure of the psyche, projected naively into the heavens by the ancients who "lacked epistemological criticism," as Jung told us in last week's assignment. The source of the imagery is the structure of the psyche. And the structure that those ancient natural philosophers projected into the heavens is this series of concentric circles with the earth at the center. Well, that tells us, first of all, that ancient man was identified with the Self, doesn't it, if we take the earth as the ego—I won't justify that now, but take it on faith for the moment that the earth be considered the ego, and the sun, moon and planets be considered the archetypal factors of the collective unconscious.

The idea was that as souls came into earthly existence they descended from the upper, heavenly realms through the various gateways of the planetary spheres, and the last gateway was the moon. As soon as they got below the moon they were in the realm of the earth, and they were incarnated. The moon was conceived as a kind of funnel between heaven and earth—all the heavenly influences descending to earth were funneled through the moon. And it worked the other way around: souls departing from earth, moving upward, went through the gateway of the moon in the reverse direction.[19]

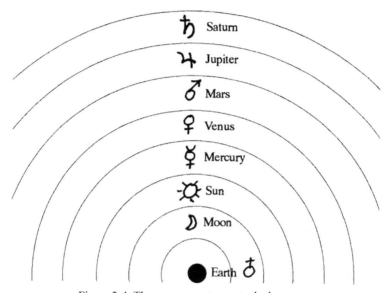

Figure 2-4. The moon as gateway to the heavens.

Since the moon was the heavenly planet closest to the earth, it shared in the earth's materiality, and that's what makes the moon so dubious—it's not a clean, pure, celestial entity; it's been contaminated by earthy matter.

Frances Wickes, in her book *The Inner World of Choice,* reports a very interesting example of moon symbolism:[20]

> A man wakes in the clutches of nameless fear. In his sleep he has been running, running across an endless desolate plain. In sharp memory he is back in the room where he slept until he was five years old. He is also back in a recurrent childhood dream that first made darkness a region of terror and dread.

And the dream is this:

> My mother is the moon; she is a huge funnel. She is chasing me across a great empty space to suck me in; I run and run, faster, faster, but always she is just behind me. I

---

[19] This ladder of the planets or the spheres is somewhat analogous to the Sefirotic Tree.
[20] *Inner World of Choice,* pp. 111f.

come to the edge of the world and jump off. I am falling down, down into darkness. While I am falling, I wake in terror.

It's a good example of how the archetypal images are such stark, living realities during childhood. The danger here is that the little ego will be sucked back up and returned to its celestial origins. That's the basic image: the moon as a funnel, as a kind of vacuum cleaner, is going after him. And if it gets him, it will suck him back up into the upper regions. In other words, it will disincarnate him and he'll lose his coagulated ego.

The moon, therefore, as the gateway to the earth, is an agent of coagulatio.[21] Jacob Boehme describes this aspect of the moon very well. He says:

> The seventh form [the seventh celestial sphere] is called Luna. The property of all the six forms lies therein and it is as a corporeal being of all the rest. For the other forms do all cast their desire through Sol into Luna, for in Sol they are spiritual, and in Luna, corporeal. So that whatever the sun is and makes in the spirit life in itself, the same Luna is and makes corporeal in itself.[22]

In other words, Luna turns it into a body, and that's how egos are made.

Jung mentions, at the end of paragraph 20, the so-called Ecclesia-Luna equation—the moon and the Church were symbolically equated. In that regard, there is a parallel in Kabbalistic symbolism. One of the synonyms for Malchuth was the knesset—the believing community of Israel. And Malchuth, as we saw, was also called the moon. So here again the ecclesiastical community, the believing community, is identified with the moon.

The same thing comes up in the patristic allegories.[23] Jung talks about the patristic idea that at the end of time the moon will fail—because the moon is such a very dubious entity anyway—and when it fails, the Church will also die.

This is quite important symbolism for an understanding of collective psychology. The Church, or the believing community, would correspond symbolically to whatever group an individual can identify with in order to reinforce his or her psychological being. Such community identifications correspond to the gateway of the moon through which the individual soul has an opportunity to enter into incarnation.

There are times when identification with a group is absolutely crucial to the incarnation and development of the individual ego. There are other times, at a different phase of psychological development, when this is not so, when the moon is going to die. And when it dies, the Church will die with it. The Church puts off that day till the end of time—it projects it pretty far into the future. The dying of the Church, or the dying of the moon, would correspond to a situation in which

---

21 See Edinger, *Anatomy*, chap. 4.

22 *The Signature of All Things*, pp. 96f. (modifed and shortened).

23 Patristic refers to the early Church Fathers (Latin *pater* = father).

an individual's identification with a group had served its purpose, had lived itself out, and the time had come for that particular *participation mystique* to die.

Jung gives examples of how Luna personifies changeability, the mutability principle; the moon doesn't stay the same from one night to the next—each night it is a little different. Thus it pertains to birth, death, transition and changes of all kinds. This mutability and change takes us to our sixth image.

6. Wounding

Change wounds the principle of constancy. Change is a traitor to everything that promises to endure. The process of incarnation of a given psychic content also exposes it to corruption and, ultimately, to death. This relates to a picture that Jung refers to in paragraph 23. It's a picture of Christ being wounded by a mermaid who holds a lance (figure 2-5).

Jung connects the mermaid symbolically with the moon, and Christ with the sun. The moon was thought of as an entity capable of wounding the sun: the sun could drown in the lunar fountain, for instance. Thus, the sun—or spirit principle—is wounded by an encounter with the matter principle. This is all associated with egohood: whatever incarnates as an earthbound, specific ego is inevitably subject to wounding.

Figure 2-5. Christ being wounded by a mermaid.

The symbolism of wounding is an important part of individuation. The ego is always wounded by its initial major encounter with the unconscious. In fact, on first encounter, the shock is terrible. This wounding is an absolutely necessary feature—it's not an unfortunate accident that might, by careful consideration, be avoided. No, it's built into the archetypal structure of the psyche itself. It's inevitable, and it is expressed by many different images. Jung refers to some of them in our assignment: Ra wounded by the snake, the worm, that Isis put in his path; the sun darkened by Luna; Eve tempted by the serpent.

Jung also alludes to other alchemical images that we'll look at in more detail later: the bite of the mad dog, another example of wounding by the unconscious; Cupid with his arrows, wounding the hearts of his victims. These are all examples of the theme of wounding which is associated with the symbolism of the moon and belongs to mortificatio symbolism.[24]

7. Kenosis

Kenosis is a Greek word meaning "emptying." This theme comes out of the idea that, in the course of the month, the moon darkens as she approaches the sun. The thought was that she voluntarily empties herself of her light and pours it into the sun. Jung points out, in paragraph 29, that this idea parallels the kenosis doctrine of the Church, which derives from a passage in Paul's Epistle to the Philippians. Bear with me a few minutes longer here because this is an important image and I want to communicate it to you if I can. In the second chapter of Philippians, Paul says to the disciples:

> In your minds you must be the same as Christ Jesus:
> His state was divine,
> yet he did not cling
> to his equality with God
> but emptied himself
> to assume the condition of a slave,
> and became as men are;
> and being as all men are,
> he was humbler yet,
> even to accepting death,
> death on a cross.
> But God raised him high
> and gave him the name
> which is above all other names.[25]

The basic idea here is that the incarnation of Christ took place through a vol-

---

[24] See Edinger, *Anatomy*, chap. 6.
[25] Phil. 2: 5-9, Jerusalem Bible.

untary process of emptying: he emptied himself of his divinity in order to become man. This is the so-called kenosis doctrine. It describes the process of the incarnation, embodiment, of the ego, and it has parallel images in other symbolic traditions. For example, there is the bodhisattva doctrine of Buddhism. A future or potential Buddha who has achieved enlightenment—a bodhisattva—declines nirvana even though it's available. The bodhisattva declines it, is emptied of enlightenment and returns to the world out of compassion for humanity. That's a version of kenosis.

Jung was fond of another beautiful Chinese example: the image of Kwannon, Goddess of Kindness (figure 2-6). Jung speaks of her in *The Vision Seminars:*

Figure 2-6.
Kwannon,
Goddess of Kindness.

In most cases . . . [love] isn't concerned with kindness, it is just a hellish possession [He's talking about "falling in love," you see], but love *should* have to do with kindness—I am pleading for love.

> In the East, where they know as little about that kind of love as we do, they have a beautiful symbol for it in Kwannon, the Goddess of Kindness. She gives nourishment to all living beings, even to the evil spirits in hell, and to do so she must go down to hell; but it would frighten the devils if she were to appear there in her heavenly form and, as the Goddess of Kindness, she cannot permit that to happen; so, having such an extraordinary regard for the feelings of the devils, she transforms herself into an evil spirit and takes the food down in that guise. There is a beautiful traditional painting where she is represented in hell as a devil among the devils, giving them food; but there is a fine thread going up from her head to a heavenly being above, who is herself in all her splendid fury. [Something like that woman's dream of the foundling child with umbilical cord going up to heaven!] That is the psychological attitude which real love suggests.[26]

Now here's an image really worth thinking about. It's one way of expressing the assimilation of the shadow—the willingness to take on the appearance of an evil spirit in order to nourish the evil spirits in hell. It's another example of kenosis, emptying.

One more: the so-called doctrine of *Tsimtsum*, according to the Kabbalah of Isaac Luria. Gershom Scholem describes this doctrine as follows:

> It means. . . that the existence of the universe is made possible by a process of shrinkage in God. . . . If God is "all in all," how can there be things which are not God? How can God create the world out of nothing, if there is no nothing? . . . God was compelled to make room for the world by, as it were, abandoning a region within Himself, a kind of mystical primordial space from which He withdrew in order to return to it in the act of creation and revelation.[27]

In other words, God had to empty out a part of himself in order to make room for the creation of the earth. Another example of the image of kenosis.

The reason I'm making so much of this symbolism is that it refers to the original state of identity between the ego and the Self. This identity has to be "emptied out" if the ego is to have a separate place of its own.

You see, we all start out in a state of identification with God, with assumptions of omnipotence and of oneness with the universe. We all start as the center of the universe. A very lengthy, laborious process of emptying that original state of identification is required if one is to develop a conscious, responsible ego that knows its own limitations.

---

[26] *The Visions Seminars,* vol. 1, p. 215.
[27] *Major Trends in Jewish Mysticism,* pp. 260f.

3

Paragraphs 31 to 41

Today we have a relatively brief assignment—a respite from the first two—ten pages instead of twenty. I've pulled out these six images as the chief ones:

1. Mani and the Manichaean myth.
2. Sweating and the inflammation of desire.
3. The Manichaean wheel of light.
4. "The Devil and His Grandmother."
5. Paradoxes.
6. The symbolism of the point, and within that category, the text that talks about the jot of Monoïmos.

Before I launch into those images, I want to draw your attention to a correction that should be made in the translation. I'm indebted to Sigrid McPherson for this one and others I will point out; she's gone through the German version carefully and noted some of the major aberrations. This one is certainly significant psychologically. It's in paragraph 31, in the sentence, "From these books Mani concocted his pernicious heresy which poisoned the nations." That should read, "It is said, according to Christian tradition, that from these books Mani concocted his pernicious heresy." That's quite a significant proviso, you see. If you read that as it is, it's as though Jung were stating the "pernicious heresy" as a fact, which is a serious distortion of his statement.

1. Mani and the Manichaean Myth

Mani, the founder of Manichaeism, lived in the third century A.D. According to our very fragmentary biographical information, he was an orphan (which connects with the symbolism of the orphan image we talked about last time). He was adopted by a rich widow, and one of his cognomens was "son of the widow" (so there's a connection with the widow symbolism also). According to legend, he learned much of his doctrine from his adoptive mother, who is supposed to have transmitted to him books she had received from her dead husband.

Now Mani is quite an important figure for the Western psyche, even though you may never have heard of him. He's important historically because he has been a major collective shadow figure for Western consciousness. Ever since Augustine, who lived and functioned about a century after Mani, Mani has been saddled with the projection of evil.

Augustine was a Manichaean until he converted to Christianity, and you know how it is with converts—they flip-flop and somersault, and then they become particularly vituperative about the position they've left. That's characteristic of the symbolism of the opposites, you know, and that's the way it was with Augustine and Manichaeism. He did a great deal to identify Mani with the devil. I would remind you that it was Augustine who originated the Christian doctrine of *privatio boni,* about which Jung says a good deal.[28] The basic idea of that doctrine is that evil doesn't really exist as a substantial entity; it's just the privation of good, it's just the absence of the real thing—it doesn't have any real substance in itself.

Mani's doctrine said just the contrary: Mani asserted that evil had the same degree of reality and was a principle with the same substance as was good. So you can see why Augustine was so against him. But Augustine is one of the creators of the collective Christian psyche and hence, for that particular psychic position, Mani is the arch-heretic and the personification of evil itself. The reason for this is that he acknowledged the reality of evil. It's an early illustration of a profound psychological fact that whenever someone sees the reality of evil and points it out, makes an issue of it—"Hey look, look at that"—that person runs the grave risk of being identified by the collective psyche with the evil being pointed out. So be very careful about pointing out evil; notice it, and think to yourself, "Ah, there it is," but, as a rule, keep it to yourself.

So the image of Mani has been associated with darkness. And, as Jung points out in paragraph 32, the combined image of Mani and his mother the widow corresponds to the alchemical image of the black Ethiopian and the veiled woman. Jung associates the black Ethiopian to the black sulphur, the son of the prima materia. He says that this black sulphur "is the activated darkness of matter." In other words, if we translate that into its psychological meaning, he symbolizes the dark consciousness that rises from below, in contradistinction to the bright consciousness that descends from above. The image of Christ has taken on the symbolism of that light good consciousness that descends from above, and the figure of Mani is a kind of counterpoint to the figure of Christ—he's the dark consciousness that rises from below.

As depth psychologists, it is the very nature of our professional work to deal with the *un*conscious—the regions below. We're going to be very familiar with the dark consciousness that is acquired through contact with the depths. This is very different from the light spiritual consciousness one acquires by embracing the spiritual wisdom of a highly structured and formulated religion or philosophy, spiritual wisdom that descends from the Olympian heights, so to speak. The one is rooted in the dark, empirical realities of actual human existence; the other derives from the sublimated state of the elevated, abstract spirit. I don't mean to knock the light consciousness—I just mean to set it in its larger context in relation to its opposite.

---

28 See, for instance, *Aion,* CW 9ii, pars. 74ff.

The theme of the missing father comes in here—Mani, as son of the widow, has no father. And the father, in the symbolic and psychological sense, personifies collective spiritual wisdom. If he's present to any appreciable extent, he will keep the son out of the dark maternal depths, and the way he does that is by instituting the psychological incest taboo. That keeps the son connected with the upper, father-spirit, and not having much to do with the dubious, incestuous connections to the mother, who is associated with matter.

Let me give you a general outline of the Manichaean myth. I have condensed this from the account given by Hans Jonas in his book, *The Gnostic Religion,* which I recommend to all of you. He has a lengthy chapter on Mani and Manichaeism, and the entire book is the best concise account in English of the whole range of Gnostic symbolism.

In the beginning, according to the Manichaean myth, there were two natures, two whole worlds of being: the world of Light and the world of Darkness. The good principle dwelt in the world of Light, and was called "Father of Greatness"; and the evil principle dwelt in the land of Darkness, and was called "King of Darkness." Initially, these two realms existed side by side and had no connection—they'd never heard of each other.

But at a certain point, the world of Darkness got a glimpse of the world of Light and was fascinated; the world of Light was such an agreeable place, and the world of Darkness was such a miserable place—all that lived in the world of Darkness were in agony. As soon as it glimpsed the world of Light, its envy and greed were excited; it wanted what was present in the beautiful world of Light, it wanted to merge with it. To bring that about it therefore attacked the world of Light.

This stirred the Light out of its repose. Until it was attacked, it hadn't even known that the world of Darkness existed; then it learned about the presence of that world very abruptly, very disagreeably. The world of Light had to respond to this attack, and what it was required to do was to create something out of itself. In order to meet the aggressor, the Godhead was obliged to produce a special "creation" representing an aspect of himself. This special creation was called Primal Man, and Primal Man was assigned the task of defending the world of Light against the aggressor, the world of Darkness.

So Primal Man went out to do battle with the world of Darkness, but in the battle he was defeated. Or, by other accounts, the defeat was a voluntary one: Primal Man sacrificed himself on purpose and allowed himself to be consumed "as a man who has an enemy mixes a deadly poison in a cake and gives it to him."[29] By this device, Primal Man, or Soul of the Light world, managed to stop the attack of Darkness, and the Darkness was satisfied by what it was able to devour—or by other accounts, it was poisoned by the Light it devoured. Anyhow,

---

[29] Jonas, *The Gnostic Religion,* p. 218.

the attack stopped. But it was stopped at the price of having the Light substance captured by Matter.

This was hardly a satisfactory state of affairs; it was not a satisfactory resolution from the standpoint of the Light world because now "Soul mingled with Matter"; and Soul "was as it were bound like a wild beast, or . . . put to sleep as by a spell." By mixing with Matter "the Soul became subject to the affections of Matter and against its true nature, was degraded to sharing in evil."[30] Thus, in order to rescue the lost Light substance, the Godhead was now obliged to create the whole cosmos as a great mechanism for the separation and redemption of the imprisoned Light.

That's the essence of the Manichaean myth, and I think you can see immediately that it is a profound image of one aspect of psychic reality.

After the defeat of Primal Man and the mingling of the Light substance with the Dark world, several procedures were instituted. One of them takes us to our next image.

2. Sweating and the Inflammation of Desire

A divine Messenger was sent to the lower world, where the Light substance was imprisoned, with the idea that maybe the Light substance could be extracted from the Darkness and stolen back. The method used by the divine Messenger was the so-called "seduction of the Archons." (The Archons were the children of Darkness who were carrying the stolen Light.)

In order to seduce the Archons, the Messenger took on an alluring form: if the Messenger was dealing with a male Archon, the Messenger took on a female form; otherwise the Messenger took on a male form. Then, by seductive procedures, the Archons were aroused sexually and forced to release their Light, either by sweating it out of them, or by ejaculation. Thus the Light substance was expelled by the process of seduction—by the inflammation of desire. Let me read you a passage about this from Jonas:

> [The Messenger came down and made himself] visible to all the Archons, the children of the Darkness, the male and the female. And at the sight of the Messenger, who was beautiful in his forms, all the Archons became excited with lust for him, the male ones for his female appearance and the female ones for his male appearance. And in their concupiscence they began to release the Light of the Five Luminous Gods which they had devoured. . . . The escaping Light is received by the angels of Light, purified, and loaded onto the "ships" to be transported to its native realm.[31]

---

[30] Ibid., p. 220.
[31] Ibid, pp. 225f.

This image of the inflammation of desire is very relevant psychologically. It's interesting to note that there is a somewhat more complex alchemical picture corresponding to this very imag. It comes from the alchemical treatise *Splendor solis,* and shows a great alchemical retort inside of which is a little homunculus with a dragon (figure 3-1). In one hand the homunculus has a pair of bellows with which he fans the flame of the fiery dragon; in the other hand he has a water bottle with which he extinguishes the flame. That makes it a little more complex than the Manichaean image, but the same theme is at work—the inflammation of desire.

Figure 3-1.
The fire of the dragon.

There is another alchemical theme, the sweat box, which makes the same point (figure 3-2). In this picture, the king is sitting in a great sweat box while the fire is being stoked beneath him. He's being exposed to an intense heat which sweats the aqua permanens out of him. It's another version of the inflammation of desire.

How might we apply this image psychologically? Certainly one aspect of the analytic process, in which one opens up the unconscious and exposes the ego to the contents of the unconscious, makes visible various desires that had long been dormant. It is as though the archons, living in the unconscious, had been cut off

Figure 3-2. The king in the sweat box.

from conscious life. Then consciousness sends a messenger down to them and allows them to entertain these forbidden desires which were the cause of their banishment. A kind of sweat box is generated that can lead to the extraction of the light stuff imprisoned in the unconscious complexes. That's one way of seeing it, anyway.

Another effort to reclaim the Light imprisoned in the Darkness leads us to our third image.

3. The Manichaean Wheel of Light

It's really quite a beautiful concept, this wheel of light. The Zodiac is a great wheel that the sun traverses in its yearly circuit—it goes through the whole wheel of the Zodiac. According to the Manichaeans, that whole cosmic wheel of the Milky Way—the Zodiac—is a great engine of cosmic salvation. They thought of it as like a water wheel with buckets that catch the water as it revolves. The idea was that this great Manichaean light wheel dipped down into the dark region of the earthly realm, scooped up light that was imprisoned in that darkness and carried it to the upper realm. It was a circulation process. The light was taken and carried up, then emptied into the moon-ship. The moon-ship transported it still higher and emptied it into the sun. So the moon was thought of as a great tanker in which to transport light.

The Manichaean creed and Manichaean ethics were built into this whole mythological symbolism in a very concrete way: the Manichaean believers thought of themselves as part of that great light wheel, and each individual was a bucket in the great wheel engaged in the process of recovering the lost light. It's just a magnificent image and it is too bad they had to spoil it by taking it so concretely!—because, I'm sorry to have to tell you, they thought they could accumulate the lost light by eating the right foods! Certain foods had more light in them than other foods. If they ate the right foods, then they'd take that light into their body, digest it and the light would become part of them. One of the foods that was particularly high on their light list was melon. Now my fantasy—it's no more than a fantasy, but in this realm fantasies can pass for evidence!—is that the reason they chose melons was that the multiplicity of seeds would be analogous to all the seeds of light imprisoned in matter. That's my guess.

In paragraph 34, Jung points out that the Manichaean light wheel is a grand image of the alchemical process of circulatio. This alchemical operation can be understood psychologically to refer to a circumambulation of all aspects of one's being. If you go through the whole cycle, it's a process that brings about a separation or a manifestation of light. Light gets extracted from darkness. But the Manichaean myth, psychologically considered, is limited: the two principles of Light and Darkness are separated at the beginning, and are still separated at the end. There's never a coniunctio in the Manichaean system; it does not picture a final synthesis.

This myth of the recollection of the scattered particles of light is similar to an alchemical image that came up in our first assignment (paragraph 12) but which I didn't have time to discuss. It's the image of Mercurius as the original man who is disseminated throughout the whole physical world. The alchemist's task was to gather together all the disseminated fragments of Mercurius and restore him to his original unity. In an important footnote (paragraph 6, note 6), Jung deals with "the idea of uniting the Many into One." He gives several examples of how some of the Church Fathers, especially Origen, elaborated that theme.

4. "The Devil and His Grandmother"

In paragraph 32, Jung states that Mani and his mother the widow "form a pair roughly comparable to the devil and his grandmother." This is a reference to the Grimm fairy tale, "The Devil and His Grandmother."[32] It's very relevant psychologically, and I'll give you the gist of it.

Three soldiers desert from the army because of low pay, and they hide in a wheat field. They expect the army to move on but it doesn't, and they are in great danger of being captured. If they're captured, they'll be hanged. At this point the

---

[32] *The Complete Grimm's Fairy Tales*, no. 125, pp. 563ff.

devil makes his appearance and offers to rescue them on the condition that, after seven years, they'll become his possession. They agree, and the devil then gives them a whip which, when they crack it, makes gold—so they can live in wealth. He also tells them that they will even have a chance to escape him if they can solve a riddle he'll give them at the end of the seven years.

For seven years everything goes swimmingly, but at the end of that time they begin to worry. One of the men finds his way to an old woman who lives in the woods. I won't go into details of how that happens—we'll say fortune leads him there. It turns out that this old woman is the devil's grandmother—and she's quite friendly. She shows him the way to the basement and says to him, "Conceal yourself there, you can hear everything that is said here; only sit still, and do not stir. When the dragon [her son] comes, I will question him about the riddle. He tells everything to me so listen to his answer."

Here's the riddle: "I will take you with me to hell. There you shall have a meal! If you can guess what kind of roast meat you will have to eat, you shall be free. . . ." The answer is that a dead dogfish will be the roast. Then, "But what will your spoon be?" "The rib of a whale that is to be our silver spoon." "And do you also know what your wineglass is to be?" "An old horse's hoof is to be our wineglass."

A very interesting fairy tale. The knowledge of the depths that some fairy tales open up—when you have eyes to see it—is just astonishing. This one starts with three men deserting the army. I think we could say that psychologically the army would symbolize highly structured, uniform, collective, masculine, paternal functioning. The deserters abandon their state of subordination to that psychic condition, and in the course of abandoning it they incur a mortal risk. This rebellious abandonment of the collective, traditional, established authority amounts to an individualistic rebellion that constellates the devil—the negative, rebellious, renegade masculine. They must deal with him if they are to survive. If they don't take him up they will be caught—so it is appropriate that they make their deal even though it's dangerous. We can think of the whip that makes gold as ego power functioning, which offers a brief foreshadowing in ego terms of the true gold-making power of the Self. That's the whip—a power image.

The contact with the devil's grandmother suggests the possibility of establishing one's own relation to the unconscious and thereby getting beneath the devil, so to speak. You're under the trap door in the basement, listening from below.

Then comes the important feature of the riddle, and with it a major symbolic image that expresses one aspect of the ego's encounter with the unconscious. The encounter with the unconscious presents the ego with a riddle, and the classic example is the riddle of the sphinx. This is a life and death issue because if the riddle is posed and one doesn't answer it, one forfeits one's life; whereas, in the Oedipus story anyway, if the riddle is answered, the sphinx is destroyed. The riddle theme is an ordeal for consciousness that, in effect, establishes whether or not the ego has sufficient potential consciousness to go on to the next stage of development.

I understand the riddle in our story to be a reference to the Messianic banquet, where the flesh of Leviathan and Behemoth—symbolizing the primordial primitive psyche—will be eaten "by the pious."[33] The dogfish is a primitive shark. In comparative anatomy, one is obliged to study the anatomy of a whole series of animals in the evolutionary sequence in order to see how the anatomical structure changes. The dogfish is the first specimen in that study—the most primitive. So the dogfish roast corresponds to serving up Behemoth and Leviathan in the Messianic banquet. In addition, we have a reference to the Leviathan—the whale—in the whale's rib that will be used as a spoon. The horse's hoof used as the wine glass suggests a more developed specimen on the evolutionary ladder, but it too is theriomorphic.

Taken as a whole, I see the imagery as corresponding to the assimilation of the primordial psyche. As that is achieved, one is released from the threat of being possessed by the autonomous devil content because it will have been subsumed into the larger consciousness of the whole.

To translate this story into our own times and into tonight's subject matter, we might say that the time has come to assimilate the Manichaean myth to the modern mind. We no longer have to treat Mani as the devil, and we no longer have to use the term "Manichaean" or "neo-Manichaean" as a negative epithet, which is done by all collective orthodox religious thinkers. If we have digested the primordial psyche, we'll be released from the danger of devil possession.

As you may know, Jung has been called Manichaean, and it's no compliment. It's erroneous; he's not Manichaean. The essential feature of all Manichaean systems is an eternal dualism, you see. In no sense at all is Jung Manichaean, except in the sense that he takes evil seriously, as a substantial entity.

5. Paradoxes

The whole of chapter II of *Mysterium* is entitled "The Paradoxa," and, as you've probably seen—or soon will —alchemy is absolutely riddled with paradoxes. A paradox is an affront to the logic of consciousness, so it's a deliberate defeat for the rational ego. I would urge you to be on the lookout for paradoxical images in dreams. They are very common and indicate that the issue of individuation is now relevant to the dreamer. Paradoxes point to the Self.

Let me give you just one marvelous description of the paradoxical nature of Mercurius which Jung quotes in his essay, "The Spirit Mercurius." Mercurius describes himself in these words:

---

[33] See Edinger, *The Creation of Consciousness: Jung's Myth for Modern Man*, p. 111.

I am the poison-dripping dragon, who is everywhere and can be cheaply had.[34] That upon which I rest, and that which rests upon me, will be found within me by those who pursue their investigations. . . . My water and fire destroy and put together; from my body you may extract the green lion and the red. But if you do not have exact knowledge of me, you will destroy your five senses with my fire. From my snout there comes a spreading poison that has brought death to many. . . . I bestow on you the powers of the male and the female, and also those of heaven and earth. The mysteries of my art must be handled with courage and greatness of mind if you would conquer me by the power of fire, for already very many have come to grief . . . . I am the egg of nature, known only to the wise, who in piety and modesty bring forth from me the microcosm . . . . given only to the few, while the many long for it in vain. . . . By the philosophers I am named Mercurius; my spouse is the [philosophic] gold; I am the old dragon, found everywhere on the globe . . . . father and mother, young and old, very strong and very weak, death and resurrection, visible and invisible, hard and soft; I descend into the earth and ascend to the heavens, I am the highest and the lowest, the lightest and the heaviest; often the order of nature is reversed in me, as regards colour, number, weight, and measure; I contain the light of nature; I am dark and light; I come forth from heaven and earth; I am known and yet do not exist at all; . . . all colours shine in me, and all metals. I am the carbuncle of the sun.[35]

Later in that essay Jung summarizes the multiple aspects of Mercurius. Let me remind you that he's talking about the unconscious, so these aren't just abstruse irrelevancies for us. He says:

(1) Mercurius consists of all conceivable opposites. He is thus quite obviously a duality, but is named a unity in spite of the fact that his innumerable inner contradictions can dramatically fly apart into an equal number of disparate and apparently independent figures.

(2) He is both material and spiritual.

(3) He is the process by which the lower and material is transformed into the higher and spiritual, and vice versa.

(4) He is the devil, a redeeming psychopomp, an evasive trickster, and God's reflection in physical nature.

(5) He is also the reflection of a mystical experience of the artifex that coincides with the *opus alchymicum.*

(6) As such, he represents on the one hand the self and on the other the individuation process and, because of the limitless number of his names, also the collective unconscious.[36]

---

[34] Here is the dragon that came up in "The Devil and His Grandmother."

[35] *Alchemical Studies,* CW 13, par. 267.

[36] Ibid., par. 284.

6. The Image of the Point

We first learn about the point as an entity when we study geometry. And I would remind you that the origin of geometry is the psyche—none of the geometrical forms or propositions exist in the outer world. There are in nature no points or lines or planes or regular solid figures. Those things are all projected by the psyche onto nature in order to manipulate and deal more effectively with it. And so it is with the point.

It is very interesting to go back to the original geometricians, the ancient Greeks, and see how they thought about the point. The pre-Euclidean Pythagoreans were the earliest ones to do any systematic work with geometry, and they defined a point as "a monad with position added." Their notion of a monad—and this is another projection—was that it was a kind of semidivine personification of unity or singleness or oneness; that's what they called a monad. It belongs to the realm of the eternal forms and doesn't actually have visible existence in the physical world. The point was conceived as the first incarnation of the monad—a monad that comes into being due to the fact that it has position. Euclid started out his *Elements* by defining the point. For the creation myth of geometry, it's as if the point were Genesis, chapter one, verse one. It is the origin of the universe. The point is that which has no parts (Euclid's definition) which could be translated as "that which is indivisible." In other words, it's an individual—that which cannot be divided. It has position but no extension; and without extension, it cannot be cut into parts.

Plato defined a point as the beginning of a line, the *arche* of a line (and *arche* is the same word that is used for the prima materia). Here is an illustration of the geometrical theorem that a moving point generates a line (figure 3-3). The point itself has no extension, but as the point moves it generates a line—an extended point. And as a line moves, it generates a plane. And as a plane moves, it generates a solid. That's a creation myth. By a threefold movement of a point—the first move creates a line, the second move creates a plane, and the third creates a solid—the net effect is to draw a three-dimensional cross on physis, on matter. In figure 3-3 I've indicated in a three-dimensional representation the three vectors of movement at right angles to each other. A three-dimensional cross is imposed on matter, and this brings it into manifestation.

Figure 3-3.
Three vectors,
creating a
solid body.

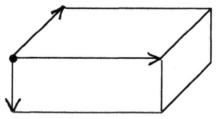

Now the first term of that process is the "point"—the monad with position added. What makes this symbolism so important is that the point is a major symbolic image for the Self. It comes up as such in dreams, and if you're familiar with this symbolism you'll be more likely to pick it up; otherwise it might go completely unnoticed.

Jung refers to the fact that the point was equated symbolically with fire and light (paragraph 41) and it is this symbolic equation that connects it to next week's image of the *scintillae,* the sparks shining in the darkness.

Finally, in paragraph 38, Jung quotes a very interesting text from Hyppolytus concerning the point. This is the text that I call the jot of Monoïmos and it reads as follows:

> Monoïmos . . . thinks that there is some such Man of whom the poet speaks as Oceanus, when he says: Oceanus, origin of gods and origin of men. Putting this into other words, he says that the Man is all, the source of the universe, unbegotten, incorruptible, everlasting; and that there is a Son of the aforesaid Man, who is begotten and capable of suffering, and whose birth is outside time . . . . This Man is a single Monad.

There's the monad that lies behind the point.

> Uncompounded and indivisible, yet compounded and divisible; loving and at peace with all things yet warring with all things and at war with itself in all things; unlike and like itself, as it were a musical harmony containing all things; . . . showing forth all things and giving birth to all things. It is its own mother, its own father.
> . . . The emblem of the whole man . . . says Monoïmos, is the jot or tittle.

And the jot or tittle is the point.

> This one tittle is the uncompounded, simple, unmixed Monad, having its composition from nothing whatsoever, yet composed of many forms, of many parts. That single, undivided jot is the many-faced, thousand-eyed, and thousand-named jot of the iota. This is the emblem of that perfect and invisible Man. . . . The Son of the Man is the one iota, the one jot flowing from on high, full and filling all things, containing in himself everything that is in the Man, the Father of the Son of the Man.

As with most of these texts, this is a little circuitous; the image the text is describing needs to be focused. This text says basically that there is a great jot, the Monad, who is the origin of everything. He corresponds to Oceanus, the origin of gods and men, and is everlasting, incorruptible and unbegotten. Born from him is a lesser jot called Son of Man, who is begotten and capable of suffering. So there are two points: the original invisible point—the Monad—and the lesser point, a geometrical entity representing position coming into manifestation. The relation between them could be seen psychologically as the relation between the Self and the ego—the great jot and the little jot.

4

Paragraphs 42-50

Tonight we will consider four major images:
1. Multiple luminosities; the *scintillae* (fiery sparks shining in the darkness).
2. Multiple eyes; *oculi piscium* (fishes' eyes).
3. The Eye of God.
4. Undressing.

Before I start, I want to mention one translation correction in note 72 of paragraph 44 (seven lines from the bottom): "body/sign" should read "body/tomb."

l. Multiple Luminosities; *Scintillae* (Fiery Sparks Shining in the Darkness)

The first three major images are really variations of the same central idea: the image of lights shining in the darkness. This is a very important image for depth psychology and Jung discusses it extensively in his important theoretical essay, "On the Nature of the Psyche." I want to read a few sentences from the section of that essay entitled "The Unconscious as a Multiple Consciousness." Here is the image of shining sparks of light in the darkness, the *scintillae,* which Jung applies to the nature of the psyche:

> The hypothesis of multiple luminosities rests partly. . . on the quasi-conscious state of unconscious contents and partly on the incidence of certain images which must be regarded as symbolical. [37]

In other words, archetypal images. He then refers to alchemy:

> Thus the *Aurora consurgens,* Part II, says . . . Know that the foul earth quickly receives white sparks. These sparks Khunrath explains as "radii atque scintillae" [the roots and sparks] of the . . . world-soul, which is identical with the spirit of God. . . . One such spark is the human mind. . . . [In another text it is said that] in the "Water of the Art" . . . there are to be found the "fiery sparks of the soul of the world as pure [essential forms of things]." These [forms] correspond to the Platonic Ideas, from which one could equate the *scintillae* with the archetypes on the assumption that the Forms "stored up in a supracelestial place" are a philosophical version of the [archetypes]. One would have to conclude . . . that the archetypes have . . . a certain effulgence or quasi-consciousness, and that numinosity entails luminosity. Paracelsus seems to have had an inkling of this. . . . [He says:] "And as little as aught can exist in man without the divine numen, so little can aught exist in man without the natural lumen. A man is made perfect by numen and lumen and these two alone. . . . Without them man is nothing."[38]

---

[37] *The Structure and Dynamics of the Psyche,* CW 8, par. 388.
[38] Ibid.

This really expresses in a nutshell the essential nature of the synthetic aspect of Jungian analysis. There's also a reductive aspect of analysis—analysis on the one hand and synthesis on the other. When we're dealing with psychological synthesis we're dealing with the process that brings into awareness the presence of the numen and the lumen—the numinous intensity of the archetypal image and the light, the consciousness, the insight, that glows out of it.

The statement that the sparks are the "roots and sparks of the world soul" parallels remarkably an image in Jung's last recorded dream before he died: "A square of trees, all fibrous roots, coming up from the ground and surrounding him. There were gold threads gleaming among the roots."[39] The "roots and sparks of the world-soul." It's exactly the same image.

This image of the multiple little numinosities shining in the darkness has two aspects: one aspect is that darkness is not all dark—there is light in the darkness; the other is that that light is in a state of multiplicity. This indicates that unconscious complexes, which almost always have at their core an archetypal image, have a certain consciousness. As the complex is assimilated, that latent consciousness is extracted so to speak from the complex. The fact that the lights are in a state of multiplicity—scattered, random—means that they are at odds with one another and they call out for unification.

That unification does in fact take place along with the ego's encounter with these lights. As they come into conscious awareness, the unity of the ego that perceives them has the effect of unifying the multiple sparks and this is accompanied by a constellation of the Self as a unity. Just how this takes place is a mystery, but if you're alert to this process in yourself and in patients, you can demonstrate that it does happen. The unconscious in its initial manifestations appears to us as a multiplicity; but the more deeply the ego commits itself to relating to it and understanding it, the more the unconscious manifests as a unity.

As with so much of alchemical imagery, this image derives originally from ancient Greek philosophy. The notion was that above the seven planetary spheres, in the region of the fixed stars, the earth was enveloped by a sphere of fiery ether. The stars were seen as little holes in the vault of heaven through which we got peeks of that sphere of fiery ether, which was thought to be the region of the Divine Logos, the Nous. Later, in the Christian conception, this notion was associated with the Holy Spirit.

One historian of philosophy describes it this way:

> All round the world was an envelope of the fiery ether, pure and unmixed, but it also penetrated the whole mass [of the earth] as its soul. The orderly working of Nature was its operation: organic beings grew according to regular types, because the Divine Reason in them was a *logos spermatikos*, a formula of life developing from

---

[39] Barbara Hannah, *Jung: His Life and Work: A Biographical Memoir*, p. 347.

a germ. Even upon earth some of the divine fire retained its pure essence—the reasonable souls, each one a particle of fiery ether, which dwelt in the hearts of men.[40]

All these little sparks of the divine fiery ether that were scattered about in the earth were thought of as expressions of the anima mundi, the world-soul, which permeated not only organic beings but also inorganic matter. This was responsible for the laws of nature, you see, so that everything was orderly and not chaotic. The alchemists inherited this image and thought they were bringing it into manifestation in their laboratory and in their retort.

This same image from Greek philosophy was applied to the myth of Christ in the first chapter of the Gospel of John which reads:

> In the beginning was the Word [the Logos; it's the same divine fiery Logos], and the Word was with God, and the Word was God. . . . All things were made by him; . . . In him was life; and the life was the light of men. And the light shineth in darkness; and the darkness comprehended it not.[41]

That's the world-soul shining in the darkness and in this passage it is identified with Christ.

This image of lights shining in the darkness shows up in dreams and it's important to recognize it; if you don't, it can't have its effect. Such a dream indicates that the psyche of the dreamer is ready for a real step in individuation, ready to relate to the unconscious as a light-bringer. It indicates that the time has come for the ego to realize that it, the ego, is not the sole source of light—the assumption we all start with and which dies very hard.

I have some dreams and other material as examples of this image of multiple luminosities shining in the darkness. Here is one:

> There is a darkness, but with a luminosity in it, not describable. A darkness somehow glowing. Standing in it is a beautiful golden woman, with an almost Mona Lisa face. Now I realize that the glow is emanating from a necklace she is wearing. It is of great delicacy: small cabochons of turquoise, each circled in reddish gold. It has a great meaning for me, as if there were a message in the complete image if only I could break through its elusiveness.[42]

This is an image of the multiplicity of lights which are unified by their being strung on the same necklace. I interpreted that dream, that figure, as representing Sophia shining out of the darkness of her embrace with Physis.

There's another important example of this image in Adler's case history, *The*

---

[40] Edwyn Bevan, *Stoics and Sceptics,* p. 43. *Logos spermatikos* means "seed-word," the word as little seeds that would be planted in the dark earth and would grow like plants.

[41] John 1: 1-5, Authorized Version.

[42] See Edinger, *Ego and Archetype,* pp. 217f., for further discussion of this dream.

Living Symbol. At a certain point in her work, the patient had an active imagination in which she was wrestling with a large angelic figure who had strange inhuman eyes. Here's how Adler describes a portion of this experience:

> The patient went on to concentrate on the struggle with the angel. She felt the urge to look at the angel as closely as possible, and the feature that fascinated her most was his eyes, which right from the beginning she had felt to be particularly powerful. When . . . she looked "with all possible concentration" into the eyes of the angel . . . . [she] "could see, through the angel's eyes, a night sky with stars; but not the sky as we see it above us, but the sky as you would see it if you were in the midst of it." . . . It was . . . "an extraordinary and ecstatic experience: . . ." She felt that this experience could be expressed only by "an abstract painting," and she proceeded to paint it the same evening.[43]

The painting is called "The Night Sky Mandala" (figure 4-1), and the patient described it this way:

> She saw the "framework" of the golden circle with the two intersecting axes as representing a three-dimensional sphere. . . . "It represents the framework which holds the scheme of things together." The tiny point in the center she understood as the "eye."[44]

And within the larger circumference was the night sky and the multiple luminosity of stars.

Figure 4-1
The Night Sky
Mandala.

You see the night sky *is* the original image for the multiple luminosities of sparks of light shining in the darkness. And it is as though that experience and that image has been seen as a reflection on earth, in matter, and in the psyche. Sometimes one even gets dreams that use this reflection image literally: the

---

[43] *The Lving Symbol,* pp. 219f
[44] Ibid., p. 220.

dreamer will dream of looking into the water, a well or some reflective surface, and the night sky is mirrored there. Such a dream is an exact parallel to the old alchemical saying: "Heaven above / Heaven below / Stars above / Stars below / All that is above / also is below / Grasp this / And rejoice."[45]

For Adler's patient, this particular decisive experience signified a break-through which led to the insight that there is consciousness in the unconscious. What started out as multiple luminosities turned, in the course of her working on that active imagination, into a unified luminosity—the two are combined. You have both the multiplicity of stars and also the unifying mandala image super-imposed on them—the Eye of God on top of the multiple sparks.

Here is another example, somewhat abbreviated, dreamt by a woman of about fifty:

> I found a small bowl about the size of a sea shell, an ordinary shallow Grecian-like bowl with a black rim. When I turned it over, I found the outside to be very unusual with many cloudy white patches. As I looked, I realized that the white patches were galaxies of stars. There were small pinpricks of white like the Milky way. Every time I looked at this bowl, it got larger and more intricate.

The outer aspect of the bowl, you see, has taken on the quality of the night sky.

> I was aware that the underside was much too large to fit the top side. I felt it was mine and I was going to keep it. [This is an ominous turning.]
>
> In a later scene a dusky black man, a Nubian, dressed in a turban and loin cloth, like Gandhi, approaches me. He has a dusty chocolate colored dog—I think it may be Cerberus. I clap my hands to make them leave but they won't and I realize I'm sort of a captive. At first I don't take them seriously but the man causes the dog to make increasingly threatening gestures. Finally I was convinced and I said, "All right, what do you want?" Then it occurred to me that he wanted the bowl.

A year or two later this woman was found to have carcinoma of the lung which was operated on successfully and has not recurred. I don't know for sure that there's a connection between this dream and that fact but I know from other experiences that the basic theme of clinging to something that is too big for the ego is one that does come up in the psychology of some cancer cases. Anyhow, I bring this up because it's an example of the image of the multiple luminosities of the night sky reflected in an earthen bowl. The bowl is a piece of earth which, if the ego tries to relate to it in the wrong way, puts the ego in great danger.

I want to mention a visionary experience that Jung refers to here in footnote 63 of paragraph 42. It's an image reported by Frances Wickes:

> I looked upon space and I beheld darkness. In that darkness moved mysterious forces. Not like the gods . . . but strange primeval beings born before the gods of

---

[45] Often quoted by Jung; see, for instance, "The Psychology of the Transference," *The Practice of Psychotherapy,* CW 16, par. 384.

human form. They were hooded in darkness. Through their fingers they drew the threads of blackness and ever wove them back and forth. I saw the rays that they made like the rays that stream inward from a many-pointed star or the converging of the lines of a many-sided crystal, but these rays were not of light but of darkness, and the darkness seemed to draw all things into it. Thus I knew that they were weaving a great void that had no form nor boundaries.

Then from the center of the void rose a single shaft, whether of stone or of a gray and lifeless tree I could not tell. As the shaft rose the creatures [the black creatures] fell away till nothing was left but the void with the shaft standing in the midst. Then I saw that on the shaft there hung a human figure that held within itself all the loneliness of the world and of the spaces. Alone, and hoping for nothing, the One hung and gazed down into the void. . . drawing all solitude unto itself. Then deep in the fathomless dark was born an infinitesimal spark. Slowly it rose from the bottomless depth and as it rose it grew until it became a star. And the star hung in space just opposite the figure, and the white light streamed upon the Lone-ly One.[46]

Frances Wickes associated this vision with the myth of Odin. So that wisdom might be born, he hung over the void for nine days on Yggdrasil, the cosmic tree. An image like this gives us some indication of how the ego's encounter with the darkness somehow helps the germinating seed of light become visible.

2. Multiple Eyes; *Oculi Piscium* (Fishes' Eyes)

At this point the multiple luminosities turn into multiple eyes like fishes' eyes, *oculi piscium*. It is a major transition from the discovery of lights shining in the darkness of the unconscious to the discovery of eyes looking at you from that darkness. The presence of eyes indicates that the light residing in the unconscious has a subject. Concerning this image, in paragraph 45 Jung says: "The eyes indicate that the lapis is in the process of evolution and grows from these ubiquitous eyes."

The story of Argus and Io is a mythological parallel to the multiplicity of eyes. Jung doesn't refer to this myth in *Mysterium,* but he does in his essay "On the Nature of the Psyche."[47] Let me give you the essence of that myth.

Io was a mortal woman who had a love affair with Zeus, and thus aroused Hera's jealousy. In an effort to keep Io secret from Hera, Zeus changed Io into a heifer. But Hera wasn't fooled, and she ordered Argus, the Hundred-Eyed One, to guard Io. At no time did all of Argus's eyes sleep—some were always open. (That's also a crucial feature of fishes' eyes—there are no eyelids—they're always looking at you.) At the order of Zeus, Hermes killed Argus but then Hera had Io tormented by a gadfly. Io was forced to wander from place to place until

---

46 *The Inner World of Man,* p. 245.
47 *The Structure and Dynamics of the Psyche,* CW 8, par. 394.

ultimately she was restored by Zeus to her human form.[48]

I want to draw your attention to this basic myth because of what it tells us psychologically about the phenomenology of the eyes of the unconscious. It is particularly instructive to note that when Argus the watcher was killed, the experience of being watched was replaced by the experience of being goaded by a gadfly. I understand that to mean if one is under the scrutiny of the unconscious (if the Self has been constellated and is looking at you) and if one refuses to acknowledge that fact and to relate to it appropriately (you turn your back on it, repressing the whole experience—killing Argus, so to speak) then the experience of being looked at is replaced by being nagged by an obsessive complex.

More frequently it works the other way around—we see the nagging, goading complex first. That's what the patient comes in with, you see. Then, as that is analyzed, we find at its core the fact that the unconscious is requiring attention. The individual discovers that there is a subject, a meaningful, purposeful, knowing subject, at the heart of the complex. In other words, an eye.

3. The Eye of God

This is the same image, the same phenomenon, except now it has been unified, it's not a multiplicity. It refers to the experience of being seen and known by an other in the unconscious.[49] The Eye of God is a particularly important image in Egyptian religion. Rundle Clark has this to say:

> The Eye of the High God is the Great Goddess of the universe in her terrible aspect. Originally it had been sent out into the Primeval Waters by God on an errand. . . . The Eye is the daughter of the High God. When it [the daughter Eye] returned, it found that it had been supplanted in the Great One's face by another—a surrogate eye—which we can interpret as the sun or moon. This was the primary cause for the wrath of the Eye and the great turning-point in the development of the universe, for the Eye can never be fully or permanently appeased. The High God . . . turned it into a rearing cobra, which he bound around his forehead to ward off his enemies [figure 4-2][50]

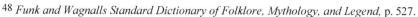

Figure 4-2
Egyptian Eye of God.

EYE OF HORUS

---

[48] *Funk and Wagnalls Standard Dictionary of Folklore, Mythology, and Legend,* p. 527.
[49] See Edinger, *Creation of Consciousness,* pp. 41ff.
[50] *Myth and Symbol in Ancient Egypt,* pp. 220f.

Figure 4-3
The uraeus
or rearing
cobra.

You'll recall that in Egyptian iconography one of the royal attributes is the uraeus, the rearing cobra (figure 4-3). That's the displaced eye. This myth gives us a picture of the profound ambiguity that accompanies the acquisition of ego consciousness. What is it that replaces the Eye of God? It is the human ego. When the ego dares to exist as an autonomous center of awareness, the Eye of the Self is profoundly offended and in this myth becomes a rearing cobra.

There's a similar idea expressed in a remarkable image that comes from Simon Magus. Jung describes it in his essay "Transformation Symbolism in the Mass,"[51] which he refers to in *Mysterium,* note 62 of paragraph 42. It's hard for us to follow up all these references—we've already got just about as much as we can handle without doing that—but there are a lot of riches in the references, and here's an example. Just listen to this:

Here's Simon Magus's idea, somewhat simplified. The divine fire of the Logos, or the *pneuma,* which resides in the soul of the individual (and this corresponds to the divine fire of the Stoic philosophers) is the flaming sword of Genesis 3: 24. Now the flaming sword of Genesis 3: 24 was set up when Adam and Eve were expelled from the Garden of Eden: in order to prevent them from returning, an angel was placed at the gateway with a fiery sword, which turned in every direction. Simon Magus's idea is that that fiery sword turning in all directions is the divine fire of the Logos in the individual. In other words that sword serves the

---

[51] *Psychology and Religion,* CW 11, par. 359.

same function as the rearing cobra does in the Egyptian myth. The light of the Self has turned into a hostile, threatening entity because ego consciousness has been born. Both of these images refer to the fact that the birth of ego consciousness alienates the ego from the Self.

One can go along blissfully unaware of this state of affairs. You read the myths but they don't register as long as they are not activated in your own psyche. But if a certain degree of psychological development is required of an individual, then these myths come to life. When, in later life, the mature ego starts to reestablish a long-lost connection to the Self—to the inner light, to the Eye—the initial contact is accompanied by profound anxiety. It's the anxiety of meeting that rearing cobra or that turning fiery sword. Thus it is that Eye of God dreams are almost always anxiety dreams. It is no fun to be looked at by the Eye of God. I give a few dream examples in *The Creation of Consciousness,* which I don't need to repeat here.

I do want to say a bit about the psychopathology of the Eye of God, as the basis of paranoia. The chief feature of paranoia is that the inflated ego, because of the activation of this archetype, projects the Eye of God into the environment so that the ego has the experience of being watched, listened to and persecuted. Whenever you encounter images of eyes in patients' dreams, drawings or paintings and that sort of material, keep this possibility in mind. Some paranoid tendency may be starting to manifest. Be on the lookout for that.

The myth of Io and Argus is also relevant to paranoid symptomatology. Argus's watching of Io is replaced by the gadfly's persecution of her; being watched and being persecuted are two different aspects of the same phenomenon. It's not hard to activate such a thing. If I pick out one person and spend quite a bit of time watching . . .

Comment: You've activated it already!

Yes, that person starts to get uncomfortable! This archetype gets activated, you see. It's the Io-Argus gadfly. So being looked at and being persecuted are very closely connected. I know that in New York, when you're riding the subway or out in collective situations, you avoid eye contact because it can be interpreted as persecutory. Who do you think you're looking at? Keep your eyes to yourself! The paranoid patient is in the condition of Io: persecuted, watched and reduced to the state of being nagged and goaded.

4. Undressing

The image of undressing occupies an inconspicuous place in this material and some of you may not even have noticed it. I've plucked it out of paragraph 43, where Jung cites an alchemical text which says:

> When you place a twelve-year-old boy side by side with a girl of the same age, and dressed the same, you cannot distinguish between them. But take their clothes off and the difference will become apparent.

Then in note 66 Jung says:

The motif of undressing goes back to the Song of Songs . . . 5: 3: "I have put off my coat, how shall I put it on?" The undressing symbolizes the extraction of the soul.

In paragraph 44, note 72, he mentions another alchemical text that refers to undressing:

There was a certain man, who was of use for nothing, and could not be kept under guard: for he broke out of all prisons, nay more, he made light of all punishments; yet a certain simple, humble, and sincere man was found, who well understood his nature, and counselled that he be deprived of all his garments and made naked.

Evidently he then would become tractable. Jung says that "according to the text . . . the undressing signifies putrefaction." That's all he says—this just comes from footnotes—but the reason I wanted to make a little more of it is that the theme is such an important one in the analytic process.

One aspect of analysis is an undressing. We often think of clothing symbolism in dreams as referring to the persona. If we are interpreting the dreams in an external sense, inappropriate nakedness or inappropriate dressing can often be interpreted as a reference to an inadequate persona. That will be one perfectly valid level of interpretation.

But from the internal standpoint, the image of undressing has a rather different meaning. Here we meet the idea that it refers to the extraction of the soul, or to the process of putrefactio.[52] Clothes can signify the body or the particular incarnation out of which an individual is living. Thus if one dreams that clothes are removed and one is naked, it can mean that the naked, essential psyche is being brought into visibility.

The whole symbolism of taking off and putting on clothes is a common theme connected with death dreams. Dying is often pictured as the changing of one's garments. A few days before a woman died she dreamed she was going to attend a fashion show. A few days before my father died I dreamed I met him nattily dressed in a new suit. If we apply this theme to the psychological transformation process, then dreams of nakedness or of changing clothes usually mean quite a sizable psychological transition, related to death and rebirth.

---

[52] See Edinger, *Anatomy,* pp. 147ff.

5

Paragraphs 51-103

Tonight the major images are these:
1. The riddle.
2. The tomb.
3. The Enigma of Bologna, and its seven interpretations.
4. The tree and the tree numen.
5. The grave numen.
    a. The dream of the black and white magicians.
    b. The Senior text.
6. The myth of Cadmus.

Tonight's assignment is particularly difficult so don't be disheartened if you have had some difficulty with it. It does provide a beautiful example of the way Jung is able to extract the psyche out of a certain kind of material and I hope to make that visible as we proceed.

1. The Riddle

This whole section concerns an alleged inscription on a tomb which, although found to be spurious, nonetheless for several centuries evoked a great deal of attention. It took the form of a riddle—another word for enigma. The theme of the riddle is important in folklore and other material from the unconscious. The classic example is the riddle of the sphinx which confronted Oedipus. Just a couple of weeks ago we encountered it in the fairy tale, "The Devil and His Grandmother." The devil presented his victims with a riddle which, if they could solve it, would release them from his grasp. With the help of his grandmother they did solve it, you remember.[53]

In the Old Testament there are two major examples of the riddle archetype. The whole Samson story has at its base a riddle:

Out of the eater came what is eaten, and out of the strong came what is sweet. [54]

The other major example in the Old Testament is that of the riddles the Queen of Sheba presented to King Solomon.[55]

This is the way the unconscious almost always presents itself to the ego—as a riddle. When the unconscious manifests itself we constantly ask ourselves, "What does this

---

[53] See above, pp. 51f.
[54] Judges 14: 14, Jerusalem Bible; discussed in Edinger, *Bible and the Psyche,* p. 72.
[55] Ibid., pp. 95ff.

mean?" Every dream is a riddle. Ultimately, I think behind all these manifestations lies the riddle of human existence itself. Alexander Pope in his poem, "An Essay on Man," gives expression to this ultimate enigma. Here are the relevant lines:

> Know then thyself, presume not God to scan;
> The proper study of Mankind is Man.
> Plac'd on this isthmus of a middle state,
> A Being darkly wise, and rudely great:
> With too much knowledge for the Sceptic side,
> With too much weakness for the Stoic's pride,
> He hangs between; in doubt to act, or rest,
> In doubt to deem himself a God, or Beast;
> In doubt his Mind or Body to prefer;
> Born but to die, and reas'ning but to err;
> Alike in ignorance, his reason such,
> Whether he thinks too little, or too much:
> Chaos of Thought and Passion, all confus'd;
> Still by himself abus'd, or disabus'd;
> Created half to rise, and half to fall;
> Great lord of all things, yet a prey to all;
> Sole judge of Truth, in endless Error hurl'd:
> The glory, jest, and riddle of the world!

This poem is also appropriate reading while we're talking about Jung's chapter titled "The Paradoxa," since the paradox of man is the essence of those verses.

2. The Tomb

The inscription we're dealing with is on a tomb and the tomb is a symbol of the unconscious. I would remind you, for instance, of the first illustration in *Man and His Symbols:* a tunnel going down into the tomb of one of the Egyptian pharaohs (figure 5-1). The tomb, for one thing, signifies the world of the dead. It's also closely connected symbolically with the womb: it's not only the repository of the dead person but symbolically connotes the birth of the resurrected individual. And in alchemy the tomb was one of the images used to describe the alchemical vessel. They spoke of it as their tomb because it's the container of the transformation process, and the basic feature of that process is death and rebirth. All of this pertains to the image of the tomb with its inscription.

Another way to put it is that the tomb symbolizes the psychic background of existence. The living ego is surrounded by the image of the tomb: on the one hand, the tomb signifies the grave of the ancestors—the womb out of which our psyche has been born—our connection with the past. On the other hand, the tomb signifies that empty hole to which we shall go when we die, thus completing the circle that connects us with the ancestors. So the tomb symbolizes the psychic background and the psychic environment of existence.

Figure 5-1
Entrance to the tomb
of the Egyptian
pharaoh Rameses III.

Concerning the phrase "psychic background," I want to draw your attention to a particularly pregnant sentence in paragraph 55 where Jung says:

> [The author of the epitaph never] dreamt that . . . it would lead his contemporaries and successors to question the nature of the psychic background—a question which, in the distant future, was to replace the certainties of revealed truth.

That's what depth psychology does. Depth psychology is research into the psychic background, and it's just such research that replaces the metaphysical certainties of past ages.

3. The Inscription and Its Interpretations

Let me start by reading the inscription (paragraph 51). There are two figures and rather than calling them by their whole names, I'm going to call them Crispis and Priscius; that's a little easier to remember.

> . . . *Crispis*, neither man nor woman, nor mongrel, nor maid, nor boy, nor crone, nor chaste, nor whore, nor virtuous, but all.
> Carried away neither by hunger, nor by sword, nor by poison, but by all.—
> Neither in heaven, nor in earth, nor in water, but everywhere is her resting place.

   . . . *Priscius*, neither husband, nor lover, nor kinsman, neither mourning, nor rejoicing, nor weeping, (raised up) neither mound, nor pyramid, nor tomb, but all.
   He knows and knows not (what) he raised up to whom.
   (This is a tomb that has no body in it.
   This is a body that has no tomb round it.
   But body and tomb are the same.)

Jung makes the very colorful remark in paragraph 52 that this inscription served "as a flypaper for every conceivable projection that buzzed in the human mind." That's a particularly good image I think—flypaper. If you're on the lookout for it, there's flypaper hanging around everywhere. It's all over the place. I don't even know how many of you are familiar with flypaper. Probably it's not even used much in the modern world, but in the old days a curl of flypaper would hang down from the ceiling—sticky stuff—and as soon as the fly touched it he was a goner, and by the end of the day you'd have this curl of flypaper just black with flies. In the old barber shops and saloons, country stores and butcher shops— places like that. Jung is attracted to this inscription, the Enigma of Bologna, because it's a particularly vivid example of psychological flypaper. Just by its very nature, a mysterious, enigmatic entity draws psychological flies to it and they stick. Once you get that idea, you see that such entities provide valuable opportunities for exploring the phenomenology of the psyche.

Now what did this piece of flypaper attract? In order to simplify and systemize somewhat the sizable amount of data Jung brings together, I have separated out seven different interpretations projected by various commentators onto this flypaper. Let me say a word or two about each of them.

1. The alchemical interpretation. The Enigma was the focus of a good bit of attention from alchemists. Although various details went into it that Jung explores thoroughly, in essence the alchemical interpretation is that the inscription refers to the process of transforming the prima materia into the lapis. Crispis, the deceased one buried in this tomb, represents the prima materia, buried in the tomb of the alchemical vessel by the alchemist, by the philosopher Priscius, who made the vessel, the tomb. The prima materia went through the alchemical process of transformation and emerged as the lapis, that multifaceted paradoxical thing which is not just this or that "but all."

2. The personalistic or reductive interpretation. According to this interpretation, Crispis, who is buried in the tomb, was a promised wife of Priscius. Sometimes in antiquity a daughter would be espoused to a prospective husband while she was still in the womb—she hadn't been born yet. That was the case with Crispis and unfortunately she was miscarried before she was born so that she never became a wife (paragraph 67). In that case the whole inscription is reduced to a mishap in personal life—a personalistic interpretation.

3. The spiritualistic interpretation. Priscius was a real man, but Crispis was an evil spirit by whom he was possessed and that evil spirit turned into a hamadryad—a spirit dwelling in a tree (paragraphs 69ff). We might also call this interpretation a mythological one because Jung amplifies it with a discussion of the myth of Cadmus. The spiritualistic or mythological interpretation thus says that the inscription refers to a creature, Crispis, who is a spiritual or mythological entity linked to or inhabiting a tree.

4. *The philosophical interpretation.* According to this, Crispis is a personification of the philosophical idea of the anima mundi. She represents the entity who creates the eternal form of things and who is described in this remarkable phrase: "She has within herself the 'selfness' of all mankind" (paragraph 93). In other words, she is a personification of Plato's realm of eternal ideas or what was spoken of as the intelligible universe by the Neo-Platonists. That's the realm of eternal forms or potentialities, the mirror image of which goes to make up created things on earth. This interpretation would have to have been projected by a philosopher.

5. *The erotic interpretation.* Crispis is a whore or a nymphomaniac who was a victim of the divine Eros. Jung takes the occasion in paragraph 98 to note that the erotic interpretation in its general form is still one of the available options among modern schools of psychotherapy.

6. *The ecclesiastical interpretation.* According to this, the monument refers to the Church. About this Jung makes a very trenchant remark in paragraph 100. He says, despite the utterly "threadbare" arguments brought forward for it, that the idea does have some merit from the psychological standpoint because:

> The symbol of the Church in part expresses and in part substitutes for the secrets of the soul which the humanistic philosophers projected into the . . . inscription.

That's worded very precisely—"The symbol of the Church in part expresses and in part substitutes for all the secrets of the soul which the humanistic philosophers projected into the . . . inscription."

7. *The psychological interpretation.* In this interpretation, Crispis is the collective unconscious that undergoes transformation when it is discovered. Here is what Jung says in paragraph 101:

> The interpretive projections we have been examining are . . . identical with the psychic contents that dropped out of their dogmatic framework at the time of the Renaissance and the Great Schism [the Reformation schism], and since then have continued in a state of secularization where they were at the mercy of the "immanentist" principle of explanation, that is, a naturalistic and personalistic interpretation. The discovery of the collective unconscious did something to alter this situation, for, within the limits of psychic experience, the collective unconscious takes the place of the Platonic realm of eternal ideas. Instead of these models giving form to created things, the collective unconscious, through its archetypes, provides the *a priori* condition for the assignment of meaning.

That's the totality of paragraph 101. It is a very important paragraph and I hope you will reread it and reflect on it. The basis of Jungian psychology is in this paragraph, and once you get it, you've got it! Until you do get it there will be a tendency to float in regard to such matters as archetypes and the collective unconscious and abstruse things like that. The psychic contents that dropped out of their dogmatic framework at the time of the Renaissance and the "Great Schism" have dropped into the unconscious of man and are therefore now available for empirical observation and elaboration by psychological means.

These seven different interpretations are really a kind of summary of the various approaches to the psyche. I suppose there could be a few more—there could be a literary interpretation and a painterly one, maybe a musical one—but by and large most of them are here.

4. The Tree and the Tree Numen

You remember that one of the interpretations was that Crispis was a hamadryad, a tree spirit. Here are some examples of the tree image that Jung brings up from alchemy in his essay "The Philosophical Tree"[56]: the tree in the midst of a fountain; the tree in the middle of the nuptial bath; the tree or pillar at the center of a pool from which a serpent descends in some cases, or sometimes a mermaid; the image of the cosmic pillar at the center of the bath (figure 5-2) ; the image of the world tree; the Sefirotic Tree that I spoke about in lecture two.[57]

In the ancient Hindu scriptures, the Upanishads, we find this remark about the cosmic tree:

> There is that ancient tree, whose roots grow upward and whose branches grow downward—that indeed is called the Bright, that is called Brahman, that alone is called the Immortal. All worlds are contained in it, and no one goes beyond.[58]

The same image comes up in the Bhagavadgita, where we find these verses:

> There is a fig tree
> In ancient story,
> The giant Ashvattha,
> The everlasting,
> Rooted in heaven,
> Its branches earthward;
> Each of its leaves
> Is a song of the Vedas,
> And he who knows it
> Knows all the Vedas.[59]

---

[56] See *Alchemical Studies*, CW 13, pars. 304ff.

[57] See above, fig. 2-3, p. 39.

[58] *Katha Upanishad*, II, 6, 1; quoted in *Mysterium*, par. 158, note 211.

[59] Quoted in "The Philosophical Tree," *Alchemical Studies*, CW 13, par. 412.

Figure 5-2. The cosmic pillar at the center of the bath.

We often find a tree spirit associated with these tree images, perhaps in the form of a snake—sometimes curled around the tree—or perhaps a feminine personification. This is an image of the psyche as an objective, organic process. It's a kind of self-portrait of the psyche as a whole, this image of the cosmic tree accompanied by some kind of hovering spirit that lives in it or dwells in its vicinity. We find the same image in Genesis where the Tree of the Knowledge of Good and Evil was the dwelling place of the serpent who tempted Adam and Eve (figure 5-3). The tree numen would correspond to the autonomous spirit—that moving, living entity that accompanies the objective reality of the psyche.

Figure 5-3. The Tree of the Knowledge of Good and Evil.

5. The Grave Numen

The grave numen is a similar spirit that hovers around the grave, the tomb. The idea is that the grave is haunted by a ghost or a spirit—that's the grave numen. It's often pictured as a serpent. And just as with the tree numen, this image refers to the autonomous living presence, an objective psychic entity, that hovers around the unconscious. Jung brings up several examples I want to talk about.

a. The dream of the black and white magicians (paragraph 79)

Jung quotes this dream at least five times in the *Collected Works,* and he discusses it at some length in "Archetypes of the Collective Unconscious."[60] I urge you to read that because it's very relevant material. The fact that he presents it so many times indicates the importance he attaches to this particular dream. It was dreamed by a young theology student who was having doubts about his faith:

> [The dreamer] was standing in the presence of a handsome old man dressed entirely in *black*. He knew it was the *white* magician. This personage had just addressed him at considerable length, but the dreamer could no longer remember what it was about. He had only retained the closing words: "And for this we need the help of the *black* magician." At that moment the door opened and in came another old man exactly like the first, except that he was dressed in *white*. He said to the white magician, "I need your advice," but threw a sidelong, questioning look at the dreamer, whereupon the white magician answered: "You can speak freely, he is an innocent." The black magician then began to relate his story. He had come from a distant land where something extraordinary had happened. The country was ruled by an old king who felt his death near. He—the king—had therefore sought out a tomb for himself. There were in that land a great number of tombs from ancient times, and the king had chosen the finest for himself. According to legend, a virgin had been buried in it. The king caused the tomb to be opened, in order to get it ready for use. But when the bones it contained were exposed to the light of day, they suddenly took on life and changed into a black horse, which at once fled into the desert and there vanished.

That's the grave numen—the black horse that was residing in the tomb and became visible when the tomb was opened.

> The black magician had heard of this story and immediately set forth in pursuit of the horse. After a journey of many days, always on the tracks of the horse, he came to the desert and crossed to the other side, where the grasslands began again. There he met the horse grazing, and there also he came upon the find on whose account he now needed the advice of the white magician. For he had found the lost keys of *paradise,* and he did not know what to do with them.

This dream can be discussed at different levels and from different standpoints, but I want to consider it from the standpoint of the state of the Western God-

---

[60] *The Archetypes and the Collective Unconscious,* CW 9i, pars. 70ff.

image. The white magician—the good, benevolent God-image—has reached the end of his resources and must now call on his dark brother, who is the devil. Remarkably, the devil has simultaneously discovered a need for his light brother and is coming to meet him. Here a reciprocal movement is going on simultaneously. This suggests that when the time is right the conscious and unconscious dominants come to meet each other.

The death of the old dominant is indicated by the fact that the king is about to die. This corresponds to the fact that the God-image, the collective dominant of the Western psyche, is moribund. In preparation for its death, it opens up an ancient tomb; in other words it opens up the unconscious. This activates the feminine principle which had been dead and buried in that very same tomb, in the unconscious. As the tomb is opened, the unconscious is penetrated by consciousness, and as consciousness ventures into it, a revitalization occurs: the grave numen, represented as the black horse, is resurrected and becomes visible.

It was Plato who established for the Western psyche the basic symbolism of the image of the black horse. In his symbolic image of man as a charioteer controlling a white and a black horse, the black horse represents the evil passions.[61] If one follows the evil passions, one is lead into the desert. This is just where our dream horse went and where the magician had to follow him—into the desert, a place of alienation and the wilderness experience.[62] But remarkably enough this dark experience also leads to the discovery of the keys of paradise, to the discovery of a connection to the lost wholeness—the Self.

For this image Jung supplies the profound amplification of the passage from Isaiah which speaks of the Messianic age when the opposites will be reconciled: "The wolf also shall dwell with the lamb, and the leopard shall lie down with the kid."[63] This Messianic age, this coming of the Self, is reached after the death of the old God-image, after pursuing the dark horse of the passions into the desert, and after opening up the tomb that had long been sealed. In other words it follows as a consequence of the exploration of the unconscious. In the process, there is a reconciliation between the light and dark aspects of deity, and the two aspects of the magician figure.

A great deal more could be said about that dream, but this gives you some hint as to why Jung quotes it so many times and why he considers it so important. In talking about it in "Archetypes of the Collective Unconscious" Jung says that it's hard to understand nature sometimes. Why would nature give this innocent fellow a dream like that? But then Jung says *he* was listening and *he* got what it meant! So another way to see it is that the young theology student was functioning as a

---

61 See Plato, "Phaedrus," in *The Collected Dialogues,* pp. 499ff
62 See Edinger, *Ego and Archetype,* chap. 2.
63 Isa. 11: 6, Authorized Version.

kind of agent by which nature communicated with Jung. Somebody was listening in, so the dream was not lost.

b. The Senior text

This is our second example of the grave numen. Jung divides it into two parts and it's easy to lose your way. The first part is quoted in paragraph 77 and it is continued in paragraph 80. I'm not going to read the original because I'm afraid it will confuse you more. Instead I'll summarize the text.

The image is that a child is to be born. (Remember, this is an alchemist speaking so the child is the *filius* that's to be born out of the alchemical retort.) A house must be built for its birth, and this house is the alchemical vessel. The text says that this house is actually a tomb inhabited by either witches or serpents, or both, who feed off the blood of sacrificed black goats. The witches/ serpents are the symbolic images of the grave numen.

These infernal creatures fight with each other, copulate with each other, and conceive and give birth all in an unholy composite, a mess. The text says they remain in this state, in the tomb-house, for forty days. A period of forty days has a great many symbolic associations and one is that it is the symbolic length of the opus. At the end of it, the male serpents cast their semen on the white marble, or "into the image [or spirit that dwells in the marble]." Ravens gather this semen and carry it to the tops of the mountains. The ravens then become white and they multiply.

This describes a process going on in the alchemical retort; it's easy to forget that because the imagery gets so picturesque. The child to be born out of this tomb-vessel is the lapis, the son of the philosophers. But the contents in the vessel are black, evil, reptilian: serpents, witches and blood of black goats. It's a real witches' brew. But that vivid feature is also what makes it so valuable for us psychologically, because it corresponds to a certain aspect of unconscious stuff when first encountered—it's very noxious. And it is crucial that this noxious stuff be contained for the forty-day period. If it seeps out into the environment, the result is all sorts of evil, vicious, paranoid activity. That is the meaning of the black horse: the evil passions that go to make up the grave numen; that nefarious stuff living in the background of the psyche, in the vicinity of the tomb. It's an aspect of the dark primordial psyche. But if it's subjected to the forty days of containment (corresponding to Christ's forty-day temptation in the wilderness), then it is transformed.

That transformation is described by the interesting image of the serpent's se-men being cast onto the white marble. You recall that we met that same image in the Manichaean myth: the image of the seduction of the Archons in which the Light, previously swallowed by the Archons, was extracted from them by seduc-tive means so they ejaculated it out again.[64] The creative power is extracted from

---

[64] See above, pp. 49f.

the dark contents—from the reptilian level of the psyche—and transferred to the upper realms, to the ravens. It's a sublimatio image.[65] The effect on the birds who gather it up is to transform them from black birds to white birds. Then the multiplicatio can take place.[66]

This pictures what happens at certain times in a depth analysis. One can encounter pockets of just this kind of dark stuff quite suddenly and unexpectedly. If you are already familiar with it and have some inkling about it, then you're not so apt to be thrown off by it. "Oh yes, I recognize this! It belongs to the Senior text." It can be very helpful to have such images available.

6. The Myth of Cadmus

The myth of Cadmus comes up as another example of the tree numen. Again we have a serpent associated with a tree. Let me give you an outline—a little different from the version Jung uses but the content is basically the same.

Cadmus was the son of the king of Phoenicia. His sister, Europa, had been carried off by Zeus and Cadmus was sent off by his father to recover her. In the course of his wanderings he came to Thrace. Here his mother, who had come with him, died. Cadmus went for counsel to the Delphic Oracle and was advised not to seek his sister anymore but to follow a cow he would meet and to found a city on the spot where the cow lay down.

He proceeded to do as he was told. He intended to sacrifice the cow and sent his companions to a spring for the necessary water. There they encountered a serpent who guarded the spring and it killed them. Cadmus then struggled with this serpent or dragon (in Greek the word "dragon" means serpent—it's an equivalent image). After great effort he killed the dragon and spitted it against an oak tree (figure 5-4). As Jung says in paragraph 85: "It represents the banishment of the dangerous daemon into the oak." This is where the connection to the tree and the tree numen comes in.

At the command of Athena, after the death of the dragon Cadmus sowed the dragon's teeth in the ground. From the teeth, a host of armed men sprang up who proceeded to fight and kill each other, all except five. Those last five survivors helped Cadmus to build the city of Thebes and when that task had been accomplished Cadmus was given Harmonia, the daughter of Ares and Aphrodite, to be his wife.[67]

Jung has such a neat interpretation of this myth that I want to read it to you. This is from paragraph 86:

---

[65] See Edinger, *Anatomy,* chap. 5.

[66] Ibid., pp. 227f.

[67] *Funk and Wagnalls Standard Dictionary,* p. 179.

Figure 5-4. Cadmus spitting the serpent.

The psychological meaning of the myth is clear [clear to Jung!]: Cadmus has lost his sister-anima because she has flown with the supreme deity into the realm of the suprahuman and the subhuman, the unconscious.

—into the suprahuman because she's taken off by Zeus, but into the subhuman because she's taken off by Zeus in the shape of a bull, and because she later is turned into a cow.

At the divine command [Cadmus] is not to regress to the incest situation, and for this reason he is promised a wife. His sister-anima, acting as a psychopomp in the shape of a cow (to correspond with the bull of Zeus), leads him to his destiny as a dragon-slayer, for the transition from the brother-sister relationship to an exogamous one is not so simple.

In other words, the dragon fight stands between the incestuous level of libido organization and the exogamous level.

But when he succeeds in this, he wins "Harmonia," who is the *dragon's sister.* The dragon is obviously "disharmony," as the armed men sprung from its teeth prove. These kill one another off as though exemplifying the maxim of Pseudo-Democritus, "nature subdues nature," which is nothing less that the *uroboros* conceptually formulated. Cadmus holds fast to Harmonia while the opposites in projected form slaughter one another. This image is a representation of the way in which a split-off conflict behaves: it is its own battle-ground.

This is very important stuff. When one engages a major complex that activates or contains the dragon component, you activate the conflict of the opposites—the armed men that sprang from the dragon's teeth.

It is crucially important at that point to hold fast to a state of harmony in the ego while the complex is undergoing a process of self-destruction. In other words it's crucial not to identify with the process of transformation going on in the complex. To identify with it would correspond to getting into the middle of the armed men who are destroying one another: you'd go down with them because you'd have fallen into identification with them. "Cadmus holds fast to Harmonia while the opposites in projected form slaughter one another. This image is a representation of the way in which a split-off conflict behaves: it is its own battle-ground."

Now that's the very same idea as the previous one of containing that infernal chaotic turmoil of the witches/serpent stuff within the vessel-tomb for forty days. The containment is what's crucial. Consciousness experiences what is going on in the unconscious but doesn't identify with it. A very difficult thing to do but absolutely crucial.

6
Paragraphs 104-133

Before starting tonight's material, I have two translation additions to draw to your attention. The first is near the end of paragraph 111 in the sentence that reads ". . . from which come all the motions of the will and . . ." It should read: ". . . from which come all the motions of the will and the drive to life (the principle of all appetition)." The "drive to life" is an important phrase—Jung is defining the nature of Sol, and the drive to life is one of its features.

The second addition is at the end of paragraph 128 where a sentence that adds color and amplification has been omitted. Following the sentence that ends ". . . switching on the electric light," add this:

> What was meant by Sol and Luna was well put with Goethe's words:
>> And even if the day is laughing to us clear and reasonable,
>> The ghosts in the web of dreams do nightly entwine us.[68]

The major images in tonight's material are these:
1. The Vision of Arisleus: an incest fable.
2. The symbolism of Sol:
   a. The sun and its shadow.
   b. Sol as father and son.
   c. The threefold sonship of Basilides.
   d. The sun as ego and the sun as Self.

In the introductory section of tonight's assignment, Jung makes some pregnant remarks about the relation between the sexes that I want to draw to your attention. He's talking about the symbolism of the coniunctio and the fact that the figures of male and female are the major images which symbolize the opposites that come together in the coniunctio. In paragraph 104 he says this:

> We are inclined to think of this primarily as the power of love, of passion, which drives the two opposite poles together, forgetting that such a vehement attraction is needed only when an equally strong resistance keeps them apart. Although enmity was put only between the serpent and the woman (Genesis 3:15),[69] this curse nevertheless fell upon the relationship of the sexes in general. Eve was told: "Thy desire shall be to thy husband, and he shall rule over thee." And Adam was told: "Cursed is the ground for thy sake . . . because thou hast hearkened unto the voice of thy

---

[68] *Faust,* part 2, act 5, "Midnight."

[69] "And I will put enmity between thee and the woman, and between thy seed and her seed; it shall bruise thy head, and thou shalt bruise his heel." (Authorized Version)

wife." (3:16f). Primal guilt lies between them, an *interrupted state of enmity.*

This is a picture of the state that exists between the opposites in general; the relation between the sexes is only a particular example of that more general phenomenon.

l. The Vision of Arisleus: An Incest Fable

As an aspect of the primal guilt lying between the sexes, Jung goes on to speak of the fact that an initial union between them takes on a guilty, negative aspect represented by the symbolism of incest. In alchemical imagery, the classic example of this is the Vision of Arisleus and Jung talks about this as though we are thoroughly acquainted with it, which assumes a little too much! So I am going to summarize the Vision of Arisleus for you. He discusses it in *Psychology and Alchemy* in two places.[70] As this is a fundamental image in alchemy, it is important to know it thoroughly. It will also be relevant for amplification in dream analysis.

The basic story is this: the *Rex marinus*, the king of the sea, has a kingdom under the sea and he lives down there at the bottom. The trouble with that kingdom is that nothing prospers and nothing is begotten; there are no births because only like mates with like. For things to be born, opposites have to unite—like needs to mate with unlike. When like mates with like, as is the case in the kingdom under the sea, there is no procreation.

In this state of affairs, the king calls for help from the philosopher Arisleus, and asks him to come down for a consultation—a house call so to speak. Arisleus, true to his call, descends to the bottom of the sea. He sizes up the situation and informs the king that the two children hatched from the king's brain, Gabricus his son and Beya his daughter, need to be mated.

So what's happened is that Arisleus the philosopher (the alchemists called themselves philosophers) has made a brave descent into the underworld in order to bring this advice to the king so that the kingdom would prosper. However when the king takes his advice and Beya and Gabricus are united, Beya "embraced Gabricus with so much love that she absorbed him completely into her own nature, and divided him into indivisible parts."[71] So, by following the advice of the philosopher, the king's son has died.

Now Arisleus is in trouble. In punishment for this apparently disastrous advice, Arisleus and his companions are imprisoned in a triple glass house, together with the corpse of the king's son. (This triple glass house is the alchemical retort.) They are enclosed in this glass vessel and subjected to intense heat and every kind of terror for eighty days. In one version, the vessel they're imprisoned in is the womb

---

70 CW 12, pars. 435-440, 449-450.
71 Ibid., par. 439, note 49.

of Beya. In another version, Beya asks to join the other prisoners, so there's some variation; but the basic point is the containment in the glass vessel and being subjected to intense heat.

After suffering from this intense heat, like the three figures in Nebuchadnez-zar's furnace (Daniel 3: 11-30),

> Arisleus and his companions see their master Pythagoras in a dream and beg him for help. He sends them his disciple Harforetus, "the author of nourishment."[72]

This disciple brings Gabricus back to life with the miraculous food of life—resurrects him. Pythagoras then says to Arisleus:

> Ye write and have written down for posterity how this most precious tree is planted, and how he that eats of its fruits shall hunger no more.[73]

Well, that's the vision of Arisleus. Now let me make a few comments about it to help fix it in your mind and connect with its psychological relevance. The kingdom under the sea is of course the unconscious, and it is unfruitful because the opposites have not yet come into existence—light and dark, male and female haven't yet been separated. Another way to put it is that the world parents are in a state of eternal cohabitation.

There must be ego consciousness to bring about the separation of the opposites, and that's what happens when Arisleus, the ego, descends into the unconscious. We don't even learn that the opposites Gabricus and his sister Beya exist until Arisleus has gone there—only then is their existence discovered. And that means his descent brings about the separation of opposites.

Now that they do exist, it is advised that they unite. But when they come together there is an apparent failure—Gabricus dies. This is the theme of the lesser coniunctio,[74] which refers to a premature union of insufficiently separated opposites. You remember in talking about the death coniunctio a few weeks ago I brought up the example of Goethe's romantic novel, *The Sorrows of Young Werther*.[75] The Vision of Arisleus is another death coniunctio. In other words, it's unconscious incest. Goethe's Werther was an example of the same thing: Werther's yearning for his beloved Lotti was an unconscious incestuous longing for containment in the mother. The living out of unconscious incest tendencies is always followed by a catastrophe. But when incest occurs consciously it refers to the union of the ego with its origin, psychologically and subjectively; when that happens consciously—when one knows what one's doing—then out of that union is born the Philosophers' Stone.

---

[72] Ibid., par. 449.
[73] Ibid.
[74] See Edinger, *Anatomy,* pp. 212ff.
[75] See above, p. 38.

Following the death of Gabricus comes the imprisonment of Arisleus and his companions, and the ordeal of intense heat—the calcinatio—which lasts for eighty days; in other words, two times forty—the symbolism of the number forty is important here. As a result of enduring that period of intense heat and terror, that affect-laden condition, the Self manifests in the figure of Pythagoras. It's as though the energy lost by the ego during its confinement flows into the Self, activating it and allowing it to make itself visible. As that takes place, the messenger brings the immortal food—the nourishing contact with the Self—which then has the effect of reviving Gabricus.[76]

Pythagoras instructs Arisleus to write about "how this most precious tree is planted, and how he that eats of its fruits shall hunger no more." That tree corresponds to the Tree of Life in the Garden of Eden. The opposites, once separated, must be united again in the conscious coniunctio in order to recover the lost state of original wholeness symbolized by the Garden of Eden.

But this whole process is experienced as incest, and so proceeding with it amounts to a breach of the ego's most profound taboo. Jung talks about the great ambiguity for modern man of the whole incest problem which Freud in his discovery of the Oedipus archetype was the first to stumble over. In paragraph 106 he speaks of three ways of handling this problem:

> We see the contrast between alchemy and the prevailing Christian ideal of attempting to restore the original state of innocence by monasticism and, later, by the celibacy of the priesthood. The conflict between worldliness and spirituality, latent in the love-myth of Mother and Son, was elevated by Christianity to the mystic marriage of sponsus (Christ) and sponsa (Church), whereas the alchemists transposed it to the physical plane as the coniunctio of Sol and Luna.

He's talking here about the fact that the unconscious has an urge to promote incest. Anyone who has any relations with the unconscious comes up against this fact. Christianity attempted to deal with the problem by transferring the incest issue to the metaphysical level, by elevating it to the mystic marriage of Christ and the Church. The alchemists, on the other hand, transferred the incest problem to the physical plane—as the coniunctio of Sol and Luna—which they thought of as material in the alchemical flask. Jung continues:

> The Christian solution of the conflict is purely pneumatic [spiritual], the physical relations of the sexes being turned into an allegory or—quite illegitimately—into a sin that perpetuates and even intensifies the original one in the Garden. Alchemy, on the other hand, exalted the most heinous transgression of the law, namely incest, into a symbol of the union of opposites, hoping in this way to bring back the golden age. For both trends the solution lay in extrapolating the union of the sexes into

---

[76] One is reminded of Jung's dream of June 1914, recounted in *Memories, Dreams, Reflections*, p. 176.

another medium: the one projected it into the spirit, the other into matter. But neither of them located the problem in the place where it arose—the soul of man.

This really puts the matter in a nutshell. The incest problem is dealt with either by projecting it into spirit, by projecting it into matter, or by facing it as a psychological reality. You can spiritualize it, materialize it, or face it as psychological reality. The first two, spiritualizing or materializing it, though they worked in earlier times, are evasions for modern man.

2. The Symbolism of Sol

The alchemists conceived of Sol as a concrete substance and we can understand they're talking about a substance of the psyche. Sol was thought of as the central celestial fire; it's the fructifying source of heat and light and the root of the life drive. (That's why I wanted to be sure to get the "drive to life" into the translation.) Some of the many metaphors used to describe Sol are light, heat, sulphur, redness, gold, fire and certain kinds of fruit—especially oranges and lemons!

Sol is thought of as the central source and, appropriately, its alchemical symbol is a circle with a dot in the center. The same symbol is used for gold because they are thought to be of the same substance. Gold is the terrestrial sun-stuff spun into the bowels of the earth by Sol's endless revolutions around the earth.

In man, Sol represents the central source of divine fire. In paragraph 113, Jung says that, according to Dorn, "Just as the physical sun lightens and warms the universe, so, in the human body, there is in the heart a sunlike arcanum from which life and warmth stream forth." I think that image must have been at the back of the minds of the early anatomists when they named a major complex of autonomic nerve ganglia in the epigastric region, the solar plexus. When we are exposed to intense affect, that solar plexus glows inside; you can feel the heat of it—that's the inner sun.

a. The sun and its shadow

In the midst of the symbolism of Sol, we learn that not only is it associated to the Deity and the creative source of fire and life, but it also has many parallels with hell and the devil. We learn that there is a *Sol niger,* a black sun; there are not only bright sun rays but also dark sun rays. Thus one of the alchemical texts says that you must extract the sun ray from its shadow.

I have a painting done by a patient of mine many years ago when I was working in Rockland State Hospital. There isn't time to go into the details of the case—the patient had had a psychotic break, but at the time I was seeing him he'd compensated. This is the final picture of a series (figure 6-1). It's indeed a quaternary mandala-like image and the patient specifically stated it was the sun. He's written "sun beam" in four different languages. It's a funny looking sun, emitting as much blackness as light—an example of the sun and its shadow, corresponding precisely to the alchemical image.

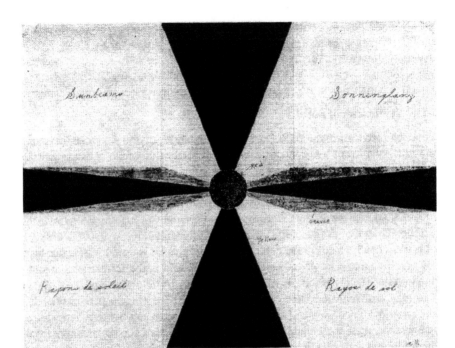

Figure 6-1. The black sun *(Sol niger).*

As Jung tells us in paragraph 117, the basic meaning of Sol is consciousness, and yet part of the symbolism of consciousness is blackness. Here is an example of this phenomenon, dreamt by a black professional woman:

> A black woman was caught in a bright searchlight and was being accused of a crime. The evidence of her guilt was that she cast a black shadow on the ground when in the field of this bright searchlight.

As Jung mentions, we don't literally see black sun rays streaming from the sun, but we do see shadows whenever a material object interposes itself in the pathway of the light. The shadow doesn't exist unless a substantial object blocks the light; then the shadow is created.

Jung takes this fact to be profoundly significant psychologically. As long as an individual does not function out of substance, as long as he or she does not demonstrate material weight but exists as a kind of flimsy, wispy, transparent, indefinite entity, there'll be no shadow. And shadow is what is attached to all that is evil and reprehensible—nobody wants to be associated with a shadow because it means carrying guilt. Yet the only way to avoid casting a real shadow is not to have any materiality. Jung makes a great deal out of that physical image as a symbol of the nature of psychological being. If one is going to have weight and substance and be definite, one will drag a shadow along at the same time. That's all symbolized by the idea of Sol having both bright and black rays.

[At this point there was a comment from the audience about an anorexic girl.]

That's very true; if she gets thin enough, she won't cast a shadow.

Another dangerous aspect of the Sol principle is that since it's fire, too much of it can be destructive. The right amount is life-giving warmth and too much of it is annihilating. An example of that is found in the myth of Amor and Psyche. As Psyche's second task, Venus ordered her to get a wisp of wool from a special flock of sheep with golden fleece. A friendly reed growing by the river gave Psyche this advice:

> [Do not] at this hour approach those terrible sheep. For they borrow fierce heat from the blazing sun and wild frenzy maddens them, so that with sharp horns and foreheads hard as stone, and sometimes even with venomous bites, they vent their fury in the destruction of men. But [wait] till the heat of the noonday sun has assuaged its burning, and the beasts are lulled to sleep by the soft river breeze, . . . And, when once the sheep have abated their madness and allayed their anger, go shake the leaves of yonder grove, and thou shalt find the golden wool clinging here and there to crooked twigs.[77]

In talking about this image, Neumann says: "The rending golden rams of the sun symbolize an archetypally overpowering male-spiritual power which the feminine cannot face."[78] It's an example of the destructive aspect of Sol.

The positive aspect of Sol shows up in the phenomenology of certain religious and mystical experiences. William James has brought together quite a few examples of such experiences, the majority of which have to do with intense illuminations, intense light. Here is one:

> All at once the glory of God shone upon and round about me in a manner almost marvelous. . . . A light perfectly ineffable shone in my soul, that almost prostrated me on the ground. . . . This light seemed like the brightness of the sun in every direction. It was too intense for the eyes. . . . I think I knew something then, by actual experience, of that light that prostrated Paul on the way to Damascus. It was sure a light such as I could not have endured long.[79]

That would be an example of Sol.

Other examples come up in nuclear explosion dreams. Nuclear explosions, you know, are miniature suns. I came across a remarkable dream of this nature some years ago. A middle-aged woman some years into analysis dreamt:

---

[77] Erich Neumann, *Amor and Psyche: The Psychic Development of the Feminine,* pp. 43f.
[78] Ibid., p. 99.
[79] *The Varieties of Religious Experience: A Study in Human Nature,* pp. 246f.

We were in a room something like a bomb shelter and also a fortified city of an ancient, holy town such as Acre or Jerusalem. In this room I'm among a privileged company. We sit crouching, waiting until we hear the terrible explosion of the Bomb descending on the outer world. . . . It happens. The din and the shaking take over and then they recede. Then we've been told that so long as we stay inside the walls and don't open the huge bronze doors, that everything within the shelter will remain free from radiation, and there will be no death by contamination. But a group of five of us, feeling our hermetically sealed room is itself fated, and being filled with curiosity to see the ruined outer world, run to the doors anyway and proceed to pull them open. That is, four of them do. When we turned the last corner in the inner corridor I lost my nerve and fell behind to watch at a distance while the others watched the world.

After great difficulty they finally get these huge bronze doors open and as they open with a great creaking noise they let in light—burning, blinding, bitter-tasting, acrid-smelling, deafening, suffocating, white light, which is radiation. That's how it appeared to the four at the doors. [The dreamer is still looking around the corner, from a distance.] I see that by their reactions, but to me, at my observational distance, it streams in as something warm, bright, golden and rejuvenating as the sun.

It doesn't take the four long to decide that they've seen all they need to see, and soon they are bracing their shoulders against the doors to close them again. That's when I step out of my corner. I stand in the middle of the corridor waiting for their return, and being so situated, I catch the first comer, one of the women, and embrace her warmly. She looks at me, startled but moved, and says, "Don't you realize that now, through touching me, you too are contaminated?" I nod my head. "Yes, I do know," but that was the point. I wanted to share her contamination; I wanted to indicate love, sympathy, admiration and a desire to be kin to all the consequences of the new human condition.

Then I asked her: "What did you see outside?" And she answers: "Only a lot of broken glass." Next we go about preparing for the deaths we feel sure will result from the exposure at the gates. First to go, in little white coats as if they were doctors or scientists, is a small group of old men who are at the age to be dying a natural death anyway. Then it is others but, incredibly, there is no mass death. It's going to take a life-time for us all to die. We have become mortal, freed from the bind of stagnation and immortality. Through growth and decay we can change. The bomb shelter can now become a holy city.

This dream indicates that the patient, who had been hiding out from life and had remained essentially in an unborn condition, is finally exposed to the intense effects of conscious existence. With that exposure, she is both born as a conscious being and at the same time starts to die as a corruptible mortal. Those two go together. Exposure to the principle of Sol both shatters the paradise state of ego-Self identity and also sets up the possibility of achieving, on a conscious level, the incorruptible nature of the preworldly paradise—represented by the bomb shelter that's now turned into a holy city. She's born into psychological existence and at the same time exposed to the reality of death; those opposites go hand in hand.

I think the basic imagery and message of this nuclear bomb dream is applicable to all such dreams, so it's something to keep in mind.

b. Sol as father and son

In paragraph 121 there is a discussion of the symbolism of Sol in which he's described both as a father and as a son of Mercurius. One text says that Mercurius is the origin of Sol; in other words, he's the father of Sol. Another text says that Sol is the father of Mercurius as the lapis, just as Luna, the moon, is the mother of Mercurius, the lapis. Jung charts these relations:

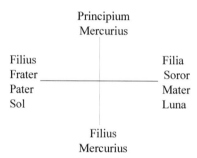

Principium
Mercurius

Filius   Filia
Frater   Soror
Pater   Mater
Sol   Luna

Filius
Mercurius

You must always remember that Mercurius is the personification of the autonomous unconscious. The original Mercurius is Mercurius as prima materia—it's the unconscious in its original unconscious state. Mercurius as the lapis is the unconscious when the ego has related to it consciously. Out of the original Mercurius, Sol and Luna emerge as the pair of opposites; when those opposites are again united, they give birth to Mercurius the son—the filius Mercurius—which is equivalent to the lapis.

Jung then, in paragraphs 122 to 124, compares this alchemical sequence, this quaternity, with the Christian image:

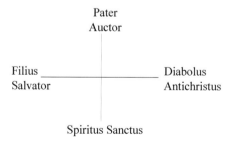

Pater
Auctor

Filius   Diabolus
Salvator   Antichristus

Spiritus Sanctus

This is the implied Christian image—it's not quite the one you find announced in churches—but it's the same idea as the alchemical image. God the Father—God the origin—divides into two sons: the good son Christ, and the bad son, the devil. The reconciling fourth is the Holy Ghost or the Kingdom of God. Jung points out here that in both schemas the rhythm is in three steps; although the product is a quaternity, the rhythm is threefold.[80]

c. The threefold sonship of Basilides

In paragraph 124 Jung speaks of the "third sonship" of Basilides and I thought you ought to know what that refers to. He discusses this image in considerably greater detail in *Aion*,[81] but even there it's not totally clear and, as it's such an interesting image, I thought this would be a good occasion to bring it up.

Basilides was a second-century Gnostic and his creation myth is represented in the diagram (figure 6-2). According to this creation myth, the nonexistent God uttered the creative word: "Let there be light." As he uttered that word he deposited a cosmic seed. That cosmic seed then divided into three parts, three sons

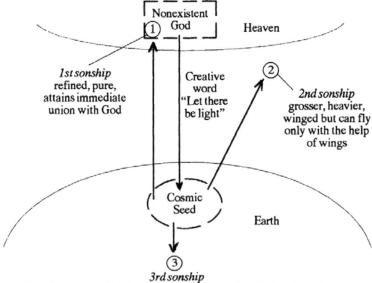

Figure 6-2. The threefold sonship o f Basilides.

---

[80] For a discussion of this see Edinger, *Ego and Archetype*, "The Trinity Archetype and the Dialectic of Development," pp. 179ff.
[81] CW 9ii, pars. 118ff.

—that's where the triple sonship comes in. The first son shot right back up and rejoined the nonexistent God from which he had come. The second sonship was described as grosser or heavier. Although he was winged, he was not pure spirit so he couldn't shoot up all the way. He got just half-way up. And the third sonship had no powers of flight at all. He was formless, unpurified and intermixed with the undiscriminated seeds of all things. He was a "panspermia"—a matrix of all possibilities and utterly entangled in the darkness of materiality. Those are the three sonships of Basilides.

What makes this so interesting psychologically is that it is an image of ego development. The ego is the son or the daughter of the unconscious and this creation myth of Basilides tells us that that has a threefold structure. At the initial point of birth of the ego, one part never separates from its origin at all—it remains unborn, in the state of complete ego-Self identity. That's the first "son." Part three, the third "son" falls totally into matter, into the concrete, manifest existence. Only the second "son" achieves an intermediate position between the opposites and thus is able to perceive the opposites. Only this portion is truly conscious. I don't have time to say any more than that but I think on reflection you can see it's quite suggestive psychologically.

d. The sun as ego and the sun as Self

I do have to say a word or two about the way Jung ends this section on Sol. In paragraph 129 he says that Sol is the principle of consciousness. Since the ego is the center of consciousness, that makes Sol the ego. Then, in paragraph 131, he goes on to say:

> Although the alchemists came very close to realizing that the ego was the mysteriously elusive arcane substance and the longed-for lapis, they were not aware that with their sun symbol they were establishing an intimate connection between God and the ego. As already remarked, projection is not a voluntary act; it is a natural phenomenon. . . . If, therefore, it is this nature that produces the sun symbol, nature herself is expressing an identity of God and ego. In that case only unconscious nature can be accused of blasphemy, but not the man who is its victim.

And at the end of the section (paragraph 133) he says this:

> I must point out to the reader that these remarks on the significance of the ego might easily prompt him to charge me with grossly contradicting myself. He will perhaps remember that he has come across a very similar argument in my other writings. Only there it was not a question of ego but of the *self*. . . . I have defined the self as the totality of the conscious and the unconscious psyche, and the ego as the central reference-point of consciousness. It is an essential part of the self, and can be used *pars pro toto* [part for the whole] when the significance of consciousness is borne in mind. But when we want to lay emphasis on the psychic totality it is better to use the term "self." There is no question of a contradictory definition, but merely of a difference of standpoint.

So the sun as the symbol of consciousness represents both the ego and the Self. The reason for that double representation is that the Self cannot come into conscious, effective existence except through the agency of an ego. Needless to say it can come into plenty of effective existence without an ego but it can't come into *consciously* effective existence without the agency of an ego. That's why it is unavoidable that the symbolism of Sol, as the principle of consciousness, represents both the ego and the Self.

Figure 6-3.
The earth between the sun and its shadow *(Sol niger)*.

7

Paragraphs 134-153

I want to begin with a translation correction near the end of paragraph 145. The sentence that starts on the tenth line from the top of page 123 should have an addition to it so it reads as follows:

> The Eastern idea of atman-purusha corresponds psychologically to the Western figure of Christ who, *on the one hand*, is the second Person of the Trinity and God himself but, *on the other hand*, so far as his human existence is concerned, conforms exactly to the suffering servant of God in Isaiah. [Italics show additions.]

That clarifies an important sentence whose meaning otherwise is a little blurred.

Tonight we have one major image—sulphur—with its various symbolic implications. Subsumed under that major image are four other images:

1. Sulphur duplex: the positive and negative aspects of sulphur.
2. The four major effects of sulphur: it consumes; it coagulates; it corrupts; it tinctures and promotes maturation.
3. An alchemical active imagination concerning Sulphur.
4. An alchemist's dream of Sulphur wounded.

Last week we talked about Sol, and tonight's material is really a continuation of the symbolism of Sol because sulphur was thought of as Sol's terrestrial embodiment. The chemistry of sulphur is very relevant to its symbolism and I was tempted to bring some sulphur tonight and set up a few chemical demonstrations. Instead, as we proceed I'll draw your attention to some of the relevant physical properties of sulphur.

Most of us know sulphur as the so-called flowers of sulphur—powdered sulphur—but it shows up in nature in crystalline form as a hard yellow rock. Miraculously, as far as most rocks are concerned, this rock burns! That's why it was called the burning stone. The word sulphur is supposed to have derived from a Latin term meaning burning stone. And the word brimstone is the Anglo-Saxon term for burning stone. So brimstone is a synonym for sulphur.

The fact that it is a brilliant yellow color connects it with Sol symbolism. And the fact that it is so readily combustible made it, in the minds of the alchemists, practically equivalent to fire itself.

A prominent feature in the chemistry of sulphur is that it generates unpleasant smelling gasses. Hydrogen sulphide for instance—that's the smell of rotten eggs, the sewer smell and the main constituent of flatus. Sulphur dioxide, a product of burning sulphur, is a main constituent of smog. It's also the main cause of acid rain, which develops when industrial smokestacks emit sulphur dioxide.

Both hydrogen sulphide and sulphur dioxide immediately tarnish metals—they form sulphide compounds, many of which are black. If, for instance, you drop a penny into a solution that has a little hydrogen sulphide in it, it immediately turns black. So it's very easy to see how the idea of the corrupting effect of sulphur could come about. Also, sulphur is the central ingredient of gunpowder. So much for its chemical manifestations.

As for the psychological qualities attached to sulphur, as I've already said it's been considered the earthly manifestation of Sol. Jung speaks of it as representing the principle of desirousness, will, compulsion and the "motive factor in consciousness." There are various places (you may already have noticed this) where, after vast quantities of symbolic amplification, Jung will give us a short paragraph summing up very succinctly all the psychological symbolism. Such is the case with paragraph 151:

> With this I would like to conclude my remarks on sulphur. . . . [And then he gives us the real punch line!] Sulphur represents the active substance of the sun or, in psychological language, the *motive factor in consciousness:* on the one hand the will, which can best be regarded as a dynamism subordinated to consciousness, and on the other hand compulsion, an involuntary motivation or impulse ranging from mere interest to possession proper. The unconscious dynamism would correspond to sulphur, for compulsion is the great mystery of human life. It is the thwarting of our conscious will and of our reason by an inflammable element within us, appearing now as a consuming fire and now as life-giving warmth.

When it comes out explosively, it comes out as gunpowder. When it comes out more gradually, it might come out as the match that lights the fire to ignite our stove or our candle. Matches used to be made principally of sulphur, though it's not so much the case now.

1. Sulphur Duplex

Jung brings in a great deal of imagery to demonstrate that sulphur was thought of as both good and evil. In its negative aspect it's associated with the devil— brimstone is a component of hell. And the fact that sulphur tends to corrupt or blacken whatever it touches connects it with the devil and negative factors. The positive aspect of sulphur is its association with Christ and the Holy Ghost (paragraph 145). It's described in paragraph 140 as the "painter of all colours."

These two aspects correspond to the double symbolism of fire: there's a heavenly or celestial aspect and a lower or infernal aspect. In the apocryphal Gospel of Thomas, Christ identifies himself with fire: "He who is near me is near the fire."[82] In Luke he identifies himself as an incendiary: "I came to cast fire

---

82 Robert M. Grant, *The Secret Sayings of Jesus,* p. 180.

upon the earth; and would that it were already kindled."[83] He's calling himself a match to ignite the world, you see; he's identifying himself with the fire. But since for our aeon Christ is the most developed symbolic manifestation of the Self, his identification with the fire of sulphur also connects sulphur with the Self.

The devil on the other hand represents the contrary aspects of fire: the torturing fire of hell and purgatory where brimstone is supposed to be the chief ingredient. So these speak to the imagery of sulphur duplex.

2. The Four Basic Effects of Sulphur

a. Sulphur consumes

In other words, it brings about the calcinatio.[84] It is the fire principle itself, so it is an image of libido, of life energy.

The alchemists thought of everything as being composed of a triad of substances: mercury, sulphur and salt. mercury is spirit, sulphur is soul, salt is body. Soul—sulphur—is the animating principle, the principle of life which has as its basic feature energy, symbolized by fire.

As elaborated in patristic imagery, the symbolism of fire connects with human sinfulness. According to this imagery, if the basic life urge is sinful, then sin feeds hell-fire and burns itself away. We have an example of this imagery in a remark of Paul's in Corinthians. This is the scriptural source for the doctrine of purgatory, the ecclesiastical location of brimstone. In this passage Paul speaks of the house one builds for oneself and the nature of its foundation:

> For no other foundation can any one lay than that which is laid, which is Jesus Christ. Now if any one builds on the foundation with gold, silver, precious stones, wood, hay, stubble—each man's work will become manifest; for the Day will disclose it, because it will be revealed with fire, and the fire will test what sort of work each one has done. If the work which any man has built on the foundation survives, he will receive a reward. If any man's work is burned up, he will suffer loss, though he himself will be saved, but only as through fire.[85]

Saint Augustine has commented on that passage:

> [The man who builds with wood, hay, and stubble is the man involved in lust and carnal desire, but] for so long as he does not prefer such affection or pleasure to Christ, Christ is his foundation, though on it he builds wood, hay, stubble; and therefore he shall be saved as by fire [even though his lusts are consumed]. For the fire of affliction shall burn such luxurious pleasures and earthly loves . . . and of this fire the fuel is bereavement, and all those calamities which consume these joys.[86]

---

[83] Luke 12: 49, Revised Standard Version.

[84] See Edinger, *Anatomy,* chap. 2.

[85] 1 Cor. 3: 11-15, Revised Standard Version.

[86] Augustine, *City of God,* 21: 26.

That's what we might call the Western version of sulphurous calcinatio. An Eastern version of the same symbolism is found in the Buddha's Fire Sermon which I want to read to you. He's talking to his disciples:

> All things, O priests, are on fire. And what . . . are these things which are on fire? The eye, O priests, is on fire; forms are on fire; eye-consciousness is on fire; impressions received by the eye are on fire; and whatever sensation, pleasant, unpleasant or indifferent, originates in dependence on impressions received by eye, that also is on fire. . . . With the fire of passion, say I, with the fire of hatred, with the fire of infatuation; with birth, old age, death, sorrow, lamentation, misery, grief and despair are they on fire. The ear is on fire; sounds are on fire; . . . the nose is on fire; odors are on fire; . . . the tongue is on fire; tastes are on fire; . . . the body is on fire; things tangible are on fire; . . . the mind is on fire; . . . ideas are on fire; . . . mind-consciousness is on fire; impressions received by the mind are on fire; and whatever sensation, pleasant, unpleasant or indifferent, originates in dependence on impressions received by the mind, that also is on fire. And with what are these on fire? With the fire of passion, . . . with the fire of hatred, with the fire of infatuation; with birth, old age, death, sorrow, lamentation, misery, grief and despair are they on fire.

And here, skipping a bit, is his prescription of how to escape being on fire:

> The learned and noble disciple conceives an aversion for the eye, conceives an aversion for forms, conceives an aversion for eye-consciousness, conceives an aversion for the impressions received by the eye; and whatever sensation, pleasant, unpleasant, or indifferent, originates in dependence on impressions received by the eye, for that also he conceives an aversion. Conceives an aversion for the ear, an aversion for sounds, . . . conceives an aversion for the nose, conceives an aversion for odors; . . . conceives an aversion for the tongue, conceives an aversion for tastes, . . . conceives an aversion for the body, conceives an aversion for things tangible. . . . etc.[87]

This adds up to the same thing as the Western version but it doesn't do it via the agency of hell. It does it by figuring it out with the head.

It's a more subtle and sophisticated version of the same thing. These are two examples of how two major collective psychological standpoints traditionally have dealt with the psychology of sulphur. They both express the fact that sulphur consumes. That's what I'm talking about—the tendency for the fiery aspect of the psyche to consume itself.

b. Sulphur coagulates

Certain alchemical recipes specify sulphur as an agent of coagulatio.[88] The basic idea psychologically is that desire coagulates. The psychologically unborn

---

[87] Henry Clarke Warren, *Buddhism in Translation*, pp. 352f.
[88] See Edinger, *Anatomy*, pp. 85ff.

abstract person, you see, isn't yet fully in life. Earth and earthly existence are a product of desire, of coagulatio, brought about by sulphur. That means that such an unborn abstract person has to discover where his or her sulphur is—where desire is—and then go with it.

Too often it can happen that abstract, spiritualized, unborn people read the apostle Paul or the Buddha's Fire Sermon and use such wisdom to avoid the process of coagulatio. Real wisdom is expressed in those statements, but it's mature wisdom, wisdom that applies only after you've been through the full fires of desirousness. It should not be used as a device to by-pass the life process.

c. Sulphur corrupts

This corresponds to the chemical fact that by forming black sulphides sulphur tends to blacken many of the metals it touches. And of course the evil-smelling gases it generates bring in the idea of corruption and foulness, too. Thus, because of these chemical hooks, the symbolism of mortificatio gets projected onto sulphur. The corrupting aspect of sulphur would correspond to the fact that mortificatio is an inevitable consequence of coagulatio. That which is born into incarnate, mortal existence is also doomed to die and to undergo corruption. It is the nature of elemental desirousness that first it leads into life, where it's perceived as sin, guilt and misery. That then leads to the corrupting aspect of sulphur and to the fact that it promotes the nigredo—the blackening.

d. Sulphur tinctures and matures

Some of the sulphides are black but others produce some of the most brilliant colors of the painter's palette. Cadmium yellow, for instance, is cadmium sulphide, a standard of painters. Bismuth sulphide is brown; arsenic sulphide is yellow; tin sulphide is orange; mercuric sulphide is red; zinc sulphide is white; copper and silver sulphides are black. You can tell that by the tarnish that forms on your silverware. You don't get nice pretty colors on your silverware—you get the blackening that corresponds to the symbolism of corruption. But the beautiful yellow, orange and red sulphides provide the hook for the projection of sulphur as the great painter of nature who paints all the colors.

That leads us to another feature of desirousness: desirousness is what gives life its color, its attraction. If desirousness is cut off at the root, as Paul and the Buddha would have it, then everything is gray—there's the ambiguity.

Along with the tincturing we have the idea that sulphur promotes maturation (paragraphs 142-143). The tincture is a synonym for the elixir and the elixir is the liquid form of the Philosophers' Stone. The fact that sulphur tinctures and matures means that it's identified with the Self, with wholeness. That connects with Jung's remark in paragraph 151 about sulphur as "compulsion . . . the great mystery of human life."

Then, in paragraph 153 Jung gives us this pregnant sentence: "Compulsion . . . has two sources: the shadow and the Anthropos." Now I'd put it a little differently. I'd say compulsion has one source—the Self—but that a relatively undeveloped person will experience compulsion through the shadow, through the personal complexes. In that respect the source of compulsion is the shadow. In such a case it's our complexes that set us on fire. It's our complexes that first demonstrate to us that we're not master in our own psychic house, because usually we don't choose to be set on fire. Something happens and we discover suddenly that we're on fire—somebody says something and we're enraged. That would be an example of compulsion coming at us from the shadow.

We first experience sulphur through the shadow because sulphur is the inflammable element, but after a lengthy period of analyzing our complexes, hopefully we then get to their core which is an archetype. The archetypal energy—the fire—the sulphur that's at the root of the complexes, derives from the Self. Then we begin to experience compulsion, what sets us on fire, not as a product of our complexes but as an expression of the Self.

Here the important idea is that the compulsive dynamism of all complexes derives from the Self. When you see that, then you don't have a complex anymore, which does not mean however that you aren't subject to inflammable affects. Not at all! But it does mean you're experiencing them on a different level and they become part of an ongoing dialogue with the Self. Before one sees that such things derive from the Self, one is in constant danger of being possessed by a complex— in other words, of catching on fire from the inflammability of the sulphur in the complex. Well, that's my elaboration of Jung's succinct remark, "Compulsion . . . has two sources: the shadow and the Anthropos."

3. An Alchemical Active Imagination

Jung mentions this dialogue starting in paragraph 140, but he mentions it very briefly and I thought it would be interesting and instructive to hear a fuller version. Jung doesn't call it active imagination but that's what I am calling it. The text comes from a treatise concerning sulphur in *The Hermetic Museum*.[89] I'm going to read it to you, interspersed with a few interpretive observations.

In this account an alchemist was obsessed with sulphur and he had the idea that sulphur was the essential ingredient for the Philosophers' Stone. After a series of depressing failures he began taking long walks.

> [One day on such a walk] all his thoughts were absorbed by the subject of Sulphur, and when he remembered the words of the Sages, who say that the substance is vile and common, and its treatment easy, when he recollected the vast amount of time, labour, and money which he had vainly spent upon it [we sometimes think that about

---

[89] "The New Chemical Light," in A.E. Waite, *The Hermetic Museum,* vol. 2, pp. 149ff.

a lengthy analysis!], he lifted up his voice, and in the bitterness of his heart, cursed Sulphur. Now Sulphur was in that grove, though the Alchemist did not know it. But suddenly he heard a voice which said: "My friend, why do you curse Sulphur?" He looked up in bewilderment: nobody was to be seen. "My friend, why are you so sad?" continued the voice.

Alchemist: Master, I seek the Philosopher's Stone as one that hungers after bread.

Voice: And why thus do you curse Sulphur?

Alchemist: My Lord, the Sages call it the substance of the Stone; yet I have spent all my time and labour in vain upon it, and am well nigh reduced to despair.

We curse our complexes, don't we? They won't go away. We work and work on them and they are still there—that element of inflammability keeps setting us on fire again and again. Despair, in this case, seems to be the gateway that leads to hearing the new element, the Voice. It's interesting that the alchemist had to reach the state of despairingly cursing Sulphur before Sulphur spoke up—before the autonomous psyche manifested itself in a way perceivable to the ego.

Voice: It is true that Sulphur is the true and chief substance of the Stone. Yet you curse it unjustly. For it lies heavily chained in a dark prison and cannot do as it would. Its hands and feet have been bound, and the doors of the dungeon closed upon it, at the bidding of its mother, Nature, who was angry with it for too readily obeying the summons of every Alchemist.

That's how Waite translates this: ". . . its mother, Nature, who was angry with it for too readily obeying the summons of every Alchemist." But Jung in paragraph 140 says Sulphur "was imprisoned because in the view of the alchemists he had shown himself too obliging toward his mother." And one person competent in the German language translates it: ". . . too *obstinate* toward his mother." So it lends itself to considerable ambiguity. The German word *willfährig* has a double-edged meaning and it can be taken different ways.

Voice: It is now confined in such a perfect labyrinth of a prison, that it can be set free only by those Sages to whom Nature herself has entrusted the secret.

Alchemist: Ah! Miserable that I am, this is why he was unable to come to me! How very hard and unkind of the mother! When is he to be set at large again?

Voice: That can only be by means of hard and persevering labour.

This imprisonment of Sulphur is a very interesting development; it is the same theme as in the fairy tale "The Spirit in the Bottle."[90] The original manifestation of Sulphur—the crude and vulgar sulphur—must indeed be bottled up. It must undergo transformation if it's going to get out of the animal level of existence. That's why the early aspect of the analytic process is largely a procedure in which

---

[90] See "The Spirit Mercurius," *Alchemical Studies,* CW 13, pars. 239ff.

primitive affects are analyzed reductively. This means in effect that the ego is required to take responsibility for such fiery behavior. It must be bottled up, confined, because civilized people don't throw their crude vulgar sulphur around freely—that's not done. So nature and instinct are subjected to an encounter with the spirit principle. This has the effect of condemning crude sulphur and labeling it as sinful. One properly feels guilty about burning freely with this crude sulphur and that's how Sulphur gets locked up.

The active imagination continues:

Alchemist: Who are his gaolers?

Voice: They are of his own kindred, but grievous tyrants.

This tells us that the same basic level that causes sulphur to burn also extinguishes it. In other words one instinct is in conflict with another. The instinctual, archetypal level of the psyche is made up of opposites and when one side gets out of hand, its contrary bottles it up.

The alchemist asks some more questions about the nature of Sulphur and then asks what Sulphur can do:

Voice: He can perform a thousand things, and is the heart of all. He can perfect metals and minerals, impart understanding to animals, produce flowers in herbs and trees, corrupt and perfect air.

Isn't that interesting! Sulphur is corrupting our air; it will be interesting to see how it can perfect it.

Voice: In short, he produces all the odours and paints all the colours in the world. . . .

Alchemist: Master, is he old?

Voice: Know, friend, that Sulphur is the virtue of the world, and though Nature's second-born—yet the oldest of all things. To those who know him, however, he is as obedient as a little child.

I have to skip over some of this—the alchemist learns more about the nature of Sulphur, the tincturing and maturing nature of Sulphur. Here's an important feature I do want to get in:

Alchemist: Master, cannot those quarrels between him and his gaolers be composed?

Voice: Yes, by a wise and cunning craftsman.

Alchemist: Why does he not offer them terms of peace?

Voice: He cannot do so by himself: his indignation gets the better of his discretion.

Alchemist: Why does he not do so through some commissary [intermediary]?

Voice: He who could put an end to their strife would be a wise man, and worthy of undying honour. For if they were friends, they would help, instead of hindering each other, and bring forth immortal things.

Alchemist: I will gladly undertake the duty of reconciling them.

That line is fine, but it goes down from there because he goes on to say:

For I am a very learned man, and they could not resist my practical skill. I am a great Sage, and my Alchemistic treatment would quickly bring about the desired end.

He immediately falls into an inflation, although at first he does exactly the right thing. When the ego discovers the conflict of the opposites in operation, it should "undertake the duty of reconciling them"—Sulphur and his jailers. But the prospect of being the mediator of such a grand enterprise got the better of him. Here's how it ends:

Alchemist: If I find his prison, shall I be able to deliver him?

Voice: Yes, if you are wise enough to do so. It is easier to deliver him than to find his prison.

Alchemist: When I do find him, shall I be able to make him into the Philosopher's Stone?

Voice: I am no prophet. But if you follow his mother's advice, and dissolve the Sulphur, you will have the Stone.

I understand the dissolving of Sulphur to mean psychologically that one frees the affect from the complexes in which it first expresses itself. If one can succeed in doing that, then Sulphur is freed so to speak, and in its free form it is seen to be a manifestation of the Self. Then the Philosophers' Stone has been at least glimpsed.

4. The Alchemist's Dream of Sulphur Wounded

The active imagination ends but the text continues. The alchemist falls asleep and has a dream that Jung talks about in paragraph 144 and that I want to say just a little about.

In this dream the alchemist sees two men who are identified as Sulphur and Sal (salt). These two men quarrel and Sal gives Sulphur an incurable wound. Then a bit later the alchemist discovers the corpse of Sulphur and takes a piece of it to operate with alchemically. As Jung points out, Sulphur is called both "medicina" and "medicus"—both medicine and physician. This double reference leads Jung to the theme of the wounded healer (paragraph 144, note 157).

Just as Sulphur was imprisoned in the active imagination, so now in the dream he's wounded and even killed by the encounter with his opposite.

I think in this context Sulphur would represent the hot fiery principle, and Sal would represent the cold watery principle—it is a variation of the Sol and Luna theme. The idea is that one opposite is wounded or killed by the encounter with its contrary, just as Gabricus disappeared in the womb of Beya. At a certain stage of development sulphur, as desirousness, must be wounded, killed, frustrated, or bottled up.

Jung describes this vividly in his *Visions Seminars,* where he talks about the transformation of anima and animus devils, which are synonymous with sulphur. Let me read it to you:

> In this transformation it is essential to take objects away from those animus or anima devils. They only become concerned with objects when you allow yourself to be self-indulgent. *Concupiscentia* is the term for that in the church. . . . On this subject the great religions come together. The fire of desirousness is the element that must be fought against in Brahmanism, in Buddhism, in Tantrism, in Mani-cheanism, in Christianity. It is also important in psychology.
>
> When you indulge in desirousness, whether your desire turns toward heaven or hell . . .

He means that if you desire something with positive affect, that would be turning toward heaven; if you hate it and are going to get even with it, that's turning toward hell.

> . . . you give the animus or the anima an object; then it comes out into the world instead of staying inside in its place. . . . But if you can say: Yes, I desire it and I shall try to get it but I do not have to have it, if I decide to renounce, I can renounce it; then there is no chance for the animus or anima. Otherwise you are governed by your desires, you are possessed. . . .
>
> But if you have put your animus or anima into a bottle you are free of possession, even though you may be having a bad time inside, because when your devil has a bad time you have a bad time. . . . Of course he will rumble around in your entrails, but after a while you will see that it was right [to bottle him up]. You will slowly become quiet and change. Then you will discover that there is a stone growing in the bottle . . . . Insofar as self-control, or non-indulgence, has become a habit, it is a stone. . . . When that attitude becomes a *fait accompli,* the stone will be a diamond.[91]

And with those wise words, I'll end.

---

[91] *The Visions Seminars,* vol. 1, pp. 239f.

8
Paragraphs 154-178

Tonight our subject is the symbolism of the moon, and I will talk about seven major features of that symbolism:

1. The moon as mediator and intercessor between the realms.
2. The moon is associated with plants and promotes fertility and healing.
3. It promotes coagulatio.
4. It promotes solutio because it is associated with images of water, sap and dew.
5. It is associated with animals, especially cold-blooded animals and the dog.
6. The moon's noetic aspect.
7. The symbolic equation between Luna and the Church: the so-called Luna-Ecclesia equation.

You'll remember that in the second class there was some brief discussion of Luna in connection with the symbolism of the widow.[92] Now Jung is venturing into a much more exhaustive treatment of this symbolism.

For the last two assignments we've been talking about the symbolism of Sol and the associated symbolism of sulphur. Tonight we turn from Sol to Luna. So we're dealing with the two major personifications of the partners of the con-iunctio—sun and moon—which in alchemy are specifically associated with the opposition of the sexes. The sun is conceived of as masculine and the moon as feminine. We can say that the moon, Luna, is a personification of the feminine principle.[93]

We hear a lot of talk about the feminine principle these days, and this material in *Mysterium* gives us an opportunity to approach the question of what the feminine principle is from a strictly empirical standpoint rather than from the standpoint of a preconceived theory. It gives us the chance to examine what the psyche itself says in alchemy about the nature of the moon, how the psyche itself describes the feminine principle.

Perhaps the best way of approaching it is to notice what particular effects are attributed to Luna. One thing quickly becomes apparent: Luna or the feminine principle is much more difficult to define than is the masculine principle. That would correspond to its nature which doesn't lend itself to definition. What we can do is examine the effects of Luna as elaborated in alchemical symbolism.

---

[92] See above, pp. 34ff.

[93] For a detailed elaboration of moon symbolism, see M. Esther Harding, *Woman's Mysteries: Ancient and Modern.*

1. The Moon as Mediator and Gateway Between the Realms

First of all there is the fundamental idea that the moon is the mediator, intercessor and gateway between the realm of celestial influences and the earthly realm. I would remind you again of the geocentric image of the universe in which, according to antiquity, the moon was set.[94]

The planetary spheres are arranged concentrically around the earth, and the moon's sphere is closest to the earth. Therefore all influences, all transmission of material or effects between heaven and earth must pass through the moon. That's the only way to get to earth from the upper regions—you have to go through the moon. In psychological terms, we can say that the feminine principle is the funnel or gateway between the personal and the transpersonal psyche. And what is communicated between those two realms can be positive or negative. Lunacy can be transmitted, for instance. Or grace can be transmitted, usually symbolized by dew which is thought to drip off the moon down to the earth.

In one of his seminars Jung gives us a negative example of what is transmitted by the moon.[95] It's a story about a man in bed in the middle of the night who saw moonlight streaming in. He had the thought that he could crouch in that moonlight and bay like a dog and still wouldn't be mad because he knew what he was doing. But then he did it, and he became mad. That story, you see, is a kind of parable of one aspect of moon functioning.

A quite opposite kind of image came up in a remarkable dream. This was dreamt by a woman shortly after taking her husband to the hospital for an emergency abdominal operation—he had an acute abdominal crisis and had his gall bladder removed. Here is the dream:

> She's standing in a circular room in the center of a building. The room is actually a disc-like platform that's equipped with life-support systems and it's attached to a center core so that the platform can be moved up and down in the building. Then it's been moved to the topmost floor. To her amazement she sees that the roof has opened up and "we're in the midst of a huge galaxy of stars, like the Milky Way. And even more amazing is that all the individuals and equipment on the disc are being recharged by the stars." And she's overwhelmed with the effects of this view; she looks around and nobody else seems to notice—they're all too busy—she's the only one that sees it. She tries to speak but she's overwhelmed with the living, pulsating, blood-filled warmth of the vision.
>
> As she's waking, she's trying desperately to find a visual image to get a hold of what she's experienced. What she sees is a huge udder which is the Milky Way. "And I think that it's nourishment for all of us."

There's no actual mention of the moon in this dream, but the huge udder takes

---

[94] See above, pp. 40f.
[95] *Analytical Psychology: Notes of the Seminar Given in 1925,* p. 97.

its place. The celestial influences correspond to the planetary powers that communicate their effects down through the moon to the earth. This dream is an exact representation of the remark from an alchemical text that Jung quotes in paragraph 154: "The earth 'receives' the powers of the stars, and in it the sun generates the gold."

This woman had a vision of the archetypal forces assisting the whole hospital operation that was caring for her husband in his emergency situation. It's a beautiful example of how, at urgent times, the archetypal psyche can be activated in a helpful way, and also of those lines of Hölderlin that Jung is fond of quoting: "Where danger is, there arises salvation also."[96]

Figure 8-1.
"The earth 'receives' the powers of the stars, and in it the sun generates the gold."

---

[96] From "Patmos"; see, for instance, *Symbols of Transformation,* CW 5, pars. 630ff.

2. The Moon Promotes Fertility, Healing and the Growth of Plants

In folklore, planters are advised to consider the phases of the moon—the full moon is best for planting above-ground crops and the dark of the moon is best for planting root crops. Medicines are supposed to have their best effect when they're taken at the full moon. Erich Neumann gives a very nice account of the psychological implications of this feature of moon symbolism in his essay, "On the Moon and Matriarchal Consciousness." I want to read you some passages from it because Neumann catches the flavor so well:

> The common identification of our ego with patriarchal head-consciousness and the corresponding unrelatedness to matriarchal consciousness often leads to our not knowing what is really happening to us. . . . We find out [only] later that we have been deeply impressed by things, situations, and people . . . . The saying of Heraclitus holds true: "Nature loves to hide itself."
>
> The moment of conception is veiled and mysterious, often submitted to by the ego of matriarchal consciousness without any awareness on the part of the head-ego. But a deeper introspection, taking dreams, images, and fantasies into account, will show that in the matriarchal consciousness the moment and the event have been registered . . . .
>
> There is much meaning in the veiling of these moments of conception which are often so vitally important. Growth needs stillness and invisibility, not loudness and light. . . .
>
> It is not under the burning rays of the sun but in the cool reflected light of the moon, when the darkness of unconsciousness is at the full, that the creative process fulfills itself; the night, not the day, is the time of procreation. It wants darkness and quiet, secrecy, muteness, and hiddenness. Therefore, the moon is lord of life and growth in opposition to the lethal, devouring sun. The moist night time is the time of sleep, but also of healing and recovery. . . . The moon-god, Sin, is a physician . . . . The realms of healing and healer, healing plant and recuperative growth, meet in this configuration. It is the regenerating power of the unconscious that in nocturnal darkness or by the light of the moon performs its task, a *mysterium* . . . from out of itself. . . . This is why healing pills and herbs are ascribed to the moon, and their secrets guarded by women, or better by womanliness, which belongs to the moon. [97]

3. The Moon Promotes Coagulatio

As is evident from the moon's position between the earth and the upper regions, all descending entities that are destined to incarnate—to take on material form, earthly existence—have to pass through the moon in order to achieve incarnation. That's the symbolic reason why the Virgin Mary is equated with the moon. She served the function of the moon to bring about the incarnation of Christ.

---

[97] In *Spring 1954,* pp. 83ff.

To expand on this a bit, it's expressing the psychological fact that any specific form, manifestation or structure which solidifies our life energies into some particular concrete expression belongs to the nature of the feminine principle. So one of the features of the feminine is that it concretizes—that's another word for incarnating, for coagulating. Any entity—it might be patriotism to a country, it might be service to a Church, to a community or particular institution, to some particular cause, to a family, a vocation, an avocation or to a personal relationship—any particular form that is capable of enlisting our commitment, of concretizing our life energy, pertains to the feminine principle. Even such apparent abstractions as science or wisdom or truth or beauty or liberty are examples of the coagulating power of Luna if they actually have the power to organize one's life energy in a concrete way and evoke a commitment from the individual.

To say it another way, the power to evoke a commitment of libido is a form of relationship energy, and that ties in with the fact that Jung has defined the feminine principle as the principle of relatedness. Thus we can say that relationship, in the broadest sense of the word—the capacity to relate—is a feature of coagulatio, it promotes coagulatio.

4. The Moon Promotes Solutio

But the moon also promotes solutio because of its association with water, the sea, the tides, the sap of plants and with dew. So in some circumstances it can coagulate, and in some circumstances it can dissolve; in some circumstances it can concretize and bring into reality psychic potentials, and in some cases it has the effect of dissolution.[98]

There are two sides to solutio: one side is when something hard is melted and made soft and gentle, and that's the aspect where grace and renewal is brought by the dew of the moon, or by the water of the moon. But in other cases the solutio aspect is a negative and dangerous feature, and that's illustrated by the myth of Diana and Actaeon.

5. The Moon, Cold-Blooded Animals and the Dog

Actaeon was a young hunter out with his pack of dogs when by accident he came upon Diana, the moon, naked in her bath. To punish him for her embarrassment, she turned Actaeon into a stag who was then dismembered by his own dogs. In other words he was subjected to dissolution.

This myth is an example of the symbol complex of moon-water-bath-dissolution. Actaeon would represent the young ego that prematurely stumbles upon the full intensity of the archetypal lunar principle and cannot stand the effects of it. He undergoes dissolution from the impact of that encounter—he's fragmented and

---

[98] For more detail on solutio, see Edinger, *Anatomy,* chap. 3.

dismembered by the dogs. One could say that he falls into an identification with the instinctual factors the dogs represent. Dog, water and moon are all symbolically synonomous. (We're going to be talking extensively next week about the symbolism of the dog—an important part of moon symbolism.)

This same image of moon, water and being attacked by animals is illustrated in a significant picture reproduced in *Psychology and Alchemy* (figure 8-2). In this picture there is the upper region with all those curlicues, and coming down through it is the sun. Beneath the sun is the moon, and liquid drips from that moon-form. That's the lunar dew, the lunar water, coming out of the moon and baptizing a male and female pair below. At the same time as they are being baptized by this lunar water, they are also being bitten in the heel or calf by animal-like figures on either side.

So they are going through an experience similar to that of Actaeon—they're falling into the moon bath and are being bitten by the instinct animals. Simultaneously we also see a frog, one of the cold-blooded creatures associated with the moon, coming up from the bath. The frog very often represents, or points to, the process of transformation.

Figure 8-2. Brother-sister pair attacked.

Figure 8-3. Tarot moon card.

Another example of the same sequence is the Tarot card entitled the Moon (figure 8-3). In this card the moon is dripping dew down to the earth, and two dogs or wolves are looking up at the moon; crustacean-like creatures are crawling out of the water toward the moon. That's part of the same symbolism.

The myth of Endymion is another moon myth that illustrates a different side of the dangerous aspect of the moon. Endymion was a shepherd who was lying asleep one night in a cave when Selene the moon saw him, and came down to lie by his side. In order to keep him to herself, she kissed his closed eyes and he fell into a deep sleep from which he's never awakened. So the moon can visit him whenever she chooses, you see. This is a version of the story of the mother and her perpetually young son-lover. Of course the way that's achieved is that the son-lover has to die young, and then he never grows old.

I think John Keats is an example of someone who identified with that archetype —he lived only to the age of twenty-six. He wrote a long narrative poem entitled "Endymion," and to give you the feeling of a certain kind of poetic lunar quality let me read you the beautiful first verses.

> A thing of beauty is a joy forever:
> Its lovliness increases; it will never
> Pass into nothingness; but still will keep
> A bower quiet for us, and a sleep
> Full of sweet dreams, and health, and quiet breathing.
> Therefore, on every morrow, are we wreathing
> A flowery band to bind us to the earth,
> Spite of despondence, of the inhuman dearth
> Of noble natures, of the gloomy days,
> Of all the unhealthy and o'er-darkened ways
> Made for our searching: yes, in spite of all,
> Some shape of beauty moves away the pall
> From our dark spirits. Such the sun, the moon,
> Trees old and young, sprouting a shady boon
> For simple sheep; and such are daffodils
> With the green world they live in; and clear rills
> That for themselves a cooling covert make
> 'Gainst the hot season; the mid-forest brake,
> Rich with a sprinkling of fair musk-rose blooms:
> And such too is the grandeur of the dooms
> We have imagined for the mighty dead;
> All lovely tales that we have heard or read:
> An endless fountain of immortal drink,
> Pouring unto us from the heaven's brink.

"An endless fountain of immortal drink"—that's the moon dripping its dew. And since Keats was a moon man, he could see it and feel it and communicate it.

6. The Moon's Noetic Aspect

Starting in paragraph 160, Jung brings up a matter that is complex and rather difficult to communicate. He talks about the fact that the moon was associated with certain terms such as Ennoia and Epinoia and Sapientia. He then goes ahead to elaborate on those matters but as they are less than crystal clear I wanted to say a few words about them. Ennoia and Epinoia were personal names equated with the moon. They come from Gnosticism and are derivatives of the word Nous. And as Jung says, they refer to the Nous-like aspect of the moon.

Nous, a term from ancient Greek philosophy and Gnosticism, is very difficult to translate exactly. It has qualities similar to the Logos but it is not equivalent to it. It's a spiritual entity thought to have a creative, generative power that moves in from the celestial transpersonal realms of the universe and comes down to earth. When it manifests on earth it creates mind and reason and order, and all that is spiritual and human as opposed to brute matter.

It's very interesting that the symbolism of the moon should include a noetic aspect—ordinarily one thinks of the phenomenon of the creative spirit as being a part of masculine symbolism—but here it is. And the evidence of etymology points to the same symbolic fact. In Greek, the word *mene* was the word for moon. The root of that word got transmitted to Latin and generated the Latin word *mensis* which means month. You can see there the root of our word menses or menstrual periods. The same root appears in the Latin word *mens,* meaning mind, with its genitive, *mentis;* and *mentis* is the root for our word mental. The same root is in the word *mensura* which means measure. So moon, month, mind and measure all belong to the same symbolism.

This tells us that in some psychological sense the moon and what's symbolized by it, namely the feminine principle, create time, measure and mind. You might look at it this way: the contents that are emerging from the collective unconscious into the ego, passing through the lunar factor from the eternal atemporal realm to the ego realm, acquire the qualities of time, space, quantity and measurement as they come into conscious existence. These qualities are the categories of consciousness. They're the ground work of mentation, of mental life or functioning. They are part of the process of incarnation, promoted by the moon.

In paragraph 159 Jung makes a provocative statement. He says:

> The moon is a favourite symbol for certain aspects of the unconscious—though only, of course, in a man. In a woman the moon corresponds to consciousness and the sun to the unconscious. This is due to the contrasexual archetype in the unconscious: anima in a man, animus in a woman.

He drops that and goes on. Erich Neumann has a somewhat different idea. He suggests that the sun is the principle of consciousness for both men and women. As I try to review my experience in this matter, the more I reflect on it the more complicated it becomes. I think both statements are true, but in this, as with all matters dealing with the feminine principle, we cannot be too precise. We have to allow ourselves to function in the moonlight where things are indistinct.

I'd put it this way: the conscious ego of a woman, at least under usual circumstances, is more comfortable and related to the moon because the moon is compatible with a woman's consciousness, with the conscious personality. For a man, the conscious ego is as a rule more compatible with the sun. But, looked at from a different angle, we could also say that Neumann is right—that strictly speaking the principle of consciousness is the same for both men and women. That leaves the matter less than crystal clear, and I think to be true to the nature of the imagery we're talking about, we'll have to leave it that way.

Relevant to this whole question is the dream of a woman who was a biological research scientist—she was about thirty and single at the time:

> A young male friend called me to the window to watch a phenomenon in the sky. As we watched we saw the moon, and from behind the moon another body was emerging, like a second moon. But suddenly the second body began to explode in spectacular colors that looked like an H-bomb explosion. We thought we were watching the birth of a new sun and this thought was very frightening, for if a new sun were being created, its heat and radiation might kill us all. All at once, during another explosive event, a piece of the new body was thrown into space and landed in our apartment. We ran out as fast as we could, being afraid that it might be radioactive.

Well, this talks about the moon, about the appearance of a second moon, and about a new sun being born. The analytic hours just prior to this dream had been spent discussing the patient's fear of men, starting as a child. Her mother had transmitted to her the fear of a man who had exposed himself to children in a tunnel under the street. And the patient had had recent fantasies of being attacked by a man. This woman's ego development was defective—you might say her lunar ego had not yet been born. And I see this dream as an expression of the birth of that lunar ego. In fact, after a good bit of work that development did take place—she was able to marry and have children, and the full feminine experience became available to her.

But even in the midst of this dream of the birth of a lunar ego—a piece of the moon falling down to earth—we also have the idea that a new sun is being born. You see how the two ideas get slipped in; so we can't be too dogmatic about it.

Question: Do you think the image of the two moons also suggest the birth—something coming into consciousness?

Well, we often think that when something is paired it means it is coming into consciousness, right.[99]

---

[99] See Marie-Louise von Franz, *On Divination and Synchronicity,* pp. 105ff.

7. The Symbolic Equation Between Luna and the Church

I want to say a few words about the so-called Luna-Ecclesia equation, the moon-Church equation. In Christian symbolism both Mary and the Church are equated with the moon. A very valuable study of the patristic symbolism of such matters as the moon can be found in a book by Hugo Rahner to whom Jung refers in paragraph 173. In the chapter on moon symbolism, Rahner writes the following:

> The Church, like a true mother, receiving into herself the rays of the Christmas sun [the new-born sun at Christmas time], and being in this respect an imitator of the Blessed Virgin, gives birth to Christ, for in baptism she gives life to the faithful. In doing so she transforms mere earthly "psychics" into the race of "pneumatics," into a people filled with the spirit.[100]

That's Gnostic jargon. In other words she transforms earth-bound creatures into spiritual creatures. According to the Gnostics there were three kinds of people: there were sarkics, psychics and pneumatics. The sarkics were the bodily ones—they're all *sarkos*. The psychics don't have quite the same meaning as our use of the word psyche; they're the watery ones who are a little better than the sarkics but not as good as the first rate pneumatics. The passage continues:

> By this action the Church becomes comparable to Selene [the moon] who receives the light of the sun, transforms it after the manner of a mother and so, as mistress of all waters upon the earth, brings new life into the world.[101]

This is one example of the Church-moon equation. Jung brings in other examples and there are great many in the patristic literature.

This issue is quite important psychologically, because the reference here to the Church refers to all sacred communities, all collective ethnic and religious containers. All such communities serve as a mother-moon for those who are contained by them: the Church is comparable to the moon who receives the light of the sun, transforms it like a mother and so brings new life into the world.

In other words, the moon-Church functions as a mediator. For those contained in the Church or the sacred community, immediate contact with the sun could be killing. They need a mediator, and that's the function that Luna-Church performs. That function is positive when it serves the individual's need. So long as one has no developmental urge that requires breaking out of that level of containment, the function of the sacred community is completely positive.

If, however, the urge for a greater level of development should appear within the individual, then the moon-like containing function of the religious community turns negative. We see striking examples of that in regard to various religious cults. They function as sacred communities for lost souls, giving them a sense of

---

[100] *Greek Myths and Christian Mystery,* p. 161.
[101] Ibid.

meaning, containment and orientation. Everything is fine as long as the containment is comfortable. But if such a person should have the inner require- ment for a greater degree of individual development and should decide to leave the cult, then he or she is in trouble—they don't let 'em go so easily. That would be an example of the moon turning from a dispenser of the grace of lunar dew into the devouring funnel of the dream I told you of in an earlier lecture.[102]

Question: Would that be the negative side of coagulatio?

I don't think containment itself refers specifically to coagulatio; but there's so much overlap—so in part, yes. But here I think the imagery is more liquid. It's more the imagery of fish swimming around in the ecclesiastical pond. As long as they're meant to be fish, they're fine, but if one or two of them happen to be lung- fish they have to start climbing out on dry land; then the pond becomes something negative.

Now even though it threatens to be confusing, I must add one further aspect here. As the lowest so-called planet, the closest one to the earth, the moon is sometimes equated with the earth. In that case we have the symbolic equation that the moon equals the earth, because the moon is the most earthly of all the so- called planets. From this standpoint, the moon is equated with the ego.

Let me give you another quote from Rahner in which he speaks about Plotinus (a Greek Neo-Platonist circa 204-270 A.D.). In Plotinus's cosmology there was a triad of major factors: the One, the Nous and the All Soul. The One was the source of all existence—a kind of invisible essence. It emanated a dynamic principle, the Nous. And the third entity, created by the Nous, was the All Soul or Mind. In talking about this, Rahner gives us this remark from Plotinus:

> We see therefore that the One is comparable to the light, the second [the Nous] . . . to the sun, and the third [the Soul or Mind] . . . to the moon which receives its light from the sun; for the spirit is something super-added to the soul, and casts a glow over it if the soul itself be spiritual.[103]

What that is saying, translated into psychological terminology, is that from one standpoint, the ego as receiver of the transpersonal energy from the collective unconscious is analogous to the moon.

In dealing with this imagery one has to keep a fluid, relativistic attitude. An image can mean one thing in one context, one set of circumstances, and something else when related to another set of images. At times the moon will be the transmitter to the ego. At other times, in a different symbolic context, it takes on the qualities of the ego itself because it receives its light and energy from a source outside itself just as the ego does.

---

[102] See above, lecture 2, pp. 41f.

[103] *Greek Myths,* p. 158; from Plotinus, *The Aeneads,* V, 6, 4.

9
Paragraphs 179-213

Our scheduled assignment for tonight is paragraphs 179 to 213, but as I'm going to be covering dog symbolism in its entirety we'll go from 174 to 213.

Before we go into tonight's material, I have some translation corrections to bring up. Near the end of paragraph 188 the text reads: "incest, as we have said before, is nothing but a preliminary form of the unio oppositorum." Jung doesn't say "nothing but." The German is better translated "has the significance of" or "signifies." So cross out "is nothing but" and put in "signifies."

In paragraph 192, seven lines from the top of page 162, the translation reads: ". . . like a blind man leading the blind with somnambulistic certainty into the ditch." The German text, instead of "ditch," reads "into the void where all the paralyzed ones follow him."

And one more, paragraph 205, third line: instead of "interpretation from above downwards," cross out the phrase "from above" so it reads simply "interpretation downwards."

Tonight's material concerns the symbolism of the dog. As we are still dealing with the over-all subject of the moon, this whole section on the dog is a subordinate category to moon symbolism. There are seven items I am going to speak about—actually seven plus one, which is significant, isn't it!

1. Hecate, hell and the underworld.
2. The dog as pursuer.
3. The dog as the despised and insignificant one.
4. The dog as guardian.
5. The dog as companion and *familiaris*—familiar spirit.
6. The text that starts, "Pull down the house."
7. Another text that starts, "If thou knowest how to moisten this dry earth . . ."

But before I go into those images, I want to talk about the myth of the extraction of the mandrake root. This came up in the previous assignment in connection with moon-plant symbolism but it actually fits better into the dog section. Jung refers to it in paragraph 158 and footnote 208. The mandrake is one of the plants associated with the moon, and the whole story of the extraction of the mandrake root is so interesting symbolically that I'm going to go into it a bit.

This imaginary plant is supposed to be shaped like a man without a head. One text says: "It needs only a soul breathed into it to become a little human being."[104] In other words it's a kind of homunculus growing as a plant in the ground. It's

---

[104] Rahner, *Greek Myths*, p. 233.

thought to be an aphrodisiac, a narcotic, an anesthetic, exceedingly poisonous on occasion—it can cause madness—and when a magician extracts it he then can work magic with its root.

Certain alchemical texts for the creation of the Philosophers' Stone have a parallel symbolism to the extraction of the mandrake root. The text quoted by Rahner says, "The little red man in the ground cries, 'Help me and I will help thee.' " The Philosophers' Stone makes a similar remark to the alchemist.[105]

It is very difficult to extract the mandrake root and in order to succeed you must follow a rigorous ritual. You can work only at night, by the light of the moon—that's where the moon symbolism comes in. The first task of course is to find the plant. Fortunately the plant helps because it glows in the dark. Once the plant is found, the digger must draw three circles around it and then turn westward. He brings an assistant with him who must dance round the plant murmuring erotica.

Because this plant belongs to Hecate who has the black dog as her attribute, a black dog must be used in the process of removing the mandrake root. This is how it's done: first the earth is dug away from around the root and the root is then tied to the tail of the black dog. The rhizotomist, the root extractor, remains some distance away. He doesn't get too close to the plant at this point. He calls the dog and the dog runs to him. It's a little like the way, as children, we'd remove a loose tooth—you'd tie one end of a thread around it and tie the other end to a doorknob, then open the door or something like that. So he calls the dog, the dog runs to him, and the root is pulled out.

This is the moment of greatest peril and urgency; at the moment of extraction the mandrake utters a scream which is death for men to hear. The rhizotomist must be sure to hold his ears as he calls the dog so that he doesn't hear the scream. Then the black dog dies. There are two versions of how this happens. According to one, the dog perishes at the moment of the extraction—the scream kills him. According to the other version, the rhizotomist sacrifices the black dog after it's done its job.[106]

Now isn't that a fascinating account? If you keep this story in mind I think there'll be occasion to use it every now and then when dreams come up that allude to some aspect or other of this sequence. Let me say just a few words about each of these operations.

I think of the mandrake root itself as an image of the original Self, the whole man, buried in a state of *participation mystique.* Or one could say that it is the

---

[105] "Protect me, and I will protect thee; give me my own, that I may help thee." ("The Golden Treatise of Hermes," in M. Atwood, *Hermetic Philosophy and Alchemy,* p. 128)
[106] See Rahner, *Greek Myths,* p. 233; also Edward Whitmont, "The Magical Dimension in Transference and Countertransference," pp. 176ff.

Self, buried at the core of one's central complex.

The work must be done at night because it's only in the darkness that one can see the faint glow of the plant. That would suggest to me that it has to be done when the ego is eclipsed. As long as the ego is emitting light and is functioning out of daytime consciousness, it's not going to be able to perceive the faint light glowing in the unconscious. Drawing three circles around the plant suggests magic protective circles—creating a kind of temenos that centers, focuses and delimits the attention and energy being poured into the procedure.

Turning westward—the direction of sunset, the land of the dead—suggests that the ego must be oriented toward the downgoing phase of life rather than the rising phase of life. In other words it's a second half of life operation.

The assistant must dance around, murmuring erotica: that suggests to me the deliberate evocation of coniunctio energies.

The earth must be dug away from the root: that suggests there must first be an analysis of the personal, concrete context of one's central complex in order to loosen the immediate earth around it.

Then the crucial event: the root is pulled out by being attached to the tail of a black dog. Both the mandrake and the black dog are associated with the moon and so the idea is that the root must be extracted by something of its own nature. The black dog suggests a dark affect which is harnessed to a specific purpose. That's the most provocative image of all—using a black dog to extract the root. No prissy fooling around will accomplish this particular task—it's a dark job.

The scream of the mandrake that one must not hear is like the song of the sirens that one may not listen to. This indicates that there is a time to be open to the unconscious and a time to be closed to it. It reminds me of Psyche's descent to the underworld when, at a certain point, she is told she must not extend pity to one of the victims of the underworld as he reaches out to her. She is obliged to turn away from him and close her ears to his entreaty.[107] There are certain times in dealing with the unconscious when one must close one's ears to more humane considerations.

Finally at the end the black dog is sacrificed. This suggests that the dark affect which was permitted to function for a specific purpose in a specific setting must now be sacrificed. This is of vital importance; if it doesn't happen, the black dog rather than the human being is the extractor. That would amount to the mandrake extracting the operator rather than the operator extracting the mandrake. Very provocative symbolism.

Now, the imagery in *Mysterium* on the dog, beginning with paragraph 174, is very rich indeed and you will have ample opportunity to use it in dream interpretation. It has immediate practical application and is worth knowing well.

---

107 See Neumann, *Amor and Psyche,* p. 48.

Psychologically the dog might be called the theriomorphic personification of the unconscious. It's the theriomorphic aspect of the moon—the way she manifests on the animal, earthy level—and there are a number of different facets to this symbolism.

1. The Dog's Association to Hecate, Hell and the Underworld

Cerberus, the dog of hell, is the guardian dog of the underworld and an embodiment of the underworld itself. Anybody going into the underworld or coming out of it must throw a sop to Cerberus in order not to be devoured by him. You have to give him something else to devour, you see. You throw him a hunk of meat to divert his attention so he won't chew you up.

If you feel your way into that symbolism it will give you some real wisdom about how to deal with the unconscious, how you get into it. You don't get into it by maintaining your conscious moralistic attitudes; you have to throw a sop to the powers of darkness in order to get in.

Although we don't see it so much in our so-called civilized state, in antiquity dogs were carrion eaters. That's one of the features of the underworld aspect of dogs, you see—they consumed the dead. In dreams the appearance of a vicious dog or a black dog can generally be thought of as a reference to Cerberus, to the dark and dangerous aspect of the unconscious which must be treated with care and respect, given its due, its sop.

2. The Dog as Pursuer

An important feature of the dog is that it scents out quarry and hounds it to death. I think for instance of fox hunting with a pack of dogs—you couldn't hunt a fox without the dogs. Psychologically, the ultimate quarry of the dog as pursuer—the hunting dog—is the ego. Actaeon experienced this when his dogs turned on him. And this aspect of dog symbolism brings up the whole theme of the hunter and the hunted.

You might say that the dog is the hunting aspect of the psyche. Sometimes it is allied to the ego and sometimes the ego is what's being hunted; sometimes the ego is going to be hunting with the hounds and sometimes it's going to be running with the fox. You might say that the dog corresponds to a complex that hounds you and won't let you get away.

Ultimately, such hounding comes from the urgency of the Self, and the best poetic example I know of that symbolism is Francis Thompson's "Hound of Heaven."[108] In that poem, God is represented as a great hound. I'll read you a few lines just to give you the feel of it.

> I fled Him, down the nights and down the days;

---

[108] Francis Thompson lived from 1859 to 1907. The poem was written about 1900.

> I fled Him, down the arches of the years;
> I fled Him, down the labyrinthine ways
> Of my own mind; and in the mist of tears
> I hid from Him, and under running laughter.
>   Up vistaed hopes I sped;
>   And shot, precipitated
> Adown Titanic glooms of chasmed fears,
> From those strong Feet that followed, followed after.
>   But with unhurrying chase,
>   And unperturbéd pace,
> Deliberate speed, majestic instancy,
>   They beat—and a Voice beat
>   More instant than the Feet—
> "All things betray thee, who betrayest Me."

And he goes on running away through a good many stanzas. He's finally cornered by the great hound, he can't escape it any more, and at the end of the poem he turns around and faces his fate:

> Halts by me that footfall:
> Is my gloom, after all,
> Shade of His hand, outstretched caressingly?
> "Ah, fondest, blindest, weakest,
> I am He Whom thou seekest!
> Thou dravest love from thee, who dravest Me."

3. The Dog as the Despised and Rejected One

The dog has been associated with the human community for a remarkably long time—since early Paleolithic times, so it's been a member of the human community almost from the beginning. But it is the lowest member, and the word dog in colloquial speech has always expressed opprobrium. "You dirty dog!" You don't ever call anybody a clean dog. In antiquity, male prostitutes were called dogs; and "son of a bitch," of course, is a current derogatory term that's dangerous to throw around too freely.

It is all the more surprising then to learn that one of the synonyms for the Philosophers' Stone is *filius canis*. Now that sounds pretty good in Latin, but it means son of a bitch! You begin to sense what a real paradox this entity is.

4. The Dog as Guardian

In paragraph 176, Jung quotes a passage from Hippolytus:

For the Logos is a dog . . . who guards and protects the sheep against the wiles of the wolves, and chases the wild beasts from Creation and slays them, and begets all things. For Cyon [dog], they say, means the Begetter.

That is an example of the enantiodromia that the imagery of the Self brings about. From dog as something despicable, we move to the dog as the creative Logos and begetter of all things.

The same symbolism is attached to the idea of the dog as a shepherd that guards the sheep, so the dog in this role has the same attributes as the image of the Good Shepherd. This sacred and profound aspect of the dog was projected into the heavens. Sirius, the brightest star in the sky, is the chief star in the constellation Canis Major—the Big Dog. That star, the Dog Star, was worshipped in ancient Egypt and special rituals were connected with its rising.

5. The Dog as Companion and Familiaris

This is another aspect of the dog as the Self, and this particular aspect has its classic example in Goethe's *Faust*. The whole of *Faust,* but particularly the beginning part, is so eminently psychological that you should all be thoroughly familiar with it. It will offer itself many times as amplification material.[109]

The *Faust* drama starts out with Faust in his study in a state of despair because all his studies have led him to sterility and emptiness. In the second scene he's out walking in the fields with his assistant, Wagner, and they encounter a dog. I want to read you a little bit about that meeting.

FAUST
D' you see a jet-black dog now scampering wide
Through corn and stubble?

WAGNER
Him I have espied
Some time ago, but gave him not a thought.

FAUST
Look closer now, with care, and say what sort
Of beast you think he is.

WAGNER
Why, Sir, a hound
Of poodle breed who snuffs his way around
To find his master.

FAUST
Mark the spiral trail
With which he comes from far, yet ever nigher
Encircling us: unless my senses fail
His track is traced with little tongues of fire.

WAGNER
Some optical illusion, Sir, maybe:

---

[109] See Edinger, *Goethe's* Faust: *Notes for a Jungian Commentary.*

He's nothing but a poodle-dog to me.

FAUST
It seems like magic tracing of a snare,
Or meshes in our future pathway spread.

WAGNER
I'm sure he seeks his master everywhere,
And frets to find two strangers here instead.

FAUST
The circle narrows, brings him near.

WAGNER
A dog, Sir,—see, no phantom have we here!
He growls, misdoubts, and settles on his hocks,
And wags his tail: all canine orthodox.[110]

Faust gives in to Wagner's common sense, but it turns out that that black poodle is the first manifestation of Mephistopheles who follows Faust home, slips inside his door, and then appears later, you see. So whenever you encounter a black dog in a dream, especially one that's following or indicates that he has some interest in the dreamer, think of *Faust* and the first manifestation of Mephistopheles—because that's what the dreamer is going to be in for.

Of course we have a lot of dreams of positive, companionable dogs too, and such things are of major importance because they signify the emergence of a positive connection with the Self.

Occasionally, I've encountered blue dog dreams and this corresponds to the image in a text Jung quotes in paragraph 174. As quoted, it begins "Hermes said . . ." This is quite a relevant text and I want you to add a sentence to the beginning of it—the text makes more sense if you have the preceding sentence. That sentence reads: "And Hermes said to his father, Father, I am afraid of the enemy in my house. And he said, My son, take a Corascene dog. . ."

Now I want to read that whole passage, including the added sentence:

And Hermes said to his father, Father, I am afraid of the enemy in my house. And he said, My son, take a Corascene dog and an Armenian bitch, join them together, and they will beget a dog of celestial hue [a blue dog], and if ever he is thirsty, give him sea water to drink: for he will guard your friend, and he will guard you from your enemy, and he will help you wherever you may be, always being with you, in this world and in the next.

I'm going to stop there because that's as much as serves my purpose.

The psychological point is that the recipe is evoked in response to an expression of fear "of the enemy in my house." This is a recipe for relief from anxiety.

---

[110] Goethe, *Faust,* pp. 68f.

"Father, I'm afraid of the enemy in my house." I'm afraid—something is making me anxious—there's something around in the house of my psyche. And the answer is, "It's okay, son, take a Corascene dog and an Armenian bitch, bring them together, they will beget a blue dog and he will guard you from your enemy in the present world and in the next." In other words, the dog's guardian function will carry beyond temporal existence into the transpersonal realm.

This term "Corascene dog"—nobody knows what it refers to; it may indicate a geographical name. But the idea is that the opposites must be united, and the process of uniting the opposites, that coniunctio, will generate the blue dog guardian that will rescue you from anxiety. Now that's left in a state of symbolism; you still have to apply it concretely, but you've got a beginning anyway. This text, then, is an example of the dog as companion—actually the eternal companion.

Question: What about the sea water?

Well, that indicates that it flourishes by being fed the unconscious—maybe something like active imagination.

6. "Therefore Pull Down the House"

This is a dog text Jung quotes in paragraph 179:

> Therefore pull down the house, destroy the walls, extract therefrom the purest juice with the blood, and cook that thou mayest eat. Wherefore Arnaldus saith in the Book of Secrets: Purify the stone, grind the door to powder, tear the bitch to pieces, choose the tender flesh, and thou wilt have the best thing. In the one thing are hidden all parts, in it all metals shine. Of these [parts], two are the artificers, two the vessels, two the times, two the fruits, two the ends, and one the salvation.

As Jung says in paragraph 180, "This text abounds in obscurities." But I think we can get the psychological gist of it. It's referring to an extraction procedure. The phrases "pull down the house" and "grind the door to powder, tear the bitch to pieces" describe the process of breaking up a previous concretion, a previous coagulatio of the libido, and extracting the essence from it.

This is the way that we can best understand dreams in which buildings are being destroyed—an extraction procedure is going on. I see this imagery most commonly with immature young people who repeatedly dream that their parents' home is being destroyed. The libido that's bound up in a dependent attachment to the parents, to the original family home, has to be extracted. So the recipe is "pull down the house," and "grind the door to powder, tear the bitch to pieces."

I think the last sentence, ". . . two are the artificers, two the vessels, two the times, two the fruits, two the ends, and one the salvation," emphasizes the fact that coming to consciousness involves, in a very profound way, the number two. Although the ultimate goal and consequence of consciousness is oneness, the way it emerges and comes about is by twoness, namely by the ego confronting an other.

One cannot achieve consciousness without another, and of course the two aspects of the other are the outer other and the inner other. They constellate one another and both are needed.

For instance, in paragraph 181 Jung mentions the theme of the adept and his *soror mystica*—his mystical sister. And there's a whole alchemical book called *Mutus liber,* which is nothing but pictures that show an opus being performed by a man and wife (figure 9-1). One is often asked in public lectures if individuation can take place without an analyst. I think the answer has to be yes, probably it can, but it can't take place without an other. Jung is reported to have said to somebody who didn't intend to go into analysis, or didn't have the opportunity: "You have to talk to somebody and if you get hard put to it, talk to the stove!"

You constellate an other by so doing, you see; you can't just talk to yourself, you have to have an other.

Figure 9-1. Alchemist and *soror mystica.*

7. "If Thou Knowest How To Moisten This Dry Earth"

This text and the commentary that follows it is really a high point of *Mysterium.* There's no other place in all of Jung's writings where he gives an alchemical text this kind of full and concrete psychological interpretation. His extensive commentary is in my opinion equivalent to a personal analytic hour with Jung.

All you have to do is to imagine that you had this text as a dream—and you might very well have had it because it is of such general reference and validity that any one of us could have dreamed it; it has that general applicability. And with this dream in hand, you go to your hour with Jung and he interprets it for you. It will apply to every single one of you and I'm going to read it.

> If thou knowest how to moisten this dry earth with its own water, thou wilt loosen
> the pores of the earth, and this thief from outside will be cast out with the workers

of wickedness, and the water, by an admixture of the true Sulphur, will be cleansed from the leprous filth and from the superfluous dropsical fluid, and thou wilt have in thy power the fount of the Knight of Treviso, whose waters are rightfully dedicated to the maiden Diana. Worthless is this thief, armed with the malignity of arsenic, from whom the winged youth fleeth, shuddering. And though the central water is his bride, yet dare he not display his most ardent love towards her, because of the snares of the thief, whose machinations are in truth unavoidable. Here may Diana be propitious to thee, who knoweth how to tame wild beasts, and whose twin doves will temper the malignity of the air with their wings, so that the youth easily entereth in through the pores, and instantly shaketh the foundations of the earth, and raises up a dark cloud. But thou wilt lead the waters up even to the brightness of the moon, and the darkness that was upon the face of the deep shall be scattered by the spirit moving over the waters. Thus by God's command shall the Light appear.[111]

Now I realize on first reading that's confusing and difficult to understand. But I'm going to summarize it, and it's very much worth whatever study it takes to get hold of it because of the marvelous interpretation that follows. You see it's a recipe—we must always remember that all of these stories in these alchemical texts are recipes. They're telling the alchemist what to do in his alchemical retort, and we can understand them as psychological recipes.

This recipe begins by telling us to "moisten this dry earth." That means you must activate the unconscious. Now it often happens, if you succeed in activating the unconscious, that you might rather have your dry state than the moist condition that comes up, but if that's the case then you won't get any farther in the recipe. So the first thing is to activate the unconscious.

Then, once that's happened, the recipe starts talking about a thief with poisonous arsenic. In other words, the activation of the unconscious brings up something negative, difficult and dark along with it. As Jung informs us in paragraph 191, this thief with his poisonous arsenic is desirousness, crude desirousness and the power motive—that's the crude sulphur. That's what comes up along with the activation of the unconscious. The other major thing that comes up with the activation of the unconscious is this very desirable item, the fountain of Diana, and this is an image of the Self in its feminine, Eros aspect.

So here you have these two entities: the fountain of Diana and the thief with his poisonous arsenic. What it amounts to is that you can't get to the fountain because the thief is in the way—so there is a kind of tantalizing quality.

The recipe then informs us that the fountain of Diana is safe to approach only when it's been purged of its connection with the thief. Only when the individual has been purged of ego motives, purged of greedy desirousness and power motives, is it safe to approach the fountain of Diana.

Then we hear about a winged youth who is yearning to unite with the fountain

---

[111] *Mysterium,* pars. 189-211, interspersed with Jung's commentary.

of Diana. This will be an image of potential Self-realization. You might even think of him as the god Eros himself. So as the thief is dealt with, the winged youth is able to make an entry into the fountain.

But his first entry has negative consequences because it brings darkness and an earthquake: "the youth easily entereth in through the pores," but then "instantly shaketh the foundations of the earth, and raiseth up a dark cloud." So no sooner is that coniunctio consummated—the winged youth and the fountain of Diana brought together—than there's an earthquake and a dark cloud. These are not very auspicious events; but gradually the darkness is dispersed "by the spirit moving over the waters"—that's the same spirit that was present at the Creation.

This image, then, signifies the birth of the enlarged personality. Jung puts that consequence very beautifully in paragraph 209:

> The earthquake sends up a dark cloud: consciousness, because of the revolution of its former standpoint, is shrouded in darkness, just as the earth was at Christ's death, which was followed by a resurrection. This image tells us that the widening of consciousness is at first upheaval and darkness, then a broadening out of man to the whole man.

Figure 9-2. The fountain of life.

10
Paragraphs 214-244

The major images in tonight's assignment are the following:

1. A Paracelsus text: The moon as the "great poisonous mirror of nature."
2. The image of the basilisk.
3. The beginning of salt symbolism, which will continue next time. Under salt symbolism I will talk tonight about four items:

    a) The triad sulphur-mercury-salt and its transformation into a quaternity.

    b) The Christian Trinity changed into a quaternity.

    c) The Assumption of the Virgin Mary.

    d) The *Pandora* picture.

Before we begin, I would like you to add the following sentence to note 395, which comes at the end of paragraph 239: "Origen's writings gave rise to the view that 'even the Devil will someday be saved.' "[112] That's such an important idea that I wanted you to be sure to get it in.

1. The Moon as the "Great Poisonous Mirror of Nature"

This very striking text of Paracelsus is quoted in paragraph 215. I'm going to read a few sentences from it to remind you of its content and flavor:

> Through his imagination the timid man has made his eyes basilisk-like, and he infects the mirror, the moon, and the stars, through himself at the start, and later on so that the moon is infected by the imagining man.

Paracelsus then goes on to say not only does the man infect the moon but the moon infects the man. "Thus man in turn will be poisoned by this mirror of the moon." And the reason he's poisoned is that "a pregnant woman at the time of menstruation" looks at the moon,

> [and] stains and damages the mirror by looking into it. For at such a time she is poisonous and has basilisk's eyes ... [because of the menstrual and poisonous blood] which lies hidden in her body.... [Because as the basilisk is caused and born from the menstrual and poisonous blood of a woman, thus the moon in the sky is the eye of the basilisk of heaven.]

This is an astonishing image, and a vivid and striking expression of the concretized psychological experiences out of which medieval man lived. It is also an image of a certain relationship to the objective psyche which I want to illustrate by a diagram (figure 10-1).

---

[112] *Aion,* CW 9ii, par. 171, note 29.

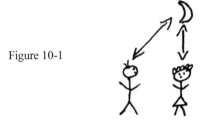

Figure 10-1

The menstruating woman is on the right and above her is the moon. The idea is that she looks at the moon and, because of the poisonous nature of her menstrual blood (which is moon stuff anyway; we know that from etymology—menses means month, which means moon), she infects the moon with its own stuff so to speak. And when the man looks at that infected mirror—the moon—then it functions like the eye of a basilisk (which I'll talk about in a moment) and it poisons him.

Now the image is incomplete here, because this would be the fantasy product of a man's psychology. If you were to complete it, you would have a fourfold structure: you would have the sun above and behind the male figure, and the moon above and behind the female figure—sun and moon representing the archetypal masculine and feminine principles which lie behind the masculine and feminine egos of woman and man respectively (figure 10-2).

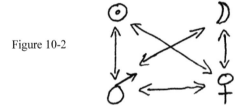

Figure 10-2

Then we have what Jung, in "The Psychology of the Transference," calls the marriage quaternio, the fourfold structure. Various possible connections are illustrated in the diagrams Jung presents (figures 10-3, 10-4).[113]

Figure 10-3. The marriage quaternio.

---

[113] *The Practice of Psychotherapy,* CW 16, pars. 422 and 437.

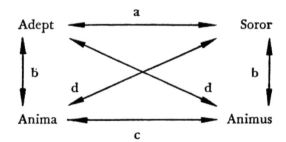

Figure 10-4.
Relationship patterns.

These diagrams show the kind of dynamic that exists in any male-female relationship in which the coniunctio is constellated.

Of course this particular text of Paracelsus emphasizes only the negative aspect of the moon. Yet that negative aspect is a reality, because for the immature ego the contrasexual archetypal principle is experienced as a very dangerous and threatening entity that must be guarded against.

A classic example of that came to my attention many years ago. I was working with a young man and we had reached a stage where the personal unconscious had been pretty well analyzed. Then he had a dream of just one sentence, and he awoke in terror. The sentence was: "Psychoanalysis is of the moon."

A short time later he decided he'd had enough analysis for the time being, and terminated. You see he wasn't yet ready for the moon; his psychology corresponded to this Paracelsus text. If he took a look at the moon, he'd be poisoned by the great basilisk eye of heaven. The same thing happens in feminine psychology: if a young woman has too heavy an encounter with the solar principle it can terrify her.

2. The Basilisk

The basilisk is mentioned in this text and I want to say a little more about that as an image. Here are some of the things *Funk and Wagnalls* says about it:

> A fabulous reptile of . . . legend and folktale whose breath and look were fatal. Physical descriptions of the creature differ [but it usually had an aspect of a serpent some way or another]. . . . [It] was thought to be hatched from a cock's egg on which a toad or serpent had sat and which preferably had matured in a dunghill or amidst poisonous materials; the glance of the basilisk was fatal . . . ; its breath was poisonous to all plants and animals; . . . It walked upright and, in some instances, was winged. . . . [In some representations it] depicted as having the head of a cock, wings and feet of a fowl, and barbed serpent's tail. Such was the power of the glance that the basilisk could kill itself by looking in a mirror.[114]

---

[114] *Standard Dictionary*, p. 117.

That's very interesting—how often do we as analysts function by holding up the mirror to the basilisk! As it peeks out of the unconscious of the patient, it sees itself in the mirror of the analytic process.

And there's also the interesting feature that, although human beings are killed if they look directly at the basilisk, they can look at it with a mirror—the same way that Perseus could look at Medusa. There's also another interesting feature— it's just a marvel what wonderful psychological insights are embedded in these legends—"If a man saw the basilisk before it saw him, the basilisk would die." I don't think that needs any commentary.

As we're a little short of time tonight, I'm going to skip an example of basilisk psychology that's in Shakespeare's *The Winter's Tale.* Anybody interested can read Act 1—the relevant material is there—and of course if you're hooked by it, then you have to read the whole story!

3. The Symbolism of Salt

This section, I would remind you, is still under the larger subject of the symbolism of the moon; salt symbolism belongs to lunar symbolism.

a) The sulphur-mercury-salt triad and its transformation into a quaternity

One feature of the very rich symbolism of salt is that in alchemy it was con- sidered to be one item in a triad, the so-called *tria prima*. The idea was that ev- erything in existence is made up of three materials: sulphur, mercury and salt. Sulphur was associated with inflammability of course; it was very much identified with fire. Mercury was thought to be the essence of metalicity—the unique features of metals that separate them from crude rocky matter. The fact that metal is fusible, that it melts and can be molded—these were all thought of as miraculous properties when metals were first discovered. So mercury was thought of as representing the essential nature of metal.

Salt was very much associated with ashes; a certain kind of salt—potash, for instance—was found in ashes. It was not flammable, it was fixed, and so it was very much identified with earthly matter.

These three entities—sulphur, mercury and salt—became identified, especially in the minds of the Paracelsian alchemists, with the three entities of human matter: the soul, the spirit and the body. Sulphur was associated with the soul, mercury with the spirit and salt with the body.

In paragraph 235, Jung talks about this triad and points out that because mer- cury—Mercurius—was bipolar, the triad becomes a quaternity. That is illustrated in figure 10-5, where the two aspects of Mercurius are separated out: Mercurius as the lapis—that's the spiritual or celestial aspect of Mercurius—and Mercurius as the serpent. Sulphur and salt are on either side. You see this is what happens when an operative image that was largely unconscious in the minds of the alchemists is scrutinized by Jung's twentieth-century consciousness. The effect of that scrutiny is to split the opposites; what had previously been perceived as a trinity becomes a quaternity.

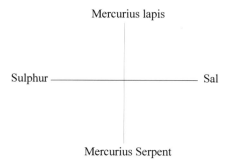

Figure 10-5. Mercurius quaternity.

b) *The Christian Trinity changed into a quaternity*

Jung goes on, in paragraph 237, to make a parallel between the alchemical quaternity, derived from the alchemical trinity, and the Christian Trinity which becomes a quaternity as the notion of the Assumption of the Virgin Mary comes into effect. That Assumption, which was an operative conviction in medieval Christendom, was finally promulgated as a dogmatic fact in 1950. The transformation is illustrated in figure 10-6: the Christian Trinity—God the Father, God the Son and God the Holy Ghost—by the addition of the Virgin Mary, turns into a quaternity.

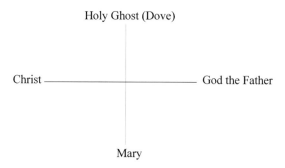

Figure 10-6. Christian quaternity.

c) The Assumption of the Virgin Mary

As you know, Jung gave a great deal of attention to this image. He discusses it much more extensively in "Answer to Job," where he speaks of the dogmatization of the Assumption as "the most important event in Church history since the Reformation,"[115] but in our material tonight (paragraph 237) he says this:

> For a long time there had been a psychological need for . . . [the Trinity to become a quaternity], as is evident from the medieval pictures of the Assumption and Coronation of the Virgin; it was also responsible for elevating her to the position of mediatrix, corresponding to Christ's position as the mediator . . . . The recent promulgation of the dogma of the Assumption emphasizes the taking up not only of the soul but of the body of Mary into the Trinity, thus making a dogmatic reality of those medieval representations of the quaternity which are constructed on the following pattern [figure 10-6]. Only in 1950, after the teaching authority in the Church had long deferred it . . . . did the Pope, moved by a growing wave of popular petitions, feel compelled to declare the Assumption as a revealed truth. All the evidence shows that the dogmatization was motivated chiefly by the religious need of the Catholic masses. Behind this stands the archetypal numen of feminine deity.

When we compare the two quaternities, the Virgin Mary is equivalent to salt: salt (the "white foliated earth" of many alchemical recipes)[116] was the earth factor, and likewise in ecclesiastical symbolism Mary was the flesh that brought about the incarnation of the Deity. So what we have here, psychologically understood, is the entry of the purified principle of materiality into the conception of totality—the totality image of the quaternity.

Another way of putting it is that the Assumption of the Virgin Mary symbolizes the assimilation of the materiality principle into the Western psyche. It's the very principle left out of Christian symbolism as it has developed over the past two thousand years. The materiality principle—the principle of egohood, the principle of the flesh, everything that pertains to the concreteness of personal, individual, fleshly, incarnated existence—all this is symbolized by the materiality principle. But materiality does have to be purified before it can undergo this Assumption— it has to be "white foliated earth." And that purification would correspond to a thorough analysis. When it's analyzed, then it's ready to be incorporated into the conception of totality.

d. The Pandora picture

This takes us, as it did Jung, to a remarkable picture from Reusner's *Pandora* (figure 10-7). I want to spend some time talking about it because it's very important. It contains, in a nutshell, the essence of alchemy and its relation to

---

115 *Psychology and Religion,* CW 12, par. 752.
116 *Mysterium,* par. 154, note 181; see also Edinger, *Mystery of the Coniunctio,* pp. 91f.

Figure 10-7.
The *Pandora* picture: "A Mirror Image of the Holy Trinity."

Christian symbolism; and of course alchemy was born in relation to Christian symbolism, as Jung tells us in his introduction to *Psychology and Alchemy.* Alchemy served as a kind of counterbalance or compensation for the Christian standpoint prevailing on the conscious level.

The Pandora picture, as I call it, is titled, in Latin and in German, "A Mirror Image of the Holy Trinity." To start with, let's just look at it and see what it shows us. First of all, it's an approximate square—it's quadrilateral anyway—and the four corners are occupied by the symbols of the four evangelists: the eagle, the symbol of John; the lion, symbol of Mark; the ox, symbol of Luke; and the angel, symbol of Matthew. The symbols of the evangelists in the four corners is characteristic of all Christian mandalas and quaternities. In the center section we have a second quaternity: God the Father, God the Son, God the Holy Ghost as a dove, and Mary, crowned as the Queen of Heaven. Those figures correspond exactly to the quaternity in figure 10-6.

Question: Which one is the Father and which one is the Son?

Well, that's a little ambiguous; in fact it's even more complicated because one of them is labeled "Sapientia," but rather than go into the full complexities of the picture, I'm simplifying it a little bit.

In the lower section of the picture there's a shieldlike outline, and pictured in that shield is a lump of matter. From this lump, a crowned and haloed figure pulls out a monstrous creature. The monster also has a haloed human head; it has snakes for arms, wings and the body of a fish.

Here's what Jung says in paragraph 238 about this picture:

> Underneath the coronation scene [is] a kind of shield between the emblems of Matthew and Luke, on which is depicted the extraction of Mercurius from the prima materia. The extracted spirit appears in monstrous form: the head is surrounded by a halo, and reminds us of the traditional head of Christ, but the arms are snakes and the lower half of the body resembles a stylized fish tail. This is without doubt the *anima mundi* who has been freed from the shackles of matter, the *filius macrocosmi* [son of the great world] or Mercurius-Anthropos, who, because of his double nature, is not only spiritual and physical but unites in himself the morally highest and lowest. The illustration in *Pandora* points to the great secret which the alchemists dimly felt was implicit in the Assumption. The proverbial darkness of sublunary matter has always been associated with the "prince of this world," the devil.

To my mind, the striking thing about this picture is the image of the birth of the monster out of the lump of matter. It is describing the essence of the alchemical transformation process, and it's shocking to find it represented in this form.

It's as though the lower procedure on earth, in which this monster is being pulled out of the lump, parallels or even brings about the Assumption and Coronation of Mary in heaven. That's what's so shocking about the juxtaposition of these two images. And the fact that the whole picture is in the form of a classical

Christian mandala, with the symbols of the four evangelists in the corners, suggests to me that we are dealing with the total Christian Weltanschauung.

It's interesting, the thoughts that pop into one's head—the idea I just had was that this foreign body of the alchemical transformation process that we find occupying the center of the Christian mandala is like a cuckoo's egg that's been laid in somebody else's nest. It's been laid in the nest of the Christian mandala and something unexpected is going to hatch out of it!

I think it signifies that the central myth and God-image of the Western psyche, by virtue of this alchemical process that's been inserted into it, is giving birth to a new entity. It signifies the emergence in the modern psyche of science and materialism on the one hand, and the discovery of the unconscious and the process of individuation on the other. The original form of the Christian mandala had the Trinity in the center, but this one, because of the addition of Mary, has a quaternity. Earth and materiality, the principle of egohood and coagulatio, has gained a representation in heaven, in the archetypal realm.

In addition to depicting that abstract fact, the picture also shows us a representation of the earthly process which brings about the Assumption of the Virgin Mary. That process begins with a lump of crude matter—that's what we've got here, a lump—and, as Jung says in the passage I read, that's the prima materia. If I try to make that a little more explicit, I think we could say that this lump signifies all the problematic, "lumpy" realities of incarnated existence. Every hard, disagreeable fact we stumble up against, from within or from without, can be thought of as part of this lump.

I don't know any better summary description of that lumpiness than the one Shakespeare gives us in *Hamlet*. Hamlet, you remember, protested vigorously against incarnated existence. He didn't want to be coagulated. He was the one who said, "Oh that this too too solid flesh would melt, thaw and resolve itself into a dew!"[117] This is how Shakespeare describes the lump:

> The slings and arrows of outrageous fortune, . . .
> The whips and scorns of time,
> Th' oppressor's wrong, the proud man's contumely,
> The pangs of dispriz'd love, the law's delay,
> The insolence of office, and the spurns
> That patient merit of th' unworthy takes, . . .
> [Leaving us]
> To grunt and sweat under a weary life.[118]

Now out of this lump a bizarre creature is being pulled by a crowned and haloed figure. What should we understand this figure to represent? My suggestion is that

---

[117] Act 1, scene 2.
[118] Act 3, scene 1.

we might call it the Christified ego. What I mean by that is an ego functioning under the aegis of the Self, the crown and halo being symbols of the Self, of wholeness. And if that line of thought is right, then the ego is doing on earth what Christ is doing in heaven. Christ in heaven—in the archetypal realm —is crowning the Virgin Mary; there, the principle of materiality and egohood is being glorified. But on earth, the task of realizing that glorification is taking place through the redemption and transformation of concrete personal existence by the individuating ego; in other words, by an ego that's consciously living out the process of continuing incarnation.[119]

That leaves us then with one more figure to explain: the monstrous creature being extracted from the lump. We know that the alchemists meant this picture to represent the extraction of Mercurius, and Jung says that this monstrous creature represents the anima mundi who has been freed from the shackles of matter, the *filius macrocosmi,* or Mercurius-Anthropos.

The more chemical, literal-minded alchemists thought of this procedure quite concretely as representing the extraction of the metal quicksilver from its ore. By heating mercury ore, you can sublimate and extract the mercury from it; that's the chemical image that lies behind this idea.

One way of seeing the image psychologically is that it corresponds to the extraction of the autonomous spirit from concrete events. For instance, discovering the meaning of a mood or an unconscious obstacle, a problem or distress of some kind. Extracting meaning from any manifestation of the lump releases the autonomous spirit, Mercurius, from its concrete imprisonment in matter.

In simplest terms, this monstrous creature is a picture, as seen from below, of the emergence of the Self. On the other hand, the quaternity, represented by this picture and by what's going on in heaven, is a representation of the emergent Self as seen from above. Symbolic images of the Self, such as this quaternity-creating one of the Coronation of the Virgin Mary and her entrance into heaven, are beautiful, grand and numinous. But the living experience of the Self is very different indeed. The living experience of the Self is a monstrosity (figure 10-8). It's a coming together of opposites that appalls the ego and exposes it to anguish, demoralization and violation of all reasonable considerations. That's what a monstrosity is—a violation of everything we've come to expect as natural and reasonable and normal. This is how the Coronation of the Virgin in heaven looks from the standpoint of the limited, earthbound ego—it looks like the emergence of a monstrosity out of a lump.

There's another way one might put it. You could say that the Pandora picture illustrates, from two levels simultaneously, the process of the transformation of God. You see, that's the essential meaning of the alchemical transformation pro-

---

119 See Edinger, *Creation of Consciousness,* pp. 83ff.

cess. In various texts, veiled in one way or another, the prima materia that was to undergo transformation was identified as God. (We'll have an example of that later when we examine Ripley's *Cantilena.*)[120]

So on the upper level, God is transformed by the entrance of the feminine element, which changes the Trinity into a quaternity. On the lower level the ego, in the service of that transformation process, is transforming its concrete life into a part of the divine drama. It thereby becomes an example of the continuing incarnation, and promotes the glorification of the materiality principle as it is represented in the upper layer of the picture.

Question: Would you repeat that last sentence?

Well, what I was saying was that the Pandora picture illustrates the process of the transformation of God from two levels simultaneously—the upper level and the lower level. And where the ego lives its life—its concrete, personal, nitty-gritty, lumpy life—that's all to be found inside this shield structure. That's where we live, you see. But in the course of that living, if consciousness is being created, that living is bringing about the divine drama that's going on up above, where the quaternity is being created out of the Trinity.

Figure 10-8.
Union of opposites
as a monstrosity.

11
Paragraphs 245-275

Tonight's assignment is a continuation of the symbolism of salt, and there are six major items that I shall speak about:
1. Salt associated with bitterness.
2. Salt associated with the sea.
3. Salt associated with ashes, and the salt-spirit.
4. The Red Sea, and the Exodus.
5. The Serpent-Chariot text.
6. Ezekiel's Vision.

1. Salt and Bitterness

Last week we talked about salt as the white earth; and, because the white earth is what helps to coagulate and bring matter into incarnated real existence, that image connected salt with the Virgin Mary. A widespread quotation in alchemical literature is "Sow your gold in white foliated earth"—it's a coniunctio image.

In tonight's material, Jung talks about the bitterness associated with the symbolism of salt. This immediately tells us that if salt as the white earth has something to do with the coagulatio process, then that process must also be a process producing bitterness—those two go together. And that helps to explain why coagulatio—the body, things pertaining to the body—has had such a bad name in the current aeon. In order to be something real and definite, to have a body and have a real incarnated existence, one must expose oneself to the bitterness of salt that accompanies that material existence.

2. Salt and the Sea

Another image Jung discusses is the association of salt with the sea. That, of course, is a natural connection because the sea is composed of salt water. Jung makes the observation that throughout the Middle Ages the word *mare*, which means sea in Latin, was thought to derive from *amaro* which means bitter, so the two are connected etymologically.

In paragraph 255 Jung quotes a very nice compilation of sea symbolism as it appears in the patristic writers. Let me read you a little bit of that. As I'm reading, remember that I am reading about the symbolism of the sea. These images will be applicable every time you encounter a dream that involves the sea—a person falling into it, or waves lapping over one's house, or whatever.

[According to] St. Augustine: . . . "the sea is the world." It is the "essence of the

138

world, as the element . . . subject to the devil." St. Hilary says: "By the depths of the sea is meant the seat of hell." The sea is the "gloomy abyss," the remains of the original pit, and hence of the chaos that covered the earth. For St. Augustine this abyss is the realm of power allotted to the devil and demons after their fall. It is on the one hand a "deep that cannot be reached or comprehended" and on the other the "depths of sin." For Gregory the Great the sea is the "depths of eternal death." Since ancient times it was the "abode of water-demons." There dwells Leviathan (Job 3: 8) who in the language of the Fathers signifies the devil. . . . St. Jerome says: "The devil surrounds the seas and the ocean on all sides." The bitterness of salt-water is relevant in this connection, as it is one of the peculiarities of hell and damnation which must be fully tasted by the meditant in Loyola's *Exercises.*

Psychologically, the sea is an image of the unconscious. So the unconscious, which our whole aeon has been trying to rise out of and to establish a spiritual counterposition toward, has had attached to it all the negative, demonic and dangerous aspects of existence.

3. Salt and Ashes, and the Salt-Spirit

Then in paragraph 247 we have the association of salt being equivalent to ashes. This connects salt with the end-product of the calcinatio process. At the end of the calcinatio everything that can burn is burnt away and only ashes are left. And ashes belong to the symbolism of bitterness: defeat, failure and the sackcloth and ashes of mourning all belong to that experience of bitterness.

But in alchemy the other side of the ash symbolism is that ashes were also associated with the "vitreous body"—the glassy body left behind at the end of the calcinatio process. It corresponds to the "glorified body" which is immortal—the indestructible residue that's left over from the calcinatio. So it's an image of the immortal Self that is refined and can endure the fire.

There's a significant text in paragraph 247 concerning this matter:

"Sublime with fire, until the spirit which thou wilt find in it [the substance] goeth forth from it, and it is named the bird or the ash of Hermes. Therefore saith Morienus. Despise not the ashes, for they are the diadem of thy heart, and the ash of things that endure."

And Jung adds:

In other words, the ash is the spirit that dwells in the glorified body.

It's texts like that, and there are others scattered around, that connect the ashes of mourning and defeat to a crown—"Despise not the ashes, for they are the diadem."

Jung's added remark that "the ash is the spirit that dwells in the glorified body" leads him into a discussion of the salt-spirit as an earth-spirit that leads one into chaos. In other words, that salt-spirit at first leads one into the very things that the sea symbolized for the patristic writers—into chaos.

Here's what Jung says in paragraph 252 about this salt-spirit:

> It is the spirit of the chaotic waters of the beginning, before the second day of Creation, before the separation of the opposites and hence before the advent of consciousness. That is why it leads those whom it overcomes neither upwards nor beyond, but back into chaos. This spirit corresponds to that part of the psyche which has not been assimilated to consciousness and whose transformation and integration are the outcome of a long and wearisome opus.

Jung then goes on to say that this return to chaos is a necessary part of the opus and that it corresponds to the bitterness. All this of course has direct relevance to what happens when one opens up the unconscious in the analytic process: the ego is led, by that salt-spirit of the unconscious, back to the chaos at the beginning of creation, before the separation of opposites.

4. The Red Sea

The equation of salt and sea then leads us into the rich symbolism of the Red Sea and, starting in paragraph 256, Jung spends quite a bit of time with this. Here I've charted some of the symbolic connections within the symbolism of the Red Sea (figure 11-1). This can be a helpful method for visualizing the interrelated images in a symbol complex—it's easy to get lost in these networks of interconnections if you don't visualize them in some concrete way. I'll talk about some of these as we go along but I won't go through the chart item by item.

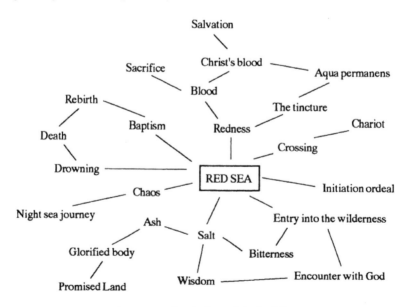

Figure 11-1. Symbolism of the Red Sea.

The Red Sea has three basic sets of symbolic meanings. 1) It's a sea, so it has all the symbolism of the sea that I've already alluded to. 2) It's red, which associates it with blood, and with all the red symbolism of alchemy which made it an image for their red "tincture." 3) The Red Sea is an important component in the Exodus story of the Old Testament. So all the symbolism associated with that story is drawn into the symbolism of the Red Sea.

Those of you who were at the Old Testament class last year will remember all this, but it doesn't hurt to review it.[121] The first thing one thinks about when the image of the Red Sea comes up is the story of the Exodus. This, you remember, came about on orders from Yahweh to Moses who then, after some difficulties, led the Israelites out of their slavery in Egypt and into the wilderness. There they wandered for forty years and experienced the theophany of Yahweh on Mt. Sinai; eventually they settled in the promised land of Canaan.

The first stage of this journey out of Egypt was the crossing of the Red Sea, and that crossing separated the Israelites from the pursuing Egyptians. The Israelites got across but, as the Egyptians in their chariots entered the passage, the sea came together again and drowned them. The image of the chariot belongs to the whole Red Sea symbolism, and that comes up later in our material.

This whole story is a profound representation of the individuation process, and so it's inevitable that it's going to be used by the alchemists. The alchemists had an uncanny sense of what was psychically relevant. Since they were working right out of the psyche themselves, they were drawn to all material that came from the same source they were working from. Mythology of all kinds flowed right into the alchemical imagination and became part of the imagery they used to describe their procedures.

Crossing the Red Sea doesn't lead to the Promised Land directly. It leads first to the wilderness, and then to the encounter with the numinosum. Only after that does it lead to the Promised Land.[122] So the idea that's represented here is a descent into the unconscious which causes an initial state of disorientation and alienation—symbolized by the wilderness—but which then leads to an encounter with God, and eventually on to a new home—a new level of consciousness.

It's quite interesting that in the Biblical account, the first stop after the Red Sea was a place called Marah—Marah means bitterness. Not only was the water bitter there, but also it was the place where bitter grumblings took place.[123] So the Red Sea and the symbolism of salt and bitterness all come up in this Biblical context, too.

The connection of bitterness with the descent into the unconscious is part of

---

[121] See Edinger, *Bible and the Psyche,* pp. 51ff.
[122] See Edinger, *Ego and Archetype,* pp. 43ff.
[123] Exod. 15: 23, 24.

the individuation journey. It is important to appreciate that fact because bitterness is such a prominent feature of our work with patients. We are constantly being barraged by bitter complaints. If we can remember this symbolism and apply it to our everyday work, then we're working out of a larger context. That larger context, slowly but surely, has a healing effect on the bitter complaints that are being expressed out of a narrow context. The larger context gradually loosens up and expands the narrow context, and calms and heals the bitterness.

Talking about this matter in paragraph 258, Jung quotes a passage from Meister Eckhart:

> "And who can be nobler than the man who is born half of the highest and best the world has to offer, and half of the innermost ground of God's nature and God's loneliness?"

Here Eckhart is equating the wilderness with God's loneliness. Then he goes on:

> "Therefore, the Lord speaks in the prophet Hosea: I will lead the noble souls into the wilderness, and speak into their hearts."

There are a lot of other examples of bitter wilderness experiences which are followed by an encounter with the numinosum. You remember Elijah, when he was in a suicidal depression, fled into the wilderness to Mt. Horah (figure 11-2).

Figure 11-2. *Elijah Being Fed by the Ravens* (detail) by Washington Allston.

Elijah was fleeing to escape Jezebel's wrath. It was in that wilderness that Yahweh came to him and gave him his next assignment.[124] And, of course, the outstanding Biblical example of the bitter wilderness experience that precedes an encounter with the numinosum is the Book of Job.

Listen to what the alchemist Michael Maier says about the result of the encounter with the transpersonal dimension following an experience of bitterness:

> There is in our chemistry a certain noble substance, in the beginning whereof is wretchedness with vinegar, but in its ending joy with gladness. Therefore I have supposed that the same will happen to me, namely that I shall suffer difficulty, grief, and weariness at first, but in the end shall come to glimpse pleasanter and easier things.[125]

Jung goes into another set of important Gnostic associations to the Red Sea in paragraphs 256 and 257. I want to underscore these because they are so relevant psychologically. First of all, Jung notes that Augustine connected the Red Sea with baptism, and adds:

> According to Honorius of Autun, "the Red Sea is the baptism reddened by the blood of Christ, in which our enemies, namely our sins, are drowned."

In that symbolism, the passage through the Red Sea is a kind of solutio ordeal, involving a death and rebirth, on the other side of which is salvation.

But what I want to mention most particularly is in paragraph 257 where Jung talks about the Peratic interpretation of the Red Sea. The Peratics were a sect of Gnostics and, according to their interpretation, the Red Sea drowned the Egyptians because the Egyptians were "non-knowers." As Jung says, "The other side of the Red Sea is the other side of Creation" according to these Gnostics, and if you are a "knower" then you make it across to the other side—you don't drown. When you arrive on the other side, in the desert, then, according to this Gnostic interpretation, you're "outside of generation." "There, the 'gods of destruction' and the 'god of salvation' are all together."

That is how the Gnostics described the desert on the far side of the Red Sea, and Jung comments:

> The Red Sea is a water of death for those that are "unconscious," but for those that are "conscious" it is a baptismal water of rebirth and transcendence. By "unconscious" are meant those who have no gnosis, i.e., are not enlightened as to the nature and destiny of man in the cosmos. In modern language it would be those who have no knowledge of the contents of the personal and collective unconscious. The personal unconscious is the shadow and the inferior function, in Gnostic terms the sinfulness and impurity that must be washed away by baptism.

---

[124] 1 Kings 19-20.
[125] Quoted in *Psychology and Alchemy*, CW 12, par. 387.

This would refer to analysis of the personal unconscious. Jung continues:

> "Unconscious" people who attempt to cross the sea without being purified and without the guidance of enlightenment are drowned; they get stuck in the unconscious and suffer a spiritual death in so far as they cannot get beyond their one-sidedness.

All that is directly relevant to our everyday clinical work, as is this:

> To do this they would have to be more conscious of what is unconscious to them and their age, above all of the inner opposite, namely those contents to which the prevailing views are in any way opposed.

Now listen to this: if you ever have to cross the Red Sea, this could be life or death knowledge for you—he's telling you what enables you to get across. You have to be more conscious of what you've been unconscious of and what your *age* is unconscious of:

> Above all . . . the inner opposite, . . . those contents to which the prevailing views are in any way opposed. This continual process of getting to know the counterposition in the unconscious I have called "the transcendent function" . . . . But an alteration is possible only if the existence of the "other" is admitted. . . .
>
> We should get along a lot better if we realized that the majority views of "others" are condoned by a minority in ourselves. Armed with this psychological insight, which today no longer has the character of revelation since common sense can grasp it, we could set out on the road to the union of the opposites and would then, as in the Peratic doctrine, come to the place where the "gods of destruction and the god of salvation are together." By this is obviously meant the destructive and constructive powers of the unconscious.

Jung then goes on to say that "this *coincidentia oppositorum* forms a parallel to the Messianic state of fulfillment described in Isaiah 11: 6ff. and 35: 5ff." But it brings with it this event:

> Everyone who becomes conscious of even a fraction of his unconscious gets outside his own time and social stratum into a kind of solitude. . . . But only there is it possible to meet the "god of salvation."

All this belongs to the symbolism of the Red Sea, and most of those ideas are incorporated, or summarized, in my chart (figure 11-1).

5. The serpent-chariot Text

This is a continuation of the symbolism of the Red Sea, which in turn is part of the symbolism of salt. You always have to keep in mind where you are so you don't get lost! In paragraph 260 we have an interesting text to which Jung gives a very fine interpretation:

> Take the serpent, and place it in the chariot with four wheels, and let it be turned about on the earth until it is immersed in the depths of the sea, and nothing more is

visible but the blackest dead sea. And there let the chariot with the wheels remain, until so many fumes rise up from the serpent that the whole surface . . . becomes dry, and by desiccation sandy and black. All that is the earth which is no earth, but a stone lacking all weight. . . . [And when the fumes are precipitated in the form of rain,] you should bring the chariot from the water to dry land, and then you have placed the four wheels upon the chariot, and will obtain the result if you will advance further to the Red Sea, running without running, moving without motion.

We have to keep reminding ourselves that all these alchemical texts are chemical recipes, and they are referring to a process in which a vessel has some stuff put in it and then that material is subjected to various operations. So this text is discussing an alchemical laboratory operation. That helps you keep your bearings with such strange images.

A serpent is put in a chariot and then certain things are done to it. One can see the chariot as the alchemical vessel, and the serpent as the prima materia—the stuff—that's put into it. The serpent corresponds to the salt-spirit that leads into chaos, the primordial psyche, which must undergo transformation in the vessel.

First of all the chariot is immersed in the sea. It's subjected to a solutio. In other words, the unconscious comes over it. It's then subjected to a dessication—a drying out process. And finally, after a second inundation from rain, it's brought out from the sea on to dry land. The wheels are replaced, and then the text says it proceeds to the Red Sea, meaning it makes the transition out of the unconsciousness of Egypt to the encounter with the numinosum on the other side of the Red Sea. Advancing to the Red Sea would correspond to the process of making the crossing.

Jung discusses this at some length, and the most striking thing he gets to is that what is being transformed is nothing less than the God-image. Now how does he arrive at that idea? He arrives at it by way of the vision of Ezekiel, the major amplification of the image of the chariot. (The chariot, you remember, is one of the features of Red Sea symbolism because it was the chariots of the Egyptians that took them into the sea where they were drowned.)

6. The Vision of Ezekiel

Jung's discussion of the vision of Ezekiel starts in paragraph 269. This will be old hat to those of you who were in the Old Testament seminar,[126] but it doesn't hurt to hear this over and over again, since it's absolutely fundamental to the Western psyche. Here, somewhat abbreviated, is Ezekiel's vision as it is described in the first chapter of the Book of Ezekiel:

I looked; a stormy wind blew from the north, a great cloud with light around it, a fire from which flashes of lightning darted . . . . In the centre I saw what seemed four

---

[126] See Edinger, *Bible and the Psyche*, pp. 124ff.

animals. . . . Each had four faces, each had four wings. . . . [Each had a human face, a lion's face, a bull's face and an eagle's face. And their wings were spread about.]

Between these animals something could be seen like flaming brands or torches, darting between the animals; the fire flashed light, . . .

I looked at the animals; there was a wheel on the ground by each of them, . . . The wheels glittered as if made of chrysolite. . . . Their rims seemed enormous . . . and all four rims had eyes all the way round. When the animals went forward, the wheels went forward. . . . Over the heads of the animals a sort of vault, gleaming like crystal, arched above their heads; under this vault their wings stretched out to one another, . . . [and they made a great noise.]

Above the vault over their heads was something that looked like a sapphire; it was shaped like a throne and high up on this throne was a being that looked like a man. . . . And a light all round . . . [and] something that looked like the glory of Yahweh. [127]

This is called the chariot vision of Ezekiel. It's the basis of a whole body of Jewish mysticism called Merkabah mysticism and that word, I understand, means chariot throne. The imagery of this vision was taken up in Christian mandalas in the symbols of the four evangelists who became the supporting pillars for the throne of Christ. So this vision of Ezekiel is the basis of Jewish mysticism and plays a prominent role in the symbolism of the Kabbalah, and it's the basic image of Christian mandalas. And we see from the serpent-chariot text that it also shows up kind of surreptitiously in alchemical symbolism.

Finally, Jung uses this image as the basis for his most complex and differentiated formulation of the Self as he describes it in *Aion* (figure 11-3).[128] In a letter to James Kirsch he states explicitly that this model is based on the vision of Ezekiel.[129] At the risk of inundating you I am going to say a few words about Ezekiel's vision. That's the constant danger in trying to relate to *Mysterium Coniunctionis*—the danger is drowning.

Jung derives this formula of the Self from a complex discussion and interpretation of Gnostic material. (I should say that Jung does not have the central star in his diagram. His delineation is just the four squares without the central star. I added that to emphasize the centrality that is generated by this circulating formula; Jung speaks of it as a dynamic entity that circulates both at each corner and also as a whole.) What I hope to do is to give you enough of an idea of what this formula refers to so that it may stick in your mind and not just fall out. It has to be anchored in something that you can get hold of and that's meaningful; otherwise it will just fall out as though you'd never heard of it before.

---

[127] Ezek. 1: 4-28, Jerusalem Bible.
[128] CW 9ii, pars. 410f.
[129] Jung, *Letters,* vol. 2, p. 118.

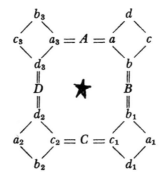

Figure 11-3.
Formulation
of the Self.

There are four entities here, represented by A, B, C, D. They appear in the larger circle and also—as the sequence of a, b, c, d—they appear in each of the smaller corners. The idea is that these four smaller mandalas were originally a linear sequence, 1, 2, 3, 4; I'm going to speak about each of them in a moment. But that linear sequence, in the fashion of the uroboric serpent, turned back on itself—put its tail in its mouth and came back where it started from—and turned into a circular process.

In simplified form, what we're talking about here are four different types of quaternities, mandala images, that show up in patients' material. We're not dealing with remote abstractions that have no clinical relevance.

One way of visualizing the fourfold sequence that was initially linear is to think of it as a downward movement of an energy that starts from above. (You could equally think of it as an upward movement from energy that starts from below, but let's do one thing at a time.) If you think of it as a downward energy that goes through four different levels of manifestation, you then have four different kinds of quaternity imagery. These four levels can be described in descending order as the spirit level, the animal level, the vegetable level and the mineral level. Spirit, animal, vegetable, mineral.[130]

If you pay attention to your clinical material and are on the lookout for quaternity imagery—which I think we all are since it indicates that the totality is somehow being constellated and it's an auspicious image—you'll find just about all quaternities can be put into one or more of these four categories. If you encounter a quaternity on the spirit level, that emphasizes light and spirit symbolism. It has heavenly, ethereal, light qualities, so it's very uplifting and spiritualizing. Jung calls this the Anthropos Quaternio. The animal level, the next level down, is what Jung calls the Shadow Quaternio; it emphasizes shadow symbolism and is of a darker nature. It may have human figures in it, but they're approaching the

---

[130] See *Aion,* CW 9ii, chap. 14, "The Structure and Dynamics of the Self," espec. pars. 369ff.; also Edinger, *Lectures on Aion,* lectures 21-22.

animal quality. Or it will have overtly animal figures, because humans, of course, are animals—they belong to the animal level too.

The third level that I'm calling the vegetable level is what Jung calls the Paradise Quaternio; that emphasizes plant symbolism, garden symbolism: the Virgin Mary as a closed garden, for instance, the garden with a fountain in the center. That belongs to the vegetable quaternity level.

The bottom level is the mineral level—Jung calls it the Lapis Quaternio—and at that level one finds inorganic symbolism: crystals, abstract forms that belong to the inorganic world and are not obviously animated.

Now what Jung has done, based on the Ezekiel vision, is to elaborate in this abstract formulation what it would look like to visualize these four different modes or levels of quaternity within a single process. That then generates a center, by virtue of the movement around it, which incorporates all those levels—that's why I put in the star. Although he didn't put the star in his image, it's implied in the text and in the way he talks about it.[131]

The reason it's important to talk about such matters—though I don't pretend to understand fully what I'm talking about myself—is that I think we should all strive, however we can, to be small, original investigators into the objective psyche. This is a whole new world that's opening up for investigation and it's done not on the basis of big government grants to huge research institutions. It's done in the solitude of individual work on one's own psyche, or by mutual work on a one-to-one basis in the analytic process. This is the only way that research in depth psychology can take place. And it redeems the noble enterprise of scientific research from the collective mania, the swallowing up of the individual functioning, that results from the mass government and academic efforts.

I'm hoping to make every one of you into an original investigator of the objective psyche. That's why I think it's worth trying to understand these matters that Jung is doing his very best to communicate to us. But we have to apply our very best attention in order to understand, and then be on the lookout to see how the material within ourselves and within our patients fits into such images as the one we've been examining. If you're on the lookout for it, you're going to find these four different kinds of quaternities. That's been my experience.

I'll just remind you, so you don't forget: we got to this from the serpent-chariot text. The chariot that underwent transformation in the alchemical text corresponds to the divine chariot of the vision of Ezekiel. That vision has gone through stages of transformation through the centuries, and now, by Jung's research, it has been transformed into this rotating mandala.

---

[131] *Aion,* CW 9ii, pars. 410f.

12

Paragraphs 276-314

Tonight's material, although still a continuation of salt symbolism, digresses from the main body of that symbolism. You remember that in talking about salt we were led to the sea, and a particular text concerning the sea led us to the Red Sea. In tonight's material Jung deals with a text by Michael Maier which also has the Red Sea as a major image. This is what I call the Perigrinatio text and it takes up all of tonight's assignment.

In talking about this text I will refer to five major items:

1. The horizontal journey through the four quarters, and the problem of three and four.

2. The discovery of the four-colored animal, the so-called Ortus.

3. The vertical journey through the seven planetary spheres.

4. The *Shepherd of Hermas.*

5. The Emerald Tablet of Hermes. (Do not confuse Hermas and Hermes—they're two different names.)

Since all of this week's assignment concerns Maier's Perigrinatio text, and since that text is scattered throughout the assignment, I want to condense and summarize it for you.

This is a story about an adept, the alchemist who wrote the text, who embarks on a series of travels. He goes first to the north which is Europe; then he goes to the west which is America; he then goes to the east which is Asia. And now he has just one place left to go, namely south which is Africa, and so he heads south. The idea seems to be that he has to touch all the bases. On his way south he encounters a statue of Mercury pointing to Paradise. He gets a brief glimpse of Paradise but that doesn't last very long.

He then proceeds to Africa which is "parched, sterile and empty"—a very disagreeable place. In fact, as Jung says in paragraph 279, it has just about all the attributes of hell. In this place called Africa all the species mingle with each other—they don't keep to their own kind. As there are only a few watering places, all the different species of animals cohabit with one another. Consequently new and bizarre creatures are being created all the time. When he arrives by the Red Sea, the adept learns that an animal named the Ortus is nearby. This strange creature is composed of four different colors: red, black, white and streaks of yellow. He also learns that the Ortus is thought to be related to, or maybe even identical with, the phoenix.

Now here's where the Red Sea comes in—this is the excuse for bringing in this text—it brings up the Red Sea. Near the Red Sea he encounters the Erythraean Sibyl. (That just means Red Sibyl—she lives near the Red Sea.) The Erythraean Sibyl, a prophetess who lives in a cave, tells him to go to the seven mouths of the Nile in order to seek Mercurius; that's what he's been seeking all along—Mercurius.

Jung informs us, based on Maier's description, that these seven mouths of the Nile correspond to the seven planets. Therefore visiting each of them corresponds to visiting each of the seven planetary spheres.

He goes through them all, one by one, but Mercurius is not to be found. After visiting all seven, he then retraces his steps, and when he gets back to the first house—the house of lead or Saturn—lo and behold! there he finds Mercurius. Mercurius wasn't there on his first visit, but after making the ascent and then coming back down again he found him. We're then told that he had numerous conversations with Mercurius but the content of those conversations is not reported. That's the story Jung comments on extensively, and which I'll discuss in a condensed and abbreviated way.

1. The Horizontal Journey through the Four Quarters

The first aspect of the story describes a horizontal journey through the four quarters. This corresponds to imagery one encounters now and then in which there'll be a circular field divided into four sections. Life activities of some sort will be going on in three of them but the fourth one will be blank or void, or black and threatening (figure 12-1). In some cases the fourth quarter is labeled "terra damnata" or "chaos" or something like that. That's how Maier's journey starts out—he travels north, west and east and has no problems; but when he goes south he runs into this fourth quarter.

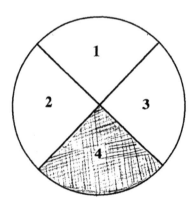

Figure 12-1.
The threatening
fourth quarter.

This corresponds to the fundamental alchemical theme of the three and the four which comes up frequently in every depth analysis. In the course of trying to achieve some consciousness of one's wholeness, one must work his or her way through all four functions. The first function is the superior function—that doesn't present any trouble because one's there to start with and most of life has been lived there. So the superior function, that's a piece of cake.

Very often the auxiliary function, number two, is also quite accessible because with a reasonably well-developed individual usually two functions are in pretty good shape. He or she will have a good judgmental function, either thinking or feeling, and a good perceptive function, sensation or intuition. So number two is not very hard. Number three starts to get difficult, and getting into some kind of living relation to it usually requires a good bit of analysis.

But number four, that's the big one. The reason it's so difficult is that number four, the inferior function, has undergone essentially no development at all—it's more or less continuous with the whole collective unconscious. So when the inferior function is touched in any major way it drags the whole collective unconscious along with it.

Touching the inferior function also means that the ego is confronted with the opposites in their extreme form. It's confronted with the opposites in a lesser form when dealing with the second and third functions, but the fourth function challenges totally the superior function and the whole mode of life operation around which the ego has been organized. It turns all the ego's values upside-down. That means, then, that an encounter with the fourth function opens up the individual to the chaos of "Africa" as it's described in this text.

It's not uncommon to encounter dreams that involve traveling in the four directions, or sometimes traveling in one or more directions, and I think it's good to be on the alert for dreams that make special mention of directional matters. Let me give you a couple of examples.

I remember a patient who had a distorted typology. This happens every now and then—you can never be absolutely certain about it, it's hard to pin down with utter certainty—but it does seem that occasionally a certain kind of traumatic childhood can distort an individual's natural typology, and I think that happened with this woman. If she had been able to go her natural way she would have been a feeling type, but her childhood circumstances were such that she was distorted into a thinking type. What put me on to that idea was a series of dreams in which directions were trying to be reversed, for instance something that was oriented north was trying to be reoriented south.

For example, to give you a flavor, she dreamt: "I am looking out of my window gazing north. A great twister-tornado forms and moves south." Another one: "I'm driving south in a car. I see the mushroom cloud of an atomic explosion and stop." So whenever one has a dream that emphasizes directions, be on the alert for something concerning typology.

Here is another particularly impressive directional dream that also has other similarities to this Perigrinatio text of Maier's:

> I'm on a trip, and on the way back from the seacoast on the north going on a north-south road [you see, paying so much attention to directions—usually dreams don't tell you exactly what direction the road is going in] we passed some tall telephone poles and on the crossbars were perched orange, pink, green and blue tropical birds, each of a different species. They had flown in from all four directions and arranged themselves symmetrically on the crossbars to form a pattern of color. All the birds faced south and they were all of a different species. They did this on five or so poles with the center pole having five cross arms and about twenty-five birds, all different.
>
> I was the only person to notice this. I thought it was the most exciting sight I'd ever seen. I remarked on it and my host said this stretch of road was famous for its birds. And back at school I resolved to revisit the birds. I planned to photograph them. I fantasized about them, I marveled at the symmetry of them, and I realized that this was the most beautiful sight I'd ever seen. The colors were so bright, pure and rare, and the birds perched in a pattern that alternated the orange, yellow, blue and green. How could the birds be so knowing?

And that was followed by a second dream—keep this image in mind:

> After many adventures trying to see the birds again [it's as though he'd gotten a brief glimpse of Paradise, like Maier], I was with my parents trying to throw away an old radio. We visited a dump which we inspected from a kind of bridge to its north. The trash seemed to be about ten feet deep, visible through fissures, but my father leaned way over and glimpsed to the bottom of the dump and it was a cesspool. It contained the blackest and foulest gummy residue. This was the hell-hole of the dump and he encouraged me to lean out and throw the radio into this *ultima Thule,* this terrible hellhole of putrefaction. I did so and I glimpsed the slimy, murky water far, far down, slanting off to the west [who puts in peculiarities like that?]. and I felt I had glimpsed the worst life had to offer.

This man was a thinking-intuitive type. West very often refers to sensation—certainly in this case it does. So feeling and sensation would be his inferior functions, and that would correspond to the south and the west.

But what's so remarkable about this dream, and the reason I bring it in here, is that it's an example of a glimpse of the four-colored animal (represented by the birds) on the one hand, followed by a glimpse of the hell-hole of the inferior function on the other. And those two go together.

When one is on the way toward totality and gets a glimpse of it—the image of totality—that potential totality then brings up with it the problem of the fourth function which is the hell-hole. The fourth function is always the hell-hole, and that's what one falls into. It just about costs one's life to climb back out of it, but having done so one then knows what it means to be whole because one has made the complete circuit.

2. The Discovery of the Four-Colored Animal, the Ortus

We learn from the text that the Ortus is found by the Red Sea. Ortus means origin, so this is the original, first animal. Like the flock of birds in the dream, it is made up of four colors: black, red, white and yellow. Jung says in paragraph 282 that this "represents the living quaternity in its first synthesis."

In other words we can think of the Ortus as the primitive or animal version of the original Self. It is wholeness that hasn't yet undergone conscious differentiation through full encounter with the ego. It would correspond, roughly, to the serpent-chariot of last week's assignment which was also a kind of primitive quaternity—a four-wheeled chariot, just as the Ortis is a four-colored animal.

And just like the serpent-chariot, the Ortus required transformation. The motif of transformation is brought up because we're informed that the Ortus is related to or may even be identical with the phoenix. The symbolism of the phoenix is going to come up again in another context, but I want to say a few words about it here because it's important imagery for dream interpretation.

Here in outline is the ancient Egyptian myth of the phoenix. It was thought to be a bird from India or Arabia, and at a certain point in its existence it would fly to Egypt. There it would signal to a priest of Heliopolis that it had arrived, and the priest would heap the altar with brushwood. The bird would then enter Heliopolis, the sacred place, mount the altar, ignite the fire and burn itself up. The next day the priest would examine the altar and find a worm in the ashes. On the second day the worm would have turned into a tiny birdling, and on the third day it would become a huge eagle which then takes flight back to its former abode.

The myth's Egyptian origin leads us to the idea that it is related to Egyptian embalming symbolism. The idea of death and rebirth is basic to the sacred embalming process of the ancient Egyptians. And this idea of creating an immortal body by first subjecting it to death through fire and then reconstituting it is the basic idea of alchemy. Alchemy is really the continuation of ancient Egyptian embalming symbolism. The transformation of the phoenix symbolizes the psychological transformation process of individuation which, like alchemy, creates a glorified, indestructible body through the same transformation process of death and rebirth that the phoenix subjects itself to. These are the imagery and ideas associated with the Ortus, you see.

Continuing with Maier's text, we are told that close by the Ortus is the Erythraean Sibyl. A sibyl is a medium or prophetess, and this image would correspond to the mediumistic anima who facilitates communication with the collective unconscious. The Sibyl advises the adept to look for Mercurius at the seven mouths of the Nile. This corresponds, as we shall see, to ascending the planetary ladder, undergoing sublimatio, and passing through the domain of each of the planetary archons.

3. The Vertical Journey through the Seven Planetary Spheres

That brings us to the vertical journey through the seven planetary houses. The horizontal journey comes first, and then when one gets to the fourth function—to Africa, as Maier did—one has to go through the vertical journey. The horizontal journey involves the number four and visiting each of the four functions. The vertical journey involves the number seven and making the acquaintance of the seven different planetary principles, the archetypal factors that go to make up the total personality. They're symbolized by the Moon, Sun, Mercury, Venus, Mars, Jupiter and Saturn.[132]

The ancient idea, you remember, is that in the course of being born on earth, a soul descends through those seven planetary spheres and picks up qualities of each of the seven planets. At death, returning to Heaven, it reverses the process and sheds each of the seven planetary influences on its trip back up.

There's an interesting poem by Henry Vaughan that speaks of this upward journey of the ascending soul. Let me read part of it to you. (This would have been written about 1650-1660.) He's taking the trip back up the seven planets.

> The power of my Soul is such, I can
> Expire, and so *analyse* all that's man.
> First my dull Clay I give unto the *Earth*,
> Our common Mother, which gives all their birth.
> My growing Faculties I send as soon
> Whence first I took them, to the humid *Moon*.
> All Subtilties and every cunning Art
> To witty *Mercury* I do impart.
> Those fond Affections which made me a slave
> To handsome Faces, *Venus* thou shalt have.
> And saucy Pride, (if there was ought in me,)
> *Sol*, I return it to thy Royalty.
> My daring Rashness and Presumptions be
> To *Mars* himself an equal Legacy.
> My ill-plac'd Avarice, (sure 'tis but small;)
> *Jove*, to thy Flames I do bequeath it all.
> And my false *Magic*, which I did believe,
> And mystic Lyes, to *Saturn* I do give.
> My dark Imaginations rest you there,
> This is your grave and Superstitious Sphaere.

Saturn was thought of as the topmost planet, so that when he got past Saturn he was free. Then, having reached that point, he can say:

> Get up my disintangled Soul, thy fire

---

[132] See above, lecture 2, pp. 40f.

Is now refin'd & nothing left to tire,
Or clog thy wings. Now my auspicious flight
Hath brought me to the *Empyrean* light.
I am a sep'rate *Essence*, and can see
The *Emanations* of the Deitie.[133]

These are the images of late medieval man for whom the ultimate achievement was to have undergone the complete sublimatio, be turned entirely to spirit and be done with it.

But of course that's not the alchemical position, so in our text Maier didn't do as Henry Vaughan did. When he'd gone through all the seven, he hadn't found what he was looking for, so he had to come all the way back down again. After ascending through all seven spheres and, in psychological terms, achieving some psychological awareness of these various archetypal factors that make up the psyche, rather than being free of them, he has to take them back on again in a new way. As he descends, he must take carry them consciously and undergo a new coagulatio. Only after coming down and returning to his starting point on earth does he find Mercurius, and he is then able to discourse with him.

4. The *Shepherd of Hermas*

Jung brings two major amplifications to this sequence of images. The first is the *Shepherd of Hermas,* and the second is the Emerald Tablet of Hermes. Let's talk first about the *Shepherd of Hermas.*

This is a text written in Rome about 140 A.D. It was very much associated with the early Christian Church, and for a while it was even part of the canonical New Testament. The main body of the text involves a series of visions of a man named Hermas, and these visions are followed by a whole set of religious instructions received by Hermas from unconscious figures.[134] Let me give you just a taste of the chief items in the story as Jung alludes to them in *Mysterium.*

The story begins with an encounter in the bath. Hermas says:

He who brought me up sold me to a certain Rhoda at Rome. After many years I made her acquaintance again, and began to love her as a sister. After some time I saw her bathing in the River Tiber, and gave her my hand and helped her out of the river. When I saw her beauty I reflected in my heart and said: "I should be happy if I had a wife of such beauty and character." This was my only thought, and no other, no, not one. After some time, while I was going to Cumae, and glorifying the creation of God, for its greatness and splendor and might, as I walked along I became sleepy. And a spirit seized me and took me away through a certain pathless district. . . . I crossed the river, and came to the level ground and knelt down and began to pray. . . . Now while I was praying the Heaven was opened, and I saw that woman

---

[133] "The Importunate Fortune," in *The Complete Poetry of Henry Vaughan,* pp. 384f.
[134] Jung discusses this text in some detail in *Psychological Types,* CW 6, pars. 381ff.

who I had desired greeting me out of the Heaven and saying: "Hail, Hermas." And I looked at her, and said to her: "Lady, what are you doing here?" and she answered: "I was taken up to accuse you of your sins before the Lord."[135]

In other words, he was guilty for having harbored lustful thoughts toward Rhoda, and so she returned to him in this vision. The lustful thoughts correspond to the Ortus, the animal level. Later, this woman identified herself as the Church. By that device the instinctual libido, activated first on a sexual level, was transferred to another level. It became spiritualized, socialized and made communal, which then led him into a commitment and loyalty to the Church.

One of the most interesting visions of this sequence is the one Jung refers to in paragraph 301, the vision of a great beast of four colors. Here is the full text:

Behold, I saw dust reaching as it were up to heaven, and I began to say to myself, Are cattle coming and raising dust? and it was about a furlong away from me. When the dust grew greater and greater I supposed that it was some portent. The sun shone a little, and lo! I saw a great beast, like some Leviathan, and fiery locusts were going out of his mouth. The beast was in size about a hundred feet and its head was like a piece of pottery. And I began to weep and to pray to the Lord to rescue me from it, and I remembered the word which I had heard, "Do not be double-minded, Hermas." Thus, brethren, being clothed in the faith of the Lord and remembering the great things which he had taught me, I took courage and faced the beast. And as the beast came on with a rush it was as though it could destroy a city. I came near to it, and the Leviathan for all its size stretched itself out on the ground, and put forth nothing except its tongue, and did not move at all until I had passed it by. And the beast had on its head four colours, black, then the colour of flame and blood [red], then golden, then white.

Black, yellow, red and white—same colors as the Ortus. It concludes:

After I had passed the beast by and had gone about thirty feet further, lo! a maiden met me, 'adorned as if coming forth from the bridal chamber,' all in white and in white sandals, veiled to the forehead, and a turban for a head-dress, but her hair was white. I recognized from the former visions that it was the Church, and I rejoiced the more.[136]

In Maier's text, after the Ortus comes the Sibyl, and after Hermas's four-colored beast comes the religious maiden, the Church. It's the same theme, and Jung is so struck by the similarity that he even wonders whether Maier might have been familiar with the *Shepherd of Hermas*. But, as there is no evidence for it, he discounts the possibility.

We've got the same four colors in both texts, but in the Hermas passage the color sequence ends with white. White is the final one because the woman is clothed in white. Going through black, red and yellow to arrive at white corre-

[135] Kirsopp Lake, trans., *Shepherd of Hermas*, in *The Apostolic Fathers*, vol. 2, pp. 7f.
[136] Ibid., pp. 61f.

sponds to going through the dark purgatorial fire to achieve spiritual purity. This is the same direction that Henry Vaughan went, the way of sublimatio, which then is the end state for that sequence.

But the alchemical sequence is different. Jung gave a very nice résumé of the alchemical color sequence which I quote at the beginning of the "Mortificatio" chapter in *Anatomy of the Psyche*. Let me repeat it here because it puts in a nutshell just what the alchemical colors mean psychologically.

> Right at the beginning you meet the "dragon," the chthonic spirit, the "devil" or, as the alchemists called it, the "blackness," the *nigredo*, and this encounter produces suffering. . . . In the language of the alchemists, matter suffers until the *nigredo* disappears, when the "dawn" *(aurora)* will be announced by the "peacock's tail" *(cauda pavonis)* and a new day will break, the *leukosis* or *albedo*. But in this state of "whiteness" one does not *live* in the true sense of the word, it is a sort of abstract, ideal state. In order to make it come alive it must have "blood," it must have what the alchemists call the *rubedo*, the "redness" of life. Only the total experience of being can transform this ideal state of the *albedo* into a fully human mode of existence. Blood alone can reanimate a glorious state of consciousness in which the last trace of blackness is dissolved, in which the devil no longer has an autonomous existence but rejoins the profound unity of the psyche. Then the *opus magnum* is finished: the human soul is completely integrated.[137]

If "the devil no longer has an autonomous existence," then this black hole has been integrated into the rest of the totality and is no longer an isolated, dissociated entity. So the sequence in alchemy is black, white, red, with gold representing the end product, whereas the sequence of Hermas is red, black, white. He starts out with the red blood of his lusting desirousness which then plunges him into the blackness of sin; he gets out of that through the sublimatio of the whitening, but then he's caught up in the sky and hasn't yet made the descent. This would correspond to the fact that the *Shepherd of Hermas* belongs to an earlier phase of development of the collective psyche, and I think we can consider that its imagery was correct for its time.

One more parallel between the Maier text and the *Shepherd of Hermas:* just as Maier finds Mercurius after he comes back down again, so Hermas encounters the shepherd after some of his visions. I'll read you a bit of that:

> While I was praying at home and sitting on my bed, there entered a man glorious to look on, in the dress of a shepherd, covered with white goatskin, with a bag on his shoulders and a staff in his hand. . . . He sat down by me, and said to me, "I have been sent by the most reverend angel to dwell with you the rest of the days of your life." I thought he was come tempting me, . . . [But] he said to me, "Do you not recognize me? . . . I . . . am the shepherd to whom you were handed over."[138]

---

[137] *C.G. Jung Speaking*, pp. 228ff.
[138] Lake, trans., *Shepherd*, p. 69.

In other words, Christ appears in the image of the Good Shepherd.

The Good Shepherd was a symbolic image that also applied to Hermes, so there's an overlap here. This was the time when, in the collective psyche, the emerging Christian symbolism was in the process of assimilating pagan symbolism and taking on some of the attributes that had belonged to it. After meeting the beast and going through the instruction of the Rhoda figure, Hermas meets the shepherd. Likewise, after meeting his beast, the Ortus, and following the advice of the Sibyl to ascend and descend the planetary spheres, Maier finds the companion of the soul, Mercurius.

Now for a few words about the other major amplification in this material: the "Tabula smaragdina," or Emerald Tablet of Hermes.

5. The Emerald Tablet of Hermes

This very succinct recipe for the Philosophers' Stone—which is what the Emerald Tablet is all about—is probably the most sacred alchemical scripture that exists. It really is a summary of the individuation process at the same time as it has its alchemical referents, and I'd suggest you paste it in your copy of *Mysterium* because it belongs with it.

Jung brings this up as an amplification because the central image in it is an ascent and descent, just as in Maier's Perigrinatio text. Let's take this opportunity to read the whole thing—there are thirteen steps—and consider briefly what it means.

1. Truly, without deception, certain and most true.

That means, in very succinct psychological translation, that the psyche is real.

2. What is below is like that which is above, and what is above is like that which is below, to accomplish the miracles of the one thing.

This is the idea of correspondences, the idea that the little world and the big world mirror each other. In other words the personal psyche, the ego, mirrors the archetypal psyche, the Self.

3. And as all things proceeded from one, through meditation of the one, so all things come from this one thing through adaptation.

Everything comes out of the original one, the original Self.

4. Its father is the sun; its mother the moon; the wind has carried it in its belly; its nurse is the earth. [Figure 12-2]

The consciously realized Self is born out of the four elements. It's the product of the four processes that the four elements refer to: calcinatio, solutio, sublimatio and coagulatio. The consciously realized Self is the son or daughter of that four-fold process.

5. This is the father of all, the completion of the whole world.

Figure 12-2.
"The wind has carried
it in its belly."

This refers to the Philosophers' Stone. And so it says the Philosophers' Stone is both the source and the goal of this recipe. The father as source, and the completion as the goal.

6. Its strength is complete if it be turned into (or toward) earth.

It must undergo coagulatio in order to be fully realized.

7. Separate the earth from the fire, the subtle from the dense, gently, and with great ingenuity.

A separatio process is required. The essential meaning must be extracted from the concrete particulars.

And here, especially, is where the reference to the Maier text comes in:

8. It ascends from the earth to the heaven, and descends again to the earth, and receives the power of the above and the below. Thus you will have the glory of the whole world. Therefore all darkness will flee from you.

This ascent followed by descent is the hallmark of the alchemical savior, as opposed to the Christian or Gnostic savior who starts in heaven, comes down and then goes back up again. The alchemical savior starts on earth, goes up and comes back to earth. The difference indicates the crucial importance that the ego has for the realization of the alchemical process.

9. Here is the strong power of the whole strength; for it overcomes every subtle thing and penetrates every solid.

This refers to the aqua permanens that penetrates everything. In other words it describes the nature of the anima mundi which has that penetrating power that can be found everywhere.

10. Thus the world has been created.

The creation of a unique, conscious, whole individual is equivalent to the creation of the world. A number of texts make that equation.

11. From here will come the marvelous adaptations, whose manner this is.

"Marvelous adaptations," *adaptationes mirabiles;* that means miracles. The personal experience takes on a miraculous quality because it's penetrated by the transcendent dimension. And when one is open to the unconscious, synchronistic events happen that correspond to these miracles, these "marvelous adaptations."

12. So I am called HERMES TRISMEGISTUS, having the three parts of the philosophy of the whole world.

This recipe is signed, signed by Hermes Trismegistus, the personification of unconscious wisdom. And it's an illustration of the fact that the unconscious comes to meet the ego through this tendency to personify. Here that absolute knowledge, that unconscious wisdom, is personified as Hermes who signs his recipe.

13. What I have said about the operation of the sun is finished.

Sun refers to gold, and so the gold has now been made.[139]

I want to conclude with a quote from Jung in which he describes just what the ascent and descent mean in real terms. This journey takes place in the dark fourth quarter I spoke of earlier, in that hell-hole where the opposites have been activated. Here's what Jung says about it in paragraph 296:

> Ascent and descent, above and below, up and down, represent an emotional realization of the opposites, and this realization gradually leads, or should lead, to their equilibrium. This motif occurs very frequently in dreams, in the form of going up- and downhill, climbing stairs, going up or down in a lift, balloon, aeroplane, etc. . . . As Dorn interprets it, this vacillating between the opposites and being tossed back and forth means being contained *in* the opposites. They become a vessel in which what was previously now one thing and now another floats vibrating, so that the painful suspension between opposites gradually changes into the bilateral activity of the point in the centre. This is the "liberation from opposites."

That "liberation from opposites" would correspond to Maier's meeting Mercurius. After he's been up and down and gone through all those different stations, then at the end he meets Mercurius, the inner guide who tells him the way to go.

---

139 The complete Latin text of the Emerald Tablet is given in Edinger, *Anatomy,* p. 231, where there is a misprint in the translation of number 3: "And as all things proceeded from one, through mediation . . ." should read: "And as all things proceeded from one, through meditation . . ." [not mediation].

13
Paragraphs 315 to 348

Tonight's material is the last of four assignments on the symbolism of salt and the major images are these:
1. Aqua permanens, *hydor theon* or divine water, and baptismal water.
2. The purifying effects of salt.
3. The preservative effects of salt.
4. The symbolic equation: salt = ash = vitreous body = glorified body.
5. The symbolic equation: salt = soul, anima mundi and Sapientia Dei.
6. Salt as Eros: wisdom and bitterness.

1. Aqua permanens, *Hydor Theon* or Divine Water, and Baptismal Water

Now we return to salt as equivalent to sea-water. The first symbolic equation leads from salt to sea-water to the baptismal water of the Church and to the aqua permanens.

As Jung says in paragraph 316, the alchemists did not hesitate to call the transformative process a baptism, and that is one of the images pertaining to the analytic process—a process of being immersed in sea-water, the aqua pontica, which at the same time is a baptism.

Baptism has two different aspects: one is to cleanse from sins, and the other is to initiate into a special, sacred fellowship. And those two things happen with every major immersion in the unconscious. One is cleansed of one's sins in the sense that by becoming conscious, radically conscious of the extent of one's shadow, one's dirt, one is purified. It doesn't mean the dirt goes away; it just means the dirt becomes clean because one is conscious of it. Conscious dirt is clean dirt as opposed to dirty dirt, which is unconscious dirt. The second aspect of baptism is that it brings about a sense of being initiated into a community, and of finding a transpersonal connection with the human community through an internal process rather than through an external process.

An alchemical phrase that was used frequently—you find it cropping up repeatedly in *Mysterium*—is the Greek term *hydor theon* (ϑδωρ θειον). This means divine water and, very interestingly, it also means sulphur water—only the context will tell you which is which. Here is an example of the profound ambiguities that run through alchemical symbolism. You'll remember from our discussion of the symbolism of sulphur that it was very much associated with the brimstone of hell. Now we learn that sulphur water and divine water are both *hydor theon*. You see how ambiguous the positive and negative aspect of divinity actually is in alchemical symbolism.

This divine water, *hydor theon* or aqua permanens, is what we might call the liquid version of the Self. One of the major sources of this image comes from the fourth chapter of John, where Christ meets a Samaritan woman at the well and asks for a drink of water. Then he says:

> If thou knewest the gift of God, and who it is that saith to thee, Give me to drink; thou wouldest have asked of him, and he would have given thee living water. . . . Whosoever drinketh of this water shall thirst again: but whosoever drinketh of the water that I shall give him shall never thirst; but the water that I shall give him shall be in him a well of water springing up into everlasting life.[140]

This is the water that has the everlasting or eternal dimension to it.

Various aspects of this image of the divine water come up in dreams. Be on the lookout whenever water or a liquid of strange or unusual quality shows up in a dream. I ran across an interesting example some time ago.

I had an analytic hour with a patient that was unusual in that the associations to the material she presented seemed to flow with unusual ease. I'm sure you'll notice, if you look out for it, that the way you function as an analyst fluctuates from patient to patient. I notice that with some patients I can be absolutely brilliant because there's something about the nature of their psychology that constellates the inner brilliance. And with others, I feel an absolute dud. I can't say *anything* right! Anyway, on this occasion things were flowing particularly well. Rich associative material was coming out, and it was being taken in and understood. The night following that hour she dreamt she was with her analyst and a stream of crystal clear water was pouring from the analyst's mouth.

So that would be an example of the *hydor theon,* the divine water, which happened to have been constellated. It doesn't belong to either of us personally, and it is a grave mistake to identify with it, but when things constellate just right, it may be activated and pour itself out. That's what happened then.

Such water isn't always positive, you know. In this case it was, but at other times it can be ambiguous or even outright negative. As the texts say, it can also be poison. In paragraph 340 Jung says that salt "contains as much evil as good." He then quotes a text from the "Gloria Mundi." This is from paragraph 341:

> The "Gloria Mundi" says that the aqua permanens is a "very limpid water, so bitter as to be quite undrinkable." In a hymn-like invocation the text continues: "O water of bitter taste, that preservest the elements! O nature of propinquity, that dissolvest nature! O best of natures, which overcomest nature herself! . . . Thou art crowned with light and art born . . . and the quintessence ariseth from thee." This water is like none on earth, with the exception of that "fount in Judaea" which is named the "Fount of the Saviour or of Blessedness." "With great efforts and by the grace of

---

[140] John 4: 10-14, Authorized Version.

God the philosophers found that noble spring." But the spring is in a place so secret that only a few know of its "gushing," and they know not the way to Judaea where it might be found. Therefore the philosopher cries out: "O water of harsh and bitter taste! For it is hard and difficult for any man to find that spring.". . . "O water, held worthless by all! By reason of its worthlessness and tortuousness no one can attain perfection in the art, or perceive its mighty virtue; for all four elements are, as it were, contained in it."

Then Jung comments on that passage:

> This is the *aqua permanens* or *aqua pontica*, the primal water which contains the four elements.
>
> The psychological equivalent of the chaotic water of the beginning is the unconscious.

And in paragraph 344 he makes this highly significant observation, just sort of slips it in quietly:

> Man's inner life is the "secret place" where the *aqua solvens et coagulans*, the *medicina catholica* or panacea, the spark of the light of nature, are to be found.

So it's our inner light—our inner life, which is also the light—that constitutes this *hydor theon*, this divine water. This is the despised place and the bitter place, but it is the secret place where that supreme value is to be located.

Somehow I want to emphasize that a little more—the words come out easily but the facts are so difficult to grasp. I keep forgetting all the time that the inner life is where the divine water is to be found. Every time I encounter a difficulty of some sort, I mobilize all the resources of my head and reason to solve it, and only when they don't work, then—Oh yes! Oh yes! there's that inner life where you find it! I don't think I'll ever learn otherwise.

As long as the head will do it, we don't turn to the inner life because the notion that there's nothing there anyway is so ingrained in us. It's only when we're really up against the wall that we're forced to turn to that neglected place we otherwise ignore.

2. The Purifying Effect of Salt

I don't have much to say about this other than that it's one of the features of salt symbolism. It corresponds to the effect of baptismal water which is supposed to remove the sins from the sinner, and to the alchemical water which removes the blackness associated with the prima materia. And, as I've said, this would correspond to becoming conscious of one's own dirt.

3. The Preservative Effect of Salt

At one time, before the invention of refrigeration, the discovery that salting preserved meat was very important for our ancestors. In connection with this symbolism, Jung refers to a Jewish legend in which Behemoth and Leviathan, those primordial monsters, are salted and preserved for the world to come (paragraph 338 and note 675). When the Messianic age comes and the Messianic banquet is laid out, these monsters who have been preserved in salt will then be served up.

Here we have the idea that salting something corruptible, such as flesh, has the effect of eternalizing it or rendering it more or less immortal. It suggests that if the coagulated psychic existence, the existential matter, that has been lived by a definite ego is subjected to the salting process, it is eternalized. This symbolism ties in, then, to the next image.

4. Salt = Ash = Vitreous Body = Glorified Body

Salt is synonymous with the ash that is left at the end of the process of calcinatio, and it is equivalent to the vitreous body left in the ash. If matter is subjected to very intense heat, everything combustible burns away and all that's left are ashes and/or vitreous bodies. A vitreous body is a little bead of glass—that's one of the contents of the ashes. This will be an image of the glorified body that takes on qualities of eternity after being subject to the refining fire, and it belongs to the symbolism of salt.

I want to talk about glass and its symbolism a little more than Jung does. It's a frequent image in dream work, and if we have a general familiarity with it, then when the image comes up we'll have a whole body of ideas to apply to it.

Vitreous body means glassy body—*vitrum* means glass. Now, the chief feature of glass is its transparency. Glass itself is invisible and there's something miraculous about it. If you'd never seen glass and were handed a piece of it, then I think you would appreciate what miraculous stuff it is. It's like solid water, for instance. In itself, it is invisible, and by virtue of its invisibility one can see things through it. So it's a symbol of a certain kind of consciousness.

Consider some of the major artifacts associated with glass: bottles, vessels, flasks, windows, mirrors, spectacles, magnifying glasses, microscopes, telescopes. Those are some of the main ones anyway. And practically all of them have to do with extending one's field of vision, or containing something in a vessel that allows one to see what's inside.

Another feature of glass is that when it is broken its sharp edges lacerate living flesh, and when ingested it is exceedingly dangerous to tender inner organs. But it is incorruptible stuff. In current jargon we could say it's not biodegradable; it will last in the ground more or less forever, the same way potsherds do.

I think the ultimate symbolism of glass is that it represents the invisible, glorified body of pure transformed consciousness. And salt is connected with this symbolism. Glass was originally made by heating sand with potash. The alchemists had no knowledge of the actual chemical constituency of glass but we now know that glass is a salt. It's a union, a combination, of an acid and a base.

Glass is actually a mixture of sodium and calcium silicates. At the risk of going too far afield, here are two chemical equations showing that glass is a salt:

1. $HCl + NaOH \longrightarrow NaCl + H_2O$

This shows how sodium chloride is made with hydrochloric acid and sodium hydroxide. An acid and a base, the basic chemical opposites, unite to form a neutral compound which is common salt.

2. a. $H_4SiO_4 + 2Ca\,(OH)_2 \longrightarrow Ca_2SiO_4 + 4H_2O$

   b. $H_4SiO_4 + 4NaOH \longrightarrow Na_4SiO_4 + 8H_2O$

Glass, which is a combination of calcium and sodium silicate, is derived in an analogous way, you see, from silicic acid and calcium hydroxide, and from silicic acid and sodium hydroxide. These are glasses, but salts at the same time.

Question: Did the alchemists know salt was made from an acid and a base?

No, they didn't; hydrochloric acid hadn't been refined at that point. They knew salt; they took it out of the ground—there are great salt deposits in Salzburg, for instance. So they knew salt as a separate entity, but they didn't know how it was created.

5. Salt Equated with Soul, Anima Mundi and Sapientia Dei

Salt is synonymous with the anima mundi, soul and Sapientia Dei. And if it is equivalent to Sapientia Dei, then that links salt with God himself. That's also implied by the preservative qualities of salt that I've already mentioned.

In addition, this ultimate imagery associated with salt is implied by its alchemical sign: a square surrounded by a circle—a mandala. So that establishes for us the idea that in alchemy salt was equated with the Self.

This corresponds to the Old Testament idea of salt's crucial role in divine sacrifice. In the second chapter of Leviticus we read:

> You must salt every oblation that you offer, and you must never fail to put on your oblation the salt of the Covenant with your God: to every offering you are to join an offering of salt to Yahweh your God.[141]

Here it seems that the salt would signify the sacrificial attitude with which the ritual must be done. It's the application of the salt itself that makes the offering sacred. We might say that by salting the offering you cover it with God's own substance, and that makes it acceptable to him.

There's a lot of folklore material with salt. Salt is thought to be a protection against evil spirits. The devil and witches never touch it, so if you throw some salt around that's apotropaic. If salt is spilled, a pinch of it must be thrown over the left shoulder. I would understand that to mean that the unconscious, the left side,

---

[141] Lev. 2: 13-14, Jerusalem Bible.

must be propitiated: if one spills, if one makes an accident, one must propitiate the unconscious by paying attention to it. So if I spill something—salt or anything else for that matter—I'll say, "Hmm, what's that trying to tell me?" Paying attention to what the unconscious has in mind would correspond, symbolically, to tossing some salt over my left shoulder.

6. Salt as Eros: Wisdom and Bitterness

We come now to the most important symbolism of all, the crowning culmination of these four assignments on the symbolism of salt: the equation of salt and Eros. Jung sums it up in paragraph 330:

> Apart from its lunar wetness and its terrestrial nature [see figure 13-1], the most outstanding properties of salt are bitterness and wisdom. As in the double quaternio of the elements and qualities, earth and water have coldness in common, so bitterness and wisdom would form a pair of opposites with a third thing between. The factor common to both, however incommensurable the two ideas may seem, is, psychologically, the function of *feeling*. Tears, sorrow, and disappointment are bitter, but wisdom is the comforter in all psychic suffering. Indeed, bitterness and wisdom form a pair of alternatives: *where there is bitterness wisdom is lacking, and where wisdom is there can be no bitterness.* Salt, as the carrier of this fateful alternative, is co-ordinated with the nature of woman. [Emphasis added]

Later, in paragraph 333, Jung explicitly equates salt with Eros. This led me to recall his remarks about the developmental stages of Eros in "The Psychology of the Transference." Here's what he says in that essay:

> Four stages of eroticism were known in the late classical period: Hawwah (Eve), Helen (of Troy), the Virgin Mary, and Sophia. The series is repeated in Goethe's

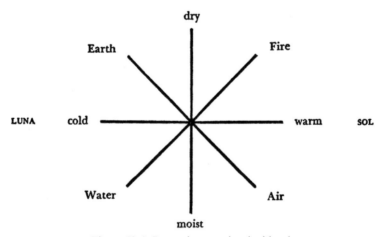

Figure 13-1. Properties associated with salt.

Faust: in the figures of Gretchen as the personification of a purely instinctual relationship (Eve); Helen as an anima figure; Mary as the personification of the
"heavenly," i.e., Christian or religious, relationship; and the "eternal feminine" as
an expression of the alchemical *Sapientia*. As the nomenclature shows, we are
dealing with the heterosexual Eros or anima-figure in four stages, and consequently
with four stages of the Eros cult. The first stage—Hawwah, Eve, earth—is purely
biological; woman is equated with the mother and only represents something to be
fertilized. The second stage is still dominated by the sexual Eros, but on an aesthetic
and romantic level where woman has already acquired some value as an individual.
The third stage raises Eros to the heights of religious devotion and thus spiritualizes
him: Hawwah has been replaced by spiritual motherhood. Finally, the fourth stage
illustrates something which unexpectedly goes beyond the almost unsurpassable
third stage: *Sapientia*. How can wisdom transcend the most holy and the most
pure?—Presumably only by virtue of the truth that the less sometimes means the
more. This stage represents a spiritualization of Helen and consequently of Eros as
such. That is why *Sapientia* was regarded as a parallel to the Shulamite in the Song
of Songs. [142]

I don't expect this to be fully grasped immediately, but these four stages are
something to reflect on, and I'm going to say a little more about them to help fix
them in your mind. They are very relevant in analytic work. The majority of our
patients are living out of the first stage, or maybe the beginnings of the second,
and don't have any inklings at all of the third or fourth stage. If one is aware of
this sequence, one will then be in a position to notice when the dreams are alluding
to these evolutionary stages of the development of Eros.

The four stages are Eve, Helen, Mary and Sapientia or Wisdom. Let me just
say a word or two about each. Eve represents Eros as it lives itself out on the
primordial, matriarchal level of the psyche, as described by Erich Neumann.[143]
This level of the psyche is basically a combination of nourishing and devouring.
It's Eros as elemental desirousness; it's Demeter before the loss of Persephone.
In terms of relation between the sexes, the goal is biological fertility and the male
principle is subordinate to the matriarchal principle—it's no more than an
instrument in the service of the Great Mother. That's Hawwah (Eve).

The second level is the Helen of Troy level. At this stage the male principle has
acquired autonomy and the opposites are now polarized. The romantic and aesthetic
factors are the prominent ones, and the goal of this level of Eros is the physical and
biological union of the opposites. So the coniunctio is the goal, but in concrete terms.

The third stage is Mary and at this stage the masculine, spiritual principle has
acquired dominance. So Mary represents spiritual motherhood and, just as the

---

[142] *The Practice of Psychotherapy,* CW 16, par. 361. See also Marie-Louise von Franz's
comments on these stages in Jung, *Man and His Symbols,* pp. 185ff.
[143] See *The Origins and History of Conciousness,* part 2, A.

Figure 13-2. Sapientia as mother of the wise.

goal of stage one—Eve—was biological fertility, so the goal of the Mary stage is spiritual fertility.

The fourth stage, Wisdom or Sapientia, is a spiritualization of Helen, just as the Mary level was a spiritualization of Eve. And, as Jung puts it, that means Sapientia represents the spiritualization of Eros as such. Here the goal is the *psychological* union of opposites. The coniunctio, as a psychological experience, is the goal of this level of Eros.

There are three steps of transformation that take place in those four stages. At the risk of oversimplifying, let me just give you a hint of what I see as symbolizing those three steps. The step between Eve and Helen is symbolized by the abduction of Persephone by Hades. The step between Helen and Mary is symbolized by the Annunciation. And the step between Mary and Sapientia is symbolized by the Assumption of Mary.

Now remember we're still talking about salt, and I thought it might be interesting to gather together some of the accumulated proverbial wisdom associated with salt. I went through *Bartlett's Familiar Quotations* and came up with many concerning salt. Let me give you some examples so you get the flavor of how salt has salted our language . . . Here's Kipling, in "Departmental Ditties":

> I have eaten your bread and salt.
> I have drunk your water and wine.

> The deaths ye died I have watched beside
> And the lives ye led were mine.

So here salt would be equivalent to soul. I've shared your life, your soul life with you, "eaten your bread and salt."

An old Spanish saying says "A kiss without a mustache is like an egg without salt." And Robert Frost, in "To Earthward," says:

> Now no joy but lacks salt
> That is not dashed with pain
> And weariness and fault;
> I crave the stain
>
> Of tears, the aftermark
> Of almost too much love,
> The sweet of bitter bark
> And burning clove.

That's an example of salt as bitterness, and it's an allusion to coagulatio.

In ancient Rome, salt was part of a soldier's pay. Petronius spoke of a man "not worth his salt." Our word salary originally meant salt-money.

Henry van Dyke:

> Individuality is the salt of common life. You may have to live in a crowd but you do not have to like it, nor subsist on its food.

Matthew 5: 13:

> Ye are the salt of the earth: but if the salt have lost his savor, wherewith shall it be salted?

In that case the salt is equal to the anima mundi. Salt represents fragments of the Deity—"salt of the earth."

Genesis, 19:26:

> [Lot's] wife looked back from behind him, and she became a pillar of salt.

That would be salt as a preservative, to be turned into an eternal statue.

Paul, in Colossians 4: 6:

> "Let your speech be alway with grace, seasoned with salt."

In this context salt would mean wisdom.

Here's a poem by Isaac Hill Bromley:

> Bring me honey of Hymettus, bring me stores of Attic salt;
> I am weary of the commonplace, to dullness call a halt!
> These dinner speeches tire me, they are tedious, flat and stale:
> From a hundred thousand banquet tables comes a melancholy wail,
> As a hundred thousand banqueters sit up in evening dress
> And salute each moldy chestnut with a signal of distress.

He calls for "stores of Attic salt." There too salt would be equivalent to soul.

In a sonnet by John Masefield:

> What am I, Life? A thing of watery salt
> Held in cohesion by unresting cells,
> Which work they know not why, which never halt.
> Myself unwitting where their master dwells?

Here salt would represent Eros as a cohesive force in which "the watery salt" holds in cohesion the "unresting cells."

It is interesting, the various facets that come up. Here's another, from Kipling's "Widow at Windsor" (referring to the Queen):

> Walk wide o' the Widow at Windsor
> For 'alf o' creation she owns.
> We 'ave bought 'er the same with the sword an' the flame,
> An' we've salted it down with our bones.

Oliver Goldsmith, in "Retaliation":

> Our Garrick's a salad; for in him we see
> Oil, vinegar, sugar, and saltness agree!

And finally, listen to Hamlet's speech in act 1, scene 2, concerning bitterness as salt:

> Frailty, thy name is woman.
> A little month; or ere those shoes were old
> With which she follow'd my poor father's body,
> Like Niobe, all tears; why she,—
> O God! a beast, that wants discourse of reason,
> Would have mourn'd longer,—married with mine uncle,
> My father's brother, but no more like my father
> Than I to Hercules. Within a month,
> Ere yet the salt of most unrighteous tears
> Had left the flushing in her galled eyes,
> She married. O most wicked speed, to post
> With such dexterity to incestuous sheets.
> It is not, nor it cannot come to, good.—
> But break, my heart, for I must hold my tongue.

Well, there are some of the flavors of salt symbolism scattered around.

14
Paragraphs 349 to 367

Tonight we start a new chapter, "Rex and Regina," and a new body of images. The central image of the king will occupy us for the next few sessions, and tonight I'm going to speak about six different features of king symbolism:

1. The emergence of divine kingship in history, and ancient Egyptian kingship—the origin of the Trinity.

2. Two aspects of the psychological meaning of kingship: the initial coming of the king; and his death and rebirth, his transformation or rejuvenation.

3. The remarkable myth of the priest-king at Nemi.

4. The myth of Osiris, an example of the rejuvenation of the king.

5. Images of the transformation, such as the killing, the drowning and the burning of the king.

6. The Allegory of Merlin.

1. The Emergence of the Institution of Kingship in History

The king is a major image in the collective psyche, and that's why it gets such a large consideration in *Mysterium*. It's not an image that comes up often in work with American patients because the American psyche does not characteristically have the image of the king in it. America was born in rebellion against kingship. (That will be an essay for somebody to write some day—the psychological significance of that fact for the American psyche.) But that doesn't mean that we're free of the archetype; it just means it takes on different clothing. For Americans, in most cases, the image comes up as the image of the president, or sometimes chairman of the board. But the same archetypal content lies behind those images—it's still the king by any other name.

The theme of the emergence of the institution of kingship in human history is very significant psychologically; it definitely signifies a major step in the evolution of the collective psyche.[144] It amounts to the emergence of an image of a central authority around which a whole nation can be ordered, and it corresponds to the emergence of the ego in the individual. The king is sort of the collective ego of the emerging nation. Those of you who attended the Old Testament course will remember how this feature was pictured in the stories of Saul and David, the first and second kings of Israel.[145]

---

[144] See John Weir Perry, *The Far Side of Madness;* also his longer study, *The Heart of History: Individuality in Evolution.*

[145] See Edinger, *Bible and the Psyche,* pp. 78ff.

In the early days when kings were first getting established—not just in Israel but in all of antiquity—the king was thought, quite concretely, to be the earthly representative of God, and therefore he had accompanying him all the trappings of divinity: the scepter, the mantle, the orb and being addressed only by superlative epithets such as "your majesty."

From the standpoint of history, the emergence of kingship represents the appearance of a central authority around which collective consciousness is ordered. The king is to the collective, national psyche what the ego is to the individual psyche. In dreams, however, the image of the king represents the Self—or an aspect of the Self, a kind of intermediary of the Self—in relation to the ego.

For most members of a primitive society, the king carried all the attributes we associate with the Self. James Frazer describes the phenomenology succinctly:

> At a certain stage of early society the king or priest is often thought to be endowed with supernatural powers or to be an incarnation of a deity, and consistently with this belief the course of nature is supposed to be more or less under his control, and he is held responsible for bad weather, failure of the crops, and similar calamities. To some extent it appears to be assumed that the king's power over nature, like that over his subjects and slaves, is exerted through definite acts of will; and therefore if drought, famine, pestilence, or storms arise, the people attribute the misfortune to the negligence or guilt of their king, and punish him accordingly with stripes and bonds . . . . Sometimes, however, the course of nature, while regarded as dependent on the king, is supposed to be partly independent of his will. His person is considered . . . as the dynamical centre of the universe, from which lines of force radiate to all quarters of the heaven; so that any motion of his—the turning of his head, the lifting of his hand—instantaneously affects and may seriously disturb some part of nature. He is the point of support on which hangs the balance of the world, and the slightest irregularity on his part may overthrow the delicate equipoise. The greatest care must, therefore, be taken both by and of him; and his whole life, down to its minutest details, must be so regulated that no act of his, voluntary or involuntary, may . . . upset the established order of nature.[146]

The phenomenology of the Self is completely visible in this description of the way primitives thought of their kings.

As Jung speaks about early kingship in the beginning of this chapter, he uses Egypt as the example of its most elaborate development (paragraphs 349-352). In Egyptian symbolism the king was definitely part of a theological trinity: there was God the Father; there was Pharaoh the king who was his son; and there was the so-called *ka* who represented the divine life-force and procreative power, and who corresponded to the Pharaoh's fourteen ancestral souls. Jung makes a point of indicating that this Egyptian trinity is the origin of the theological doctrine of the Christian Trinity, and he specifically states that the idea of the *homoousia* of the

---

[146] *The Golden Bough: A Study in Magic and Religion,* pp. 221f.

Father and the Son derives from the Egyptian symbolism.

I want to say a word or two about this idea of the *homoousia* of the Father and the Son because it is very important imagery; Jung also speaks about it in other places,[147] and I think it has considerable psychological importance.

There was a grave doctrinal dispute in the early history of the Church about a matter which, if considered superficially, could be seen as trivial. But the fact that the best minds of the period gave their greatest energies to the controversy indicates that psychologically it was a very grave matter indeed.

The dispute was over a single word in the formulation of the Christian creed: when the Trinity is described as the Father, Son and Holy Ghost, should it be stated that the Father and the Son are of the *same* substance as one another—*homoousia*—or are the Father and Son only of *similar* substance as one another—*homoiousia?*[148] This conflict wracked the Church for centuries, and the split still survives: when the Eastern and Western Churches separated, the Western Church chose *homoousia* and the Eastern Orthodox Church chose *homoiousia*. Thus, for the Western psyche, God the Father and God the Son are of the same substance (consubstantial), while for the Eastern Christian psyche, God the Father and God the Son are of similar substance but are not identical.

Consider what that means: it means that for the Western psyche—this is its basic, fundamental mythology—the ego is of the same stuff as the Self. However for the Russian psyche, which is the major representative of Eastern Orthodoxy, the ego doesn't have that same honorable position; it has a lesser position. This, I think, helps to explain the difference between the Western ego's relation to authority and the Eastern ego's relation to authority.

A small example relevant to this issue is a dream of my own. As I said, we Americans don't dream of kings, so I dream that I am President Reagan's analyst. Now remember—if you are interpreting it archetypally, anyway—that irrespective of a president's politics, it's the presidential function that will be the relevant thing here. What the dream implies is that the ego has a sizable say as to what goes on in the Self.

2. The Initial Emergence of the King, and His Rejuvenation

As I've said, the initial coming of the king corresponds to the emergence of kingship in history, and is illustrated by the Old Testament story of Saul, the first king of Israel. In an individual, this image of the first coming of the king repre-

---

[147] See, for instance, *Psychology and Religion,* CW 11, pars. 215ff.

[148] This is indicated by the *filioque* addition to the Creed in the West, which was rejected in the East. See ibid., par. 217, note 19, and par. 218. My impression is that the real dispute focused on the *filioque* doctrine, but it is a companion doctrine to the bigger one of *homoousia*—they belong together. One implies the other.

sents the appearance of the first central structuring of the psyche and the emergence of an ego with a stable inner authority and sense of autonomous identity. It generally shows up at the beginning of adolescence. Jung experienced it in his eleventh year—but he was always precocious with everything—when he suddenly walked out of a mist and realized "Now I am *myself!*"[149] In individual psychology this would correspond to the coming of the king.

It is the task of that inner king, the ego, to establish its kingdom, to augment and develop its powers of control—a task which as a rule lasts well into middle age. But then, if the developmental process has been constellated, sooner or later the time comes for the king to undergo a transformation process, a rejuvenation requiring a death and a rebirth. This theme leads to an exceedingly rich body of material directly relevant to alchemy, but there's also a lot of material that precedes alchemy. I want first to consider the magnificent work of James Frazer.

3. The Golden Bough and the Myth of the Priest-King at Nemi

Sir James George Frazer is really a major figure in the cultural history of the modern age, one of the creators of the new psychological world view. It's not that he approached his material with a specific psychological consciousness, but he did an incredible amount of spade work, digging out the images and making them available for a new understanding.

His great work, *The Golden Bough,* comprises twelve volumes, but he also accommodated us very nicely by providing an abridgment containing everything we as analysts need. I would urge you to study it because it's a vast treasure house of the psyche. He documents the way the primitive mind functions, and of course the primitive mind is the unconscious. If we know how the primitive mind functions we have information about how the unconscious functions. Let me give you a couple of appetizers, examples of the gems you can find by browsing around in Frazer.

Some of the ways that primitive doctors function is exceedingly instructive. For instance, certain French peasants were subject to a kind of gastro-intestinal disorder which they thought was caused by a disconnection of the stomach. In that event, the medicine man would be called in to reconnect the patient's disconnected stomach. The way he would go about doing that would be to disconnect his own stomach, and get into a very bizarre state—this very uncomfortable state of the disconnected stomach. Then, with a variety of gyrations and strange movements, he would go through the process of reconnecting his disconnected stomach, and in the course of doing that he'd do the same job for the patient's disconnected stomach—when he was reconnected, the patient would be reconnected too. That's one example.[150]

---

149 *Memories, Dream, Reflections,* pp. 32f.
150 *Golden Bough,* p. 21.

Another example of primitive medical practice: it was thought that under certain circumstances the primitive doctor would take advantage of his patient—there would be evidence that he had swallowed the patient's soul. The doctor would be called forth, presented with the evidence that the patient's soul was missing, and told that there was reason to believe he had swallowed it. He would then be fed emetics and be forced to vomit it up.[151] They are gems, you see.

Now the whole twelve volumes of Frazer's *Golden Bough* is an exhaustive amplification of the basic image of primitive regicide, of early communities killing their king in order to replace him with a new one. In other words it's an elaborate amplification of the basic archetypal image of the death and rebirth of the king. Here is the way the abridged version starts:

> Who does not know Turner's picture of the Golden Bough? The scene, suffused with the golden glow of imagination in which the divine mind of Turner steeped and transfigured . . . [this] natural landscape . . . of the little woodland lake of Nemi—'Diana's Mirror,' as it was called by the ancients. . . . That calm water, lapped in a green hollow of the Alban hills. . . . The two characteristic Italian villages . . . slumber on its banks. . . .
>
> In antiquity this sylvan landscape was the scene of a strange and recurring tragedy. On the northern shore of the lake. . . stood the sacred grove and sanctuary of . . . Diana of the Wood. . . . In this sacred grove there grew a certain tree round which at any time of the day, and probably far into the night, a grim figure might be seen to prowl. In his hand he carried a drawn sword, and he kept peering warily about him as if at every instant he expected to be set upon by an enemy. He was a priest and a murderer; and the man for whom he looked was sooner or later to murder him and hold the priesthood in his stead. Such was the rule of the sanctuary. A candidate for the priesthood could only succeed to office by slaying the priest, and having slain him, he retained office till he was himself slain by a stronger [man] or a craftier.
>
> The post which he held by this precarious tenure carried with it the title of king; but surely no crowned head ever lay uneasier, or was visited by more evil dreams . . . . For year in year out, in summer and winter, in fair weather and in foul, he had to keep his lonely watch, and whenever he snatched a troubled slumber it was at the peril of his life. The least relaxation of his vigilance, the smallest abatement of his strength of limb or skill . . . put him in jeopardy; grey hairs might seal his death-warrant.[152]

Frazer was so fascinated by this image of the kingship of the priest of Nemi that he started looking around for parallels to it, and the result was the whole *Golden Bough*. Frazer's fascination, I think, reflects the fact that this myth is an image of fundamental importance to the psyche, so I want to pay it a little further attention as part of our examination of the king symbolism in alchemy.

---

[151] Ibid., p. 249.
[152] Ibid., pp. 1f.

The basic idea of the priesthood of Nemi was this: Diana's temple there was served by a priest, called the King of the Wood, and he could be replaced by whomever could challenge him successfully. Within this sanctuary, this grove, grew a certain tree of which no branch might be broken. Only a runaway slave was allowed, if he could, to break off one of its boughs. If he managed to do this, he was entitled to fight the priest in single combat; and if he slew him, he reigned in his stead as King of the Wood. According to ancient notions, this fateful branch was the golden bough which, in Virgil's *Aeneid*, Aeneas broke off to gain entry into the underworld.[153]

Now the reigning King of the Wood, as Frazer describes him, is a desperate figure, in perpetual anxiety, on the lookout for his certain successor who will overthrow him and take his place. This very powerful image describes one aspect of egohood. On the one hand, the ego comes into existence by taking on— usurping let's say—the prerogatives of kingship; but then the consequence of that act is that in turn the ego is in perpetual terror of being overthrown. The image of the King of Nemi represents that very vividly. It is the best image I know to express the inner reality of paranoia in its extreme form, and it is the image that lies behind what we so blandly call defenses of the ego.

This tree, and its golden bough which must be broken off before one can claim to be the usurper, is an image of the Self. And since the king's relation to the Self is a usurped one, it's always precarious and in danger of collapse. And, according to the myth, the danger comes from a runaway slave. In other words, a revolt is to be expected from the inferior, enslaved shadow side of the psyche which will then overcome the established authority of the ego.[154]

It is important to note that the golden bough comes from the same tree from which Aeneas wrested his golden bough—his passport to the underworld (figure 14-1). The Self, represented by the golden bough, is activated by the revolt of the slave and the subsequent overthrow of the tyrannical ego. This will precipitate, as it did for Aeneas, a *nekyia*, a down going, a descent into the underworld—into the unconscious—as a part of the death and rebirth of the king.

I think this image, this myth, compensates all the positive and glittering associations that generally accompany the grand image of the king, and it also corresponds to Shakespeare's observation: "Uneasy lies the head that wears a crown."[155]

---

[153] Ibid., p. 3 (condensed).

[154] The figure of the runaway slave reminds one of the *servus fugitivus* or *cervus fugitivus* (fugitive slave or stag) of alchemy. This is a term applied to the "philosophic Mercurius. . . the transformative substance." ("The Spirit Mercurius," *Alchemical Studies*, CW 13, par. 259) In *Mysterium*, par. 188, footnote 336, Jung notes that the stag also is a "symbol of renewal."

[155] *Henry IV, Part 2*, act 3, scene 1.

Figure 14-1. Aeneas
picks the golden bough.

4. The Osiris Myth

The death and rebirth of Osiris is probably the most basic of the classical myths which pertain to the symbolism of the king's rejuvenation. I'll just remind you of the central features of this story. It has a double form. According to one version, the evil figure, Set, traps Osiris in a chest and throws it into the sea. Eventually the chest washes up on the shore of Biblos and is incorporated into a great tree. That's what we might call the solutio version of the myth.

The other version—a separatio version[156]—is that Set dismembers Osiris into fourteen fragments which are then scattered throughout the world.

Then in both versions Isis, the sister-wife of Osiris, rescues or retrieves Osiris and reconstitutes him. She gathers together all the missing fragments, all except the phallus which has been swallowed by a fish. She has to make a wooden replacement of that. The child Horus is then conceived by the reconstituted Osiris, and Horus thus becomes the rejuvenated king.

In the first version, there's a solutio and a regressive movement to the vegetative level of the psyche, a reversion to the tree. In the second version, there's a dismemberment, a breaking into pieces, a process of pulverizing and scattering.

---

[156] See Edinger, *Anatomy,* chap. 7, "Separatio."

This division into fragments would correspond to an analysis—"analysis" means literally a cutting up into little pieces, pieces small enough to be assimilated. That's part of the transformation of every major complex or every major unconscious content: it must be subjected to dismemberment—analytic fragmentation—and then reconstituted again on a conscious level.

5. Ritual Regicide in Alchemy

This whole story of Osiris is directly paralleled by the alchemical procedures which treat the prima materia in the same way as Set treated Osiris: the prima materia is subjected to solutio or separatio, to pulverization, to dismemberment.

Many alchemical pictures represent this process quite graphically. In *Psychology and Alchemy,* for instance, there is a picture titled "The Slaying of the King" (figure 14-2). The king is lying on the ground having been beaten by a mob of ruffians with clubs. We have to remind ourselves that this picture is not expressing some sociological commentary on society. It's an image of what goes on in the alchemical flask as part of the transformation process, namely the dismemberment of the king. There is a particularly good example of this theme in a text Jung discusses, so let's go to that.

Figure 14-2.
The slaying of
the king.

6. The Allegory of Merlin

I'm going to read Jung's description of this text and then talk about it. This comes from paragraph 357:

> The allegory tells us of a certain king who made ready for battle. As he was about to mount his horse he wished for a drink of water. A servant asked him what water he would like, and the king answered: "I demand the water which is closest to my heart, and which likes me above all things." When the servant brought it the king drank so much that "all his limbs were filled and all his veins inflated, and he himself became discoloured." His soldiers urged him to mount his horse, but he said he could not: "I am heavy and my head hurts me, and it seems to me as though all my limbs were falling apart." He demanded to be placed in a heated chamber where he could sweat the water out. But when, after a while, they opened the chamber he lay there as if dead. They summoned the Egyptian and the Alexandrian physicians, who at once accused one another of incompetence. Finally the Alexandrian physicians gave way to the Egyptian physicians, who tore the king into little pieces, ground them to powder, mixed them with their "moistening" medicines, and put the king back in his heated chamber as before. After some time they fetched him out again half-dead. ... They ... washed him with sweet water ... mixed him with new substances. Then they put him back in the chamber as before. When they took him out this time he was really dead. But the physicians said: "We have killed him that he may become better and stronger in this world after his resurrection on the day of judgment." The king's relatives, however, considered them mountebanks, took their medicines away from them, and drove them out of the kingdom.

Then the Alexandrian physicians arrive on the scene, and they say they can revive the king.

> The Alexandrian physicians took the body, ground it to powder a second time, washed it well until nothing of the previous medicines remained, and dried it. Then they took one part of sal ammoniac and two parts of Alexandrian nitre, mixed them with the pulverized corpse, made it into a paste with a little linseed oil, and placed it in a crucible-shaped chamber. ... Then they heaped fire upon it and melted it . ... Whereupon the king rose up from death and cried in a loud voice: "Where are my enemies? I shall kill them all if they do not submit to me!"

So we have the king, who, in an expansive state, overreaches himself. He consumes the special water, the divine water, and falls into a state of ego-Self identity. It's a kind of internal drowning, a dropsy or inflation, that causes him to fall apart. In other words the psychic authority, represented by the king, has succumbed to hybris; he collapses, and must then be subjected to the alchemical process in the vessel.

This process takes place on two different levels, represented by the two teams of physicians—the Egyptian and Alexandrian—which I would understand to represent two levels of healing power from the unconscious. Since the Egyptians get the first chance, that would indicate they are closer to consciousness; they will represent methods more familiar to the conscious standpoint. Their method consists of grinding the king into powder, mixing the powder with moistening medicines and then baking him. That method failed, it did not work.

So the second level of the healing power from the unconscious is brought on the scene, represented by the Alexandrian physicians. They grind the body to a powder again, they wash it and dry it, and then they add salt, after which they fire it. That worked, and the king was rejuvenated.

Now here's what Jung says about that—this is from paragraph 365:

> The difference between the Egyptian and the Alexandrian physicians seems to be that the former moistened the corpse but the latter dried it (or embalmed or pickled it). The technical error of the Egyptians, therefore, was that they did not separate the conscious from the unconscious sufficiently, whereas the Alexandrians avoided this mistake.

In the next paragraph Jung adds:

> [Instead of using water, the Alexandrians used] the other constituent of the *aqua pontica,* namely salt in the form of *sal ammoniac. . .* and *sal nitri* (saltpetre). Primarily the preservative quality of both salts is meant, but secondarily, in the mind of the adepts, "marination" meant the "in-forming" penetration of *sapientia . . .* into the ignoble mass, whereby the corruptible form was changed into an incorruptible and immutable one.

To state more explicitly how we might understand this image psychologically, we can say that the king who had succumbed to dropsy, to this bloated condition, was subjected to a double process—he had a twofold analysis. The Egyptian physicians provided him with a personal, reductive analysis, and the Alexandrian physicians provided him with an archetypal analysis, the crucial feature of which was the adding of salt—divine wisdom is added to the material. The Egyptian physicians included water in their procedure and, as Jung says, the *participation mystique* was not rigorously enough analyzed: "They did not separate the conscious from the unconscious sufficiently."

The Alexandrian physicians do a fuller drying process but, even more important, they apply the salt, which I would understand to mean that they make use of an understanding of archetypal realities. I think we have to assume that both these phases—the Egyptian and the Alexandrian—were required.

The fact that the initial state of the patient-king is a state of bloating would correspond to the folk wisdom that labels analysts as head shrinkers, "shrinks"— it's the same imagery. When analysts have to deal with psychological bloating, a shrinking procedure is called for.

15
Paragraphs 368 to 404

Ripley's *Cantilena*

Tonight I'm not going to list a specific set of images because the material for this week and next will have as its ordering principle an examination of Ripley's *Cantilena*. That dramatic poem offers the connecting thread on which we can hang some ideas. It's really quite a charming story. The basic idea is that there is a king who has become barren, and he's obliged to return to his mother's womb for rejuvenation by rebirth. What I intend to do is to follow the poem verse by verse and make some comments on it as we go along.

As with all alchemical material, we must keep reminding ourselves that although this poem is in the form of a dramatic story, it's actually an alchemical recipe which describes a process of transformation going on in the alchemical retort. That means for us that it is a symbolic description of an analysis.

The first two stanzas are introductory material. The meaty part starts with the third stanza. Here are verses 3, 4 and 5 (in paragraph 370):

> There was a certaine Barren King by birth,
> Composèd of the Purest, Noblest Earth,
> By nature Sanguine and Devoute, yet hee
> Sadly bewailèd his Authoritie.

> Wherefore am I a King, and Head of all
> Those Men and Things that be Corporeall?
> I have no Issue, yet I'le not deny
> 'Tis Mee both Heaven and Earth are Rulèd by.

> Yet there is either a Cause Naturall
> Or some Defect in the Originall,
> Though I was borne without Corruption
> And nourished 'neath the Pinions of the Sunne.

That's how it gets started. We are introduced to the materia that's being deposited in the vessel, and the materia announces itself to be a king, although a barren king that has lost its authority—lost its capacity to govern.

As Jung points out, this theme of the barren king that initiates the alchemical opus has many parallels with the Grail legend. It also corresponds to the usual reason for the beginning of an analysis. Something's wrong with the functioning of the psychological authority. It's barren or defective; it has lost its authority, its full capacity to rule and function effectively, so it deposits itself in the analytic vessel—the modern equivalent of the alchemical vessel.

181

The idea is that the current ordering dominant of the psyche is exhausted and must submit itself to a process of rejuvenation. Such a state of affairs is evidenced by the feeling that life has become meaningless. The individual is assailed by questions: Why? What's the meaning of my life? What am I doing? These kinds of questions are apt to emerge—at least with a reflective person—whenever the life force grows weak, whenever the natural libido slackens. As long as the libido is flowing at full force, such questions need not come up.

In fact for the healthy minded, the very presence of such questions is evidence of sickness. If you're going along at full tide of health, natural life never asks such questions, it just lives. The ability of a reflective person to ask such questions is one of the noblest aspects of humanity, yet such questions only come to the fore at moments of weakness. We need the experience of weakness in order to experience our full human potential and actually only the person who is potentially twice-born will entertain such questions. The very fact that they rise up indicates that the potential exists for the rejuvenation process, the death and rebirth process, to take place.

In "Answer to Job" Jung makes a crucial observation about the value of human weakness:

> But what does man possess that God does not have? Because of his littleness, puniness, and defencelessness against the Almighty, he possesses . . . a somewhat keener consciousness based on self-reflection: he must, in order to survive, always be mindful of his impotence.[156]

It is actually human weakness, barrenness and failure that generate the reflective capacity of consciousness. I'd even venture the hypothesis that only creatures who die, and who are therefore required to come to terms with the fact of death, are capable of consciousness. It's an interesting reflection anyway, and does give another angle to our mortality. Since we've got to accept it one way or another, we might as well put the best face on it we can!

These first verses are quite astonishing. They state explicitly that this barren king—the materia which is going to be subjected to the alchemical process—is God! The king says he won't deny that both Heaven and Earth are ruled by him. Well, that's nobody else but God, only God can say that. So what is announced right at the outset of this poem is that the prima materia identifies itself as God.

Also, a very interesting question is raised here in these initial stanzas: is this impotent condition of the king due to a natural cause or to an original defect? I think this is the essential difference between the personalistic and the archetypal standpoints of psychology. Another way of putting it is to ask whether the cause of the barrenness, the psychic conflict or problem, is due to environment or to heredity. The answer has to be both, but essentially we are dealing with an original

---

[156] *Psychology and Religion,* CW 11, par. 579.

defect: to the extent that we're dealing with the prima materia as a manifestation of God, then it has to be a defect in the ground of existence.

That ground of existence is imperfect, in a state of transition, and it requires a process of transformation. In verses 6 and 7, the barren king continues:

> Each Vegetative which from the Earth proceeds
> Arises up with its own proper Seeds;
> And Animalls, at Seasons, speciously
> Abound with Fruit and strangly Multiply.
>
> Alas, my Nature is Restricted so
> No Tincture from my Body yet can flow.
> It therefore is Infoecund: neither can
> It ought availe, in Generating Man.

These verses express the distress of the barren king or the barren God who wants to be creative but who lacks the power to create. And he contrasts his barren state with the fruitfulness of vegetative nature, indicating that the king is somehow separate from nature. He doesn't participate in the fruitfulness of nature, he belongs to another level, another order of things.

This alludes, I think, to the idea that although the alchemical opus was thought of as a continuation of nature, the alchemists thought they were just helping nature to do what she already had an inclination to do. As one alchemist put it, they were working on material on which nature "hath worked but a little." Nevertheless there was also the contrary idea that alchemy was an *opus contra naturam*—contrary to nature. This would suggest that consciousness as a human achievement could never be created by nature on her own. Something has to arise to contradict the natural flow of life if consciousness is to emerge from the conflict between the opposites.

The barren king complains, "No Tincture from my Body yet can flow." Jung observes that there is a parallel here to the blood and water that gushed from Christ's side when, on the cross, he was pierced by the spear. This association would equate the barren king with Christ and would allude to the fact that the process the king is going to go through will be analogous to the death and resurrection sequence of Christ's passion. In paragraph 372 Jung says about this:

> The analogy of the pierced Redeemer with the rock from which Moses struck water was used in alchemy to denote the extraction of the *aqua permanens* or of the soul from the lapis.

And in footnote 73 he quotes Origen who says of Christ that "unless this rock had been smitten, it had not given water."

These images suggest that the king, in the course of his transformation-rejuvenation process, is going to be subjected to a piercing or a wounding analogous to that piercing of Christ. This would correspond psychologically to the fact that the barren ego, if it's to undergo transformation, must be wounded or broken in some way in order to open up a connection with the unconscious. Only by that process of breaking or piercing can healing effects—the "Tincture"—flow.

Now of course nobody ever chooses to be wounded—that's just a little too much contra naturam—but the way it seems to work is that the wounding happens and then only afterward, with a lot of work, do we sometimes discover that the wounding has actually been valuable because it promotes an enlargement and a regeneration of the personality.

In verses 8 and 9, the sick old king continues to expostulate:

> My Bodies Masse is of a Lasting-Stuffe,
> Exceeding delicate, yet hard enough;
> And when the Fire Assays to try my Sprite,
> I am not found to Weigh a Graine too light.
>
> My Mother in a Sphaere gave birth to mee,
> That I might contemplate Rotunditie;
> And be more Pure of kind than other things,
> By Right of Dignity the Peer of Kings.

This tells us that the king is made of "Lasting-Stuffe," something eternal and indestructible. And he seems to be speaking in anticipation of his future transformed state when he says "My Mother in a Sphaere gave birth to mee, that I might contemplate Rotunditie." That's what happens when he's reborn. It is as though he's dreaming that prospect—the achievement of wholeness—he's fantasizing it, it hasn't happened yet.

The other aspect of being born from the sphere is that he's born out of the alchemical flask. About this matter, Jung says in paragraph 373:

> The "house of the sphere" is the *vas rotundum*, whose roundness represents the cosmos and, at the same time, the world-soul, which in Plato surrounds the physical universe from outside. The secret content of the Hermetic vessel is the original chaos from which the world was created. As the filius Macrocosmi and the first man the king is destined for "rotundity," i.e., wholeness, but is prevented from achieving it by his original defect.

We're told here that "the secret content of the Hermetic vessel is the original chaos from which the world was created." This implies psychologically that every analysis—if it gets down to that level anyway—works on the original chaos from which the world was created and is therefore continuing the process of world creation. To think of it that way enlarges the context of our daily work—and it's really true!

Jung says the sphere that gives birth to the transformed king is simultaneously the alchemical vessel on the one hand, and the spherical vessel of the universe on the other hand. This presents the same idea from a different angle: the alchemist and the individual in analysis, at the same time as they are creating or recreating the individual psyche, are also promoting the creation of the world. The implication is that the whole world is in a great process of psychological evolution; it's like a vast alchemical vessel.

The French poet Charles Baudelaire had a vision of this idea of the whole world as a great alchemical vessel. It's really quite a striking vision. Let me read it to you. This is in translation, of course, so most of the poetry is gone and all that's left is the stark image that gripped him. The title of the poem is "The Lid."

> Wherever he may go on sea or land,
> In atmosphere of flame or under pallid sun,
> Servant of Christ or one of Venus' band,
> Dark beggar or Croesus gleaming gold,
>
> City dweller, rustic, vagabond or settled one,
> Whether his small mind is bright or dull,
> Terror of the mystery man always bears,
> And looks above with trembling eye.
>
> Above, the sky, wall of the tomb which suffocates,
> Ceiling lit up by an opera bouffe
> Where every actor treads on bloody ground;
>
> Terror of libertines, mad hope of Eremites,
> The sky! Black lid of the great pot
> Where boils, invisible and vast, all humanity.[157]

The alchemical pot. I'm not sure whether Baudelaire grasped the notion of transformation, but he was certainly gripped by the process itself.

In verse 10, the king speaks:

> Yet to my Griefe I know, unless I feed
> On the Specifics I so sorely need
> I cannot Generate: to my Amaze
> The End draws near for me, Ancient of Daies.

Here again the text equates the king with God: he calls himself the "Ancient of Daies," a synonym for God in chapter 7 of the Book of Daniel.

It is at this point (paragraph 374) that Jung picks up this equation in his commentary and discusses the astonishing fact that the alchemists in their laboratories, probably only half consciously, were working on the transformation of God. Ripley himself was even a churchman—he was a canon of a cathedral. As Jung indicates, surely the one side of him didn't know what the other side was doing when he was writing this alchemical poem.

---

[157] Author's translation in consultation with Joanna Richardson, trans., *Baudelaire: Selected Poems.*

The king announces in these verses that he needs to feed on a certain specific kind of food. This is a reference to the alchemical process called cibatio, or feeding: the transformation going on in the vessel must be fed to keep it going. Psychologically, it means the transformation going on in the unconscious must be nourished by libido poured into it from the ego.

This archetypal idea—that an objective process outside of human existence must be fed by human efforts—has been absolutely fundamental to the primitive mentality. The major aspect of the whole phenomenon of sacrifice to the gods is based on the idea that the gods require human sacrifice in order to stay alive.

We have an amazing example of this archetypal reality in the ancient Aztecs who thought that the sun would go out unless it was constantly fed by human sacrifice. They had vast orgies in which the hearts of victims were torn out and offered as food to the sun god. This is all part of the archetypal image of feeding the objective process so that it can develop, and the alchemical notion of cibatio is another variation of that same archetypal theme.

Verses 11 and 12, the sick king still talking:

> Utterly perish'd is the Flower of Youth,
> Through all my Veines there courses naught but Death.
> Marvelling I heard Christ's voice, that from above
> I'le be Reborne, I know not by what Love.
>
> Else I God's Kingdom cannot enter in:
> And therefore, that I may be Borne agen,
> I'le Humbled be into my Mother's Breast,
> Dissolve to my First Matter, and there rest.

Now, if there were any rationalists studying this material we would have lost them long ago—they'd be driven wild by such inconsistencies as these stanzas describe. We've already identified the barren king with God, so how then can God state that he needs to be reborn in order to enter into God's kingdom?—which is what he says here. If he's God, why doesn't he just walk right in?

The answer is that God and the prima materia are composed of opposites, and what's symbolized here as "God's Kingdom" is a potential transformed state which the current manifestation of God in this text has not yet reached.

"Marvelling I heard Christ's voice, that from above I'le be Reborne, I know not by what Love." These lines allude specifically to Christ's opus of the transformation of God, in which he transformed the ambivalent Yahweh into a benevolent, loving father by splitting off his dark side, Satan.

Continuing, the poem says that in order to proceed with the process the king must submit to solutio: "I'le Humbled be into my Mother's Breast, Dissolve to my First Matter, and there rest." That solutio—a reversion to his "first matter"—amounts to a dissolution of the conscious standpoint that has become sterile and empty. This would correspond, psychologically, to the analytic lysis or dissolution of the ego's barren standpoint. The very word analysis has at its root "lysis" which means loosening, solutio, a dissolution, a breaking up into component parts, and that's what the king then announces he's going to do—he's going to submit himself to lysis.

We hear no more from the king. Now, because the king has dissolved, an objective voice in the poem announces what's happening. Verse 13:

> Hereto the Mother Animates the King,
> Hasts his Conception, and does forthwith bring
> Him closely hidden underneath her Traine,
> Till, from herselfe, she'd made him Flesh againe.

This is a kind of announcement from on high as to what's going on: it announces that the king has crawled back into the womb. He's committed incest; he's broken the most august taboo of consciousness, the taboo against returning to one's source.

Incest is a treason against all first-half-of-life values. Incest makes one a traitor to the proud autonomy of the ego. I think the dread of incest is the root source of all guilty reflections concerning solitude, self-centeredness, preoccupations with fantasies, with dreams and with the inner life. You know for many, all such self-centered, introspective occupations have a morbid quality attached to them. And now the barren king has done it, he's done it with a vengeance, he's crawled all the way back into the womb.

This is what happens in every depth analysis. The ego submits itself to an intimate relationship with its maternal origins, namely with the unconscious. It submits itself to incest and in so doing reverses all the rules and standards that the ego, in the first half of life, has been taught. It exposes itself to a very real danger—things are not tabooed without very good reason. The danger, of course, is that if you crawl back into the womb you may not get out again.

In verses 14 and 15, the objective voice is speaking:

> 'Twas wonderfull to see with what a Grace
> This Naturall Union made at one Imbrace
> Did looke; and by a Bond both Sexes knitt,
> Like to a Hille and Aire surrounding it.

> The Mother unto her Chast Chamber goes,
> Where in a Bed of Honour she bestowes
> Her weary'd selfe, 'twixt Sheets as white as Snow
> And there makes Signes of her approaching Woe.

The king has disappeared and the subject of the narrative shifts to the queen, the Queen Mother. That would mean that now the central matter is the gestation process in the unconscious. The ego is eclipsed and the autonomous archetypal process has taken over.

Here again we have an allusion to the double nature of the opus: on the one hand, it's a chemical procedure in the laboratory; on the other hand, it corresponds to the greater world, to the macrocosm, which is alluded to by the unusual image of a hill and its surrounding air. This is all taking place inside the flask, and it's also as though the earth itself is participating in the event: hill and air are uniting—earth and heaven are joining.

Once more, we have the implicit psychological idea that when one works on transforming one's own inner prima materia, one simultaneously contributes to a similar transformation of the collective psyche and of the world as a whole.

Verse 16:

> Ranke Poison issuing from the Dying Man
> Made her pure Orient face look foule and wan:
> Hence she commands all Strangers to be gone,
> Seals upp her Chamber doore, and lyes Alone.

This refers to the mortificatio or putrefactio stage of the process; but the king's return to the womb is at the same time both a death and a conception or fertilization. The dissolution of the old king—he's digested, so to speak, in the body of the queen—is simultaneously the gestation of the new king. It's something like what happens with the formation of a chrysalis as the caterpillar undergoes dissolution and is reconstituted as a butterfly.

This idea of sowing a seed that dies and then rejuvenates in another form is a basic image in alchemy. One major analogy is a passage in the Gospel of John:

> Truly, truly, I say to you, unless a grain of wheat falls into the earth and dies, it remains alone; but if it dies, it bears much fruit. He who loves his life loses it, and he who hates his life in this world will keep it for eternal life.[158]

The barren king's return to the womb corresponds to sowing himself in the earth as a seed so that, as the seed germinates, he'll grow up reborn. These verses tell us that this process of dissolution and gestation throw the queen into a state of profound introversion: "Hence she commands all Strangers to be gone, seals upp her Chamber doore, and lyes Alone." The sealing of the chamber refers to the sealing of the alchemical flask during the crucial transformation so that there's no loss by leakage.

Psychologically, this would refer to the intense internal direction of libido during a major psychic gestation. At such a time the inner process claims all one's available energy in order to complete itself. It can be quite crucial that at such times no leakage occur. There's often considerable urge to leak in order to relieve oneself of the tension—pressure builds up at such times. And although in ordinary circumstances there is no harm in releasing such pressure by going to a movie or

---

[158] John 12: 24-25, Revised Standard Version.

calling a friend, there are certain times when leakages of that sort violate the process.

As far as the analytic process itself is concerned, I think it should be a strict rule that applies consistently to both analyst and analysand that neither talk with anybody else about what goes on in the analytic hour. We're all familiar, of course, with the notion of professional confidence, and it's regularly assumed that the analyst should not talk to anybody else about his or her patients. It's not so generally realized that the same thing should also apply to the patient.

Because it's difficult to do what clearly needs to be done in a given situation, it is not uncommon for the patient to say to his or her partner, "My analyst said thus and so." That's terrible leakage. It is not permissible. One must never do anything until one is prepared to do it on one's own initiative and take responsibility for it. The fact that the analyst brought it up as a suggestion is irrelevant. The analyst isn't going to take responsibility for it—*you* have to live it. This sometimes has to be made very explicit because people don't always know instinctively that professional confidence works both ways, and the analysis really will not reach any depth if that sort of leakage takes place. So the queen "seals upp her Chamber doore, and lyes Alone."

Verse 17:

> Meanwhile she of the Peacocks Flesh did Eate
> And Dranke the Greene-Lyons Blood with that fine Meate,
> Which Mercurie, bearing the Dart of Passion,
> Brought in a Golden Cupp of Babilon.

This stanza evokes Jung's most profuse interpretive commentary—sixteen pages in tonight's assignment, and that's just for the first two lines. What is the basic idea of those first two lines that is so provocative?

The basic idea is that the queen, sealed up in her chamber, ate peacock's flesh and drank green lion's blood. That's the image, that's her "pregnancy diet," as Jung puts it, and that's what he talks about at such length. So there are really just two images here: peacock's flesh and green lion's blood.

Now what is peacock's flesh? Jung amplifies this quite richly. Let me summarize his amplifications this way:

Peacock's flesh is the *omnes colores*, the "all-colors" of the display of the peacock's tail, *cauda pavonis*.

It's incorruptible flesh—according to legend it's flesh that won't rot—so it corresponds to the *cibus immortalis*, the immortal food.[159]

The peacock is an image of resurrection and sunrise.

Peacock's flesh is an antidote for poison.

The peacock was an attribute of Juno.

---

[159] *Cibus immortalis* is a synonym for the Host in the Eucharist.

I would add to this list one more, to bring it home to personal psychology: the peacock is also an emblem of pride and vanity.

So the various associations that come up in the amplifications indicate that the peacock is a symbol of the Self, but pride and vanity are symptomatic of the ego's identification with the Self. Thus, to eat peacock's flesh means to achieve a conscious relation to the Self, and that involves, as part of the process, a dissolution of the ego's identification with the Self: if we're going to eat peacock's flesh, we're obliged to assimilate our pride and our vanity.

Now I should immediately add that the assimilation does not mean becoming humble. That is not what it means. Pride and humility are just a pair of opposites. To assimilate pride means to locate the source of pride in the Self rather than in the ego, and the same thing applies to the assimilation of the power motive. The assimilation of the power motive does not mean to become meek and mild and without effective power, not at all. It means, rather, to locate the source of one's power in the Self rather than in the ego, so that power is experienced as the voice of God, or the Self, rather than as the petty urge to dominate.

One aspect of peacock symbolism is the *omnes colores* of the peacock's tail. This leads Jung into a discussion of color symbolism, and one of his amplifications is the association of the four colors with the four temperaments.

In antiquity they distinguished four different types of psychology: the sanguine, the phlegmatic, the melancholic and the choleric. The idea was that everyone had an excess of one particular humor: the sanguine had too much blood; the phlegmatic had too much phlegm; the melancholic had too much black bile; and the choleric had too much yellow bile. So the four colors there were red, white, black and yellow.

The four colors that seem most often to emerge in modern material are red, blue, green and yellow, and, if you don't take it too rigidly, those colors can be related to the four functions in Jung's model of typology.[160]

In an approximate way, blue can be related to thinking, red to feeling, green to sensation, and yellow to intuition. This symbolism is most likely to be valid when, in dreams, the colors are associated with definite fourfold images of some kind. So the peacock's tail, which makes a display of all the colors, represents the sort of image that comes up when there is the possibility of assimilating all four functions. The whole range of colors becomes at least potentially available.

---

[160] See "General Description of the Types," *Psychological Types,* CW 6, pars. 556ff. For a summary and commentary, see Daryl Sharp, *Personality Types: Jung's Model of Typology.*

16
Paragraphs 405 to 463

Ripley's *Cantilena* **(continued)**

We ended last time in the middle of verse 17, which describes what the queen did alone in her sealed chamber. The text tells us:

> Meanwhile she of the Peacocks Flesh did Eate
> And Dranke the Greene-Lyons Blood, with that fine Meate,
> Which Mercurie, bearing the Dart of Passion,
> Brought in a Golden Cupp of Babilon.

We talked about the first line—what it means to eat peacock's flesh; now let's look at the second—what it means to drink "the Greene-Lyons Blood."

In antiquity, blood was always considered to be the vital life essence of the organism, so we can consider the blood of the lion to be the extracted essence of the lion. We might ask why a *green* lion? Jung points out in paragraph 405 that there were two kinds of lions in alchemy: a red lion and a green lion.

Green and red are the colors of the two vital life principles, chlorophyll and hemoglobin respectively. Chlorophyll is the life principle of the plant world and hemoglobin is the life principle of the animal world. So I think what we're dealing with here is an assimilation of the two kinds of vital life essence.

Let me remind you that what we are talking about isn't just abstract stuff; this is day-to-day material, tools for your analytic tool kit. Lions come up not at all infrequently in modern dreams, so there's nothing abstract or remote about these remarks. Perhaps I don't need to tell you that, but it doesn't hurt.

We've noticed, in earlier material, that the lion is symbolically associated with the sun; it's the theriomorphic aspect of Sol (paragraphs 169, 173). Another way of putting it is that it's the animal version of royalty. Jung has a marvelous passage on this subject in paragraph 405:

> [The lion] represents the king in his theriomorphic form, that is, as he appears in his unconscious state. The animal form emphasizes that the king is overpowered or overlaid by his animal side and consequently expresses himself only in animal re-actions, which are nothing other than emotions.[161] Emotionality in the sense of uncontrollable affects is essentially bestial, for which reason people in this state can be approached only with the circumspection proper to the jungle, or else with the methods of the animal-trainer.

---

[161] Our translation reads "nothing but emotions," but the German uses the less reductive "nothing other than emotions."

Then he adds a footnote, and this is vital information for analytic work because we never know when we're going to stumble over bestial affects from our patients, not to mention from ourselves:

> Contact with wild nature, whether it be man, animal, jungle or swollen river, requires tact, foresight, and politeness. Rhinoceroses and buffaloes do not like being surprised.

To drink the green lion's blood, then, would mean to assimilate, to become consciously aware of the primitive, affective manifestations of the Self and thus to submit them to transformation. This drinking of the green lion's blood is taking place during a gestation process, you remember; it's part of the gestation—the transformation—of the reborn king.

In talking about lion symbolism, Jung refers to another text as a parallel to the *Cantilena,* the so-called "lion hunt" of King Marchos. It's outline is as follows—Jung doesn't present it quite this systematically, but here's how I would put it together:

King Marchos prepares a trap to catch a lion, a pit containing as bait a magical sweet-smelling stone. The lion, attracted by this sweet smell, falls into the trap and then is swallowed by the stone, so the stone is also an animal creature. The lion is said to have fallen in love with this stone, which is also a woman—again, the images overlap. The trap is covered by a glass roof, and when the lion falls through it he falls into what is called a bridal chamber—this amounts to his falling into the alchemical vessel. It turns out that this chamber has in it a bed of coals on which the woman-stone lies. "This stone swallows the lion 'so that nothing more of him was to be seen' " (paragraph 409). The text also speaks of this process as the stepping of the pious mother over the body of her son (paragraph 386). In other words, the text speaks of incest as one image of what's going on in this strange event. Jung says about this allegory, in paragraph 410:

> As the king is represented by his animal [the lion] and his mother by the magic stone, the royal incest can take place as though it were happening somewhere "outside," in quite another sphere than the personal world of the king and his mother.

He then proceeds to discuss this theme of the "outsideness" of the process, and suggests that when one reaches the realm of incest fantasies in the psyche it should not be taken personally because, when one reaches that realm:

> [It is] as though one were entering a strange territory, a region of the psyche to which one feels no longer related, let alone identical with it; and whoever has strayed into that territory, either out of negligence or by mistake, feels outside himself and a stranger in his own house. I think one should take cognizance of these facts and not attribute to our personal psyche everything that appears as a psychic content.

These remarks strike me as methodologically very important in the analytic process. They refer to the realization that what goes on when we're dealing with incest imagery, when we're dealing with this level of symbolism, is a process pertaining to the objective psyche, not to the personal psyche. Now the ego, of course, is needed as the operator, as a conscious presence to witness what's going on—witnessing is a vital part of the procedure. But the process itself is taking place *outside* the ego, in the glass bridal chamber so to speak, and it's crucial that an awareness of this fact be maintained.

You see the great danger in any kind of depth psychological work is that the ego will fall into an identification with the activated contents of the objective psyche. The immediate effect is what we call inflation.

Inflation has two chief features, depending on whether it is positive or negative. If it's a positive inflation then one takes on a grandiose attitude. If it's a negative inflation, one takes on an attitude that I feel requires the coinage of a new word, so I've coined "guiltiose," as a parallel to grandiose. It's a crude kind of coinage but nevertheless it makes its point, because one of the major dangers of the ego's identifying with this objective material is that the ego then takes responsibility for it, either positively—which makes one grand—or negatively, which lays on the ego a burden of transpersonal guilt that is more than an individual can carry. That is why I think Jung's remarks about the "outsideness" of the process are so very important.

That takes us then to the next phrase of verse 17:

> Which Mercurie, bearing the Dart of Passion,
> Brought in a Golden Cupp of Babilon.

So this matter to be assimilated, peacock's flesh and lion's blood, is brought in the guise of Cupid and his arrows— "Mercurie, bearing the Dart of Passion." The dart of passion, the *telum passionis,* is the arrow or lance that is characteristically carried by Cupid. This means that, like St. Sebastian,[162] anyone involved in this process is obliged to be open to this *telum passionis*—willing to experience being pierced and wounded by the unconscious.

Further, we're told that the material is brought in a "Golden Cupp of Babilon." As Jung points out in paragraph 414, this refers to a particular image in the first few verses of Revelation 17 which I'll read to you. This is part of the grand and terrible vision of the Apocalypse:

> And there came one of the seven angels which had the seven vials, and talked with me, saying unto me, Come hither; I will shew unto thee the judgment of the great whore that sitteth upon many waters:

---

[162] A Christian martyr of the late third century. He was supposedly shot with arrows by Diocletian (fig. 16-1), and his martyrdom was a favorite subject in Renaissance painting. See *Oxford Dictionary of Saints,* pp. 380f.

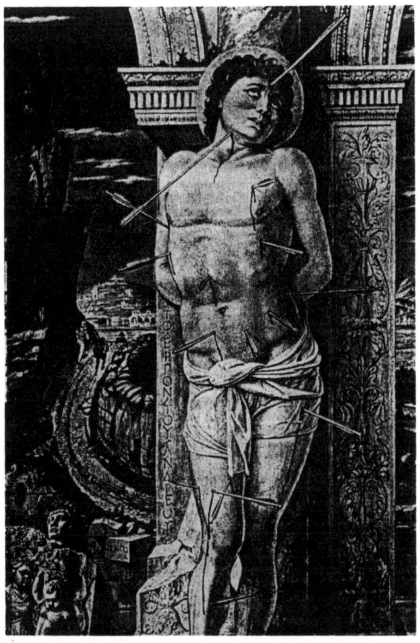

Figure 16-1. St. Sebastian pierced by arrows.

With whom the kings of the earth have committed fornication, and the inhabitants of the earth have been made drunk with the wine of her fornication.

So he carried me away in the spirit into the wilderness: and I saw a woman sit upon a scarlet coloured beast, full of names of blasphemy, having seven heads and ten horns.

And the woman was arrayed in purple and scarlet colour, and decked with gold and precious stones and pearls, having a golden cup in her hand full of abominations and filthiness of her fornication:

And upon her forehead was a name written, MYSTERY, BABYLON THE GREAT, THE MOTHER OF HARLOTS AND ABOMINATIONS OF THE EARTH.[163]

This is the famous "Whore of Babylon," historically a very well-known image of the Western psyche. It is an image of the Great Mother in her negative aspect, the matriarchal psyche looked at from its most negative side. But even though the author of the vision was expressing the most profound disgust for this negative aspect, yet it carries the image of supreme value, the golden cup, which is synonymous, symbolically, with the Holy Grail.

The golden cup brings to mind a couple of Biblical parallels. In Ecclesiastes there is reference to a golden bowl:

Remember also thy Creator . . . before the evil days come. . . . Before the silver cord is loosed, or the golden bowl is broken, or the pitcher is broken at the fountain.[164]

Here the golden bowl would correspond to the vessel of human consciousness, the ego, which is presumed to be broken at death.

We get another angle in Zechariah's vision of the candlestick of God:

[The angel] said unto me, What seest thou? And I said, I have looked, and behold a candlestick all of gold, with a bowl upon the top of it, and his seven lamps thereon.[165]

"His" refers to God, so here's another aspect of the symbolism of the golden bowl: it belongs to the lampstand of God.

I'm hoping someday we'll have available a psychological Bible which will include references of this sort. We have reference Bibles now but the type of references are all determined by theological presuppositions. We need a Bible with psychological cross-references, so when I read about the golden cup containing the abominations in Revelation, a note in the margin will say, "See reference in Zechariah to the golden bowl that is God's." But for the present we don't have such a Bible and we have to make our own.

---

[163] Rev. 17: 1-5, Authorized Version.

[164] Eccles. 12: 1 and 6, Revised Standard Version.

[165] Zech. 4: 2, Authorized Version.

Look what we come to from these amplifications: the golden cup of Babylon in Revelation contains the filthy abominations, but it's symbolic correspondence to the Holy Grail leads to quite a different content because the Holy Grail was the container of Christ's blood. And the golden bowl of the ego in Ecclesiastes is yet another angle, as is the golden bowl of God's lampstand in Zechariah. These are all varying manifestations of the same archetypal image seen from different standpoints and in different contexts.

The image of a remarkable container is an image that shows up every now and then in modern dreams. It's not always a golden bowl—it might be a dish or a cup or any particularly beautiful vessel. When such an image comes up it may refer to positive contents or to negative contents; either way, if you are familiar with the totality of the symbolism you will be able to round out the references to the dream image and see it in its full perspective.

Speaking of modern versions of this archetype, Henry James wrote a novel, *The Golden Bowl,* which concerns a woman's incestuous relationship with her father—unconsciously incestuous, James never spelled out any overt incest—and only when the golden bowl is broken is she able to separate psychologically from her father and have a more satisfactory relationship with her husband.

Verse 18:

> Thus great with Child, nine months she languishèd
> And Bath'd her with the Teares which she had shed
> For his sweet sake, who from her should be Pluckt
> Full-gorg'd with Milke which now the Greene-Lyon suckt.

She's crying. Now why would she be crying? I think that refers to the sad aspect, the grief, of giving birth—she's in the process of losing the contained child. It's the basic image of Mater Dolorosa. The deep tragedy of motherhood is that the mother has to give up possession of the child that has grown within. Part of the contents of the golden cup from which she's obliged to drink, then, will be the bitterness and pain of that sacrifice. This is the theme of much medieval art (see figure 16-2).

Verse 19:

> Her Skin in divers Colours did appeare,
> Now Black, then Greene, annon 'twas Red and Cleare.
> Oft-times she would sit upright in her Bed,
> And then again repose her Troubled Head.

Jung says about this, in paragraph 430:

> This display of colours . . . means that during the assimilation of the unconscious the personality passes through many transformations, which show it in different lights and are followed by ever-changing moods. These changes presage the coming birth.

Figure 16-2. Pietà, c. 1330.

Verse 20:

> Thrice Fifty Nights she lay in Grievous Plight,
> As many Daies in Mourning sate upright.
> The King Revivèd was in Thirty more,
> His Birth was Fragrant as the Prim-Rose Flower.

The fragrant odor, as Jung points out in paragraph 432, refers to the sweet smell of the Holy Ghost who is responsible for the regeneration process.[166] And we could consider that the mention of the primrose—"His Birth was Fragrant as the

---

[166] "In alchemy the Holy Ghost and Sapientia are more or less identical; hence the smell of flowers attests that the rebirth of the king is a gift of the Holy Ghost or of Sapientia, thanks to whom the regeneration process could take place."

Prim-Rose Flower"—is an allusion to the rejuvenation of Eros.[167] You remember Shakespeare's reference to "the primrose path of dalliance."[168] This alludes to desirousness—Eros in its elemental level—but now with the reborn king it has undergone regeneration, and I would venture to say that the rebirth of Eros leads from desirousness to object love.

In verses 23 and 24 we are reminded once again that this really is an alchemical operation:

> A burning Stove was plac'd beneath her Bed,
> And on the same another Flourishèd:
> Trimm'd up with Art, and very Temperate,
> Lest her fine Limbes should freeze for lack of Heate.

> Her Chamber doore was Lock'd and Bolted fast,
> Admitting none to Vex her, first or last;
> The Furnace-mouth was likewise Fasten'd so
> That hence no Vaporous Matter forth could go.

The queen's bed is the alchemical vessel that is being heated to promote the process, and it's a temperate heat—an incubating heat—which will promote the hatching of the egg.

This whole question of heat and the proper degree of heat is an important one for the analytic process. You know, the alchemists were very concerned that excessive heat not be used in the midst of the opus because it can destroy. Of course if there's not enough heat nothing happens. That would correspond to the affective temperature required to keep the analytic process moving, and there's no exact rule about that—it varies from one individual and from one occasion to another. But it's an issue that the analyst has to keep in mind because, although one does not have ultimate control over the process, one can throw one's weight one way or the other. Often one has to ask "Well now, what's called for?" when a particularly intense affect comes up; "Is this heat excessive and should I do what I can to alleviate and ameliorate it?" Or in certain other cases, "Is it necessary to turn up the thermostat so that the issue gets more urgent?"—because if a certain degree of urgency does not develop, nothing much happens.

Verse 25:

> And when the Child's Limbs there had putrefy'd,
> The Foulness of the Flesh was laid aside,
> Making her fair as Luna, when anon
> She coils towards the Splendour of the Sun.

---

[167] It is worth noting here that in his discussion of the Green Lion in paragraph 408 Jung points out that "the lion has among other things an unmistakable erotic aspect."
[168] *Hamlet,* act 1, scene 3.

Jung considers this is a clumsy verse which attempts to express the miraculous moment of transformation, analogous to the moment in the Mass when the bread and wine are transformed into the body and blood of Christ (paragraphs 434-435). At this moment the process takes a quantum leap from one level of manifestation to another: from the fleshly, personal, material dimension to the transpersonal, archetypal dimension. There's a leap from matters of flesh to matters of Sun and Moon—a whole different level. And the coniunctio of mother and son turns into a totally different image, the image of Luna entwining herself around the Sun.

Psychologically, at this point the individual would be freed from the humiliation and darkness of a petty, conflicted condition—the state of putrefaction. When freed from that state, one can see oneself as part of the universal, archetypal drama of continuing creation at the celestial level, the Sun and Moon level—under the aspect of eternity, so to speak. And this insight is like the immortal food, the *cibus immortalis*. That's what the partakers of the Mass are receiving symbolically. That ritual, in a literal form, is feeding them the food of immortality; it's a kind of concretistic substitute for the psychological insight born out of the process represented by this alchemical story.

Verses 26 and 27:

> Her time being come, the Child Conceiv'd before
> Issues re-borne out of her Wombe once more;
> And thereupon resumes a Kingly State,
> Possessing fully Heaven's Propitious Fate.
>
> The Mother's Bed which erstwhile was a Square
> Is shortly after made Orbicular;
> And everywhere the Cover, likewise Round
> With Luna's Lustre brightly did abound.

We're told here that at the moment of rebirth, when the king emerges out of the womb of the Queen Mother, the square bed the mother was lying on turns round or spherical. So the central image here is the circling of the square, or squaring of the circle, which has been a major preoccupation of man ever since antiquity: how to devise an arithmetic or geometric process whereby one could create a square of the same area as a given circle.

I understand that preoccupation to be an innate archetypal yearning for individuation. We might give a geometrical formula for the individuation process this way: it starts as a circle, which must be turned into a square, which must then be transformed again into a circle. Original circle, square, final circle:

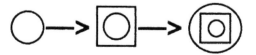

The first circle would represent the condition of initial unconscious unity that we start with when we're born. It's the state of unity in which animals live their whole existence. Then, in the course of ego development, the gradual and conscious discrimination of the four functions turns the initial circle of unconscious wholeness into a square.

According to ancient Chinese thinking, earth is a square and heaven is a circle. This would mean that squaring is a process of ego development insofar as earth, in relation to heaven, represents the ego. But, in the state of squareness, the four sides are not yet in a state of harmony and unity with each other. Harmonizing and unifying can only be achieved by a further circling of the square. First the original circle must be squared and then the achieved square must be circled in order to achieve wholeness on a conscious level.

I think it is symbolically significant that, when we try to establish a mathematical relationship between a curved line and a straight line, we're led to the whole problem of how we can determine the circumference of a circle if we know its diameter. The diameter of a circle is a straight line that determines the size of that circle, but the relationship between the length of the diameter and the circumference of that circle is governed by the factor of pi, an irrational number, which means that it has no exact numerical value.

What we have here, I think, is an image of the snaky coilings of Luna around the Sun. You see, the curved line and the straight line cannot be rationally squared up with each other because they belong to two different realms. They can be approximated, so that for all practical purposes it can be solved, but you cannot get the ideal geometrical solution because of that irrational factor.

Verse 28:

> Thus from a Square, the Bed a Globe is made,
> And Purest Whiteness from the Blackest Shade;
> While from the Bed the Ruddy Son doth spring
> To grasp the Joyful Sceptre of a King.

Here are the three color stages of the coniunctio: the *nigredo,* the *albedo* and the *rubedo;* and out of this sequential process the spherical *filius* is born, the "Ruddy Son." The Ruddy Son is symbolically equivalent to the globe, the rotundum that's born out of the square bed.

Verse 29:

> Hence God unlock'd the Gates of Paradise,
> Rais'd him like Luna to th'Imperiall Place,
> Sublim'd him to the Heavens, and that being done,
> Crown'd him in Glory, aequall with the Sun.

This reference to unlocking the gates of Paradise can be understood again in terms of the circle-square-circle sequence. Paradise is the first circle, the state of original wholeness. The full development of the ego as an earthly material manifestation would be the square, but as Jung says in paragraph 439, in the square the elements are still separate and hostile to one another.[169] So with the second circle, the four elements are unified into the quintessence and the state of original wholeness returns on a conscious level.

This would correspond to a conscious return to Paradise. It's like the Messianic kingdom in which, according to Jewish legend, the Garden of Eden manifests itself again and grapes from the Garden of Eden are served at the Messianic banquet.[170] So with the birth of the regenerated new king, the gates of Paradise are unlocked too.

Verse 30:

> Four Elements, Brave Armes, and Polish'd well
> God gave him, in the midst whereof did dwell
> The Crownèd Maid, ordainèd for to be
> In the Fifth Circle of the Mysterie.

The "Four Elements" would correspond to the four sides of the square I've been talking about, and they are now united in the fifth essence, the quintessence, which is the "Fifth Circle." This fifth circle is personified as the "Crownèd Maid" and she's Luna, or she's the representation of the coronation of the Virgin Mary— that's another "Crownèd Maid." In other words, she's the sublimated transformation of the materiality principle.[171]

Verse 31:

> With all delicious Unguent flowèd she
> When Purg'd from Bloody Menstruosity:
> On every side her Count'nance Brightly shone,
> She being Adorn'd with every Precious Stone.

The phrase, "with all delicious Unguent flowèd she," recalls the earlier verse when the barren king exclaims, "No Tincture from my Body yet can flow" (paragraph 372), but now that's all changed because the vital life juices are flowing. That's made even more explicit in the next two stanzas.

> A Lyon Greene did in her Lapp reside
> (The which an Eagle fed), and from his side
> The Blood gush'd out: The Virgin drunck it upp,
> While Mercuries Hand did th'Office of a Cupp.

---

[169] See also Jung's commentary in *Psychology and Alchemy,* CW 12, pars. 165ff.

[170] "In that hour the Holy One, blessed be He, will set table and . . . will bring them wine that was preserved in its grapes since the six days of creation." (Raphael Patai, *The Messiah Texts,* pp. 238ff; see also Edinger, *Bible and the Psyche,* p. 159)

[171] For a full discussion, see Edinger, *Transformation of the God-Image,* pp. 124ff.

> The wondrous Milk she hasten'd from her Breast,
> Bestow'd it frankly on the Hungry Beast,
> And with a Sponge his Furry Face she dry'd
> Which her own Milk had often Madefy'd [moistened or wettened].

Now here we have a bizarre contamination of alchemical and religious images, a contamination which, as Jung points out, is characteristic of unconscious processes. Since the unconscious is part of nature, it is totally indifferent to the distinctions consciousness makes. You see, this is the difference between the curved line and the straight line. This is what happens when you start trying to turn a square into a circle—you get this kind of juxtaposition of images that jar one's conscious, discriminated sensibilities.

Two images are combined: the Pietà—the dead Christ on the lap of the Virgin Mary (the Madonna and Child), and the alchemical image of the double uro-boros where two creatures are mutually feeding off one another. Altogether, it's an image of the coniunctio, a kind of bizarre image of the coniunctio as a dynamic double cibatio, a double feeding process. The queen drinks up the lion's blood that's gushing out of his side, and the lion nurses at the breast of the queen. This, in the utterly unself-conscious language of nature, is an image of the coniunctio of Sol and Luna, of Yang and Yin, of the masculine and the feminine principles, united and mutually nourishing each other. And this image is part of the transformation process which created the *filius*—the lapis—the so-called "united double nature."

Jung makes some very interesting remarks in his commentary on these verses; he talks about the phenomenon of symbolic overlapping, contamination and condensation of imagery (paragraphs 454ff). As an example, he brings in the *Hexastichon* of Sebastian Brant, two pictures of which he reproduces (figures 16-3, 16-4). This condensation and overlapping of images from totally different sources is an expression of an assimilation phenomenon. The unconscious connects images that consciousness would keep apart, and it connects them because of the innate archetypal similarity of the images—they belong together psychically even though consciousness has separated them. By making these interconnections the unconscious is, in effect, urging the ego to achieve a larger synthesis. We can see all of alchemy, really, as such an assimilation phenomenon—it uses ecclesiastical, Biblical and mythological imagery to describe chemical laboratory procedures. Things of very different provenance are contaminated with one another, intermixed and overlapped.

Perhaps the most outstanding example of this phenomenon is *Aurora Consurgens,* which I would remind you is the third part of *Mysterium Coniunctionis*. It's just incredible how that text applies a continuous stream of Biblical images to the alchemical process. It's an extreme example of the assimilation phenomenon which is such a major feature of alchemy. This is what makes alchemy so

Figure 16-3. "Third Picture of John."   Figure 16-4. "Second Picture of Luke."

important for depth psychology. It was the first sizable effort of the Western psyche to pry the archetypal images out of their theological matrix, out of their creedal context where they were set like concrete, and make them available for individual psychological experience. Depth psychology is a later and fuller effort in the same direction, but I don't think depth psychology could have evolved so far without the earlier efforts of alchemy. That is why Jung's analysis of alchemy is so important. Alchemy set the example, gave the initial evidence and impetus to the process of disengaging the psychic images from their original traditional context. This is all part of the assimilation phenomenon.

We discover this in our patients all the time. Dreams are brought that juxtapose traditionally sacred imagery with very nonsacred references. Those of you who attended my lectures on a case history presented in pictures will remember the painting of Christ discovered in a dark place in a problematic situation.[172] That image is an extreme example of what I'm talking about—it's the assimilation of two vastly different things that have been brought together, and psychologically *validly* brought together. The impetus for the painting was the saying of Christ concerning "the least of these my brethren":

---

[172] See Edinger, *The Living Psyche: A Jungian Analysis in Pictures,* p. 29.

For I was hungry and you gave me food; I was thirsty and you gave me drink; I was a stranger and you made me welcome; naked and you clothed me, sick and you visited me, in prison and you came to see me. . . . I tell you solemnly, insofar as you did this to one of the least of these brethren of mine, you did it to me.[173]

The patient took seriously the fact that Christ is to be found among "the least of these my brethern," and painted a picture to express that fact.

I consider it very important to understand how the assimilation phenomenon operates; you see, it is part of the process of turning the square into a circle.

Verses 34 and 35:

Upon her Head a Diadem she did weare,
With fiery Feet sh'Advanced into the Aire;
And glittering Bravely in her Golden Robes
She took her Place amidst the Starry Globes.

The Dark Clouds being Dispers'd, so sate she there,
And woven to a Network in her haire
Were Planets, Times, and Signes, the while the King
With his Glad Eyes was her Beleagering.

So here we have this magnificent image of the cosmic woman (figure 16-5). It reminds me of another image from Revelation:

And there appeared a great wonder in heaven; a woman clothed with the sun, and the moon under her feet, and upon her head a crown of twelve stars: And she being with child, cried travailing in birth.[174]

In this image, and in that of the transformed queen, we have the same archetypal image as the Whore of Babylon, but it has undergone transformation.

The next two verses speak about the lapis, the Philosophers' Stone, in the form of the newborn king.

Thus He of all Triumphant Kings is Chiefe,
Of Bodies sicke the only Grand Reliefe:
Such a Reformist of Defects, that hee
Is worshipp'd both by King and Commonalty.

To Princes, Priests he yields an Ornament,
The Sicke and Needy Sort he doth content:
What man is there this Potion will not bless,
As banishes all thought of Neediness?

This is an image of wholeness that heals all defects because it's complete. When one's in touch with that state—with the Self—one has everything one wants. At the bottom of all yearning is the desire for the connection with one's

---

[173] Matt. 25: 35-40, Jerusalem Bible.
[174] Rev. 12: 1-2, Authorized Version.

wholeness, and when one has that connection one doesn't have to yearn anymore. Back in paragraph 192 Jung asks: "What is behind all this desirousness?" And he answers: "A thirsting for the eternal."

Thus when one contacts the Self, which has this eternal transpersonal dimension, one is released from possession by hungry desires; one has the *cibus immortalis,* the food of immortality.

Verse 38:

> Wherefore, O God, graunt us a Peece of This,
> That through the Encrease of its own Species
> The Art may be Renew'd, and Mortal Men
> Enjoy for aye its Thrice-Sweet Fruits. AMEN.

Here the reference to the "Encrease of its own Species" refers to the process of multiplicatio. The idea was that the Philosophers' Stone had the power to reproduce itself.[175]

Figure 16-5.
The cosmic woman.

---

[175] For further amplification, see Edinger, *Anatomy,* pp. 227f.

17
Paragraphs 464 to 497

The Dark Side of the King

Tonight's material is a continuation of the imagery of the king's transformation. We have a text from Trismosin's *Splendor solis* that takes up this theme and I am going to order all my remarks around it.

First, I want you to add one sentence to the text as Jung quotes it in paragraph 465. At the beginning, preceding "The old Philosophers . . . ," add this: "When heat operates upon a moist body then is blackness the first result. For that reason the old Philosophers . . ." That makes the text a little more comprehensible.

Now I'll start by quoting it.

> When heat operates upon a moist body, then is blackness the first result. For that reason the old Philosophers declared they saw a Fog rise, and pass over the whole face of the earth, they also saw the impetuosity of the Sea, and the streams over the face of the earth, and how these same became foul and stinking in the darkness. They further saw the king of the Earth sink, and heard him cry out with eager voice, "Whoever saves me shall live and reign with me for ever in my brightness on my royal throne," and Night enveloped all things. The day after, they saw over the King an apparent Morning Star, and the light of Day clear up the darkness, and bright Sunlight pierce through the clouds, with manifold coloured rays of brilliant brightness, and a sweet perfume from the earth, and the Sun shining clear. Herewith was completed the Time when the King of the Earth was released and renewed, well apparelled, and quite handsome, surprising with his beauty the Sun and Moon. He was crowned with three costly crowns, the one of Iron, the other of Silver, and the third of pure Gold. They saw in his right hand a Sceptre with Seven Stars, all of which gave a golden Splendour.

I'll remind you once again that this is a recipe for an alchemical process going on in a flask; and the formula or scheme of the transformation process as it is described here can be outlined as follows:

1. The Blackness.
2. "His One Day."
3. The Dawn.
4. The Apotheosis.

In the beginning is the blackness, which has the synonyms of fog and stench and darkness and drowning. That's followed by a special term that shows up more clearly in parallel texts that Jung refers to, namely a reference to the One Day, "His One Day." When that One Day arrives, it leads to number three, to the Dawn, in which sunlight, perfume and many colors break through. This is the phase of the emergence of the renewed king who appears first as a worm or a snake. That renewed king then experiences his apotheosis, takes on crowns, a scepter and seven stars—he takes on celestial attributes as part of his apotheosis.

This scheme is essentially the same sequence we saw in Ripley's *Cantilena* where the king crawled back into the queen's womb and then was reborn and experienced an apotheosis. Now I want to make a few remarks about each of the stages of this scheme.

1. The Blackness

The initial term, blackness, is described as fog, darkness and drowning, indicating that the first stage of this sequence is the *nigredo* and of course it corresponds to the dark, depressed, distressing aspect of the analytic process. I don't think it can be emphasized too much how important symbolic images of darkness are for dealing practically with the darkness of the unconscious. Certainly, the experience of darkness is very widespread in analytic work, and for that reason we're particularly in need of images to symbolize and represent it.

We need to know these images in all their variety because dark moods are healed by images of darkness, not by images of light. You need only consider how you feel in a depressed state when you encounter images of lightness and good cheer; that's not what you're interested in when you are in that condition. What you're interested in are symbolic images that represent the condition you're experiencing, because they bring objectivity; they give you your bearings so you know what you're dealing with. It is therefore healing, when in a dark mood, to encounter images of darkness.

Of course they have to be the right ones, and best of all are those that come from within. With that in mind, let's consider some of the amplifications to this image—to the stage of darkness, fog and drowning—remembering that the amplifications we talk about become part of our analytic tool kit, to be used when we encounter the darkness they refer to.

There are a couple of excellent examples of this image of the initial state of darkness in that remarkable work Marie-Louise von Franz has made available to us, *Aurora Consurgens,* which we spoke of last time. I hope you all have that on your shelf and even look at it now and then. In the first parable of *Aurora Consurgens* (in other words, the beginning of the recipe) this same initial state of darkness is described in these words:

> Beholding from afar off I saw a great cloud looming black over the whole earth, which had absorbed the earth and covered my soul, (because) the waters had come in even unto her, wherefore they were putrefied and corrupted before the face of the lower hell and the shadow of death, for a tempest hath overwhelmed me; then before me shall the Ethiopians fall down and my enemies shall lick my earth. Therefore there is no health in my flesh and all my bones are troubled before the face of my

iniquity. For this cause have I laboured night by night with crying, my jaws are become hoarse; who is the man that liveth, knowing and understanding, delivering my soul from the hand of hell? They that explain me shall have (eternal) life, and to him I will give to eat of the tree of life which is in paradise, and to sit with me on the throne of my kingdom.[176]

Now the question is, who's talking here? It's Sapientia Dei in her aspect as prima materia, in her black, original state, and she corresponds here to the king who's drowning in the darkness and calling for rescue. This particular quotation could be thought of as an image of a depressed mood calling out to the ego, saying: "If you can find the meaning of the darkness you're experiencing, if you can find the significant images within this black cloud, then there is a reward and the reward is eternal life and 'to him will I give to eat of the tree of life which is in paradise and to sit with me on the throne of my kingdom.' " In other words, the reward is a connection with eternity—the transpersonal—and when that connection has been made, one is then redeemed from one's banal, purely personal life.

Let me give you another example, from the seventh parable of *Aurora Consurgens;* the same personage is speaking but by this time she has identified herself more explicitly as the Shulamite in the Song of Songs. She says:

Be turned to me with all your heart and do not cast me aside because I am black and swarthy, because the sun hath changed my colour and the waters have covered my face and the earth hath been polluted and defiled in my works; for there was darkness over it, because I stick fast in the mire of the deep and my substance is not disclosed. Wherefore out of the depths have I cried, and from the abyss of the earth with my voice to all you that pass by the way. Attend and see me, if any shall find one like unto me, I will give into his hand the morning star.[177]

Here is the same idea, you see: a calling from out of the darkness and abyss, and if the ego attends to that call it will be given a connection with the morning star.

Jung refers to these passages and he also talks about their connection with the two major psalms that associate to the theme of the call from out of the depths. Those psalms are 69 and 130 and I'm going to read parts of them.

This is all an amplification of the first phase—the blackness—and I could conceive of doing this very same thing if a dream were brought to me that alluded to this image of someone calling for rescue out of the darkness, out of the depths. I might very well dispense with personal associations—it all depends on the patient, of course, but I could imagine saying: "Well, that's a familiar theme, let me give you some examples of it." And then for the next fifteen minutes I'd do just that. With the right patient that can be just the thing to do.

So, Psalm 69; I'll just read a few verses to give you the flavor of it:

---

[176] Marie-Louise von Franz, ed., *Aurora Consurgens,* pp. 57, 59.
[177] Ibid., p. 133.

Save me, O God; for the waters are come in unto my soul.

I sink in deep mire, where there is no standing: I am come into deep waters, where the floods overflow me.

I am weary of my crying: my throat is dried: mine eyes fail while I wait for my God.

They that hate me without a cause are more than the hairs of mine head . . . .

Deliver me out of the mire, and let me not sink: let me be delivered from them that hate me, and out of the deep waters.

Let not the waterflood overflow me, neither let the deep swallow me up, and let not the pit shut her mouth upon me. . . .

And hide not thy face from thy servant; for I am in trouble: hear me speedily.

Draw nigh unto my soul, and redeem it: deliver me because of mine enemies.[178]

The last verse gives us just a hint of the redemption motif. In this case the ego is asking to be redeemed, and in the alchemical passages the prima materia is asking to be redeemed by the ego. That's the kind of shift to and fro that frequently happens when the ego has dealings with the unconscious—they hand a particular aspect back and forth to each other.

Now the other one is Psalm 130, called *De Profundis*.

Out of the depths have I cried unto thee, O Lord.

Lord, hear my voice: let thine ears be attentive to the voice of my supplications.

. . .

I wait for the Lord, my soul doth wait, and in his word do I hope. . . .

Let Israel hope in the Lord: for with the Lord there is mercy, and with him is plenteous redemption.

And he shall redeem Israel from all his iniquities.[179]

Here again is the redemption theme, expressed in the same way as in Psalm 69.

Jung talks about how these psalms are connected to the alchemical texts, and in paragraph 469 makes a very important observation about the double implication of the theme of the depths; he quotes Epiphanius, who says that Psalm 130, "Out of the depths have I cried to thee, O Lord," means:

After the saints are so graced that the Holy Ghost dwells within them, he gives them, after having made his habitation in the saints, the gift to look into the deep things of God, that they may praise him from the depths.

Do you get that? The idea is that when one is calling out of the depths one is praising God from the depths because one has been given the capacity to look into the deep things of God.

So we have a double meaning, then, of the depths: on the one side it means to fall into the fog and the darkness and to be inundated by the waters; and at the

---

[178] Verses 1-4, 14-15, 17-18, Authorized Version.
[179] Verses 1-2, 5, 7-8, Authorized Version.

same time it means to be initiated into the deep things of God. Psychologically this means that an encounter with the unconscious brings first darkness, disorientation and distress; but if one persists in scrutinizing the experience, its consequence is to enlarge the personality and bring one closer to wholeness. That would be symbolized, then, by "the deep things of God."

This double aspect of the depths is expressed very nicely in a Jewish legend concerning Jonah that I am particularly fond of. According to this legend, after Jonah was swallowed by the whale, the whale gave Jonah a kind of excursion through all the profound mysteries of the universe. The whale showed Jonah where Korah and his followers sank into the earth.[180] He showed where the Jews crossed the Red Sea. He showed him the underwater entrance to Gehenna —to Hell; he showed Jonah the mouth of the river from which all the oceans flowed, and he showed him the river of youth at the gates of the Garden of Eden. So Jonah's sojourn in the belly of the whale became an initiation into the mysteries of the universe at the same time that it was experienced in its conventional form as a disaster—as being swallowed up and lost to the upper world.[181]

Now this double, contradictory aspect of the depths leads to a very important paragraph in *Mysterium,* paragraph 470. Jung uses this paradoxical double aspect of the depths to speak about the double aspect of the opposites in general. Here's what he says:

> These contradictory interpretations of the "depths" . . . come much closer together in alchemy, often so close that they seem to be nothing more than two different aspects of the same thing. It is natural that in alchemy the depths should mean now one and now the other, to the despair of all lovers of consistency. But the eternal images are far from consistent in meaning. It is characteristic of the alchemists that they never lost sight of this polarity, thereby compensating the world of dogma, which, in order to avoid ambiguity, emphasizes the one pole to the exclusion of the other. The tendency to separate the opposites as much as possible and to strive for singleness of meaning is absolutely necessary for clarity of consciousness, since discrimination is of its essence. But when the separation is carried so far that the complementary opposite is lost sight of, and the blackness of the whiteness, the evil of the good, the depth of the heights, and so on, is no longer seen, the result is one-sidedness, which is then compensated from the unconscious without our help. The counterbalancing is even done against our will, which in consequence must become more and more fanatical until it brings about a catastrophic enantiodromia. Wisdom never forgets that all things have two sides, and it would also know how to avoid such calamities if ever it had any power. But power is never found in the seat of wisdom; it is always the focus of mass interests and is therefore inevitably associated with the illimitable folly of the mass man.

---

180 Num. 26: 10.

181 See Joseph Gaer, *Lore of the Old Testament,* p. 271.

The attitude he's expressing here is particularly important in doing analytic work. We must always keep in mind that each image we're dealing with could almost invariably lend itself either to a positive or to a negative interpretation, and which it's to be at a given time depends on the conscious condition of the patient and on the total context. We need to preserve the flexibility to go either way depending on the indications.

2. "His One Day"

Okay, all of that concerning the first stage, blackness. Now number two is this term, "His One Day."

The texts indicate—and this shows up more clearly in the subsidiary texts Jung refers to in paragraph 472 and in footnote 288 than it does in the text we're considering from paragraph 465—that the transition from the state of darkness to the dawning sunlight is said to take place in "one day" or, according to another text, it takes place on "His One Day," which refers to God. The idea here is that the Philosophers' Stone is born on the day chosen by God, on His One Day. It corresponds to the idea of the *kairos,* the right time.

This symbolic image, His One Day, has three major associations as Jung develops it in paragraphs 475 and 476. First, it's the first day of Creation, Day One; second, it refers to Easter Day, the day of the resurrection of Christ; and the third major association is that it refers to the day of Yahweh, which is on the one hand the day of the Last Judgment and on the other hand the day of the coming of the Messiah.

The idea behind this archetypal image is that the timing for the crucial transformation is chosen by the Self and not by the ego, even though it can be very helpful for the ego to have prepared itself for it so that it doesn't come as a complete surprise.

I'll give you a personal example. It was no small thing for me to reach the decision that I would pull up all the roots I had established on the East Coast and move to California. Some months before that decision came into full conscious realization, in other words before I'd even considered such a preposterous idea, I had a dream. The dream was very simple, it had just one single image to it. The image was that I was looking at the front page of the *New York Times* and in headlines larger than any headlines I'd ever seen before, something like a six-inch headline running across the whole front page of the *New York Times,* were the words "FIRST DAY."

That's all. Well, it was only some months later that I came to a fuller realization of what that meant but it was clear to me immediately that something big was cooking. My association to it was the first day of Creation. That dream would be an example of this archetypal image of His One Day, the second phase of this process.

3. The Dawn

Phase three brings the dawn and sunlight, and the play of many colors—corresponding to the peacock's tail—and brings the fragrance, the perfume, all of which is quite to be expected and there's nothing unusual about it. But an unusual feature does creep into the symbolism because, as it shows up in the various subsidiary texts, the renewed king appears as a worm or a snake. That feature, the worm, doesn't show up in the original text; it shows up in some of the parallel versions and in an outstanding parallel that Jung talks about beginning with paragraph 472—the myth of the phoenix.

According to that myth, the phoenix lived in Arabia and every five hundred years the young phoenix appeared at Heliopolis in Egypt—this is an Egyptian myth, you see. And the phoenix built a nest of twigs on the altar of a temple; there it is consumed in fire, and out of the dead phoenix crawls a worm from which the new phoenix grows.

This particular account of the phoenix comes from *Funk and Wagnalls,*[182] where there's a very interesting addendum. The author of this item says that the phoenix appears in Job 29: 18 where Job says, "I shall die in my nest and I shall multiply my days as the phoenix." Now that's not quite what the Authorized Version says. The Authorized Version, verses 18-20, says:

> Then I said, I shall die in my nest, and I shall multiply my days as the sand. My root was spread out by the waters, and the dew lay all night upon my branch. My glory was fresh in me, and my bow was renewed in my hand.

But the term translated as "sand" here should in all likelihood be translated as "phoenix," and if anybody's interested in this matter, it's discussed at length in a note to the Anchor Bible's edition of Job, translated by Marvin Pope.

The reason I'm making such an issue of this is that it gives us a specific connection of this alchemical text and the phoenix myth with the Job story—it symbolically connects the Job story with this sequence. The Job story is, in fact, a phoenix story and, as Jung perceives it, Job went through the experience of the transformation of the king involving the experience of darkness and the reversal to worm state, followed by apotheosis. In addition, the phoenix myth clearly relates to Egyptian embalming symbolism. The basic idea of that symbolism is to create an immortal body and that's also the basic idea of alchemy. The transformation of the phoenix symbolizes the transformation process of individuation which creates a glorified, indestructible body, a kind of eternal fruit or product of a consciously lived life.

As a number of texts state explicitly, the death and rebirth of the phoenix is equated with the death and resurrection of Christ, and the worm image of the new-

---

[182] *Standard Dictionary,* pp. 868f.

born phoenix is also paralleled in the Christ symbolism. For instance in Psalm 22, verse 6, which is generally considered by both Jewish and Christian scholars to refer to the Messiah—a Messianic Psalm—the Messiah is quoted as saying, "I am a worm and no man, a reproach of men and despised of the people." That amplification assimilates the passion of Christ also to this sequence.

What this material is pointing to is really the quite astonishing idea that the reborn king in alchemy, the reborn phoenix in the phoenix myth and the reborn Yahweh, the Messiah, in the myth of Christ—all three of these appear initially as a worm. That's what the material says. And it's astonishing when you look at it seriously.

I think it has to do with the fact that the transformation process, in its crucial phase, takes place at a moment of the highest constellation of the opposites, and therefore one does not get just a beautiful sequence of celestial images. That's what the one-sided rational mind would expect—a riding off into the celestial sunset—but that's not what the living imagery does. The living imagery juxtaposes one right after the other: the worm, the lowliest form of life we can conceive of on the one hand, and the celestial apotheosis on the other. And they are right together, the most exalted and the most despicable.

You see according to the Christian symbolism, Christ went through the worm experience of humiliation in the process of death and rebirth of the God-image, which was then followed by his being crowned with glory just as in our text the king is crowned with glory. And according to the alchemical symbolism these images also pertain to Mercurius. But Mercurius is a duplex figure—there's an upper Mercurius and a lower Mercurius. The lower Mercurius is imprisoned in matter and the upper, volatile Mercurius descends and suffers itself to be fixed and imprisoned—coagulated—which then helps in the rescue of the lower Mercurius, the worm. The outcome is that the worm, the serpent Mercurius, is crowned or glorified, just as Christ's resurrection and ascension was a crowning glorification of the worm. This sequence of events is indicated by the frequent image in alchemy of the crowned serpent.[183] It indicates that the upper Mercurius and the lower Mercurius have been brought together (paragraphs 478ff).

As I've indicated, there is a kind of overlap or parallel in many ways between this alchemical symbolism and the Christian symbolism. We have here a further example of the assimilation phenomenon we talked about last time. You know Jung discusses at considerable length, in *Psychology and Alchemy,* the whole theme of the alchemists' parallel of the Philosophers' Stone to Christ.[184] And here, in paragraph 485, he quotes what I think is probably the finest, most extensive example of the assimilation of Christian symbolism into alchemy.

---

[183] See above, p. 28, fig. 1-6.
[184] CW 12, chap. 5.

In this text, found in Waite's *Hermetic Museum*, an alchemist describes the transformation process going on in the alchemical flask in terms of the Passion of Christ. The effect of this kind of description and this way of thinking is to take the imagery that had been totally embedded in the dogma and ritual and extended traditional ceremony of the Church—remember, this was done several hundred years ago—pry it right out of that religious context and put it into the alchemical context. By doing that, the imagery becomes available for modern depth psychology.

Here's what the alchemist says:

And firstly it is here to be noted, that the Sages have called this decomposed product, on account of its blackness . . . the raven's head. In the same way Christ (Isa. 53) had no form nor comeliness, was the vilest of all men, full of griefs and sicknesses, and so despised that men even hid their faces from him, and he was esteemed as nothing. Yea, in the 22nd Psalm [Vulgate] he complains of this, that he is a worm and no man, the laughing-stock and contempt of the people; indeed, it is not unfitly compared with Christ when the putrefied body of the Sun lies dead, inactive, like ashes, in the bottom of the phial, until, as a result of greater heat, its soul by degrees and little by little descends to it again, and once more infuses, moistens, and saturates the decaying and all but dead body, and preserves it from total destruction. So also did it happen to Christ himself, when at the Mount of Olives, and on the cross, he was roasted by the fire of the divine wrath (Matt. 26, 27), and complained that he was utterly deserted by his heavenly Father, yet none the less was always (as is wont to happen also to an earthly body through assiduous care and nourishing) comforted and strengthened (Matt. 4, Luke 22) and, so to speak, imbued, nourished, and supported with divine nectar; yea, when at last, in his most sacred passion, and at the hour of death, his strength and his very spirit were completely withdrawn from him, and he went down to the lowest and deepest parts below the earth (Acts 1, Eph. 1, I Peter 3), yet even there he was preserved, refreshed, and by the power of the eternal Godhead raised up again, quickened, and glorified (Rom. 14), when finally his spirit, with its body dead in the sepulchre, obtained a perfect and indissoluble union, through his most joyful resurrection and victorious ascension into heaven, as Lord and Christ (Matt. 28) and was exalted (Mark 16) to the right hand of his Father; with whom through the power and virtue of the Holy Spirit as true God and man he reigns and rules over all things in equal power and glory (Ps. 8), and by his most powerful word preserveth and upholdeth all things (Hebr. 1) and maketh all things one (Acts 17). And this wondrous Union and divine Exaltation angels and men, in heaven and on earth and under the earth (Philipp. 2, I Peter 1) can scarce comprehend, far less meditate upon, without fear and terror; and his virtue, power, and roseate Tincture is able even now to change, and tint, and yet more, perfectly to cure and heal us sinful men in body and soul: of which things we shall have more to say below. . . . Thus, then, we have briefly and simply considered the unique heavenly foundation and corner-stone Jesus Christ, that is to say, *how he is compared and united with the earthly philosophical stone of the Sages* [so all that stuff that's gone before is now being applied to the Philosophers' Stone], *whose material and preparation, as we have heard, is an outstanding type and lifelike image of the incarnation of Christ.*

Jung follows this with an important summary in paragraph 492:

> If the adept experiences his own self, the "true man," in his work, then, as the [above] passage . . . shows, he encounters the analogy of the true man—Christ—in new and direct form, and he recognizes in the transformation in which he himself is involved a similarity to the Passion. It is not an "imitation of Christ" but its exact opposite: an assimilation of the Christ-image to his own self, which is the "true man." It is no longer an effort, an intentional straining after imitation, but rather an involuntary experience of the reality represented by the sacred legend. . . . It is the real experience of a man who has got involved in the compensatory contents of the unconscious by investigating the unknown, seriously and to the point of self-sacrifice.

4. The Apotheosis

The apotheosis is the state of crowning, when celestial attributes are applied to what had previously been a worm. Here the imagery indicates that divine eternal and cosmic qualities are being attached to the materia, to that which has undergone transformation. It comes as a consequence of the coniunctio. In other words, we can say that the worm and king are now one—the highest and lowest have been united; another way of putting it is that power and weakness have been transcended in a third thing.

This reminds me of a passage of Paul's in 2 Corinthians that I think is very relevant psychologically. In this passage he's been talking about the fact that he'd been granted special divine revelations, and then he goes on to say:

> As to the extraordinary revelations, in order that I might not become conceited I was given a thorn in the flesh, an angel of Satan to beat me and keep me from getting proud. Three times I begged the Lord that this might leave me. He said to me, "My grace is enough for you, for . . . [power is completed *(teleitai)* in weakness]." And so I willingly boast of my weaknesses instead, that the power of Christ may rest upon me. Therefore I am content with weakness, with mistreatment, with distress, with persecutions and difficulties for the sake of Christ. For when I am powerless it is then that I am strong.[185]

Now if we were to translate that into psychological language he might say this: "I'm content with weakness, distress and failure of all kinds for the sake of wholeness, for when I am powerless then the Self has room to manifest."

I think the operative phrase here is "power is completed in weakness." It's an image of the coniunctio—weakness and power juxtaposed, you see, right together with each other.

---

[185] 2 Cor. 12: 7-10, New American Bible (modified).

18
Paragraphs 498 to 531

Last time, I spoke of the four stages in the transformation of the king. Number one was the stage of fog, darkness and drowning; number two was "His One Day," the first day of creation, the day of Yahweh; number three was the dawn, the emergence of the sunlight, the many colors and the renewal of the king as a worm or a snake; and number four was the apotheosis, the crowning and the scepter and the seven stars.

In tonight's material, which goes over that same sequence once again, we have two sections: "The Relation of the King-Symbol to Consciousness," and "The Religious Problem of the King's Renewal." They are a kind of oasis of straight interpretation and give a little respite from the otherwise dense network of symbolic imagery.

In these sections Jung discusses two levels of psychological meaning in the sequence of the transformation of the king. One is the level of individual psychological experience, and the other is the meaning of the process as it applies to the collective psyche—the meaning of the historical, cultural transformation process that is symbolized by the death and rebirth of the king.

Let's first consider the individual meaning: I think we can say that the symbolic sequence of the death and renewal of the king is the basic image of the individuation process and therefore of every depth analysis. Jung outlines the sequence in paragraph 523. Let me just go through that and remind you of it.

1. "Sick king, enfeebled by age, about to die." Jung says that corresponds to the "ego-bound state with feeble [psychic] dominant." In other words the psychic dominant, the center around which the psyche has been living, has lost its life-punch; it's enfeebled and in a decrepit state.

2. "Disappearance of the king in his mother's body, or his dissolution in water." This corresponds to the ego's encounter with the unconscious: either it's an ascent of the unconscious in which the unconscious inundates the ego, or it is a descent of the ego, in which the ego goes down to meet the unconscious. Either way there's an encounter between the two and the king disappears in the bath.

3. "Pregnancy, sick-bed, symptoms, display of colours." That corresponds, as Jung puts it, to "conflict and synthesis of conscious and unconscious."

4. "King's son, hermaphrodite, rotundum." These correspond psychologically to the formation of a new dominant which is accompanied by circular symbols of the Self—mandala images, for instance.

That's Jung's outline, which he presents after he has described different aspects of this process quite vividly.

1. The Relation of the King-Symbol to Consciousness

Starting in paragraph 501, Jung says the situation is aptly expressed by the planet simile:

> The king represents ego-consciousness, the subject of all subjects, as an object. His fate in mythology portrays the rising and setting of this most glorious and most divine of all the phenomena of creation, without which the world would not exist as an object. For everything that is only is because it is directly or indirectly known, and moreover this "known-ness" is sometimes represented in a way which the subject himself does not know, just as if he were being observed from another planet, now with benevolent and now with sardonic gaze.

Then, skipping over to paragraph 504, the description continues:

> Pitilessly it is seen from another planet that the king is growing old, even before he sees it himself: ruling ideas, the "dominants," change, and the change, undetected by consciousness, is mirrored only in dreams. King Sol, as the archetype of consciousness, voyages through the world of the unconscious, one of its multitudinous figures which may one day be capable of consciousness too. These lesser lights are, on the old view, identical with the planetary correspondences in the psyche which were postulated by astrology. . . . When the king grows old and needs renewing, a kind of planetary bath is instituted—a bath into which all the planets pour their "influences." This expresses the idea that the dominant, grown feeble with age, needs the support and influence of those subsidiary lights to fortify and renew it.

Going on to paragraph 505:

> In this alchemical picture we can easily recognize the projection of the transformation process: the aging of a psychic dominant is apparent from the fact that it expresses the psychic totality in ever-diminishing degree. One can also say that the psyche no longer feels wholly contained in the dominant, whereupon the dominant loses its fascination and no longer grips the psyche so completely as before. On the other hand its content and meaning are no longer properly understood, or what is understood fails to touch the heart. A "sentiment d'incomplétude" of this kind produces a compensatory reaction which attracts other regions of the psyche and their contents, so as to fill up the gap. As a rule this is an unconscious process that always sets in when the attitude and orientation of the conscious mind have proved inadequate. I stress this point because the conscious mind is a bad judge of its own situation and often persists in the illusion that its attitude is just the right one and is only prevented from working because of some external annoyance. If the dreams were observed it would soon become clear why the conscious assumptions have become unworkable. And if, finally, neurotic symptoms appear, then the attitude of consciousness, its ruling idea, is contradicted, and in the unconscious there is a stirring up of those archetypes that were the most suppressed by the conscious attitude. The therapist then has no other course than to confront the ego with its adversary and thus initiate the melting and recasting process. The confrontation is expressed, in the alchemical myth of the king, as the collision of the masculine, spiri-

tual father-world ruled over by King Sol with the feminine, chthonic mother-world symbolized by the *aqua permanens* or by the chaos.

Well, it's really all right there. But what I wanted to give greater attention to—Jung alludes to it very explicitly but then goes on to other things—is the idea of Sol, the ego, being scrutinized pitilessly as though "from another planet." This is the theme of being seen by the Eye of God and I consider it an exceedingly important experience to understand thoroughly.

The ego—and consciousness itself—is born out of the initial split between subject and object. The subject is the ego and the object is the other which is first of all experienced as the world in its multitude of manifestations; then it is experienced as one's own body; and eventually, the unconscious becomes a kind of inner other.

With the split of subject and object, the ego establishes its existence as a knower, the seat of knowledge—it's the entity that sees and that knows. A major feature of ego development is the wider and wider extension of the range of the ego's knowing, and of its ability to perceive the whole world of objects as something separate from itself to be manipulated, propitiated or related to in one way or another.

But if an individual is destined for a certain level of psychological development, a time comes when subject and object are reversed. When the ego, who all its life has experienced itself as the knower, becomes the known object, then the state of subjecthood is transferred to the other, and the subject—the ego—becomes the known object perceived by that other subject.

That's what Jung refers to when he says that the king, unknown to himself, is being perceived "from another planet." When that state of affairs dawns on the ego, it is a cataclysm. The ego, in its familiar understanding of itself, disappears or dissolves or goes back into the womb of the queen, because the ego is deprived of the basis of its sense of identity, of being the subject and the knower. Instead, the other—an outer figure or the inner other, or both—becomes the center, the perceiving entity which knows the ego as an object.[186]

Now this is an event that takes place, one way or another, in all analytic work of any depth. In most psychotherapeutic situations the patient feels this state of affairs projected onto the analyst, at least to a mild degree: the analyst is experienced as that Eye of God that can pitilessly, as if from another planet, look right through you. That will have a certain limited, partial reality to it in that, presumably, the analyst will have certain objective observations about the patient that the patient won't have about him- or herself. But to a larger extent the experience is based on a projection: the analyst is carrying the projection of the Eye of God

---

[186] For a full discussion, see Edinger, *Creation of Consciousness*, esp. section 2, "The Meaning of Consciousness."

that's been constellated by the analytic process.

But, if one works regularly on dreams, the experience of being the perceived object of another consciousness will be more and more applied to the unconscious itself, because dreams are expressions of the Self and derive from a center of knowing outside the ego. Dreams are therefore events in which the ego—if it pays attention to dreams—begins to realize that it's being seen and known from another standpoint, "from another planet." In other words, in dreams the ego is the object of another knowing subject.

So serious dream work will lead inevitably, if carried far enough, to the shattering realization that one is being seen and looked at and is under constant scrutiny by the Eye of God. Of course, one can do a lot of dream work before that realization dawns; one can entertain the idea theoretically—"Oh yes, that's true"—but the full implication doesn't often penetrate. Yet if one goes far enough, sooner or later the full realization does dawn and then out of that realization, out of that reversal of centrality that the experience brings about, comes the rebirth that Jung speaks of as the formation of a new dominant.

It is at this point that circular symbols appear, and the demoralized ego, which had its props knocked out from under it, undergoes a reconstitution; it emerges with a new attitude, a religious attitude. It has now had an experience of the transpersonal other and achieves a relationship to that other center; that's what gives the ego the celestial attributes associated with the apotheosis stage of the process.

Now that, in brief outline, is the individual meaning of this symbolic sequence. The rest of my remarks will be about the collective meaning of the symbolic process of the king's death and rebirth—the death and renewal of the historical, cultural dominant of our current civilization. In other words it refers to the death and rebirth of the God-image in the collective psyche.

But just before we talk about that, I want to remind you of my conviction— and it was certainly Jung's too—that in every depth analysis where an individual goes through this experience and realizes the individual meaning of it to some extent in his or her own life, that individual is simultaneously contributing to the process of the transformation of the God-image in the collective psyche, and hence is serving more than just a personal purpose. When one is dealing with this level of the psyche one is, to some extent or another, serving the generality. This is the very conviction that Jung arrived at when he had his confrontation with the unconscious and realized, when he came out of it, that his life no longer belonged to himself alone but he was in the service of the generality.[187] And that's true of everyone who goes through this experience at some depth.

You see, just as an individual psyche is structured around a personal dominant,

---

[187] *Memories, Dreams, Reflections,* p. 192.

so a civilization is structured around a collective dominant—a God-image or operative myth. And it's abundantly evident that our age is going through a death
and renewal of its God-image. In my opinion, Jungian psychology has a crucial
role to play in this transformation process, for it is the only formalized body of
knowledge that understands what's going on in any depth and breadth.

2. The Religious Problem of the King's Renewal

In paragraphs 520 and 521, Jung talks about what is required in any process of
renewal. He says:

> Any renewal not deeply rooted in the best spiritual tradition is ephemeral; but the
> dominant that grows from historical roots acts like a living being within the ego-
> bound man. He does not possess it, it possesses him.

So the renewal must be "rooted in the best spiritual tradition"—it must have a
connection with the past. This is why it's crucial for us to understand the nature
of archetypal images and to make a connection between historical parallels and
the modern dreams we have to deal with. It's by connecting the individual's
personal life—and the images that emerge from the personal life—with the historical, symbolic, archetypal tradition that is our past—our "historical roots"—
that renewal can come about.

To illustrate the fact that the collective psyche is in this state of transition, Jung
earlier mentions two examples of the death-of-God theme: an ancient story from
Plutarch and a modern one from Nietzsche. In paragraph 510, he points out that
the modern age is analogous to what was going on two thousand years ago when
a rumor developed that the Great God Pan was dead. That rumor is recorded in
Plutarch's essay, "The Obsolescence of Oracles," where Plutarch records the
following story he had heard directly from a participant:

> He said that once upon a time in making a voyage to Italy he embarked on a ship
> carrying freight and many passengers. It was already evening when, near the Echi-
> nades Islands, the wind dropped, and the ship drifted near Paxi. Almost everybody
> was awake, and a good many had not finished their after-dinner wine. Suddenly
> from the island of Paxi was heard the voice of someone loudly calling Thamus, so
> that all were amazed. Thamus was an Egyptian pilot, not known by name even to
> many on board. Twice he was called and made no reply, but the third time he an-
> swered; and the caller, raising his voice, said, "When you come opposite to Palodes,
> announce that Great Pan is dead." On hearing this, all . . . were astounded and
> reasoned among themselves whether it were better to carry out the order or to refuse
> to meddle and let the matter go. Under the circumstances Thamus made up his mind
> that if there should be a breeze, he would sail past and keep quiet, but with no wind
> and a smooth sea about the place, he would announce what he had heard. So, when
> he came opposite Palodes, and there was neither wind nor wave, Thamus from the
> stern, looking toward the land, said the words as he had heard them: "Great Pan is
> dead." Even before he had finished there was a great cry of lamentation, not of one

person, but of many, mingled with exclamations of amazement. As many persons were on the vessel, the story was soon spread abroad in Rome, and Thamus was sent for by Tiberius Caesar. Tiberius became so convinced of the truth of the story that he caused an inquiry and investigation to be made about Pan.[188]

That's the story of how, in antiquity, they learned that the God Pan was dead. We have a modern equivalent of that event, and our modern Thamus—the pilot—is Nietzsche. Let me read you something of what he has to say. He doesn't tell us this on his own authority; the unconscious tells him to tell us—that's my reading of it. It's from *Thus Spake Zarathustra.*

At the beginning of Nietzsche's account, Zarathustra descends from his mountain retreat and is going to go among men to preach his new message. On his way down, going through the forest, he encounters an ascetic hermit, a saint:

"And what is the saint doing in the forest?" asked Zarathustra.

The saint answered: "I make songs and sing them; and when I make songs, I laugh, cry, and hum: thus I praise God. With singing, crying, laughing, and humming, I praise the god who is my god. . . ."

When Zarathustra had heard these words he bade the saint farewell and said: ". . . Let me go quickly lest I take something from you!" And thus they separated, the old one and the man, laughing as two boys laugh.

But when Zarathustra was alone he spoke thus to his heart: "Could it be possible? This old saint in the forest has not yet heard anything of this, that *God is dead!*"[189]

Then later on, Zarathustra encounters what he calls the "ugliest man," a very disgusting creature who represents the repressed, neglected, disregarded shadow aspect of humanity. And the ugliest man says this:

"Zarathustra! Zarathustra! Guess my riddle! Speak, speak! What is *the revenge against the witness?*"[190]

That's his riddle, and Zarathustra responds to the ugliest man:

"I recognize you well," he said in a voice of bronze; *"you are the murderer of God!* . . . You could not *bear* him who saw *you*—who always saw you through and through, you ugliest man! You took revenge on this witness!"[191]

That's the meaning of "revenge against the witness." There follows a lot of interchange that I'm leaving out; in effect the ugliest man says, "Okay Zarathustra, you've guessed my riddle, my worst riddle, what I did." Then he continues:

"But he *had* to die: he saw with eyes that saw everything; he saw man's depths and ultimate grounds, all his concealed disgrace and ugliness. . . . He crawled into my

---

[188] *Moralia,* vol. 5, pp. 401, 403.
[189] *The Portable Nietzsche*, pp. 123f.
[190] Ibid., p. 376.
[191] Ibid.

dirtiest nooks. This most curious, overobtrusive, overpitying one had to die. He always saw me: on such a witness I wanted to have revenge or not live myself. The god who saw everything, *even man*—this god had to die! Man cannot bear it that such a witness should live."[192]

That's an image of the state of modern man, you see, and why God is dead. And that's the state of affairs that depth analysis reverses. Instead of murdering the witness, the witness is revived and a relation to it is reestablished.

In paragraph 510, Jung speaks very effectively of the collective effects of the death of God. Because it's so relevant, I'm going to read you most of it.

Just as the decay of the conscious dominant is followed by an irruption of chaos in the individual, so also in the case of the masses . . . and the furious conflict of elements in the individual psyche is reflected in the unleashing of primeval bloodthirstiness and lust for murder on a collective scale. This is the sickness so vividly described in the *Cantilena*. The loss of the eternal images is in truth no light matter for the man of discernment. But since there are infinitely many more men of no discernment, nobody, apparently, notices that the truth expressed by the dogma has vanished in a cloud of fog, and nobody seems to miss anything. The discerning person knows and feels that his psyche is disquieted by the loss of something that was the life-blood of his ancestors. The undiscerning . . . miss nothing, and only discover afterwards in the papers (much too late) the alarming symptoms that have now become "real" in the outside world because they were not perceived before inside, in oneself, just as the presence of the eternal images was not noticed. If they had been, a threnody for the lost god would have arisen, as once before in antiquity at the death of Great Pan. Instead, all well-meaning people assure us that one has only to believe he is still there—which merely adds stupidity to unconsciousness. Once the symptoms are really outside in some form of sociopolitical insanity, it is impossible to convince anybody that the conflict is in the psyche of every individual, since he is now quite sure where his enemy is. Then, the conflict which remains an intrapsychic phenomenon in the mind of the discerning person, takes place on the plane of projection in the form of political tension and murderous violence. . . .
When [the individual] no longer knows by what his soul is sustained, the potential of the unconscious is increased and takes the lead. Desirousness overpowers him, and illusory goals set up in the place of the eternal images excite his greed. The beast of prey seizes hold of him and soon makes him forget that he is a human being. His animal affects hamper any reflection that might stand in the way of his infantile wish-fulfilments, filling him instead with a feeling of a new-won right to existence and intoxicating him with the lust for booty and blood.

This threnody for a lost god comes up in a nineteenth-century poem that I think is particularly relevant as an amplification of the collective event—Matthew Arnold's "Dover Beach." Like a lot of sensitive souls in the nineteenth century he perceived that God was dead, and had a vague sense of malaise. This poem was

[192] Ibid., pp. 378f.

written in 1851 and *Thus Spake Zarathustra* in about 1883, so there's about thirty years' difference, but that's pretty close. Let me read it to you.

The sea is calm to-night,
The tide is full, the moon lies fair
Upon the straits;—on the French coast the light
Gleams and is gone; the cliffs of England stand,
Glimmering and vast, out in the tranquil bay.
Come to the window, sweet is the night-air!

Only, from the long line of spray
Where the sea meets the moon-blanched land,
Listen! you hear the grating roar
Of pebbles which the waves draw back, and fling,
At their return, up the high strand,
Begin, and cease, and then again begin,
With tremulous cadence slow, and bring
The eternal note of sadness in.

Sophocles long ago
Heard it on the Aegean, and it brought
Into his mind the turbid ebb and flow
Of human misery; we
Find also in the sound a thought,
Hearing it by this distant northern sea.

The Sea of Faith
Was once, too, at the full, and round earth's shore
Lay like the folds of a bright girdle furled.
But now I only hear
Its melancholy, long, withdrawing roar,
Retreating, to the breath
Of the night-wind, down the vast edges drear
And naked shingles of the world.

Ah, love, let us be true
To one another! for the world, which seems
To lie before us like a land of dreams,
So various, so beautiful, so new,
Hath really neither joy, nor love, nor light,
Nor certitude, nor peace, nor help for pain;
And we are here as on a darkling plain
Swept with confused alarms of struggle and flight,
Where ignorant armies clash by night.

Arnold wrote that poem on his honeymoon. You see what he was doing was transferring all that was lost—all the needs that were no longer fulfilled, the cosmic transpersonal needs whose fulfillment had been denied him because of his lost faith, his lost God-image—he was transferring all that heavy weight of need to his personal relationship with his new wife. It's a wonder that relationship survived. It did, due to the fact that Matthew Arnold was a very conscious and high quality person, and no doubt his wife was too.

He says, in effect: "My love, let us be true to one another because there's nothing else in the universe to give us any security." Few relationships can endure such an archetypal burden. What's required, rather, is that the lost dominant—the lost God-image—undergo the renewal process that the alchemical imagery refers to, be reborn and reemerge into view.

Here's where the next passage in the *Mysterium* comes in. Jung says, in paragraph 511:

> Only the living presence of the eternal images can lend the human psyche a dignity which makes it morally possible for a man to stand by his own soul, and be convinced that it is worth his while to persevere with it. Only then will he realize that the conflict is *in him,* that the discord and tribulation are his riches, which should not be squandered by attacking others; and that, if fate should exact a debt from him in the form of guilt, it is a debt to himself.

In other words, our guilt is our treasure.

> It's a debt to himself. Then he will recognize the worth of his psyche, for nobody can owe a debt to a mere nothing. But when he loses his own values he becomes a hungry robber, the wolf, lion, and other ravening beasts which for the alchemists symbolized the appetites that break loose when the black waters of chaos—i.e. the unconsciousness of projection—have swallowed up the king.

And then comes this marvelous paragraph 512:

> It is a subtle feature of the *Cantilena* that the pregnancy cravings of the mother are stilled with peacock's flesh and lion's blood, i.e., with her own flesh and blood. If the projected conflict is to be healed, it must return into the psyche of the individual, where it had its unconscious beginnings. He must celebrate a Last Supper with himself, and eat his own flesh and drink his own blood; which means that he must recognize and accept the other in himself. But if he persists in his one-sidedness, the two lions will tear each other to pieces. Is this perhaps the meaning of Christ's teaching, that each must bear his own cross? For if you have to endure yourself, how will you be able to rend others also?

And you see that then makes the connection with Nietzsche's passage on the ugliest man. If the ugliest man, namely the shadow, submits to conscious scrutiny, then he won't have to murder God, the scrutinizer, and God can be reborn. "For if you have to endure yourself, how will you be able rend others also?"

In paragraph 530, Jung brings up another example of the death and renewal of the king, from the Gospel of John. In this case, the theme is the death of Christ and his renewal as the Paraclete or the Holy Ghost. Christ prepares his disciples for his death with these words:

> I shall ask the Father,
> and he will give you another Advocate [that means Paraclete]
> to be with you for ever,
> that Spirit of truth
> whom the world can never receive
> since it neither sees nor knows him;
> but you know him,
> because he is with you, he is in you.
> I will not leave you orphans;
> I will come back to you.
> In a short time the world will no longer see me;
> but you will see me,
> because I live and you will live.
> On that day you will understand that I am in my Father
> and you in me and I in you.[193]

And later he says:

> but the Advocate, the Holy Spirit,
> whom the Father will send in my name,
> will teach you everything
> and remind you of all I have said to you.[194]

Then he brings up the theme again, in John 16, where he says:

> it is for your own good that I am going
> because unless I go,
> the Advocate will not come to you;
> but if I do go,
> I will send him to you. . . .
> But when the Spirit of truth comes
> he will lead you to the complete truth[195]

So here the idea is stated quite explicitly that the spiritual authority figure—the king, represented by Christ—must die in order that the phenomenon of the Advocate—the Paraclete, the Holy Spirit—can be born out of his death. I would understand this to mean psychologically that a particular concrete container of a God-image must die if its renewed form is to come as an inner experience. And this corresponds to what Jung means when he speaks of the continuing incarnation of the Holy Ghost in the individual. He puts it explicitly in paragraph 531 where

---

[193] John 14: 16-20, Jerusalem Bible.
[194] John 14: 26, Jerusalem Bible.
[195] Verses 7, 13, Jerusalem Bible.

he says:

> It is easy to see what happens when the logical conclusion is drawn from the four-teenth chapter of John: the *opus Christi* is transferred to the individual. He then be-comes the bearer of the mystery.

That's it in a nutshell: "The *opus Christi* is transferred to the individual." This statement summarizes the whole goal of Jungian psychology as an assimilation phenomenon. The goal is to retrieve the archetypal images from their projection in mythological and metaphysical contexts and return these images to the psyche from which they originally came. And for the Christian myth this means that the work of Christ, the *opus Christi,* is transferred to the individual: the imagery previously enshrined in metaphysical dogma is now available so that at least the occasional individual can relate to it empirically and experientially.[196] Needless to say, that's not going to be a particularly popular undertaking.

Well, that completes what I want to say. Let me just draw your attention, however, to the fact that a paragraph has been omitted. I guess practically all of you have the second edition of *Mysterium;* if you do, turn to page vii and you'll find there that paragraph 518a, which belongs right after paragraph 518, was omitted by mistake from the first edition. Now, since we're used to considering such events as having some significance, I think we're obliged to read that paragraph, censored out by the unconscious, and see what it says.

> The reader must pardon my use of metaphors that are linguistically analogous to dogmatic expressions. If you have conceptions of things you can have no concep-tions of, then the conception and the thing appear to coincide. Nor can two different things you know nothing of be kept apart. I must therefore expressly emphasize that I do not go in for either metaphysics or theology, but am concerned with psy-chological facts on the borderline of the knowable. So if I make use of certain ex-pressions that are reminiscent of the language of theology, this is due solely to the poverty of language, and not because I am of the opinion that the subject-matter of theology is the same as that of psychology. Psychology is very definitely not a the-ology; it is a natural science that seeks to describe experienceable psychic phe-nomena. In doing so it takes account of the way in which theology conceives and names them, because this hangs together with the phenomenology of the contents under discussion. But as empirical science it has neither the capacity nor the com-petence to decide on questions of truth and value, this being the prerogative of theology.

So we'll take due note of that content.

Question: Are you going to say anything about why you think it was left out?

---

[196] See "Psychology and Religion," *Psychology and Religion,* CW 11, par. 148, where Jung says: "That is why I take these thought-forms that have become historically fixed, try to melt them down again and pour them into moulds of immediate experience."

Well, since you asked me—! On the surface of it, it's harmless enough and it doesn't seem to warrant any particular consideration, but my opinion is that it was left out because the issue underlying this passage is so explosive.

Since I don't have to be as careful as Jung about my reputation, I think I can express things a little more forthrightly. If one collects the remarks he makes in various places on the subject of psychology and theology one finds a certain inconsistency—they're not absolutely uniform. That's illustrated even in this passage by his saying, in the very last sentence, that empirical science doesn't have the "competence to decide on questions of truth and value, this being the prerogative of theology." That's throwing a sop to theology, you see. In other places he behaves a little differently.[197]

Now the strictly empirical standpoint is that the images which go to make up the metaphysical dogmas are the phenomenology of the archetypal psyche. Jung specifically states this empirical standpoint in various places—-the Kantian notion of the impossibility of metaphysical knowledge.[198] So, to the extent that one is an empiricist, there's nothing to be said about metaphysics at all, as long as it is on the metaphysical level. But psychologically one can understand metaphysical imagery as the projection of the archetypal psyche onto the metaphysical plane.

The reason it's difficult to be that explicit—that rigorous—in widely distributed published works is that such a viewpoint does violence to a large number of individuals whose connection to archetypal images is via metaphysical dogmas, and Jung does not want to do violence to anybody. I believe that's why, at the beginning of *Psychology and Alchemy,* he puts the motto: "The bruised reed he shall not break, and the smoking flax he shall not quench. . . ."

Jung is very sensitive to the psychological needs of individuals at all levels of development; for those for whom it is psychologically proper to have the strictly empirical viewpoint, he puts it forth in various places, but in other places he muddies the waters. This whole issue, a highly explosive one, is what I believe lies behind that omitted paragraph.

---

[197] See, for instance, his letter to Bernhard Lang in *Letters*, vol.2, pp. 375ff.
[198] Ibid.

19

Paragraphs 532 to 569

In tonight's material we have the subject of Regina, the queen, the feminine version of the royal figure. And I'm going to take this opportunity to say a few words about the whole question of the ego's relation to the masculine and feminine principles in the case of a man and in the case of a woman.

Then we will start chapter V, "Adam and Eve": Adam as the original substance, his fourfold nature, and the symbolism of the statue.

1. Regina

The subject of the queen—Regina—brings up the royal feminine principle, consort and partner to the royal masculine, symbolized by the king. I think it is the very nature of the feminine principle to be problematic when it comes to rational and articulate description—it refuses to be caught in a concept—so we will just have to circumambulate this image as best we can.

What I want to discuss in particular stems from the remark Jung makes in paragraph 536: "The queen corresponds to the soul (anima) and the king to spirit, the dominant of consciousness." Then in footnote 428 he adds: "This is true only of the male artifex. The situation is reversed in the case of a woman."[199] Now I want to try to clarify this remark; the danger is that when one ventures into this subject, rather than clarifying it one just obfuscates it more. Nonetheless, I'm going to make the effort, and I've made a drawing that illustrates the ideas I'm going to try to express (figure 19-1).

The question is, how the ego of a man and the ego of a woman typically relate to the masculine and feminine principles—in other words, to the father and mother archetypes? I think we all sense that it is not exactly the same; a woman's ego, in a general way, has a different way of relating to these two archetypal entities than the usual man's ego does. This is an issue we should all have in mind as we work on cases, in the hope that the data we gather can help to elucidate it. Here are some thoughts I've had, based on my experience.

It's my impression that, in general, the man's ego is heavier, so to speak, on the masculine side. Usually it has a bigger dose of the masculine principle connected to it; this then causes it to lean toward the feminine side of the circle representing the unconscious, because we know that a compensatory relation prevails between consciousness and the unconscious. If consciousness has quite a

---

[199] For a discussion of this "reversal" from a woman's standpoint, see Rivkah Sharf Kluger, "The Queen of Sheba in Bible and Legends," in *Psyche and Bible,* pp. 137ff.

strong tendency in one direction, the unconscious, by and large, tends to compensate that by emphasizing the contrary direction.

So if you have a masculinized ego then the unconscious of that individual is going to be more prominently feminized; that's shown in the drawing by the fact that the masculine ego, on the left, has a closer connection to the feminine aspect of the unconscious.

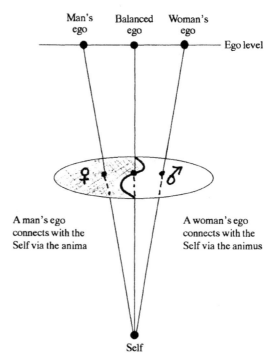

Figure 19-1.
Relations between
the ego and the Self.

Contrarily, the woman's ego is usually heavier on the feminine side. It's a feminized ego, as a rule, and thus it has a tendency to lean in the opposite direction so that masculinity will be constellated in the unconscious.

In Jungian terms we can say that the ego of a woman usually meets the unconscious via the animus—a masculine personification of the unconscious—and the ego of a man usually meets the unconscious via the anima, which can be defined as a feminine personification of the unconscious.

Needless to say, these matters are not strictly uniform—there's immense individual variation. If a man has a somewhat feminized ego then it's likely that a masculine figure will mediate the unconscious for that individual, at least temporarily. And if a woman has a masculinized ego, then a feminine figure is apt to mediate the unconscious for that woman.

I think the usual condition is that one gets a partial glimpse of wholeness (represented in the drawing by the Self underlying the twofold division) through the archetypal principle of the same sex, but a more intense experience of wholeness through the archetypal principle of the opposite sex.

Jung refers to some of these matters in paragraphs 539 and 540, which I want to read and speak to because there are not very many places in this book where Jung makes a specific connection between the alchemical images he's talking about and the psychology of individuals; we have to make the most of those descriptive passages when we come to them.

In effect, Jung asks himself: "Now what do the figures Rex and Regina mean in the psychology of the individual?" He has already indicated that the king has a connection to ego consciousness in the case of the man, and he says that the queen relates to the anima. Then, in paragraph 539, he goes on to say:

> The anima in her negative aspect—that is, when she remains unconscious and hidden—exerts a possessive influence on the subject. The chief symptoms of this possession are blind moods and compulsive entanglements on one side, and on the other, cold, unrelated absorption in principles and abstract ideas. The negative aspect of the anima indicates therefore a special form of psychological maladjustment. This is either compensated from the conscious side or else it compensates a consciousness already marked by a contrary (and equally incorrect) attitude. For the negative aspect of the conscious dominant is far from being a "God-given" idea; it is the most egoistic intention of all, which seeks to play an important role and, by wearing some kind of mask, to appear as something favourable (identification with the persona!). The anima corresponding to this attitude is an intriguer who continually aids and abets the ego in its role, while digging in the background the very pits into which the infatuated ego is destined to fall.

Now, in terms of my drawing, Jung is referring to a case where the ego of a man falls into an identification with the queen—with the anima—and then is in the grip of an anima mood. And, as all observation will verify, anima moods have a remarkably queenly demeanor. They assume royal status, you see, so that the image of the queen is absolutely apt; but when it manifests in identification with the ego, it's not very agreeable because it's not accompanied by consciousness — that's the crucial missing entity.

And of course the same pertains to the woman's ego when she falls into animus possession. Such possession likewise has a very kingly way of behaving—it makes arbitrary judgments ex cathedra; it operates in an absolutely kingly fashion. The two images are visible to those who have eyes to see, especially in their negative, unconscious manifestation.

But then comes the very nice paragraph 540 in which Jung says:

But a conscious attitude that renounces its ego-bound intentions—not in imagination only, but in truth—and submits to the suprapersonal decrees of fate, can claim to be serving a king [and I can add, or a queen]. This more exalted attitude raises the status of the anima from that of a temptress to a psychopomp. The transformation of the kingly substance from a lion into a king has its counterpart in the transformation of the feminine element from a serpent into a queen. The coronation, apotheosis, and marriage signalize the equal status of conscious and unconscious that becomes possible at the highest level—a *coincidentia oppositorum* with redeeming effects.

This really puts the psychological nature of the transformation in a nutshell, and the only thing that distinguishes the condition as described in paragraph 539 from the condition described in paragraph 540 is consciousness.

If consciousness intervenes in regard to anima or animus possessions, then those moods are broken and the possessing agent is perceived to be the autonomous psyche itself and actually a manifestation of the center, the Self. With that realization, royal status is not lost, the king and queen retain their royalty—because they are indeed royal—but the ego no longer identifies with that royalty and, as Jung puts it, then the "conscious attitude . . . renounces its ego-bound intentions . . . in truth and submits to the suprapersonal decrees of fate, [and] can claim to be serving a king."

Question: Is fate the Self?

Yes, fate is the Self.

Let me give you an interesting example of how the Self can manifest through the feminine archetype in a man who is one-sidedly intellectual. There was a case of a mathematician whom I saw under somewhat unusual circumstances. He was doing very high level classified research in a government project but his marriage broke up and he collapsed. He had to get some help, but he was under constant FBI surveillance. I'd never had that before in analysis, and I can't say it's particularly auspicious!

The unconscious obliged us in this situation by condensing the process into a very brief period of time and we got through it fast. Here is the decisive dream that brought about the transformation and enabled him to regain his balance and go back to work:

> An elegant, queenly woman is arriving in a Rolls Royce, and the royal coat of arms is engraved on the panel of the car. The coat of arms is the symbol for infinity [∞].

That's the whole dream. But in working on it his first association to the queen was the phrase "Mathematics is the queen of the sciences." He was a mathematician, that was his life, and he really had a transpersonal commitment to that subject. This dream put him back on track, you see; it put him back in touch internally with what he was serving, so that, as Jung says, such an individual "submits to the suprapersonal decrees of fate, and can claim to be serving a king" or a queen. He could go back to serving his queen with the coming of this dream.

It reestablished his connection with the Self, via the feminine principle.

This man's relation to mathematics corresponds to the way Jung describes the alchemists' relation to their art. He says, in paragraph 543:

> The Queen of Sheba, Wisdom, the royal art, and the "daughter of the philosophers" are all so interfused that the underlying psychologem clearly emerges: the art is queen of the alchemist's heart, she is at once his mother, his daughter, and his beloved, and in his art and its allegories the drama of his own soul, his individuation process, is played out.

It's that degree of relation to the psyche, I think, that we should all be striving for, because after all, the alchemists are our forerunners.

One of the texts Jung talks about in paragraph 534 brings up imagery indicating that for the masculine ego, the feminine principle is very often experienced as a surrounding medium, corresponding to the image of the heavens that surround and contain the sun.

For the feminine ego, the related image would be the experience of the masculine principle as a fertilizing, penetrating spirit, symbolized for instance by a ray, a spear, an arrow, a phallus, or something that penetrates or opens up, or injects intoxicating, inseminating matter—as in the mythological story of Danaë inseminated by Zeus via a shower of gold (figure 19-2).

Figure 19-2.
Danaë and the shower of gold.

2. Adam as the Original Substance and His Fourfold Nature

Now we move on to chapter 5, "Adam and Eve." Jung starts out by talking about Adam as the representation of the Anthropos, the original Self. It's the image of original unconscious wholeness and for this reason, according to the texts and the symbolism, Adam has a fourfold nature. Let me give you a couple of examples of this fourfold nature of Adam.

According to one text cited by Jung (paragraph 552, footnote 26), God collected from the four corners of the earth the dust from which Adam was made. Another text, quoted in paragraph 552, says:

> And they saw God take a grain of dust from the whole earth, and a drop of water from the whole sea, and a breath of wind from the upper air, and a little warmth from the nature of fire. And the angels saw how these four weak elements, the dry, the moist, the cold, and the warm, were laid in the hollow of his hand. And then God made Adam.

Jung then brings up several other examples of the tetradic or fourfold nature of Adam, which corresponds with the familiar symbolism of the quaternity.

Another aspect of Adam symbolism noted by Jung is that the word "Adam" itself means red earth (paragraph 585, footnote 157). In many texts he is associated with clay and dust—his very name represents the matter that God molded into a figure. Genesis 2: 7, tells us: "God formed man of the dust of the ground, and breathed into his nostrils the breath of life." (AV) And in Genesis 1: 27 we read: "God created man in his own image, in the image of God created he him; male and female created he them." (AV) Both these passages indicate that Adam is composed of two factors. In other texts he's composed of four factors, but in these texts he's composed of two; clay and breath, according to the one account, or earth and image, according to the other. So matter and spirit are united in the creation of Adam.

We don't encounter very many Adam dreams but some years ago I came across a particularly impressive one:

> I was invited to a party for Adam and Eve. They had never died. They were the beginning and the end. I realized this and accepted their permanent existence. Both of them were enormous, overscale, like Maillol's sculptures. They had a sculptural and not a human look. Adam's face was veiled or covered and I longed to know what he looked like. I dared to try to uncover his face and I did. The covering was a very heavy layer of peat-mosses, or some sort of vegetable growth. I pulled it away just a little and peeped behind. His face was kind but frightening—it was like a gorilla or giant ape of some sort.[200]

This dream verifies what Jung's material brings out, namely that the image of

---

[200] See Edinger, *Ego and Archetype,* p. 207.

Adam stands at the beginning as the prima materia and also at the end, as the culmination of the process. Dreams like this give us empirical data as to the nature of the primordial psyche—that's what makes them particularly valuable.

Question: What sort of feeling response did the dreamer have?

These dreams were more than he could relate to in a really effective way. This man was destined to die a short time after the remarkable series of dreams I recorded in *Ego and Archetype.*[201] In the course of the whole series he was beginning to develop something of a religious attitude toward the transpersonal dimension but they were much too big for him to assimilate. It was as though they came from another planet.

3. The Statue

In the next section Jung goes into the symbolism of the statue because in certain texts Adam is described as a statue that God breathed the breath of life into. So I am going to go into this image in some detail.

We don't see many dreams about statues—I think in modern dreams it's more likely to be a doll; at least, I take the image of a doll to mean something analogous. Certainly the statue is a very apt example of an eternal image, of an archetype. That will be especially the case if it is made of really durable material such as marble or bronze because then it will survive for eons. Statues made of stone are connected with the whole stone symbolism of alchemy, the Philosophers' Stone, and the statue then becomes a synonym for the lapis.

In the material, the image of the statue and the pillar overlap; the Greek caryatids, for example (figure 19-3), combine those two images—statues that are also pillars. This overlap between statue and pillar comes up in Manichaean eschatology. Jung quotes a reference to that in paragraph 567:

> [The Father of Greatness] made the messenger and Jesus the radiant and the Virgin of Light and the Pillar of Glory and the gods. . . . The fourth time, when they shall weep, is the time when the statue . . . shall raise itself on the last day. . . . At that same hour, when the last statue shall rise, they shall weep. . . . The first rock is the pillar . . . of glory, the perfect man, who has been summoned by the glorious messenger. . . . He bore the whole world and became the first of all bearers. . . . The intellectual element. . . [gathered itself] into the pillar of glory, and the pillar of glory into the first man. . . . The garments, which are named the Great Garments, are the five intellectual elements, which have [made perfect] the body of the pillar of glory, the perfect man.

Now I must explain what image that text refers to, as it's not absolutely clear. The Manichaean idea is that in the last days, when the Manichaean faithful—the elect—have done all their work and gathered together all the lost particles of

---

[201] Ibid., pp. 199ff.

Figure 19-3. Caryatids on the Acropolis of Athens.

light that it is their task to gather, then what's called here the "first man" and the "perfect man" are united; they come together in the form of a statue-pillar. That's the entity that crystallizes out in the last days.

The first man and the perfect final man manifest in this statue-pillar and then all of the gathered light that has been brought together from the earth streams out of this statue-pillar into the heavens where it came from. That's the culmination of the Manichaean eschatology.[202] Then the perfect state of affairs will be reestablished—the way things were before the original fall, you see. The final end for the Manichaeans was not a unification of the light and the darkness, but a final irrevocable separation of the two, and it's brought about through their statue-pillar image. That has, then, certain parallels to the alchemical lapis: the statue is the final product of the Manichaean opus just as the Philosophers' Stone is the final product of the alchemical opus.

When one thinks about it, the experience of a statue must have been numinous for early humanity in its childhood. For early man to see the likenesses of humans or animals—who are not humans or animals, yet look like them—would have an effect on the unconscious that I expect would really activate the arche-typal dimensions that were very close anyway. I think that's why Yahweh forbade the making of statues or images by the Israelites.

We know that in the early period of sculpting there were no portrait statues, statues of individual human beings; there were only statues of mythological or

---

[202] See Jonas, *Gnostic Religion,* pp. 234f.

divine figures. The common people probably could not distinguish between the god that was being represented and the earthly, concrete image of that god. So for the ancients and the early people the statue *was* the god, and the early Christian fathers berated the pagans bitterly for worshipping gods of wood and stone. They heaped scorn and contempt on them for thinking their wooden gods or their stone gods were actually the effective presence.

Yet that psychology isn't completely gone yet; it's still alive. For instance, there is a bronze statue of St. Peter in St. Peter's Basilica in Rome, and that statue has a large depression in its great toe which comes from being kissed by millions of the faithful over hundreds of years.

An important statue myth is that of Pygmalion and Galatea. Let me read you that story from Ovid, because I consider it to parallel the alchemical opus.

Ovid speaks of Pygmalion as being sort of disillusioned, unhappy about women and their faults, and so he lived unmarried and "long was without a partner of his couch."

> [But] meanwhile with wondrous art he successfully carves a figure out of snowy ivory, giving it a beauty more perfect than that of any woman ever born. And with his own work he falls in love. The face is that of a real maiden, whom you would think living and desirous of being moved, if modesty did not prevent. So does his art conceal his art. Pygmalion looks in admiration and is inflamed with love for this semblance of a form. Often he lifts his hands to the work to try whether it be flesh or ivory; . . . He kisses it and thinks his kisses are returned. He speaks to it, grasps it and seems to feel his fingers sink into the limbs when he touches them; and then he fears lest he leave marks of bruises on them. Now he addresses it with fond words of love, now brings it gifts pleasing to girls, shells and smooth pebbles, little birds and many-hued flowers, and lilies and coloured balls, . . . He drapes its limbs also with robes, puts gemmed rings on its fingers and a long necklace around its neck; pearls hang from the ears and chains adorn the breast. All these are beautiful; . . . He lays it on a bed spread with coverlets of Tyrian hue, calls it the consort of his couch, and rests its reclining head upon soft, downy pillows, . . .
>
> And now the festival day of Venus had come, which all Cyprus thronged to celebrate;. . . Pygmalion, having brought his gift to the altar, stood and falteringly prayed: "If ye, O gods, can give all things, I pray to have as wife— . . . one like my ivory maid." But golden Venus (for she herself was present at her feast) knew what that prayer meant; and, as an omen of her favoring deity, thrice did the flame burn brightly and leap high in air. When he returned he sought the image of his maid, and bending over the couch he kissed her. She seemed warm to his touch. Again he kissed her, and with his hands also he touched her breast. The ivory grew soft to his touch and, its hardness vanishing, gave and yielded beneath his fingers, as Hymettian wax grows soft under the sun, . . . The lover stands amazed, rejoices still in doubt, fears he is mistaken, and tries his hopes again and yet again with his hand. Yes, it was real flesh! The veins were pulsing beneath his testing finger. Then did the Paphian hero pour out copious thanks to Venus, and again pressed with his lips

real lips at last. The maiden felt the kisses, blushed and, lifting her timid eyes up to the light, she saw the sky and her lover at the same time. The goddess graced with her presence the marriage she had made; and ere the ninth moon had brought her crescent to the full, a daughter was born to them, Paphos, from whom the island takes its name.[203]

That is the story of Pygmalion and Galatea. George Bernard Shaw worked it over too. Like the alchemists creating the Philosophers' Stone, Pygmalion succeeded in creating a living statue. That's what the Philosophers' Stone claimed to be, a living stone. This is an image, as I understand it, of the process in which one pours loving attention into the psyche and brings the soul to life—the archetypal soul—by those efforts.

There is another statue story with a little different angle to it—Don Giovanni. In the first scene of Mozart's opera, Don Giovanni kills Don Pedro, the father of one of his many amorous conquests. At the end of the opera, he meets the statue of Don Pedro on his grave and rashly orders his servant to invite the statue to dinner. The statue indicates its acceptance by a nod.

That nod is a reference to the fact that in antiquity it was thought that the statues of the gods replied to earnest questions made to them by nodding. If you have a very serious question and maybe even make a pilgrimage to the god—it may not be just the home-town version, you may have to travel—you're probably tired and wrought up from the trip. With the urgency of the issue, whatever it is (it must be pretty serious if you're going to take it to the god), you stare at the statue of the god and if you see it nod then you've got an answer. That's the source of our word "numinous"—that's why I bring it in here—which derives from the old Latin word *numen,* "a nod"—the nodding of the god when it is questioned.

That's what the statue of Don Pedro does. It nods when it's invited to dinner. And that night the clinking statue arrives at Don Giovanni's door. According to Mozart's story, Don Giovanni refuses to repent, and so the statue pulls him into hell. This is a kind of obverse of the Pygmalion and Galatea story. In Pygmalion's case his devotion to his art and to his love constellates auspiciously the archetypal psyche—the statue—and brings it to life with positive effects. Don Giovanni's inflated and cynical attitude constellates the archetypal psyche—the statue—in its negative aspect and it comes to life with negative effects, leading Don Giovanni into a purging calcinatio in the underworld.

But there is another way of looking at it. Both Pygmalion and Don Giovanni are lovers, and the statue coming to life in each case has something to do with the matter being loved. It is perhaps significant that Don Giovanni had to deal with a male statue whereas Pygmalion dealt with a female statue. That would suggest, according to my earlier description, that Don Giovanni's ego was somewhat

---

[203] *Metamorphoses,* vol. 2, book 10, pp. 83, 85.

feminized, which I think is indeed commonly true in cases of Don Juanism. So it fits our way of thinking.

If a man's ego is not carrying its full masculinity and therefore is somewhat feminized, then what is apt to happen is that the anima is masculinized, or even in some cases completely invisible, with an overlay of the unrealized masculinity. This is the condition of many male homosexuals. Alternatively, if a woman's ego is not carrying its full femininity, then the animus is feminized, or even invisible, with an overlay of unrealized femininity.

The rule is that what ought to be conscious—according to the inner requirements of the individual—and is not, falls into the unconscious and contaminates the anima or animus. Then we get dream images of a masculinized anima in a man or a feminized animus in a woman because animus and anima are being obliged to carry those contents the ego is failing to carry consciously.

Finally, I want to give you a couple of modern examples of the statue experience. Freud had one. He wrote a paper in 1914 entitled "The Moses of Michelangelo." It was originally published anonymously but eventually it came out that it was Freud's paper and Freud's experience. In this paper he gives a rather detailed interpretation of the posture of the Moses sculpture, which I'm not going to go into, but here is the personal reference. He writes:

> Another one of these inscrutable and wonderful works of art is the marble statue of Moses, by Michelangelo, in the Church of S. Pietro in Vincoli in Rome. As we know, it was only a fragment of the gigantic tomb which the artist was to have erected for the powerful Pope Julius II. It always delights me to read an appreciatory sentence about this statue, such as that it is "the crown of modern sculpture" (Hermann Grimm). For no piece of statuary has ever made a stronger impression on me than this. How often have I mounted the steep steps of the unlovely Corso Cavour to the lonely place where the deserted church stands, and have essayed to support the angry scorn of the hero's glance! Sometimes I have crept cautiously out of the half-gloom of the interior as though I myself belonged to the mob upon whom his eye is turned—the mob which can hold fast no conviction, which has neither faith nor patience and which rejoices when it has regained its illusory idols.[204]

I think we can understand this experience of Freud's as an experience of the numinous Self as manifested in Moses; Freud obviously had a negative relation to that entity because he experienced it in accusatory form. Following the rule laid down by Jung—the unconscious shows the same face to the ego as the ego shows to the unconscious—the fact that Freud had rejected the transpersonal dimension of the unconscious means that that aspect of the unconscious is going to be experienced as rejecting him in turn.

Finally I want to mention a statue experience of my own that also happened in

---

[204] *Collected Papers,* vol. 4, pp. 259f.

Italy. Is there something about Italy? Well, I guess there are more statues there for one thing!

This took place in Florence at the Medici Chapel which is attached to the Church of St. Lorenzo. One of the tombs in that chapel is adorned by the reclining figures of Twilight and Dawn, carved by Michelangelo. Twilight is a male figure draped on one side of the tomb and Dawn is a female figure draped on the other side (figure 19-4). I arrived at that chapel right about noon one day in 1958, and astonishingly it was deserted. I was all alone. I sat down on a stone bench and just looked at that figure and suddenly it seemed to come alive. I was gripped by the conviction that it was actually alive and that lasted maybe five or ten minutes. Then it slowly faded away.

Now the circumstances may be relevant: in the summer of 1958 I was thirty-six years old, a fledgling analyst and on my first trip to Europe. I had just come from Zürich after attending the First International Congress where I had met Jung for the first time and had had a couple of conversations with him. Now, as I consider it in retrospect, I understand that experience to have been the harbinger of my emerging vocational commitment. It's probably significant that the statue was titled Dawn. It is about as near to perfection as anything can be, which would have to be the case to get such a solid sensation type as myself to think it had come to life! Anyway, it's another example of the theme of the living statue.

Next week our assignment is a little shorter than usual so I'm going to ask you also to read the Song of Songs and/or the chapter on that subject in my book *The Bible and the Psyche*. We're going to be talking about an alchemical text that makes considerable use of the Song of Songs.

Figure 19-4.
Michelangelo's
Dawn.

20

Paragraphs 570 to 595

Tonight's assignment has these major images:
1. The figure of Adam as wise man and first alchemist.
2. Adam in a series of eight.
3. The polarity and androgyny of Adam.
4. Adam as Anthropos.
5. We will begin an examination of Eleazar's text.

Before starting, I have an additional remark concerning the matter of Adam as statue. I want to draw your attention to a Gnostic text Jung quotes in footnote 64 to paragraph 566. This is a passage from Hippolytus:

> The Chaldaeans say the same thing about Adam; and they assert that he was the man whom the earth brought forth alone, and that he lay unbreathing and unmoved as a statue . . . an image of him on high who is praised as the man Adamas, begotten of many powers.

In that passage Adam is explicitly identified with an inert statue—waiting to have his soul breathed into him, so to speak. In Hippolytus that particular text is immediately followed by this passage:

> In order, therefore, that finally the Great Man from above may be overpowered "from whom," as they say, "the whole family named on earth and in the heavens" has been formed, to him was given also a soul, that through the soul he might suffer; and that the enslaved image may be punished of the Great and most Glorious and Perfect Man, for even so they call him.[205]

The idea expressed here is that the evil demiurge who created Adam imprisoned in him the image of the heavenly Anthropos, and that image is what's referred to as "the Great Man from above." He imprisoned this image of the heavenly Anthropos with the intention of punishing it.

Now, you'll remember last week I spoke of the Manichaean myth of the war between the powers of light and darkness.[206] But from the standpoint of the upper god, the fall of this image of the Anthropos into matter and the incarnation of the soul of the Anthropos in the clay statue image of Adam was to have the effect of poisoning the darkness from within. The suffering of the Anthropos image imprisoned in the soul of Adam is thus a part of the redemption drama of the divine or transpersonal aspect of the psyche.

---

[205] Hippolytus, "Elenchos," V, 2.
[206] See also above, lecture 3, pp. 49f.

Do I make that clear? Do you get that? I see there is some question about it! I think this is so significant psychologically that I want to try to communicate it—that's why I brought it up. The basic idea of the text I just quoted is that the inert statue—the first Adam—was imbued with a soul which is the image of the heavenly Anthropos. The text says that the soul, that image, was put into the original Adam in order to make the heavenly Anthropos suffer. That was the evil demiurge's intent, to make it suffer—it was a prisoner of war he was going to torture. But the consequence is quite different, because the heavenly deity has another plan: he intends to poison the powers of darkness by allowing the light soul to enter into the lower realm. And although the suffering of the soul does take place, it is for the purpose of redemption, the net goal being the reconciliation of the conflict that goes on between the realms.

My view is that anything helps which sheds a little light, a little understanding, on why earthly existence is so damned hard. And I think this myth does shed some light on that.

Okay, now going on to tonight's assignment. It continues the examination of the symbolism of Adam.

1. Adam as Wise Man and First Alchemist

Jung states that a lot of material indicates that Adam was associated with primal wisdom and was also, in some alchemical material, thought to be the first alchemist. It is even thought that he brought the Philosophers' Stone out of Paradise. There is a very interesting story in the Kabbalah about Adam's book of wisdom and Jung alludes to it in paragraph 572. Let me read a somewhat expanded version of that myth.

In the fifth book of Genesis there is mention of a so-called book of the generations of Adam, and the Kabbalists interpret that to mean the following:

> It is supposed by the Zohar to signify that there was a Secret and Supreme Book, the source of all, including the Hebrew letters. . . . It expounded the Holy Mystery of Wisdom and the efficiency resident in the Divine Name of seventy-two letters. It was sent down from heaven by the hands of the angel Raziel and Adam was entrusted therewith. . . . The gift placed Adam in a superior position to that of any celestial being . . . [because he became acquainted] in this manner with Supernal Wisdom, and the Celestial Choirs came down to be present when he read the book. He was cautioned, however, to conceal it, and he seems therefore to have studied it in silence. . . . [This book] was clasped in his hands when he was driven out of the Garden of Eden, but thereafter it vanished, and for long and long he lamented the loss of his treasure. Ultimately it was given back to him. . . : he returned to its study and bequeathed it to his son Seth, who entrusted it to later messengers, so that the Secret Doctrine might be spread through the world.[207]

---

[207] A.E. Waite, *The Holy Kabbalah,* pp. 16f.

This particular myth is something to keep in mind when one encounters dreams containing images of an ancient or remarkable book. Such an image is symbolically analogous, when amplified with this myth anyway, to the image of Adam: the original wisdom that connects the psyche with its celestial, transpersonal origins. That's one of the implications of the image of Adam.

2. Adam in a Series of Eight

Adam also fits into the symbolic context of the series of eight. For instance, in paragraph 573 we learn that certain texts consider Adam as the first of a series of eight incarnations of the "true prophet": Adam, Enoch, Noah, Abraham, Isaac, Jacob, Moses and Christ. Jung points out that this theme is paralleled by the Taoist series of eight mortals, seven of whom are immortal sages residing in heaven—represented with long beards—and the eighth, a girl who sweeps up fallen flowers. Jung remarks that this once more is an example of that old problem of the three and the four—the famous Axiom of Maria[208]—transposed to the level of the seven and the eight: seven are more or less uniform and established, but the eighth is something novel, different and unexpected.

Jung then moves to another parallel of the same image—this time in Gnosticism—where the seven archons of the Pleroma, which combined are called the Hebdomad, are then completed in an eighth which is Sophia, the feminine element. This changes the Hebdomad to the Ogdoad, the eightfold Pleroma.

That reminds Jung of a Gnostic chart described by Origin, "the diagram of the Ophites," which shows the universe in ten concentric bands or circles (paragraph 574). The interesting feature of this particular chart, which Jung says is indeed a mandala, is that both the outermost circle—the circumference—and the center are called "Leviathan." The text describing this Ophite chart states that Leviathan "is the soul that has permeated the universe."

So this image of the total universe—an image of psychic totality—has Leviathan as its center and as its circumference. That corresponds to one of the descriptions of God often referred to by Jung: "God is a circle whose centre is everywhere and the circumference nowhere."[209] This tells us in psychological terms that Leviathan, which we can recognize as a symbolic image of the primordial psyche (the collective unconscious or archetypal psyche in its abysmal aspect) is the center and circumference of the human psyche. That's a manifestation of deity—the same discovery Job made, as Jung points out. That's all implied in this diagram of the Ophites.

It's also interesting that a parallel to this diagram of the Ophites is found in

---

[208] See below, lecture 23, pp. 276f.
[209] See, for instance, "A Psychological Approach to the Dogma of the Trinity," *Psychology and Religion,* CW 11, par. 229, note 6; also *Mysterium,* CW 14, par. 41.

certain pictures of the Sefirotic Tree, which I talked about in the second lecture and will again a little later tonight. In these diagrams, the Sefirotic Tree is pictured as a series of ten concentric circles (figure 20-1); the lowest circle, the innermost, is Malchuth, and the topmost circle is Kether. So the Kabbalistic imagination came up with essentially the same image of totality as did the Gnostic imagination of the Ophites.

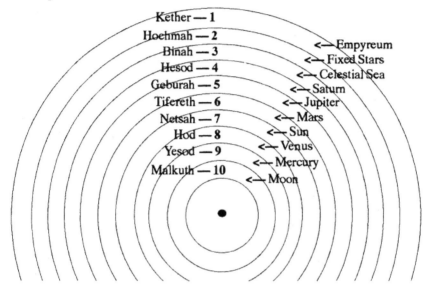

Figure 20-1. The Sefirotic Tree as a series of ten concentric circles.

3. The Polarity and Androgyny of Adam

According to the Biblical account, Eve was created out of the rib of Adam; according to certain legendary material, it is stated even more explicitly that Adam was overtly androgynous—or Eve couldn't have been created out of him.[210]

This androgyny of Adam, which requires a division at the beginning of the creation of man, is paralleled by an important myth that's found in Plato's dialogue, "The Symposium." In this dialogue, Socrates and some of his companions got together for a banquet. Their idea of amusement was to choose a subject on which each participant would give a presentation; it would be a kind of competitive series. On this occasion they decided that each person would give a presentation on the nature of Eros. It's a very interesting series—if you're not familiar with it, I recommend it highly.

---

[210] See Louis Ginzberg, *Legends of the Bible,* p. 35.

One of the participants was Aristophanes, and the main content of his presentation was that the nature of love can best be understood by an old myth which he proceeded to relate. It is sort of a Platonic version of the Adam myth and the myth about the original man. It's so relevant psychologically that I'm going to quote fairly extensively from it.

> [In this original situation, when God was first creating man] the form of each person was round all over, with back and sides encompassing it every way; each had four arms, and legs . . . two faces, perfectly alike. . . . There was one head to the two faces, which looked in opposite ways; there were four ears, two privy members, and all the other parts . . . . The creature walked upright as now. . . and whenever it started running fast, it went like our acrobats, whirling over and over.

So it sort of rolled, since it was globular in shape.

> Now, they were of surprising strength and vigour, and so lofty in their notions that they even conspired against the gods; and the same story is told of them as Homer relates of Ephialtes and Otus, that scheming to assault the gods in fight they essayed to mount high heaven.

It's a version of the Tower of Babel story, you see.

> Therat Zeus and the other gods debated what they should do, and were perplexed: for they felt they could not slay them like the Giants, whom they had abolished root and branch. . . . — it would be only abolishing the honours and observances they had from men; nor yet could they endure such sinful rioting. Then Zeus, putting all his wits together, spake at length and said: "Methinks I can contrive that men, without ceasing to exist, shall give over their iniquity through a lessening of their strength. I propose now to slice every one of them in two, so that while making them weaker we shall find them more useful by reason of their multiplication; and they shall walk erect on two legs. If they continue turbulent and do not choose to keep quiet, I will do it again, said he; "I will slice every person in two, and then they must go their ways on one leg, hopping." So saying, he sliced each human being in two, just as they slice sorb-apples to make a dry preserve, or eggs with hairs; and at the cleaving of each he bade Apollo turn its face and half-neck to the section side, in order that every one might be made more orderly by the sight of the knife's work upon him. Then Apollo turned their faces about and pulled their skin together from the edges over what is now called the belly, just like purses which you draw close with a string; the little opening he tied up in the middle of the belly, so making what we know as the navel. For the rest, he smoothed away most of the puckers and figured out the breast with some such instrument as shoemakers use in smoothing the wrinkles of leather; . . . Now when our first form had been cut in two each half in longing for its fellow would come to it again; and then they would fling their arms about each other and in mutual embraces yearn to be grafted together . . . . Thus anciently is mutual love ingrained in mankind, reassembling our early estate and endeavouring to combine two in one and heal the human sore.
>
> Each of us, then, is but a tally of a man, since every one shows like a flat-fish the

traces of having been sliced in two; and each is ever searching for the tally that will fit him.[211]

In a footnote, the translator tells us that the word translated as "tally" is the Greek word *symbolon,* which was used to refer to the half of a broken die given and kept as a token of friendship.

This is what happened to the original spherical man, according to the Platonic myth, and it is analogous symbolically to Adam being divided into two. And according to this myth, that division is the origin of love, because the divided halves yearn to be reunited; the yearning for original wholeness is the origin of love. And believe it or not, Aristophanes didn't win the prize! He wasn't considered the best; Socrates was even better. But I thought it was pretty good.

Another fundamental polarity embodied in the Adam figure is the contradiction between his physical and his spiritual nature. He's made of both clay and breath, you see, and those two features are opposites. This corresponds to the ancient formula of the Orphics who, in order to get into Paradise after they died, had to announce successfully who they were to the gatekeepers of the other world. According to the Orphic formula, when you were asked: "Who's knocking at the door?" you were supposed to answer: "I am a child of earth and starry heaven." In other words, "I'm made of clay and stars combined"—it's the same thing as Adam.[212]

There's an interestingly similar and yet different symbolism that occurs in the image of the Persian first man, Gayomart. According to the myth, which I simplify a little bit, there were originally two gods, Ahura Mazda, the good god; and Angra Mainyu, the evil one. Ahura Mazda, the good one, created Gayomart, the first man; but Angra Mainyu attacked Gayomart with the Demon of Death so that avarice, want, pain, hunger, disease, lust and lethargy were all diffused through Gayomart's body and after thirty years he died. On his death he released semen which incubated in the earth and from his body grew metals, including gold; from the gold grew a plant. This plant represented the first human couple and they were wrapped in each other's arms, their bodies united. (That would correspond to Plato's spherical man.) From that plant they then separated and became two human beings.

The conflict between Ahura Mazda and Angra Mainyu wasn't over because Ahura Mazda told them to do good, but Angra Mainyu attacked and they were poisoned with antagonism. So the battle between good and evil went on.[213]

Now, what is the difference between the Persian myth and the Biblical Adam and Eve myth? It is important to pay attention to such things because I believe the

---

[211] Plato, *Symposium,* pp. 135ff. (sections 189e-191a).
[212] See Jane Harrison, *Prolegomena to the Study of Greek Religion,* p. 573.
[213] See Joseph Campbell, *The Masks of God: Occidental Mythology,* pp. 205f.

roots of international relations can be observed in the myths of origins.

Persia of course is Iran, and according to this Persian version of the creation of man, evil is a cosmic archetypal principal that causes the fall of man and his corruption. But in the Biblical version, the source of evil and the cause of man's fall is lodged in man himself. This means then that in the Biblical myth man is being obliged to carry the opposites in the ego, so to speak, whereas in the Persian version, the origin of evil and the source of the sense of guilt and conflict resides in the divine realm. In other words, the Biblical version lodges more responsibility with the ego than does the Persian version. The implication would be that what grows out of the Biblical version involves greater ego development, albeit at the cost of greater psychological suffering.

4. Adam as Anthropos

In paragraph 590 Jung says:

> As the first man, Adam is the *homo maximus,* the Anthropos, from whom the macrocosm arose, or who *is* the macrocosm. He is not only the prima materia but a universal soul which is also the soul of all men.

Now there's an important passage in paragraph 593 about this matter of the universal soul—a very interesting piece of symbolic imagery. Jung quotes a passage from a text by Knorr von Rosenroth concerning the psychological interpretation of Adam:

> (The meaning [about Adam] is this: out of your souls was composed the microcosm of Adam). . . . Ye are Adam. (He says, as it were, that all the souls of the Israelites were in truth nothing but the first-created Adam.) And you were his sparks and his limbs.

Then Jung goes on to interpret what that means:

> Here Adam appears on the one hand as the body of the people of Israel and on the other as its "general soul." This conception can be taken as a projection of the interior Adam: the *homo maximus* appears as a totality, as the "self" of the people. As the inner man, however, he is the totality of the individual, the synthesis of all parts of the psyche, and therefore of the conscious and the unconscious. § 20 says: "And therefore our masters have said: The son of David shall not come until all the souls that were in the body (of the first-created) have fully gone out." The "going out" of the souls from the Primordial Man can be understood as the projection of a psychic integration process: the saving wholeness of the inner man—i.e., the "Messiah"— cannot come about until all parts of the psyche have been made conscious. This may be sufficient to explain why it takes so long for the second Adam to appear.

This alludes to the psychological fact that the Self, as long as it operates in a completely unconscious way, constellates and manifests in an organic collective, and the individual lives as though he or she were a part of that larger organism—

the organic collective, the collective soul. Individuals then are cells or units of the collective soul. That's how their existence is lived out. Now if an occasional individual here and there achieves consciousness of the Self, that person is ejected, so to speak, from containment in the collective soul, and is on his or her own—which is both better and worse. That's what's referred to in these remarks in paragraph 593.

Question: What's worse about it?

It's lonely; cold and lonely.

Last time, you remember, I presented an Adam dream and I have a couple more this time. Adam doesn't come up very often in dreams, I must say, but when he does you prick up your ears because you know something's going on in the depths. Here's an example of a woman's Adam dream:

> I am walking down a mountain path that leads to a stream. To my surprise I find a naked man stretched out sleeping by the side of the stream. He's large and strong; virile and bearded. His backpack and clothes are lying to the side. Somewhat frightened, my first thought is to run and retreat, but when the man awakes and looks at me, I realize he has no intention of hurting me; I know he will let me pass unharmed. I apologize for disturbing him, turn to the right and go through a tunnel. I am slowly and carefully climbing over and among huge rocks. As I am about to step on one of the rocks, I am startled to discover that the rock moves. It is in fact a naked man. As I look around, I see that there are several men among the rocks. It is difficult to distinguish them from the rocks—both are clay-colored. The men are sleeping as I enter but some of them wake up and look at me as I pass by.

Now two things establish that as an Adam dream: first, the rocks and men are clay-colored; the second and crucial thing is that her immediate association to the man was Michelangelo's Adam painted on the Sistine Chapel.

This was a middle-aged professional woman with a positive father or princess complex. I mean by that a woman in the habit of being granted what she wants and who takes it as a basis for her existence that if she really desires something, it will be forthcoming; circumstances, like a good daddy, will give it to her.

Her assumption was tested not long after this dream. She very much wanted a certain position for which she was required to be interviewed, and afterward she was denied the position. Well that did it! She fell into a rage because her bedrock assumptions about the nature of life had been challenged. That's how I understand this dream. She thought she was walking on rock, but in fact she was walking on something alive, with a will of its own, and the dream pictures that as Adam. The net result was a kind of earthquake in the psyche in which an encounter with the original man as a living entity helped to dissolve the erroneous assumptions derived from her positive father complex.

Here's another Adam dream. This one did not actually take place under my observation. The dreamer was in her early thirties at the time of the dream and in the early stage of a previous analysis.

> I was asked to be a witness to the opening of a tomb. This was the last time it was going to be unsealed. I stood in the basement at the top of a flight of stairs leading into a sub-basement. Doors opened and I could see into a room down into the sub-basement. All of a sudden a tombstone, suspended on a long rope, swung into view. It dangled there for a moment and I tried desperately to read the inscription on it. It didn't remain long but moved out of sight.
>
> The stone was old and worn, but the surroundings were not old. Did the name begin with an A? It was a short name, four or five letters. Then a man, or maybe two, appeared at the bottom of the stairs and said that I was to sign my name to show that I had been a witness to this event. I turned back, preparing to leave, and I saw a Negro man sitting on the floor. I walked past him and then turned back and said, "Wasn't I supposed to sign?" and the Negro's only response was, "Yes." He said it as though he didn't care whether I signed or not, and he wasn't especially helpful or friendly. I felt I must follow through with the assignment although it took some effort to do so. The Negro allowed me to take the paper and sign it. Then it seemed that, according to him, more was expected. I was supposed to write something elaborate. Seeing a pad of paper, I took it and went over to a desk. As I stood there I realized this was a bigger assignment than I could cope with. I needed time. Also wanted to look up a word in the dictionary. I couldn't complete it now. I must give it some thought.

Then, as she awoke, these verses came to her:

> The stone, the stone, that swings so mysteriously on its long rope,
> Let it come to rest on the rough floor so that the inscription may be read;
> And she who seeks, learn that it belongs to Adam.
> Let the old man rise from the deep and sit with her on the stone throne
> In the musty old new room, prophetic in its atmosphere.
> Let the woman put some questions to the frail and ancient sage,
> Probe the mystery of the setting, seek the meaning of the stone.
> The woman isn't equal to it; she's dumb.
> She signs her name in a large black ledger and departs.

That's the dream of a woman who had a lifetime of analysis. It took place many, many years ago and it's another Adam dream; the images of Adam, his tomb and the tombstone are all interconnected. At that early phase, at the beginning of her lifetime analytic process (it went on for thirty or forty years), the dream showed that she'd had a glimpse of the Self which brought with it an assignment that was more than she could deal with. And that indeed is how her life lived itself out. She lived a decent, conventionally productive life, but she didn't make it in terms of achieving a full connection with the inner authority. This dream lays that all out right at the very beginning.

The idea of the stone as a symbolic equivalent of Adam comes up in another myth from the Zohar concerning the mystical stone. Let me read you some of it:

This mysterious stone was originally in the throne of God, a precious stone or jewel, and it was cast by him into the abyss in order to form the basis of the world and give birth thereto. It was like a cubical stone or altar, where its extremity was concealed in the depths while its surface or summit rose above the chaos. It was a central point in the immensity of the world. The cornerstone, the tried stone, the sure foundation. It was that stone also which served Jacob as a pillow and thereafter for an altar. It was the good stone, the precious stone and the foundation of Zion. The Tables of the Law were made from it and it is destined for the salvation of the world. It is like the *lapis exilis* of the German Grail legend for it appears to be a slight stone but it is supposed to have been carried by Aaron when he entered the Holy Place and it was held in the hands of David when he desired to contemplate close at hand the glory of his master. In a sense it fell from heaven like the stone from the crown of Lucifer. Solomon was also one of those who restored it and built his sanctuary on it. And on this stone was inscribed the Divine Name before it was cast into the Abyss. . . . This mystic stone is the central point of the world and where it resides is the Holy of Holies.[214]

This would be a mythological elaboration of the tombstone image which the patient glimpsed in her dream.

5. Eleazar's Text

The reason this text comes up is that it has the figure of Adam in it—it's a further amplification of the image of Adam. Jung's discussion of it continues on into our next two assignments. I want to read Eleazar's text as a complete unit now. It starts in paragraph 591:

For Noah must wash me in the deepest sea, with pain and toil, that my blackness may depart; I must lie here in the deserts among many serpents, and there is none to pity me; I must be fixed to this black cross, and must be cleansed therefrom with wretchedness and vinegar and made white, that the inwards of my head may be like the sun or Marez [earth], and my heart may shine like a carbuncle, and the old Adam come forth again from me. O! Adam Kadmon, how beautiful art thou! And adorned with the rikmah [many-colored garment] of the King of the World! Like Kedar [the men of Kedar lived in black tents] I am black henceforth; ah! how long! O come, my Mesech [mixed drink, spiced wine], and disrobe me, that mine inner beauty may be revealed. . . . O that the serpent roused up Eve! To which I must testify with my black colour that clings to me, and that is become mine by the curse of this persuasion, and therefore I am unworthy of all my brothers. O Sulamith afflicted within and without, the watchmen of the great city will find thee and wound thee, strip thee of thy garments and smite thee, and take away thy veil. . . . Yet shall I be blest again when I am delivered from the poison brought upon me by the curse, and mine inmost seed and first birth comes forth. For its father is the sun, and its mother is the moon. Yea, I know else of no other bridegroom who should love me, because

---

214 Waite, *Holy Kabbalah,* pp. 228f. (modified and summarized).

I am so black. Ah! do thou tear down the heavens and melt my mountains! For thou didst crumble the mighty kingdoms of Canaan like dust, and crush them with the brazen serpent of Joshua and offer them up to Algir [fire], that she who is encompassed by many mountains may be freed.

Then we go on to paragraphs 622 and 624 which complete the text:

What shall I say? I am alone among the hidden; nevertheless I rejoice in my heart, because I can live privily, and refresh myself in myself. But under my blackness I have hidden the fairest green.

But I must be like a dove with wings, and I shall come and be free at vespertime, when the waters of impurity are abated, with a green olive leaf; then is my head of the fairest Asophol [gold], and my hair curly-gleaming as the [moon]. And Job says (27: 5), that out of my [earth] shall come forth blood. For it is all as [fire], shining red Adamah, mingled with a glowing [fire]. Though I am poisonous, black and hateful without, yet when I am cleansed I shall be the food of heroes; as out of the lion which Samson slew there afterward came forth honey. Therefore says Job 28: 7: . . . [No bird has known the path nor has the eye of the vulture seen it.] For this stone belongeth only to the proven and elect of God.

This is a long and difficult text but since Jung lavishes on it such a lot of attention it is evident that he considers it very important. So likewise we will examine it carefully over the next couple of evenings.

Tonight I want to draw your attention to two features. First, the speaker describes herself as the Shulamite. This will be the personification of the prima materia, or the hidden value caught in the darkness of the unconscious, who identifies herself with the beloved in Solomon's Song of Songs. That's why I wanted you to look into the Song of Songs—it will be useful for amplification.

Secondly, Adam Kadmon is mentioned in the first part of the text and I'd like to say a word or two about that. Adam Kadmon is the image of the Anthropos as it manifests itself in the Kabbalah. He's thought of as the first emanation of the En Sof and he's also thought of as the totality of the Sefirotic Tree.[215]

Now let me tell you what I mean by that. The Kabbalistic idea is that the original creative power—the En Sof which signifies infinity, that which has no end—emanates; it shines forth out of its potential. And what it emanates is Adam Kadmon, the Anthropos, a great cosmic figure of man. According to some versions, Adam Kadmon then may further emanate the whole Sefirotic Tree (figure 20-2); or in other versions the Sefirotic Tree itself can be considered as the body of Adam Kadmon. Those are two different ways of seeing it.

Here's what the Zohar says about the En Sof:

Within the most hidden recess a dark flame issued from the mystery of *eyn sof,* the Infinite, like a fog forming in the unformed. . . . Only after this flame began to as-

[215] See above, fig. 2-3, p. 39.

sume size and dimension, did it produce radiant colors. From the innermost center of the flame sprang forth a well out of which colors issued and spread upon everything beneath, hidden in the mysterious hiddenness of *eyn sof.*

The well broke through and yet did not break through the ether [of the sphere]. It could not be recognized at all until a hidden, supernal point shown forth under the impact of the final break through.[216]

It starts out as a kind of creative point and then Adam Kadmon emanates out from that.

Next week we'll engage in detail this complex and profound text.

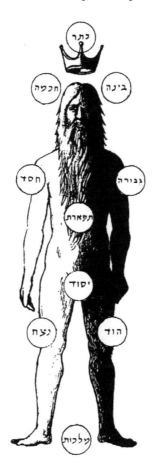

Figure 20-2.
Adam Kadmon and
the Sefirotic Tree.

---

[216] Gershom Scholem, ed., *Zohar, The Book of Splendor: Basic Readings from the Kabbalah,* p. 27.

21
Paragraphs 596-625

Tonight and next week we continue the examination of Eleazar's text. Jung gives it a lot of attention so we're also going to examine it in a fairly leisurely fashion. This is one of the alchemical texts that makes special use of the symbolism of the Song of Songs; the other outstanding example is the *Aurora Consurgens*, edited by Marie-Louise von Franz. As it is used so explicitly in the text, I want to review briefly the essential content of the Song of Songs.

Eleazar's Text: The Song of Songs

Considered from the psychological standpoint the Song of Songs, along with Ezekiel's great chariot-mandala vision,[217] can be seen as the symbolic culmination of Old Testament symbolism and as a representation of the individuation process. Let me remind you briefly of the basic sequence of images.

There are two protagonists: the Shulamite (the Bride) and her Bridegroom.

1. The Shulamite, burned black by the sun, labors in her brothers' vineyards and yearns for the Bridegroom.

2. Then lo and behold, the Bridegroom comes, leaping over the mountains like springtime.

3. But he goes again and is lost. The lonely Shulamite rises from her bed and searches the streets for her Beloved.

4. Once again she encounters him; this time the Bridegroom comes like a great royal procession, the procession of King Solomon.

5. The Bride and the Bridegroom meet in the garden and the Bridegroom praises the Shulamite, but he's wounded by her. "You ravish my heart," he says, "with a single one of your glances." Once again they separate.

6. Then the Bride is alone at night and the Bridegroom knocks at her door but she is slow to answer. When she finally does answer, he's gone.

7. She's distraught and goes out in search of him.

8. While she's searching, the watchmen come upon her, beat her and steal her cloak.

9. Finally, the Bride and Bridegroom find each other and they unite in the garden of pomegranates.

10. The poem ends with the united lovers sealed to each other in eternal love.

That's the basic plot of the Song of Songs. It's a book that has been used by all the major Western mystical traditions—very extensively in the Kabbalah—and,

---

[217] See above, lecture 11, and Edinger, *Bible and the Psyche,* pp. 124ff.

because of its psychological content, it is quite understandable that it should be picked up by the alchemists and used widely in their symbolism.

Last time I read the entire text of Eleazar which extends over several pages. I'm not going to read that again but I am going to outline it for you. You must remember that alchemical texts are very much like dreams—they emerge from the unconscious in a similar way and that means they lack the rational sequence, the order and the structure that conscious contents have. The process of assimilating either a dream or an alchemical text requires therefore that one impose a certain rational structure and order on the unconscious material so that consciousness can assimilate it. That's what we call the interpretive process. It is an essential part of assimilation because consciousness cannot build into its own structure material which has not been ordered in the categories consciousness is familiar with. That is why interpretive structuring is indispensable.

So I'm going to impose a certain amount of order on the text, which in its original form is quite disorderly—so disorderly that it can hardly be held in consciousness. You can read it through and you can't remember what you read—it has not been accommodated to the categories of consciousness.

This text has as its central character the black Shulamite who is submitting to a process which she describes twice. Her first description I would outline as having five steps:

1. She's washed by Noah.
2. She finds herself in a desert with serpents.
3. She's fixed on a black cross.
4. Her heart and head become shining and bright.
5. Old Adam and/or Adam Kadmon come forth from her.

That's the first version of the process. Then the same process is described a second time with a different sequence, this one of six steps:

1. She calls to be disrobed.
2. She announces she's guilty of the sin of Eve.
3. Watchmen strip her of her garments. (It's an exact parallel to the Song of Songs here.)
4. Her mountains are melted with Joshua's brazen serpent.
5. From her blackness comes greenness.
6. Her head turns to gold and she turns into the Philosophers' Stone.

That's the sequence of steps, described twice over, that we're going to be talking about tonight and next time.

As with all these alchemical texts, we must remind ourselves again that what's being described is an alchemical recipe, a description of a process that's going on in the alchemical retort. The black Shulamite is the personification of the prima materia that's undergoing transformation. She specifically calls herself the Shulamite, so that association is explicitly to the Song of Songs. But parallels to that same image would be Sophia caught in the dark embrace of matter, which is the Gnostic myth; or the Shekinah, the feminine presence of God, who is in exile from Yahweh, lost in the dark world, separated from her divine consort. Or she's the anima mundi, the animating spirit that permeates all things. Or, to be completely psychological, she is the primordial psyche in its dark, unregenerate, infantile state as we encounter it in analysis.

All these images and terms are different expressions for the same psychological entity. When we think of it that way and appreciate that all these facets are variations of the same thing, it helps us to realize that when we work on unconscious contents, whether in ourselves or our patients, we are simultaneously contributing to the rescue of Sophia, to the restoration of the Shekinah from her exile, and to the redemption of the anima mundi.

1. The text begins:

> For Noah must wash me in the deepest sea, with pain and toil, that my blackness may depart.

The prima materia is announcing that it must be subjected to a solutio.[218] In fact it must be subjected to a Noah's flood. And that particular image actually amounts to a death and rebirth of the world, an archetypal solutio. The alchemist here is obliged to function out of the guiding figure of Noah. Noah, you know, was the archetypal faithful one in a world of corruption. He was an important figure in the Kabbalah which equated the ark that saved Noah from the flood with the Ark of the Covenant, the dwelling place of Yahweh enshrined in the Tabernacle. This indicates that it was Noah's covenant with Yahweh, his connection with the transpersonal center, that saved him from perishing.

This suggests psychologically that the adept must perform this solutio operation out of a Noah attitude, in a covenant state with the Self; because the danger of course, when one ventures to encounter and deal with the black prima materia, is that one will be inundated and carried away by Noah's flood. If one isn't a Noah, you see, one may drown. This very first phrase that speaks of Noah alludes to that double aspect of the work.

2. Then comes an abrupt shift to a different climate. The Shulamite says:

> I must lie here in the deserts among many serpents and there is none to pity me.

After the solutio comes the calcinatio,[219] a drying process in the hot desert which includes an exposure to serpents. That image comes from a specific event, recorded in the Bible, that took place during the wilderness wanderings:

> And the soul of the people was much discouraged because of the way. And the

---

[218] See Edinger, *Anatomy,* chap. 3.
[219] Ibid., chap. 2.

people spake against God, and against Moses, Wherefore have ye brought us up out of Egypt to die in the wilderness? for there is no bread, neither is there any water; and our soul loatheth this light bread. And the Lord sent fiery serpents among the people, and they bit the people; and much people of Israel died.[220]

The fiery serpents are part of Yahweh's dark nature. The floods that he sent at the time of Noah are another version—a watery one as opposed to the hot serpentine version. So in our text, the serpents are part of the Shulamite's dark nature which must be experienced, assimilated and made conscious. After the danger of being inundated by dark flood waters comes the danger of being bitten by fiery serpents, which would correspond to intense affects that burn one up or poison one.

3. The Shulamite says:

I must be fixed to this black cross and must be cleansed therefrom with wretchedness and vinegar.

The idea of being fixed to a cross indicates that she must undergo a fourfold differentiation. It was a characteristic feature of certain of the philosophical creation myths that the original prima materia of the universe had to submit to a fourfold division, be divided into the four elements: earth, air, fire, water. That cross of the four elements constitutes the cross of *physis*—it's how matter comes into the world. The idea of being fixed is a procedure which refers to the process of coagulatio, namely a realization of the contents that are coming into consciousness.[221] The fact that the cross is black indicates its *nigredo* aspect, so we have a combination of the coagulatio operation with the symbolism of the mortificatio which is what the symbolism of blackness is associated with.[222]

The cross is also an allusion to enduring the conflict of the opposites and to Christ's crucifixion. This connection is repeated with the phrase "with wretchedness and vinegar," which refers to the hyssop and vinegar that was offered to Christ on the cross.

Let's look at this idea of the fourfold differentiation of emerging contents. One can say that each newly appearing entity that must be subjected to psychic inventory, to assimilation, is subject to four questions or four procedures, corresponding to the four psychological functions.

The first issue is the realization that something in fact does exist. Often, when a newly emerging content comes up we see it for a minute and then it's gone and something in us says, "Oh, that isn't anything, that was just a fantasy, an illusion. It doesn't have any reality." So the first step is provided by the sensation function, that says, "There's something there, there's something really there; that's *real!*"

---

[220] Num. 21: 4-6, Authorized Version.
[221] See Edinger, *Anatomy,* chap. 4.
[222] Ibid, chap. 6.

Sensation tells us that. It's a fact.

Then the thinking function will tell us what it is, what category of understanding is to be attached to it. The feeling function tells us whether we like it or not. And intuition tells us where it came from, where it's going, what it's good for and what connections it may have. If one applies all four procedures to a newly emerging content then that would correspond to fixing it on the fourfold cross, so to speak, and once that's taken place it's not likely to drop out of consciousness; it's been nailed into consciousness and it's going to stay there.

4. and 5. The Shulamite speaks of being

> made white, that the inwards of my head may be like the sun or Marez [white earth], and my heart may shine like a carbuncle, and the old Adam come forth again from me.

Here we see that the product of the preceding operations of calcinatio and mortificatio is the *albedo,* the white earth, the shining white earth, the purified principle of materiality which, like the Virgin Mary, is ready to incarnate the divine child. With that symbolism it comes as something of a shock to learn, according to the text, that what she's going to give birth to is the "old Adam."

Jung goes into some detail discussing the implications of the "old" Adam (paragraphs 596f). The term derives from the apostle Paul who in Corinthians says:

> For as in Adam all die, even so in Christ shall all be made alive.[223]

That idea leads to Adam being considered as the old Adam and Christ being considered the new Adam, or the second Adam. In Romans Paul says:

> For if we have been planted together in the likeness of his [Christ's] death, we shall be also in the likeness of his resurrection: Knowing this, that our old man is crucified with him, that the body of sin might be destroyed.[224]

That "old man" is the old Adam and is crucified with Christ.

The fact that this text made use of that phrase gives away the author's Christian psychology, you see—he was familiar with this particular imagery although he was claiming to be writing as a Jew. Jung demonstrates that he gave himself away in that regard. The author apparently meant to refer to the original "Ur-" Adam, which he equates with the Kabbalistic Adam Kadmon in the next sentence. But as Jung puts it in paragraph 598, he made a "slip" and used a term with a very different connotation for the Christian psyche. This slip indicates that his unconscious was seeking a greater wholeness, one that includes the dark, sinful old Adam whereas his Christian consciousness had a bias toward the spirit. It

---

[223] 1 Cor. 15: 22, Authorized Version.
[224] Rom. 6: 5-6, Authorized Version.

would be just the person who has that kind of spiritual bias that would be most apt to submit to the slip in the opposite direction.

The last phrase, "and the old Adam come forth again from me," is immediately followed by:

> O! Adam Kadmon, how beautiful art thou! And adorned with the rikmah [many-colored garment] of the King of the World! Like Kedar I am black henceforth.

So we see that the old Adam is immediately followed by Adam Kadmon, the Anthropos, who is called "the King of the World." Also, right after being told that the Shulamite had been made white and shining, now she calls herself black again, you see. So that the old Adam and Adam Kadmon are merged with each other, and the shining white, rejuvenated Shulamite is merged with the blackness once more.

Now Jung points out in paragraph 611 that this double pair of contraries constitutes a quaternity and he sets that up in several ways.

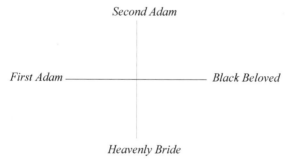

The Second Adam in this diagram would correspond to Adam Kadmon; the Heavenly Bride corresponds to the shining white Shulamite. First Adam corresponds to the old Adam, and the Black Beloved corresponds to the black Shulamite. Those terms can also be arranged in a different sequence so that the two Shulamites are over against each other, and the two Adams are over against each other. That's another version of the quaternity:

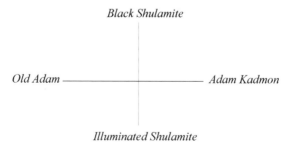

This discussion of the quaternities then leads Jung, in paragraph 619, to the symbolism of the Tetragrammaton about which I want to say a few words. *Yod he vau he: YHVH.* The pronunciation of that sequence of four letters is unknown. It was the unpronounceable name of Yahweh. More than once, when I was giving talks and seminars on Old Testament symbolism, I caused offence to some people by uttering the word "Yahweh"—that issue isn't dead yet.

But this was an item that appealed intensely to the imaginations of the Kabbalists and Jung alludes briefly to what they made of the Tetragrammaton. According to the Kabbalah, *yod* equals the Father, the Primal Point. The first *he* equals the Mother or the upper Shekinah. *Vau* or *wau* corresponds to the Son which refers to the Eternal World—that would be the intelligible world, or the archetypal world of Platonic forms in Neo-Platonic philosophy. And the second *he* corresponds to the Daughter or the Shekinah below; that would be the Shekinah in exile.

Now, as Jung points out in paragraph 619, it is highly significant that although the Tetragrammaton is made up of four letters and is therefore a quaternity, one of the letters duplicates itself and therefore the issue of the three and the four appears. And, in the Kabbalistic symbolism anyway, the letter that duplicates itself is the feminine entity. The first *he* is the Mother, and the second *he* is the Daughter, but since they have identical letters, they are not really distinguishable from each other. That corresponds to the fact that, in the masculine psyche anyway (which is the one that is making up this kind of Kabbalistic symbolism) it is the feminine aspect that is not yet differentiated; so that if Mother and Daughter can't be distinguished, I wonder if there is an incest problem.

Interestingly, the same issue comes up again in the Christian symbolism of the four letters that, according to traditional ecclesiastical art, were attached to the Cross of Christ at the time of the Crucifixion. The sign was said to read *Ieusus Nazarenus Rex Iudaeorum,* "Jesus the Nazarene King of the Jews." The initial letters of that phrase are INRI. Once again the same phenomenon pertains, namely that there are four letters but one of them is duplicated. When you're on the lookout for a pattern that repeats itself, it is very impressive how it shows up.

I want to read you what the Kabbalah, paraphrased by Waite, says about the Tetragrammaton:

> *Yod* and *He* are the Supreme Mystery, forever impenetrable. On the *Yod* are all things based, and it is never in separation from the *He.* As the prototypical male principle, it has man for another symbol. *He* is the female principle, and it has woman therefore as its emblem; it signifies many mysteries, and its true name is Shekinah. Because the letter *He* is duplicated in the Sacred Name it is said to terminate both the first and second parts thereof. The world was created by the *He,* or alternatively, by the *Yod* and *He* in the perfection of their concurrence. The *Vau* is the "free Son", and it is this which diffuses all blessings. The *Yod* unites with the *He*

as male with female, and gives birth to the *Vau* as Son. The three dwell together in unity. *Vau* is the Eternal World.

. . . [In addition to the three,] there is the *He* final which completes the Sacred Name, and this is called the Daughter. It is said of this Daughter that the *He* came down to earth. The first *He* is liberty above and the second is liberty below. The High Priest depends from the *He* which is above but the ordinary priest from that *He* which is below. . . .

The engendering of a whole world depends on these two principles. The second *He* will rise from the earth, meaning that it will be united with the Divine Hypostases in the world of transcendence. The *Vau* will be united to the *He* and when the *Vau* is thus attached, as a bridegroom to the Bride, there will be union everywhere— between the *Yod* and the *He* above, between the *Vau* and the *He* final.[225]

The idea is that there will eventually be a universal coniunctio, you see.

Question: Is the Christian Trinity based on this too? The Father, Son and Holy Spirit and then the Assumption of the Virgin?

No, the Christian Trinity is not based on this. But what you are noticing is that there is an archetypal correspondence between the two images even though they come from very different sources.

Now I want to speak a little bit about the psychological implications of these quaternities. It's evident that opposites are combined in them; specifically in this case blackness and illumination. The black Shulamite and the illuminated Shulamite; the primitive "old" Adam on the one hand—the sinful, guilt-laden aspect of man—and the transformed Adam as Anthropos on the other hand. In the state of totality represented by such quaternities, the animal psyche and the divine psyche come together. Jung speaks about this in paragraph 601:

As high as the Primordial Man stands on the one side, so low on the other is the sinful, empirical man. The phenomenon of contamination, which we meet so frequently in the psychology of dreams and of primitives, is no mere accident but is based on a common denominator; at some point the opposites prove to be identical, and this implies the possibility of their contamination. One of the commonest instances of this is the identity of the god and his animal attribute. Such paradoxes derive from the non-human quality of the god's and the animal's psychology. The divine psyche is as far above the human as the animal psyche reaches down into subhuman depths.

The connection between the god and the animal, the symbolic equivalence between them, leads then to the idea of the connection between image and instinct. Image = god; instinct = animal. I'm going to skip now to paragraph 603 and read a certain amount there because I think it's quite important.

The primary connection between image and instinct explains the interdependence of

225 Waite, *Holy Kabbalah,* pp. 207f.

instinct and religion in the most general sense. These two spheres are in mutually compensatory relationship . . . . "Religion" on the primitive level means the psychic regulatory system that is coordinated with the dynamism of instinct. On a higher level this primary interdependence is sometimes lost, and then religion can easily become an antidote to instinct, whereupon the originally compensatory relationship degenerates into conflict, religion petrifies into formalism, and instinct is vitiated. A split of this kind is not due to a mere accident, nor is it a meaningless catastrophe. It lies rather in the nature of the evolutionary process itself. . . . For just as there is no energy without the tension of opposites, so there can be no consciousness without the perception of differences.

But when the split has gone so far that the two sides, religion and instinct—or image and animal—lose connection with each other, then some kind of procedure has to be found to reconnect them. Jung says:

Corresponding customs and rites have grown up for the purpose of bringing the opposites together. These reconciling procedures are rites performed by man, but their content is an act of help or reconciliation emanating from the divine sphere   .
. . . To take a simple example: When the rice will not grow, a member of the rice-totem clan builds himself a hut in the rice-field and tells the rice how it originally grew from the rice-ancestor. The rice then remembers its origin and starts growing again. The ritual anamnesis of the ancestor has the same effect as his intervention.

He continues in paragraph 605:

Just as the rice spoils in the defective state, so too man degenerates, whether from the malignity of the gods or from his own stupidity or sin, and comes into conflict with his original nature. He forgets his origination from the human ancestor, and a ritual anamnesis is therefore required. Thus the archetype of Man, the Anthropos, is constellated and forms the essential core of the great religions. In the idea of the *homo maximus* the Above and Below of creation are reunited.

That's what generally occurs in the course of a depth analysis. The patient comes to us in this split state of sterility and division and "a ritual anamnesis" is performed, of which the first phase is a literal anamnesis. In other words we take a case history. And it has a ritual quality to it because it takes place in a formal, structured setting. We say, "Let's pour attention into the question of your origins. Where did you come from?" That's how we start. And we go through that ritual anamnesis which leads into the next stage of the ritual, the examination of dreams.

Hopefully, out of that whole procedure the wisdom of the ancestor is constellated and something of the idea of the *homo maximus,* as Jung puts it—the archetype of Man—is activated and generates a sense of wholeness that heals the split.

There is another aspect to the fact that the divine psyche and the animal psyche are linked to each other and it has direct clinical relevance. Whenever a patient—or oneself for that matter—is grappling with intense instinctual urges, whenever the animal psyche is highly activated, one should be on the lookout for the religious aspect of the phenomenon. Wherever the animal is, one should look for the god. Contrariwise, wherever the god is, one should look for the animal, because, you see, they pull us in opposite directions. The god pulls us into grandiosity, inflation, and the animal pulls us down to the earth. Whenever there is an excess of one, we need to look for its other side.

I want to draw your attention to something else. This is paragraph 611:

> We have paid due attention to the recalcitrant nature of the Shulamite's blackness. Now it is significant that the "old Adam" is mentioned at the very moment when the perfect, prelapsarian Adam, the shining Primordial Man, is obviously meant. Just as the black Shulamite misses the final apotheosis, the total *albedo,* so we lack the necessary confirmation that the first Adam is changed into the second, who at the same time is the father of the first. We cannot suppress the suspicion that, just as the blackness will not disappear, so the old Adam will not finally change. This may be the deeper reason why the expression "the old Adam" did not worry the author, but, on the contrary, seemed just right. It is, unfortunately, far truer to say that a change for the better does *not* bring a total conversion of darkness into light and of evil into good, but, at most, is a compromise in which the better slightly exceeds the worse.

This corresponds to a remark Jung makes in one of the final chapters of his autobiography, where he says something like, "I hold the anxious hope that good may prevail slightly over evil."[226]

I think this is particularly important to keep in mind because our whole two-thousand year cultural history has given us a bias toward the idea of achieving spiritual perfection, the idea that the darkness will be utterly destroyed and there will be nothing but light. That does not fit the reality of psychological experience. The factor that allows the better to slightly exceed the worse is consciousness. But consciousness doesn't turn one into a wholly light person with one's darkness banished. The only difference is that awareness accompanies the dark state. It doesn't remove it. It just allows the better slightly to exceed the worse.

---

[226] *Memories, Dreams, Reflections,* p. 359: "Life is—or has—meaning and meaning-lessness. I cherish the anxious hope that meaning will preponderate and win the battle."

22

Paragraphs 622-653

Eleazar's Text: The Song of Songs (cont.)

Tonight we shall continue with Eleazar's text, although we won't get to the end. I want to begin by repeating the entire text because it's difficult and evokes a lot of complex commentary. I'll remind you once again that it refers to a chemical transformation process going on in the alchemical flask. We have to keep reminding ourselves of that because the imagery leads us elsewhere.

The text starts in paragraph 591; the feminine personification of the prima materia is speaking:

> For Noah must wash me in the deepest sea, with pain and toil, that my blackness may depart; I must lie here in the deserts among many serpents, and there is none to pity me; I must be fixed to this black cross, and must be cleansed therefrom with wretchedness and vinegar and made white, that the inwards of my head may be like the sun or Marez [earth], and my heart may shine like a carbuncle, and the old Adam come forth again from me. O! Adam Kadmon, how beautiful art thou! And adorned with the rikmah [many-colored garment] of the King of the World! Like Kedar [the men of Kedar lived in black tents] I am black henceforth; ah! how long! O come, my Mesech [mixed drink, spiced wine], and disrobe me, that mine inner beauty may be revealed. . . . O that the serpent roused up Eve! To which I must testify with my black colour that clings to me, and that is become mine by the curse of this persuasion, and therefore I am unworthy of all my brothers. O Sulamith afflicted within and without, the watchmen of the great city will find thee and wound thee, strip thee of thy garments and smite thee, and take away thy veil. . . . Yet shall I be blest again when I am delivered from the poison brought upon me by the curse, and mine inmost seed and first birth comes forth. For its father is the sun, and its mother is the moon. Yea, I know else of no other bridegroom who should love me, because I am so black. Ah! do thou tear down the heavens and melt my mountains! For thou didst crumble the mighty kingdoms of Canaan like dust, and crush them with the brazen serpent of Joshua and offer them up to Algir [fire], that she who is encompassed by many mountains may be freed.

Then, paragraphs 622 and 624 complete the text:

> What shall I say? I am alone among the hidden; nevertheless I rejoice in my heart, because I can live privily, and refresh myself in myself. But under my blackness I have hidden the fairest green.

> But I must be like a dove with wings, and I shall come and be free at vespertime, when the waters of impurity are abated, with a green olive leaf; then is my head of the fairest Asophol [gold], and my hair curly-gleaming as the [moon]. And Job says

(27: 5), that out of my [earth] shall come forth blood. For it is all as [fire], shining red Adamah, mingled with a glowing [fire]. Though I am poisonous, black and hateful without, yet when I am cleansed I shall be the food of heroes; as out of the lion which Samson slew there afterward came forth honey. Therefore says Job 28: 7: . . . [No bird has known the path nor has the eye of the vulture seen it.] For this stone belongeth only to the proven and elect of God.

Since the text is so diffuse, let me remind you of the outline I gave you last time to help you catch the main images.

1. She's washed by Noah.
2. She finds herself in the desert with serpents.
3. She's fixed on a black cross.
4. Her heart and head become shining bright.
5. Out of her comes forth the Old Adam, who is Adam Kadmon.

Then the same process is described a second time, with six steps:

1. She calls to be disrobed.
2. She announces she's guilty of the sin of Eve.
3. Watchmen strip her of her garments.
4. She asks that her mountains be melted with Joshua's brazen serpent.
5. From her blackness comes greenness.
6. Her head turns to gold and she turns into the Philosophers' Stone.

That's the sequence. We went through the five steps of the first version last time, ending with the birth of Adam Kadmon; we're ready now to begin examining the second version of the description.

1. She calls to be disrobed. The second version begins with the phrase:

Ah! how long! O come, my Mesech [mixed drink, spiced wine], and disrobe me, that mine inner beauty may be revealed. . . .

This is a composite of several passages from the Song of Solomon, or Song of Songs. In the fifth chapter, the Song of Songs says:

The watchmen that went about the city found me, they smote me, they wounded me; the keepers of the walls took away my veil from me.[227]

They disrobe her. In the seventh chapter it says:

Come, my beloved . . . . Let us get up early to the vineyards; let us see if the vine flourish, whether the tender grape appear, and the pomegranates bud forth: there will I give thee my loves.[228]

Then, in the eighth chapter, it says:

---

[227] Song of Sol., 5: 7, Authorized Version.
[228] Ibid., 7: 11-12.

I would cause thee to drink of spiced wine of the juice of my pomegranate.[229]

So those different aspects are merged in the one phrase in Eleazar's text.

The basic idea is that the apparent blackness of the Shulamite will be resolved when she's part of the coniunctio, when she unites with her beloved; in other words, when the union of opposites has been achieved. Now, what would that mean psychologically?

I think it suggests that what we despise in ourselves, that which is laden with blackness, takes on value and undergoes a transformation to the extent that it is perceived as part of our totality. When the blackest aspects of the shadow, the most negative features of one's life and fate, are seen in relation to one's total life destiny, they change their character. They become acceptable and a meaningful part of the whole. Thus the remark: "When I'm disrobed, then my inner beauty may be revealed"—when she's disrobed as part of the coniunctio.

2. She's guilty of the sin of Eve. Eleazar's text goes on:

O that the serpent roused up Eve! To which I must testify with my black colour that clings to me, and that is become mine by the curse of this persuasion, and therefore I am unworthy of all my brothers.

In this phrase the Shulamite is tracing her black condition back to Eve, back to the crime of eating the fruit of the Tree of Knowledge of Good and Evil. In other words, her blackness derives from the original separation of the opposites that represented the birth of consciousness out of the original state of unconscious wholeness. With that event good and bad, black and white come into existence; moral consciousness is born.

3. Watchmen strip her of her garments.

O Sulamith afflected within and without, the watchmen of the great city will find thee and wound thee, strip thee of thy garments and smite thee, and take away thy veil. . . . Yet shall I be blest again when I am delivered from the poison brought upon me by the curse, and mine inmost seed and first birth comes forth. For its father is the sun, and its mother is the moon.

Here the theme of being disrobed repeats itself. In the previous passage the Shulamite has called for her beloved to come and disrobe her and reveal her inner beauty. But evidently that doesn't happen. That isn't completed, and now she's being disrobed by the watchmen with harshness. The implication remains, however, that this disrobing will still remove the blackness that clings to her. One of the symbolic meanings of disrobing, the removing of clothes, is the extraction of the soul. This corresponds to the coming forth of the first birth, to which the passage refers.

---

[229] Ibid., 8: 2.

The idea seems to be that if the first request to be disrobed by the beloved is not heeded, if it isn't done with gentleness and full awareness of the goal of wholeness, then the theme comes back in a cruder, harsher form and the disrobing actually takes on the quality of stripping. When this process gets started the accretions of the persona that have gathered must be removed. If they are not removed deliberately and gently in quest of wholeness, then they are stripped more harshly by the watchmen.

4. Her mountains are melted with Joshua's brazen serpent.

> Yea, I know else of no other bridegroom who should love, me, because I am so black. Ah! do thou tear down the heavens and melt my mountains! For thou didst crumble the mighty kingdoms of Canaan like dust, and crush them with the brazen serpent of Joshua and offer them up to Algir [fire], that she who is encompassed by many mountains may be freed.

It's as though the whole theme of being stripped, which has taken on some urgency, now shifts to another level. The Shulamite identifies herself with the whole mountain chain. As part of the stripping she now says, "Melt my mountains!" which indicates that at one level of her reality she's identified with the earth—she *is* the earth. And Jung points out in paragraph 622, the Shulamite, like the Hindu goddess Parvati, turns out to be a mountain dweller.

The name Parvati means "mountain dweller." According to Alain Danielou,[230] Parvati is the "daughter of the axial mountain [the axis of the world], from which the earth energy springs forth." He says that in Hindu symbolism "the peaks of the mountains are regarded as places from which the earth energy flows into the ether," into the upper regions. Parvati, the mountain dweller, sends forth her earth energy to the upper regions at such spots. For that reason it is not a safe for human beings to dwell on top of a hill or a mountain because they're right in the path of this energy flow. Such places are only suitable for places of worship.

This symbolism would apply to the Shulamite because we learn from the text that she's a mountain dweller and indeed is the mountain itself. I think this imagery of Parvati alludes to the inflationary aspect of anima possession. Living on the top of a hill or mountain associates to height and inflation symbolism and, according to the Parvati myth, it is in just such a spot that one is most vulnerable to infusion by that anima energy coming up from the earth. It's an expression of the fact that, for a man's psychology, just when he is off the ground and in an inflated, grandiose state, he's most vulnerable to being tripped up by the seduction of the dark anima.[231]

In the text the Shulamite is asking that her mountains be melted. That corre-

---

230 *The Myths and Gods of India,* pp. 263f.
231 See Edinger, *Bible and the Psyche,* p. 66, for a parallel in an individual's dream.

sponds to a passage in Isaiah:

> Every valley shall be exalted, and every mountain and hill shall be made low: and
> the crooked shall be made straight, and the rough places plain.[232]

In other words, the passage announces an enantiodromia in which the opposites
will be reversed.

This is what the Shulamite is calling for—that her mountains be melted
down—and she describes specifically how that's to be done: "with the brazen
serpent of Joshua." There are two references here. One is to Joshua's conquering
of Jericho by marching around the city until the walls tumble down (Joshua 6).
This reference indicates that the Shulamite not only identifies with mountains, she
also identifies with Jericho. So she's the city that must be conquered.

The other reference is to the brazen serpent which wasn't Joshua's brazen
serpent, it was Moses' brazen serpent. It alludes to that very important event,
psychologically and symbolically, during the wilderness experience in which
there was a plague of fiery serpents.[233] You remember that Moses asks Yahweh's
help in this situation. Here's what we're told about that:

> And the Lord said unto Moses, Make thee a fiery serpent, and set it upon a pole: and
> it shall come to pass, that every one that is bitten, when he looketh upon it, shall live.
> And Moses made a serpent of brass, and put it upon a pole, and it came to pass, that
> if a serpent had bitten any man, when he beheld the serpent of brass, he lived.[234]

This tells us then that the Shulamite is not only identified with mountains and
with the city of Jericho, she's also identified with the fiery serpent. And remember
that all these different symbolic synonyms are descriptions of different aspects of
the activated unconscious—that's what we're talking about, the activated
unconscious. The Shulamite informs us that among these other things she's also
a plague of fiery serpents whose poisonous effects must be overcome by the
brazen serpent of Moses.

I consider this image of the brazen serpent that heals the poisonous snake bites
to be very important psychologically. It represents the transformative, healing
symbolic image to be found in the midst of an invasion of the unconscious. It
rescues us from being poisoned or overwhelmed.

Jung has this to say about his own confrontation with the unconscious:

> To the extent that I managed to translate the emotions into images—that is to say,
> to find the images which were concealed in the emotions—I was inwardly calmed
> and reassured. Had I left those images hidden in the emotions, I might have been

---

[232] Isa. 40: 4, Authorized Version.
[233] Num. 21: 5-7. This, incidentally, was mentioned earlier in the Eleazar text: "I must lie
here in the deserts among many serpents . . . ." (See above, p. 254)
[234] Num. 21: 8-9, Authorized Version.

torn to pieces by them. . . . As a result of my experiment I learned how helpful it can be, from the therapeutic point of view, to find the particular images which lie behind emotions.[235]

I think a definite course of action, one that can be more or less regularly prescribed, is indicated under such circumstances. Whenever one is possessed by a powerful affect or mood, the first thing to do is to separate oneself from the aggravating external factor—whatever it is—and then look inside. Do active imagination, seek the image that gives expression to the nature of the inner content that grips one. If the agitation is too great one may need some help. For example, throwing the *I Ching* can be a helpful way to encourage the introverting process when it's hard to get started. If you can find the image that expresses and represents what is gripping you, it can have an almost miraculous effect. It works like Moses' brazen serpent: one is healed of the snake bite, the snake bite of primitive affect.

Let me give you a personal example. Many years ago I was visiting Rome as a sightseeing tourist. I woke up in the middle of the night in a state of anxiety, convinced that the plane I would be taking home was going to crash into the sea. Well, there was clearly no question of any more sleep while that fear was there so I tried to apply this procedure. The image that emerged was the imperious image of the feminine personification of ancient Roma who was angry at me because I had picked up some stones—I had taken some from the Palatine, a little piece from the Colosseum—and she was enraged that I had plucked some of her material and was going to steal it and take it away. She said, "You're going to discover that those stones are too heavy for you to get across the sea. I'm going to drop you right into the ocean."

Well, that was wonderful; at least I knew what I was dealing with! And I said, "Well, if you insist, I'll meekly take them back and drop them right where I found them. However, they're not very much, and you've got a lot of them. Furthermore, I can promise you that when they are taken to the New World they will promote respect for you. They will not be treated disrespectfully; in fact, they will enhance your esteem in the New World. Consider that—you see you've got something to gain."

"Okay," she said, "you can have them." And I could go back to sleep. That's all there was to it.

5. From her blackness comes greenness.

Now that the Shulamite has been subjected to these extreme procedures, being melted down and treated like a fiery serpent, there comes a whole new tone in the text which Jung picks up immediately. The text says this:

> What shall I say? I am alone among the hidden; nevertheless I rejoice in my heart, because I can live privily, and refresh myself in myself. But under my blackness I have hidden the fairest green.

---

[235] *Memories, Dreams, Reflections,* p. 177.

This particular passage evokes from Jung what I regard as one of the most beautiful pieces of writing in all his work. One can be sure that Jung is describing a profound experience of his own inner life. Here is his interpretation of that passage (paragraphs 623 and 624):

> The state of imperfect transformation, merely hoped for and waited for, does not seem to be one of torment only, but of positive, if hidden, happiness. It is the state of someone who, in his wanderings among the mazes of his psychic transformation, comes upon a secret happiness which reconciles him to his apparent loneliness. In communing with himself he finds not deadly boredom and melancholy but an inner partner; more than that, a relationship that seems like the happiness of a secret love, or like a hidden springtime, when the green seed sprouts from the barren earth, holding out the promise of future harvests. It is the alchemical *benedicta viriditas,* the blessed greenness, signifying on the one hand the "leprosy of the metals" (verdigris), but on the other the secret immanence of the divine spirit of life in all things. "O blessed greenness, which generatest all things!" cries the author of the *Rosarium.* "Did not the spirit of the Lord," writes Mylius, "which is a fiery love, give to the waters when it was borne over them a certain fiery vigour, since nothing can be generated without heat? God breathed into created things . . . a certain germination or greenness, by which all things should multiply . . . They called all things green, for to be green means to grow . . . . Therefore this virtue of generation and the preservation of things might be called the Soul of the World."
>
> Green signifies hope and the future, and herein lies the reason for the Shulamite's hidden joy, which otherwise would be difficult to justify. But in alchemy green also means perfection. Thus Arnaldus de Villanova says: "Therefore Aristotle says in his book, Our gold, not the common gold, because the green which is in this substance signifies its total perfection, since by our magistery that green is quickly turned into truest gold."

I think when Jung wrote this he must have had in mind a particular vision he had in 1939 where the combination of greenness and gold appears. Here it is:

> One night I awoke and saw, bathed in bright light at the foot of my bed, the figure of Christ on the Cross. It was not quite life-size, but extremely distinct; and I saw that his body was made of greenish gold. The vision was marvelously beautiful, and yet I was terrified[236] by it. . . .
>
> I had been thinking a great deal about the *Anima Christi,* one of the meditations from the *Spiritual Exercises* [of Ignatius Loyola]. The vision came to me as if to point out that I had overlooked something in my reflections: the analogy of Christ with the *aurum non vulgi* ["not the common gold"] and the *viriditas* of the alchemists. When I realized that the vision pointed to this central alchemical symbol, and that I had had an essentially alchemical vision of Christ, I felt comforted.

---

[236] The German word is *erschrak,* from *erschrecken,* which in the English translation is rendered as "profoundly shaken." I think "terrified" more accurately describes such a powerful experience.

The green gold is the living quality which the alchemists saw not only in man but also in inorganic nature. It is an expression of the life-spirit, the *anima mundi* or *filius macrocosmi,* the Anthropos who animates the whole cosmos. This spirit has poured himself out into everything, even into inorganic matter; he is present in metal and stone. My vision was thus a union of the Christ-image with his analogue in matter, the *filius macrocosmi.* . . . The emphasis on the metal, however, showed me the undisguised alchemical conception of Christ as a union of spiritually alive and physically dead matter.[237]

I keep a permanent marker here in *Mysterium.* I call it the "blessed greenness" page, and whenever a dream comes up involving the color green I take that page out and read it. If you are on the alert for it you'll find green dreams do come up every now and again, usually when the ego is in a state of blackness. Jung's beautiful remarks help to penetrate such blackness, as does Emily Dickinson in "Hope Is the Thing with Feathers":

> Hope is the thing with feathers
> That perches in the soul
> And sings the tune without the words
> And never stops at all.

The Shulamite continues (paragraph 624):

> But I must be like a dove with wings, and I shall come and be free at vespertime, when the waters of impurity are abated, with a green olive leaf;

This refers to the account in Genesis when the flood waters are starting to abate, where we read:

> And he [Noah] stayed yet other seven days; and again he sent forth the dove out of the ark; And the dove came in to him in the evening; and, lo, in her mouth was an olive leaf pluckt off: so Noah knew that the waters were abated from off the earth.[238]

You remember that the text began with a reference to a Noah's flood. This whole text has as its basic psychological reference an inundation by the unconscious, which corresponds to Noah's flood. Now when the inner greenness has been discovered from out of the blackness, the Shulamite speaks of being like Noah's dove, with the green olive leaf in her mouth. The Shulamite has been transformed into the dove of the Holy Ghost, or the dove of Aphrodite; those are two aspects of the same thing. She is a bringer of good tidings, green good tidings. She is "the thing with feathers," the green-feathered one, bringing good tidings to the beleaguered alchemist who is in the position of Noah in his ark, hoping that maybe the waters are finally abating and there's going to be some respite. The olive branch signifies that the flood is over and God's covenant, with its rainbow, is about to come. The *nekyia,* or inundation from the unconscious, is over.

---

[237] *Memories, Dreams, Reflections,* pp. 210f.
[238] Gen. 8:10-11, Authorized Version.

6. Her head turns to gold and she turns into the Philosophers' Stone.

Then is my head of the fairest Asophol [gold] and my hair curly-gleaming as the [moon.]

This brings up a very rich section, paragraphs 626 to 628, amplifying the symbolism of the head. The Shulamite's head has now been transformed into gold and Jung talks about the golden head, the oracular head and the crystalline head. Probably the basic point in head symbolism is that it is the round element of the human organism and it's a reference to the psyche.

Also, the great head or face is a synonym for Adam Kadmon. The Zohar describes the "Macroprosopus"[239] as a great big face:

> That head, desired by all desires, proceeding from the En Soph, the infinite and limitless one, appeared and communicated the vestments of honor. It had been formed and prepared in the likeness of a cranium and it is filled with a crystalline dew. His skin is of ether, clear and congealed. His hair is as of most fine wool, floating through the balanced equilibrium. His eye is ever open and sleepeth not, for it continually keepeth watch. Therein are His two nostrils like mighty galleries, whence his spirit rushes forth over all.[240]

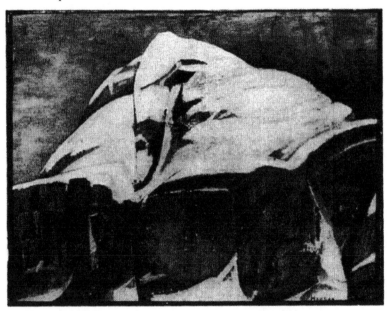

Figure 22-1. The Great Head; painting by Barbara Hannah, 1924.

---

[239] See *Mysterium,* par. 643 and footnote 347.
[240] S.L. MacGregor Mathers, *The Kabbalah Unveiled,* pp. 44-46 (condensed).

I find it particularly interesting that the head is described as that which is "desired by all desires." It reminds me of Jung's earlier remark, in paragraph 192: "What is behind all this desirousness? A thirsting for the eternal." In other words behind all desires is the desire for Adam Kadmon, the Great Head. He is the one desired by all desires.

The symbolism of the Great Head of Adam Kadmon reminds me of a story I first encountered in junior high school. I don't know whether junior high school students still have such good reading but anyway it's Hawthorne's story entitled "The Great Stone Face." It is about a boy named Ernest who grew up in a valley dominated by the Great Stone Face. Hawthorne describes it this way:

> The Great Stone Face, then, was a work of Nature in her mood of majestic playful-ness, formed on the perpendicular side of a mountain by some immense rocks, which had been thrown together in such a position as, when viewed at a proper distance, precisely to resemble the features of the human countenance. It seemed as if an enormous giant, or a Titan, had sculpted his own likeness on the precipice. There was the broad arch of the forehead, a hundred feet in height; the nose, with its long bridge; and the vast lips, which, if they could have spoken, would have rolled their thunder accents from one end of the valley to the other. True it is, that if the spectator approached too near, he lost the outline of the gigantic visage, and could discern only a heap of ponderous and gigantic rocks, piled in chaotic ruin one upon the other. Retracing his steps, however, the wondrous features could again be seen; and the farther he withdrew from them, the more like a human face, with all its original divinity intact, did they appear; until, as it grew dim in the distance, with the clouds and glorified vapor of the mountains clustering about it, the Great Stone Face seemed positively to be alive.[241]

As he develops the story, Hawthorne talks about a legend in the valley that someday a man would come there to live whose face would turn out to be exactly the same as the Great Stone Face. A number of previous valley dwellers arrive trying to claim that distinction—a great merchant, a great general, a statesman—but they don't measure up. And it finally turns out that this boy Ernest himself is the one with the face that's the same as the Great Stone Face. It's a lovely old story about the ego and the Self.

Our text continues:

> And Job says (27: 5), that out of my [earth] shall come forth blood. For it is all as [fire], shining red Adamah, mingled with a glowing [fire].

This reference indicates that the Shulamite's transformation ordeal is analo-gous to Job's.

The image of fire coming out of the earth leads Jung to bring out two major amplifications. One is the fire of hell that burns in the underworld (paragraph 632)

---

[241] *The Complete Novels and Selected Tales,* p. 1171.

and the other is the fire at the feet of the Apocalyptic Christ in the Book of Revelation (paragraph 633). Now in psychological terminology, fire equals affect; and in mythological terminology fire belongs to the gods. In other words, affect comes from the Self. Jung says in "Answer to Job": "God has a terrible double aspect: a sea of grace is met by a seething lake of fire."[242]

As he talks about the image of the Apocalyptic Christ, Jung is reminded of an alchemical picture of the Apocalyptic Christ labeled "Jezoth the Just" (figure 22-2). "Jezoth" is a variant spelling for Yesod, the ninth Sefirah of the Sefirotic Tree. This leads Jung into a long discussion of the symbolism of Yesod.

I've brought back the chart of the Sefirotic Tree.[243] I'm not going to go through it all but I'll remind you that the idea is that the divine manifestation begins as En Sof which then emanates Adam Kadmon, the Anthropos, the Primordial Man which, according to one branch of symbolism, is the Great Face. Further emanations then lead to the tenfold Sefirotic Tree.

For our purposes we can confine ourselves to the central column of that Sefirotic Tree which has Kether or Crown at the top (number 1), Tifereth in the middle (number 6), Yesod below (number 9) and Malchuth at the very bottom. These are descending manifestations of Adam Kadmon. Yesod, then, according to the symbolism, is like the genitals of Adam Kadmon, the phallus of Adam Kadmon.[244]

Now this is what has happened in the material Jung brings together here: the Apocalyptic Christ with the sword coming out of his mouth from Revelation 1: 14 (which is brought up by the image in our text of the fire coming out of the earth), through the alchemical picture of Jezoth the Just, is equated with Yesod in the Kabbalistic symbolism. And Yesod, in turn, is associated with the sexual aspect of Adam Kadmon—the creative phallic fountain, the "spout of the waters" of Adam Kadmon (paragraph 634).

Concerning these interconnections, Jung says that by following up comparisons like these one gradually dislodges images from their dogmatic, traditional matrix and makes them available for psychological understanding. Thus the comparison of the image of the Apocalyptic Christ with the Kabbalistic Yesod, which then has connections to the alchemical text, pries that image out of its original matrix. Similarly, Jung's image of the golden-green crucifix dislodges the image of Christ from its original matrix and recasts it in alchemical terms.

Such recasting and rearranging have the effect of making these images available—for the first time—for psychological understanding. We can now begin to

---

[242] *Psychology and Religion*, CW 11, par. 733; see also Edinger, *Transformation of the God-Image*, p. 114.

[243] See above, fig. 2-3, p. 39.

[244] See above, fig. 20-2, p. 251.

perceive them as psychic entities and no longer as metaphysical or philosophical or speculative entities that must be confined to the particular system in which they first appear.

Jung tells us in paragraph 650 the result when such a process is applied to the imagery of Christ's life:

> The events [of Christ's life] formulated in dogma are brought within range of psychological experience and become recognizable in the process of individuation.

We're not through with Eleazar's text, but that's as far as we'll go tonight.

Figure 22-2. Jezoth the Just.

23
Paragraphs 624-680

1. Eleazar's Text: The Song of Songs (cont.)

Before we turn to tonight's assignment we have to complete Eleazar's text. We were at the conclusion of the second version of the description of the process and in paragraph 624 we come to these lines:

> Though I am poisonous, black, and hateful without, yet when I am cleansed I shall be the food of heroes; as out of the lion which Samson slew there afterward came forth honey.

This refers to the Samson story in Judges 14. You remember that Samson killed a lion, and later when he passed the same way he found that a honey comb had developed in the carcass of the lion (Judges 14: 5-8). Our theme therefore is "Out of the strong came forth sweetness" (Judges 14:14).[245] The changing of the lion into honey is a symbolic image of a transformation mystery—the transformation of power into sweetness.

As Jung tells us in paragraph 639, the transformation of the lion into honey was also applied to the image of Christ: through his passion and death he turned his body into the food of immortality, the eternal food of the Host, the *cibus immortalis,* that is served at the Mass.[246] This would be symbolically equivalent to the honey the lion is turned into. And this is the same process that's taking place with the black Shulamite—she's turned into the food of heroes.

It is very interesting to consider what such images mean when they're nailed down to actual psychological experience. I think it has something to do with the transformation that takes place in the blackness of the psyche—in the shadow—when it's thoroughly analyzed and made conscious.

We see in our own experience and in our work with patients that as long as the shadow is for the most part unanalyzed the unconscious has, by and large, a negative, challenging or critical attitude toward consciousness. It's constantly throwing up to consciousness examples of the neglected shadow so that the ego feels nagged and criticized. Following a thorough analysis of the shadow, the nature of the unconscious is transformed; it becomes nourishing and supportive. This is another example of the psychological rule formulated by Jung that the unconscious takes the same attitude toward the ego as the ego takes toward it.

The final words of Eleazar's text (paragraph 624) are these:

---

[245] Authorized Version; see also Edinger, *Bible and the Psyche,* pp. 72ff.
[246] See above, lecture 16, p. 199.

Therefore says Job 28: 7: . . . [No bird has known the path, nor has the eye of the vulture seen it]. For this stone belongeth only to the proven and elect of God.

These final words announce the fact that we're now dealing with the Stone. This is the first time the word "stone" has been used; the Philosophers' Stone has been created. The black Shulamite's transformation is complete and she is now the Philosophers' Stone.

Simultaneously it is announced that a path has been created and has come into view: the quotation from Job concerns a path, a path no bird "has known nor has the eye of the vulture seen it." It's an invisible path, it cannot be seen by the eye of the hovering bird looking down from above—it's another kind of path. This will be one of the images, then, of the Philosophers' Stone: the path of in-dividuation. That's what flickers into view from within at a certain stage of the individuation process. One begins to become aware that there is a way, that the ego is not just on its own in making decisions, that there's an objective inner path to be followed.

The last sentence also announces that this Stone and this path belong "only to the proven and elect of God." This brings up the whole symbolism of the word "elect" which has a double reference, both passive and active.

From the passive standpoint, the idea is that God elects an elite and that status of election is invested passively in the individual. The active standpoint implies a choice and an effort by the ego: the ego must elect to seek the Philosophers' Stone and to serve it, in order to bring it into existence. On the one hand it is a gift, on the other hand it is something that must be labored for and comes as a consequence of conscious effort.

That concludes, then, the text of Eleazar and chapter V. We now turn to the final chapter, "The Conjunction," which begins with paragraph 654.

2. The Conjunction

The major part of this chapter examines various texts of Gerhard Dorn concerning the threefold coniunctio. But first, to prepare the way, Jung quotes a text from the *Hermetic Museum.* That's in paragraph 655, but to make it a little clearer I'm going to read you a slightly fuller version. Here it is, a symbolic description of the threefold process that introduces the rest of the chapter:

> The three Principles of things are produced out of the four elements in the following manner: Nature, whose power is in her obedience to the Will of God, ordained from the very beginning, that the four elements should incessantly act on one another, so, in obedience to her behest, fire began to act on air, and produced Sulphur; air acted on water and produced Mercury; water, by its action on earth, produced Salt. Earth, alone, having nothing to act upon, did not produce anything, but became the nurse, or womb, of these three Principles [i.e., Sulphur, Mercury and Salt]. . . .
>
> Whoever would be a student of this sacred science must know the marks whereby

these three Principles are to be recognised, and also the process by which they are developed. For as the three Principles are produced out of four, so they, in their turn, must produce two, a male and a female; and these two must produce an incorruptible one, in which are exhibited the four (elements) in a highly purified and digested condition, and with their mutual strife hushed in unending peace and good will.[247]

I've made a chart to represent what's being referred to (figure 23-1): the four elements, fire, air, water and earth, one on top of the other. Fire works on air and generates Sulphur; air works on water and generates Mercury; water works on earth and generates Salt.

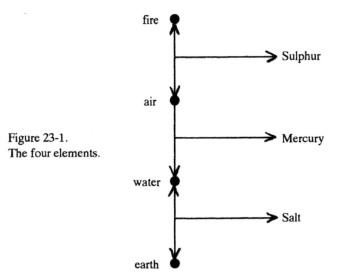

Figure 23-1.
The four elements.

These are basically number symbols, so this text is an allusion to the Axiom of Maria which concerns the whole matter of four and three. There are several versions of the Axiom of Maria; one goes like this:

One becomes two, two becomes three, and out of the third comes the One as the fourth. [248]

Another version reads this way:

One, and it is two; and two, and it is three; and three, and it is four; and four, and it is three; and three, and it is two; and two, and it is one.[249]

So they go: one, two, three, four; four, three, two, one.

---

[247] Waite, *Hermetic Museum,* vol. 2, pp. 142f.
[248] *Psychology and Alchemy,* CW 12, par. 209.
[249] Ibid., par. 210, footnote 86.

Figure 23-2.Maria Prophetissa.

This symbolism of the first four numbers of the arithmetic series has a very ancient and venerable origin. It goes back to the Pythagorean tetractys, which was a sacred symbol used by the ancient Pythagorean brotherhood and was represented thus: four rows of pebbles, four, three, two, one:

Figure 23-3.
The Pythagorean
tetractys.

Here are some things Walter Burkert has to say about the ancient tetractys:

The kernel of Pythagorean wisdom is the "tetractys," or "four-group," made up of the numbers, 1, 2, 3, 4, which add up to 10. They are represented in a pebble figure, in the form of the "perfect triangle"; . . . these four numbers contain not only the basic intervals—fourth, fifth, octave, and double octave—but also . . . point, line, plane, and solid. . . .

. . . The tetractys, a "tetrad" made up of unequal numbers, is a cryptic formula, only comprehensible to the initiated. The word inevitably reminds us of the *trictus,* the "triad" of different sacrificial animals. Is the sacrificial art of the seer involving the shedding of blood, superseded by a "higher" bloodless secret? . . . [There is perhaps a hint toward an explanation in the text that says:] "What is the oracle of Delphi?" "The tetractys, that is, the harmony in which the Sirens sing." The later tradition is more explicit: The "tetrad" of the numbers 1, 2, 3, and 4, which add up to 10 (the "perfect triangle"), contains within itself at the same time the harmonic ratios of fourth, fifth, and octave. The Sirens produced the music of the spheres, the whole universe is harmony and number. . . . The tetractys has within it the secret of the world; and in this matter we can also understand the connection with Delphi, the seat of the highest and most secret wisdom . . . . Later sources speak of . . . [the] mysterious ringing [of the bronze tripod of Apollo]. . .

The meaning of the shibboleth or *symbolon* "tetractys" can only be explained in a tentative fashion. In place of that which was connected with it from the beginning, in the form of belief or experience, the later sources give us more and more rationalizations. Some way or other the secret of the world is to be found in number.[250]

Well that gives you just a little sense of the sacred numinosity the ancients attached to the symbol of the tetractys.

Now I want to examine this image a little more carefully in relation to "the four elements" and the "three Principles." And I want to link it with the discussion, running through this final chapter, of the threefold coniunctio. So before I speak about some of the psychological implications of the tetractys let me say a few words about what the threefold coniunctio is and what it means. Jung doesn't make it too clear; he's not interested in simplifying what he presents but leaves that for others to do—he makes us work a little.

The three stages of the coniunctio are announced in a text of Dorn's that Jung quotes in paragraph 663:

We conclude that meditative philosophy consists in the overcoming of the body by mental union *[unio mentalis].* This first union does not as yet make the wise man, but only the mental disciple of wisdom. The second union of the mind with the body shows forth the wise man, hoping for and expecting that blessed third union with the first unity [i.e., the *unus mundus,* the latent unity of the world]. May Almighty God grant that all men be made such, and may He be one in All.

As you see, that's not very clear but in essence the three stages of the coniunctio are as follows.

The first stage is called the *unio mentalis,* which means "mental union." It refers to the union of the soul and the spirit which are separated from the body. The idea is that the organism is composed of three entities: body, soul, and spirit and at the beginning they are all mixed up with one another. This first stage of the coniunctio, the *unio mentalis,* brings about the union of soul and spirit over and against the body. They link up as partners and go against the body.

In the second stage, the united spirit and soul, which were previously separated from the body, are now reunited with the body. They say, in effect, we love you after all, so you can come back and join us. That's the *unio mentalis* united with

---

[250] *Lore and Science in Ancient Pythagoreanism,* p. 72 and pp. 187f.

the body.

The third stage, *unus mundus,* refers to yet another union: the united spirit-soul-body, achieved in the second stage, is now united with the world. That union brings about the *unus mundus.*

We'll be talking about those three stages in further detail as we go along, but because the same symbolism is imbedded in the imagery of the tetractys, I wanted to lay them out so you get a general idea of what they refer to.

Since this image of the tetractys was invested with such sacred meaning by the ancients, I think we can assume it carries some pretty important symbolism and psychologically is worth our consideration. I'm going to offer you certain reflections of my own about its meaning. These are tentative efforts to sketch out what may lie behind the tetractys, but what I have to say does not by any means exhaust the symbolic meaning of this image. Apply your own creative reflections and see what your unconscious comes up with.

Among other things, the tetractys can be considered as an epitome of the process of psychological development and as an analogy to the three stages of the coniunctio. As indicated in my chart (figure 23-4), I think of the process of psychological development as twofold: first, a movement down through the sequence of numbers, and second, a movement back up through the sequence.

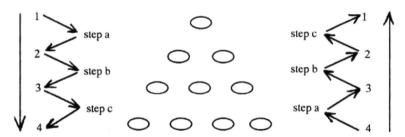

Figure 23-4. The process of psychological development.

We can think of the sequence as having four stages and three steps of transition. The original condition, stage 1, would be represented by that single little pebble at the top, which would signify the state of original wholeness before any consciousness enters the picture.

Then an event takes place, transition step a, which leads to a split, something like cell division. The original Self divides into two, corresponding to the theme of the separation of the World Parents.[251]

This brings about stage 2, the beginning of ego development, which is char-

---

[251] See Edinger, *Anatomy,* chap. 7, "Separatio," espec. pp. 183ff; also Neumann, *Origins and History of Consciousness,* chap. 3, pp. 102ff.

acterized by the separation of subject and object. Here the ego begins to experience itself as separate from the world while still being caught in the polarity between Nature (Mother) and Spirit (Father).

The next transition, step b, is full separation from the Mother (Nature).

This leads to stage 3, autonomous, independent thinking.

Transition step c then brings about separation from the Father (Spirit).

This leads to stage 4 which is characterized by independent, autonomous being, a state where original unity has been differentiated into a fourfold multiplicity and the individual is living fully in the world.

Eventually this fourth stage—living in the world—begins to pall and, as Jung puts it in paragraph 657:

> [The four elements begin] to fall apart, as it were, in four directions. As the four elements represent the whole physical world, their falling apart means dissolution into the constituents of the world, that is into a purely inorganic and hence unconscious state. Conversely, the combination of the elements and the final synthesis of male and female is an achievement of the art and a product of conscious endeavour. The result of the synthesis was consequently conceived by the adept as self-knowledge, which, like the knowledge of God, is needed for the preparation of the Philosophers' Stone. Piety is needed for the work, and this is nothing but knowledge of oneself.

So at a certain point, when one has achieved a full life in the world and, in a certain sense, full psychic differentiation, the inadequacy of that state of being becomes more and more manifest. Then the four elements start falling apart and the specific task of individuation is activated. This task of individuation can be thought of as an ascent back up through the number series of the tetractys.

The event that must take place to ascend from level 4 to level 3 is the first stage of the coniunctio, namely the *unio mentalis.* That would correspond to a reductive analysis of the shadow, a mortificatio.[252]

Here is what Jung has to say in paragraphs 671 and 672 about this process of the *unio mentalis,* the first stage of the coniunctio that corresponds to moving back up from level 4 to level 3:

> But in order to bring about their subsequent reunion, the mind . . . must be separated from the body—which is equivalent to "voluntary death"—for only separated things can unite. By this separation . . . Dorn obviously meant a discrimination and dissolution of the "composite," the composite state being one in which the affectivity of the body has a disturbing influence on the rationality of the mind. The aim of this separation was to free the mind from the influence of the "bodily appetites and the heart's affections," and to establish a spiritual position which is supraordinate to the turbulent sphere of the body. This leads at first to a dissociation of the personality

---

[252] See Edinger, *Anatomy,* chap. 6.

and a violation of the merely natural man.

This preliminary step, in itself a clear blend of Stoic philosophy and Christian psychology, is indispensable for the differentiation of consciousness. Modern psychotherapy makes use of the same procedure when it objectifies the affects and instincts and confronts consciousness with them.

That puts it all very concisely and as you go along, if you have trouble understanding just what this *unio mentalis* really is, I suggest you reread and reflect on these two paragraphs.

So the *unio mentalis* brings about a state where the ego is separated from the unconscious, and able to take an objective and critical attitude toward affects and desirousness—the spirit and soul are joined together and separated from the body. When this is achieved, level 3 of the ascent is reached.

Then the next step up is brought about by the second stage of the coniunctio. In this stage, the previously achieved *unio mentalis* is reunited with the body. Jung describes this operation in paragraphs 679 and 680:

> The second stage of conjunction, the re-uniting of the *unio mentalis* with the body, is particularly important, as only from here can the complete conjunction be attained—union with the *unus mundus*. The reuniting of the spiritual position with the body obviously means that the insights gained should be made real. An insight might just as well remain in abeyance if it is simply not used. The second stage of conjunction therefore consists in making a reality of the man who has acquired some knowledge of his paradoxical wholeness.
>
> The great difficulty here, however, is that no one knows how the paradoxical wholeness of man can ever be realized. That is the crux of individuation, though it becomes a problem only when the loophole of "scientific" or other kinds of cynicism is not used. Because the realization of the wholeness that has been made conscious is an apparently insoluble task and faces the psychologist with questions which he can answer only with hesitation and uncertainty, it is of the greatest interest to see how the more unencumbered symbolical thinking of a medieval "philosopher" tackled this problem.

So now we're at level 2 on our way up, and at this level the ego has achieved the acceptance of the opposites and is able to endure the paradox of the psyche's two-sidedness. This brings into reality the insights that Jung describes in the passage just quoted.

The event that then takes place is the third stage of the coniunctio, the so-called union with the *unus mundus*. That leads one up to level 1, in which universal unity prevails. It represents a union of the ego with the Self and with the world. Now the Philosophers' Stone as the savior of the macrocosm—the great world—has been created. At this level, time and eternity are united and synchronicity prevails. It is perfectly evident that this is a borderline state that one can only glimpse from afar; once you are totally in it you are out of the ego world as we know it. So the assumption is that that final, total translation to unity is consummated only at death—at best, that is, because death doesn't automatically bring it about either.

Those are some of my thoughts about the symbolic implications of the tetractys and about how the three stages of the coniunctio can be implied in the movement up and down the first four numbers.[253]

There is another way of seeing it (figure 23-5). Let me go through that to indicate what I have in mind. I'm again thinking of an initial descent down the four numbers followed by an ascent up the four numbers.

Stage 1 starts with the original state of oneness: the world, the body, the soul and the spirit are all identified with one another—there's no distinction whatsoever. They all go to make up the original entity and don't yet exist separately.

In stage 2, the world gets separated off; body, soul and spirit remain a unity—so two entities exist.

In stage 3, three entities exist: world and body get separated off; soul and spirit remain united.

In stage 4, all four have been differentiated but not in full consciousness.

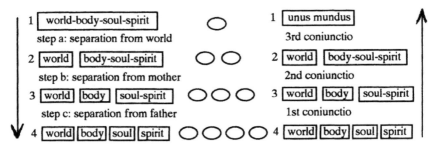

Figure 23-5. The three stages of the coniunctio.

---

[253] It is interesting to note that in slightly different formation, the same sequence can be seen in the Sefirotic Tree (see above, fig. 2-3, p. 39):

⬭	1	①	
⬭ ⬭	2	③ ②	
⬭ ⬭ ⬭	3	⑤ ④ / ⑥	
⬭ ⬭ ⬭ ⬭	4	⑧ ⑦ / ⑨ / ⑩	

The operation of more complete differentiation requires another level of separation, which takes place in the ascending sequence. Soul and spirit unite in order to separate from body and world more fully. That's the first stage of the coniunctio, the *unio mentalis*. On the one hand there's a higher level of separation but on the other hand it's the first step in a conscious synthesis. Four items turn into three items.

Then another synthesis takes place—the second stage of the coniunctio—in which three items, world, body and soul-spirit, turn into two items.

Finally, the two items, world and body-soul-spirit, are synthesized and the final result is the *unus mundus*. That's the third stage of the coniunctio.

I understand this is difficult; it's something that grows on you—you don't have to get it right away!

The *unio mentalis*, the first step on the upward path, is both a union and a separation. One way of putting it is that the separation is between the body and the spirit; in that state the soul is still attached to the body.

The second separation takes place between the body and the soul with the soul then transferring its connection from the body to the spirit. Jung tries to describe that situation in paragraph 673:

> Since the soul animates the body, just as the soul is animated by the spirit, she tends to favour the body and everything bodily, sensuous, and emotional. She lies caught in "the chains" of Physis, and she desires "beyond physical necessity." She must be called back by the "counsel of the spirit" from her lostness in matter and the world. This is a relief to the body too, for it not only enjoys the advantage of being animated by the soul but suffers under the disadvantage of having to serve as the instrument of the soul's appetites and desires. Her wish-fantasies impel it to deeds to which it would not rouse itself without this incentive, for the inertia of matter is inborn in it and probably forms its only interest except for the satisfaction of physiological instincts. Hence the separation means withdrawing the soul and her projections from the bodily sphere and from all environmental conditions relating to the body. In modern terms it would be a turning away from sensuous reality, a withdrawal of the fantasy projections that give "the ten thousand things" their attractive and deceptive glamour. In other words, it means introversion, introspection, meditation, and the careful investigation of desires and their motives.

How often we have the experience of being gripped by a material desire of some sort—a pair of shoes, a new hi-fi system, a television set, a new car—any one of "the ten thousand things." One can be gripped by the desire for something and if one goes after it unreflectingly, one may find that once one has it the desire drops away and the whole episode can be recognized as a piece of foolishness. One was caught by an illusion, a projection, and the acquisition of the object didn't really satisfy because it wasn't really what was wanted. That would be an example of burdening the body. The body knows what material things it wants and needs, and if it gets what it needs it will be satisfied.

But the soul's purposes are symbolic ones, and if the soul slips up and makes the body serve these purposes—act them out literally—then there will be disappointment. Experiences like that force one to reflect about "the ten thousand things" and "their attractive and deceptive glamour." It leads then, in Jung's words, to "introversion, introspection, meditation, and the careful investigation of desires and their motives."

I should add that such experiences happen not only with things like shoes and cars and television sets; they also happen with personal relationships! One could get married on such a basis, you know. "Marry in haste and repent at leisure."

I want to end with Jung's important remarks in paragraph 667:

> One should not be put off by the physical impossibilities of dogma or of the coniunctio, for they are symbols in regard to which the allurements of rationalism are entirely out of place and miss the mark. If symbols mean anything at all, they are tendencies which pursue a definite but not yet recognizable goal and consequently can express themselves only in analogies. In this uncertain situation one must be content to leave things as they are, and give up trying to know anything beyond the symbol. In the case of dogma such a renunciation is reinforced by the fear of possibly violating the sanctity of a religious idea, and in the case of alchemy it was until very recently considered not worth while to rack one's brains over medieval absurdities. Today, armed with psychological understanding, we are in a position to penetrate into the meaning of even the most abstruse alchemical symbols, and there is no justifiable reason why we should not apply the same method to dogma. Nobody, after all, can deny that it consists of ideas which are born of man's imagining and thinking. The question of how far this thinking may be inspired by the Holy Ghost is not affected at all, let alone decided, by psychological investigation, nor is the possibility of a metaphysical background denied. Psychology cannot advance any argument either for or against the objective validity of any metaphysical view. I have repeated this statement in various places in order to give the lie to the obstinate and grotesque notion that a psychological explanation must necessarily be either psychologism or its opposite, namely a metaphysical assertion.

And here's the punch line:

> The psychic is a phenomenal world in itself, which can be reduced neither to the brain nor to metaphysics.

That means on the one hand that the psyche cannot be explained by biochemistry, and on the other that it cannot be explained by metaphysical, religious, dogmatic formulations of any brand or creed whatsoever. It is a separate world of being and the only reason attempts are made to explain it in terms of biochemistry or metaphysics is because the explainers who make the attempt are not aware of the existence, the reality, of the psyche as a separate world of being. The very effort to explain it by those alternative means demonstrates that the psyche as a reality is invisible to the would-be explainers.

The Conjunction (cont.)

Last time we considered the three stages of the coniunctio; the Axiom of Maria; the symbolism of the tetractys; the descent and ascent of the sequence 1, 2, 3, 4; and I spoke of how the three steps of transition in the ascent of the tetractys, 4, 3, 2, 1, correspond to the three stages of the coniunctio.

Tonight I want to review and elaborate those three stages of the coniunctio. They are the epitome of the whole book and it is important that you understand them thoroughly . You remember that the first stage was called the *unio mentalis;* the second stage was referred to as the union of the *unio mentalis* with the body; and the third stage was described as the union of that previous second synthesis with the *unus mundus.*

These three stages of the coniunctio can also be thought of as three aspects of every analytic process, but they don't happen in a pure and totally differentiated way. The first stage does not have to be fully completed before shifting to the next stage and then to the third. A better way of looking at it is that these three stages, to a greater or lesser degree, are taking place simultaneously in the course of an analysis. Different aspects of the personality can be undergoing different stages of the coniunctio at more or less the same time, or right after one another. Keeping that complication in mind, let me again go over each of these stages in a little more detail.

What is called the *unio mentalis*—the mental union—is symbolized by Dorn as involving a twofold process. The first part is the union of soul and spirit; they unite and create the *unio mentalis.* Simultaneously, that union of soul and spirit is accompanied by a separation from the body. It is as though the soul and the spirit gang up against the body and separate from it, saying, in effect, "We don't want anything to do with you, body."

That's the *unio mentalis.* And, as we will see next week, one of the images for that phenomenon is decapitation—beheading, separating the head from the body. That's a stark and vivid image for the fact that everything going on in the head gangs up against the body, doesn't want to have anything to do with the body, and so separates from it. It decapitates itself, so to speak.

This symbolism of the *unio mentalis* is very closely connected with the symbolism of sublimatio.[254] As Jung says in paragraph 672, the whole operation of

---

[254] See Edinger, *Anatomy,* chap. 5.

the *unio mentalis* is "a clear blend of Stoic philosophy and Christian psychology." And when one thinks of it in historical terms, it is actually a process that has been going on in the cultural history of the West for the last two thousand years. Nietzsche made the very perceptive and waggish remark that Christianity is Platonism for the masses, which has a lot of truth in it. Plato, along with the Stoics, was a major exponent of the *unio mentalis*—the process that separates the psyche of Western man from the body.

This is an absolutely necessary first step because the body is the initial dwelling place of the chaos of the affects, the passions. The whole *unio mentalis* operation has as its basic purpose the establishment of a spiritual counterpole over and against the body. Jung gives a good description of it in paragraph 696:

> All projections are unconscious identifications with the object. Every projection is simply there as an uncriticized datum of experience, and is recognized for what it is only very much later, if ever. Everything that we today would call "mind" and "insight" was, in earlier centuries, projected into things, and even today individual idiosyncrasies are presupposed by many people to be generally valid. The original, half-animal state of unconsciousness was known to the adept as the *nigredo,* the chaos, the *massa confusa,* an inextricable interweaving of the soul with the body, which together formed a dark unity (the *unio naturalis).* [That's the original state, you see, that dark unity.] From this enchainment he had to free the soul by means of the *separatio,* and establish a spiritual-psychic counterposition—conscious and rational insight—which would prove immune to the influences of the body. But such insight, as we have seen, is possible only if the delusory projections that veil the reality of things can be withdrawn. The unconscious identity with the object then ceases and the soul is "freed from its fetters in the things of sense." The psychologist is well acquainted with this process, for a very important part of his psychotherapeutic work consists in making conscious and dissolving the projections that falsify the patient's view of the world and impede his self-knowledge. He does this in order to bring anomalous psychic states of an affective nature, i.e., neurotic symptoms, under the control of consciousness. The declared aim of the treatment is to set up a rational, spiritual-psychic position over against the turbulence of the emotions.

That is the process called the *unio mentalis.*

Needless to say, the separation of head and body is not a satisfactory end state so we are led then to stage two of the coniunctio, which involves the reconnection of the *unio mentalis* with the body. The chief recipe in tonight's assignment is about how that reconnection is achieved.

Then we come to the third stage of the coniunctio: when the *unio mentalis* and the body have been reconnected, that unity is then united with the world and brings about what Dorn and Jung speak of as the *unus mundus.* The chief feature of that condition is the phenomenon of synchronicity. I won't say anything more about that now, but perhaps a bit more will come up later.[255]

Now I want to turn to the chief content of tonight's assignment which is Dorn's alchemical recipe for the second stage of the coniunctio. That recipe has two parts: the first part concerns the production of what he calls the *caelum,* and the second part concerns the mixing operation.

First comes the production of the *caelum.* Remember that the whole procedure is meant to bring about the second stage of the coniunctio, namely the re-connection of the body with the *unio mentalis.* In other words it is a recipe for the final coagulatio so that the consciousness that has been achieved by the *unio mentalis* can be brought into living, functioning, concrete personal reality. It doesn't remain just a theoretical abstraction but comes into living, embodied operation. That's the goal of the second stage of the coniunctio.

According to Dorn's recipe, the first step in bringing this about is to produce what he calls the *caelum,* described as "a certain heavenly substance hidden in the human body" (quoted by Jung in paragraph 681). To summarize what the text describes, the adept starts with "grana" or grape-pips, the residue of a previous operation. This material is calcined, dissolved and rotated until a pure blue liquid comes to the top. This pure blue liquid is what's called the *caelum,* which is just Latin for "heaven." Dorn continues:

> Then you will see the pureness floating to the top, transparent, shining, and of the colour of purest air. . . .
>
> The caelum therefore is a heavenly substance and a universal form, containing in itself all forms, distinct from one another, but proceeding from one single universal form. Wherefore, he who knows how individuals can be led on to the most general genus by the spagyric art, and how the special virtues, one or more, can be impressed upon this genus, will easily find the universal medicine.

The idea is that one starts with this "grana" or grape-pips. This is the residue, the deposits, the stuff that's been left out when the *unio mentalis* was created. It's the bodily dregs, the despised and rejected body that the spirit and the soul have cast off. Psychologically that residue will be concrete reality, particularity, the most personal and particular and individual stuff. I understand that to be egohood in its lowest and most despised form.

This residue is then treated and purified and from it is extracted the so-called *caelum* which is also called "truth." It's heavenly stuff that exists in this lowly left-over residue. It's something like a hidden god that's caught in the darkness of matter and is drawn out by the extraction process. As Jung states specifically in paragraph 681, it's the *imago Dei* in the individual. It's the image of the Self, the

---

255 See "Synchronicity: An Acausal Connecting Principle," *The Structure and Dynamics of the Psyche,* CW 8, and Marie-Louise von Franz, *C.G. Jung: His Myth in Our Time,* chap. 12, "Breakthrough to the *Unus Mundus.*"

same image used as the ground plan for the construction of the ego. Another way to put it is that it is the universal form on which all individuals are molded.

The whole process of achieving the *unio mentalis* is a spiritualizing, abstracting, generalizing kind of process which depreciates everything that is uniquely particular and individual and derives from the desires of the individual ego. That's why all spiritual disciplines depreciate the selfish desirousness of individual being. They have to establish a position over and against that and the result then is that everything individual, self-centered and potentially self-sufficient is left behind in the residue, in the grape-pips. It's that precious, neglected value that is being extracted by the process which produces the *caelum*. Psychologically the recipe would refer to the work one must do on the attributes of egohood in preparation for stage two of the coniunctio.

In an unconscious state, the Self expresses itself through an identification with the ego. The ego and the Self are mixed up with each other, and the Self expresses itself through the pleasure and power drives of the ego. After the *unio mentalis* has been achieved, the Self, or *imago Dei,* still remains in that ego-body residue and must be rescued; that's what the extraction of the *caelum* accomplishes. The consequence is that the universal validity of egohood, one's own ego and one's own self-centered drives, are reaffirmed on a conscious and differentiated level. That's what is symbolized by the *caelum*.

It amounts to a redemption and glorification of one's own unique subjectivity which in all spiritual, intellectual and abstract systems is of no value at all. For those systems it's nothing but a unique, accidental anecdote—it has nothing to do with statistical truth, you see. But when that *caelum* is recovered, then one's own unique subjectivity and its supreme value is rediscovered.

Emerson captured it in a sentence: "To believe that what is true for you in your private heart is true for all men—that is genius."[256] There's another remark of Emerson's that is also relevant. This comes from "The Over-Soul":

> Foolish people ask you, when you have spoken what they do not wish to hear, 'How do you know it is truth, and not an error of your own?' We know truth when we see it, from opinion, as we know when we are awake that we are awake. . . . [Or as Swedenborg said:] "It is no proof of a man's understanding to be able to affirm whatever he pleases; but to be able to discern that what is true is true, and that what is false is false,—this is the mark and character of intelligence."[257]

The idea is that with sufficient self-knowledge—when in Dorn's terms the *caelum* has been produced—one is able to tell the difference between a factual, psychological observation and an arbitrary opinion based on a complex. That's

---

[256] "Self-Reliance," in *The Complete Essays and other Writings of Ralph Waldo Emerson,* p. 145.
[257] Ibid., p. 268.

always the question, you know, in evaluating purely subjective experience. How do I know that my subjective experience is not just an aberration, that it doesn't just derive from a complex, from an unconscious content of mine that I'm puffing up into a universal truth? Well, with sufficient self-knowledge, one knows. An important indication is that one perceives a given thing but has no need to insist on it or to defend it against those who don't; and one certainly doesn't have to proselytize for it. Those tendencies—to insist, to defend, to proselytize—are pretty good signs that the *caelum* hasn't yet been completely created.

The first stage of the recipe is extracting the *caelum*. Then comes the second aspect and this involves a mixing. The *caelum*, or "new heaven" as it is called, is then mixed with six additional ingredients: honey, Chelidonia or celandine, rosemary flowers, the Mercurialis plant, red lily and human blood.

Don't forget we're still involved in a recipe for coagulatio, for bringing a certain level of consciousness into fully embodied reality. And according to this alchemical recipe, the *caelum* that's been extracted from the bodily residue now must be mixed with these various ingredients.

First of all comes honey. Like all sweet things, honey is associated with co-agulatio.[258] It symbolizes the alluring sweetness that excites desire and lures one into life and reality. But as Jung mentions (in paragraph 687 and footnote 81), certain texts make clear that honey can also change into deadly poison. This refers to the fact that following one's desires can be quite dangerous at times.

Probably the most frequent images for sweetness in dreams are such things as ice cream, candy, cake, cookies and so on. As a rule, such dream images refer to regressive desirousness, childish tendencies, although dreams of chocolate, representing black sweetness, may refer to the assimilation of evil.[259]

It's a kind of coagulatio, true, but a regressive coagulatio. That kind of coagulatio calls for more effort on the *unio mentalis*. But when one is really dealing with the second stage of the coniunctio, then sweetness in dreams indicates that the time has come to bring certain conscious insights into concrete reality—to go for one's desires.

There is an interesting image in the *Odyssey* concerning honey and its incarnating aspect. In book 13 there's a description of the so-called Cave of the Nymphs. It's on the island of Ithaca, when Odysseus has finally found his way back home, and is described this way:

> At the head of the harbor, there is the olive tree with spreading
> leaves, and nearby is the cave that is shaded, and pleasant,
> and sacred to the nymphs who are called the Nymphs of the Wellsprings,
> Naiads. There are mixing bowls and handled jars inside it,

---

[258] See Edinger, *Anatomy,* espec. pp. 90f.
[259] See Edinger, *Ego and Archetype,* pp. 22f.

all of stone, and there the bees deposit their honey.
And therein also are looms that are made of stone, very long, where
the nymphs weave their sea-purple webs, a wonder to look on;
and there is water forever flowing. It has two entrances,
one of them facing the North Wind, where people can enter,
but the one toward the South Wind has more divinity. That is
the way of the immortals, and no men enter by that way.[260]

It is very interesting to follow up what some of the ancient thinkers and philosophers did with such images. For instance, Porphyry, a Neo-Platonic philosopher, wrote a whole treatise on this passage, entitled *The Cave of the Nymphs.* The cave of the nymphs, as he interpreted it, represents the entrance and exit gateways for souls entering earthly existence on the one hand, and leaving earthly existence on the other. The entrance of the cave on the north, where Homer says men enter, is where souls, about to be incarnated, descend from above down to earth. The southern gateway is where the disembodied soul exits when leaving earth and returning to heaven.

Now what makes this so significant from the standpoint of our alchemical recipe, while we're talking about honey, is that this cave has honey in it. In other words it's as though the honey attracts the souls to come down to this not-so-agreeable place—to descend into a body, to materialize. A necessary ingredient for this recipe for the second stage of the coniunctio, then, is honey. You have to pour into the flask whatever you find sweet and desirable and what you long for. While you've been going through the stage of the *unio mentalis* you had to turn your back to all that, but now the time has come to do the reverse.

Next comes Chelidonia, or celandine. In paragraph 687 Jung says:

[This plant] cures eye diseases and is particularly good for night-blindness, and even heals the spiritual "benightedness" (affliction of the soul, melancholy-madness) so much feared by the adepts. It protects against "thunderstorms," i.e., outbursts of affect. It is a precious ingredient, because its yellow flowers symbolize the philo-sophical gold, the highest treasure.

For my purposes, I would consider the golden flowers to be the chief aspect of the Chelidonia. Flowers are nature's own symbols of wholeness. I think we can say that flowers in dreams are always auspicious; they are organic mandalas and they also convey feeling and beauty. So, remembering that we are dealing here with a coagulatio recipe, the text seems to be saying that an organic mandala image has to be added to the pot.

It's not easy to get the *unio mentalis* to embrace the body; it has previously devoted all its efforts to separating from the body. An enantiodromia is required and that's not so easy because what had previously been seen as a bundle of

---

[260] Richmond Lattimore, trans., *The Odyssey of Homer,* book 12, lines 102-112, p. 201.

greeds, lust, power-striving and unconscious negatives of all kinds must now be invited back in. In order to bring about such a total reversal there must be some reason that justifies a sacrifice on the part of the purified *unio mentalis.*

My thought is that this image of the golden flowers of Chelidonia probably symbolizes that rational reason. And that reason, in a word, is wholeness. If you are going to be whole, not just a disembodied head, then you have to open your arms to the body and all it signifies.

Comment: Like it or not!

Yes, but one's also dealing with honey and desirable pretty flowers, you see, so it's not all misery.[261]

Next comes rosemary. Let me read you some of what *Funk and Wagnalls* has to say about rosemary:

> Ophelia's famous line, "Rosemary, that's for remembrance," expressed the common knowledge of the day; for rosemary has been symbolic of remembrance, fidelity, and friendship since early times, and in this connection was most frequently used as a funeral wreath and in wedding ceremonies. . . . In ancient Greece, students wore rosemary twined in their hair while studying for examinations also "for remembrance" (i.e., to strengthen their memory) . . . .
>
> Because rosemary is a plant of remembrance, it is a sovereign remedy for all diseases of the brain and is strengthening to the mind in all forms. But its uses seem to have spread to the whole head, for besides the brain, a decoction of rosemary in wine is good for loss of speech, sore eyes, and to clear the complexion. . . . A decoction of rosemary put into the beer barrel secretly was said to be a sure cure for drunkenness.[262]

The word rosemary derives from *ros marinus,* meaning "dew of the sea." The symbolism of dew associates to divine grace that drips from the moon.[263] And also, by the similarity of sound, rosemary was associated with the rose as well as with the Virgin Mary.

The major symbolism of rosemary is memory and this brings up the whole question of the role of memory in the process of individuation. It gives us an occasion to pay a little more attention to this question—it is not something we ordinarily think much about. But in antiquity, Mnemosyne, Memory, was a goddess and the mother of the Muses; so the symbolism of rosemary coming up in this recipe leads us to the realization that memory is a function of the Self.

As Freud discovered, the unconscious makes its presence very definitely felt

---

[261] An example of this imagery came up in a dream of a woman who, after many years of analysis, was dealing with this second stage of the coniunctio. She dreamt she was to eat a delicious concoction of honey, yoghurt, yellow rose petals and almonds.

[262] *Standard Dictionary,* p. 957.

[263] For further amplification of dew symbolism, see Edinger, *Mystery of the Coniunctio,* pp. 82ff.

by memory lapses. The same thing applies to Jung's Word Association Test.[264] The whole idea of memory was an important feature of Plato's viewpoint: he spoke of the process of anamnesis or remembrance—recollection—of one's past as the essential feature of self-discovery. According to the Platonic method of anamnesis, one gradually remembers or recollects the knowledge one had before birth of the world of Platonic forms, the world of the archetypes.[265]

This Platonic idea is actually the ancient philosophic precursor to the modern analytic notion of encounter with the collective unconscious. You might say that anamnesis is the basic activity of analysis in dealing with both the personal unconscious and the collective unconscious. We start a new case with a life history, a process of remembering, to the extent one can, one's personal life. And as the analysis of the personal unconscious proceeds, there is a progressive recovery of memory and a recollecting of forgotten, repressed or otherwise disregarded contents. That process continues as one deals with the archetypal level because the archetypes are the modern version, the modern equivalent, of Platonic ideas. We might say that rosemary is a crucial feature, then, of the analytic process: you've got to have rosemary, memory, for it to work.

So rosemary must be one of the ingredients of the second stage of the con-iunctio because in order to reconnect the *unio mentalis* with the body one must remember that one has a body and a past. Jung speaks somewhere about how necessary it is to hold in memory that one did this and that, even though the memories of those events make one squirm with embarrassment; all those petty, embarrassing, inferior aspects of oneself are part of one's total reality and it is important to remember them. That's who I am, I'm the person who did all those things. It's memory of that sort that gives one a body, you see. One can't float around anymore. One is grounded and weighted down with the reality. One might also say, similarly, that a knowledge of history, what the human race has done in the past, serves that same function for the collective.

The next ingredient is the Mercurialis plant. Jung tells us, in paragraph 688, that the Mercurialis plant occurs in male and female forms, and is connected with the attractive power of sexuality. So he is telling us that sexual libido is a part of the recipe.

There is another very interesting association. In the same paragraph, Jung says the Mercurialis plant corresponds symbolically to moly, the magic herb in the *Odyssey*. I want to spend a few minutes talking about that.

It comes in book 10 of the *Odyssey* and the situation is this: Odysseus has landed on Circe's island, his men have fallen under the enchantment of Circe—the witch, the enchantress—and she has turned them into pigs. Now Odysseus has

---

[264] See "Studies in Word Association," *Freud and Psychoanalysis,* CW 2, part 1.
[265] Plato, "Phaedo," 75e, in *The Collected Dialogues.*

the problem of trying to rescue them. This is a very relevant image, since we're talking about coagulatio symbolism: those men were enchanted because they were going after honey. And Odysseus is going to run into the same problem because he has to encounter Circe. The very nature of her charms is that she can play on his desirousness.

We're seeing some interesting examples of this same Circe phenomenon in current events: the new American Embassy in Moscow has been compromised because of a Russian Circe, and our TV evangelists are in some disarray because of another Circe. The honey-Circe is a serious issue and that's why the story of the moly is so relevant.

So Odysseus is now going to try to rescue his men from Circe's enchantment. He's left the ship and is heading toward Circe.

Here's what he says:

> But as I went up through the lonely glens, and was coming
> near to the great house of Circe, skilled in medicines,
> there as I came up to the house, Hermes, of the golden
> staff, met me on my way, in the likeness of a young man
> with beard new grown, which is the most graceful time of young manhood.
> He took me by the hand and spoke to me and named me, saying:
> "Where are you going, unhappy man, all alone, through the hilltops,
> ignorant of the land-lay, and your friends are here in Circe's
> place, in the shape of pigs and holed up in the close pig pens.
> Do you come here meaning to set them free? I do not think
> you will get back yourself, but must stay here with the others.
> But see, I find you a way out of your troubles, and save you.
> Here, this is good medicine, take it and go into Circe's
> house; it will give you power against the day of trouble.
> And I will tell you all the malevolent guiles of Circe.
> She will make you a potion, and put drugs in the food, but she will not
> even so be able to enchant you, for this good medicine
> which I give you now will prevent her. I will tell you the details
> of what to do. As soon as Circe with her long wand strikes you,
> then drawing from beside your thigh your sharp sword, rush
> forward against Circe, as if you were raging to kill her,
> and she will be afraid, and invite you to go to bed with her.
> Do not then resist and refuse the bed of the goddess,
> for so she will set free your companions, and care for you also;
> but bid her swear the great oath of the blessed gods, that she
> has no other evil hurt that she is devising against you,
> so she will not make you weak and unmanned, once you are naked."
> So spoke . . . [Hermes, slayer of Argos], and he gave me the medicine, which
> he picked out of the ground, and he explained the nature
> of it to me. It was black at the root, but with a milky

flower. The gods call it moly. It is hard for mortal
men to dig up, but the gods have power to do all things.[266]

So Odysseus went on his way, did as he was instructed, and was successful because he had the divine help of the moly.

Remember, Jung tells us that the Mercurialis plant is symbolically equivalent to moly. I have a lot of material amplifying moly, because it pleased me to accumulate it, but there isn't time to present it to you. The ancients were very attracted to this image. You know that whenever an important symbolic image emerges, it has a magnet-like function that activates the unconscious and encourages speculative fantasy. That's what the ancients did with the image of moly. It was equated with the divine Logos and things like that, but the important thing for us will be that it unites the opposites: although its root is black, its flower is milky white. One commentator says that it refers to *paideia,* the process of spiritual education, and the root is black because the beginnings of spiritual education are always dark and extraordinarily ill-formed. But in the later stages of the development, the flower is bright and sweet and satisfying.

I think the basic point is that it unites the opposites and if one has that herb, the organic entity that unites the opposites, then one is more or less immune to anima seductions. Seduction requires the inability, for the moment at least, to see the two sides. You see the light, but you don't see the dark, and that's what seduction consists of—the failure to carry both sides at the same time.

Next comes the red lily. In paragraph 689 Jung tells us that red and white lilies refer to male and female respectively and these are the components of the coniunctio. In this case it's the red lily, which I think is another version of the final ingredient, blood.

Blood is vital life essence. Jung alludes in paragraph 690 to the fact that there is a sinister angle to the presence of human blood in this recipe because the question comes up: if it is a magical operation, where does one get it from? As long as it's a psychological operation, one knows perfectly well where one gets it—from oneself, it's one's own blood. But if it is a magical operation, if it has been concretized and exteriorized, then one has to get it from some external source. That's the source of the widespread fantasies of the killing of children in diabolical rites.

Blood is the real stuff that brings the body and the *unio mentalis* back together. What has cost us blood, we never forget. There's a good example of the connecting power of blood in book 11 of the *Odyssey,* when Odysseus is obliged to descend to the Underworld to get advice from his deceased father. In order to call forth the spirit of the father, Odysseus has to sacrifice the blood of sheep and pour it on the ground. The blood then attracts the dead spirits and they come

---

[266] Lattimore, *The Odyssey,* book 10, lines 275-306, pp. 156ff.

rushing to lap it up. It's an example of how the unconscious is brought into connection with consciousness by the sacrifice of blood.[267]

All these things are mixed with the *caelum.* Jung summarizes the recipe's meaning in paragraph 704:

> With the honey the pleasure of the senses and the joy of life went into the mixture, as well as the secret fear of the "poison," the deadly danger of worldly entanglements. With the Chelidonia the highest meaning and value, the self as the total personality, the healing and "whole-making" medicine which is recognized even by modern psychotherapy, was combined with spiritual and conjugal love, symbolized by rosemary; and, lest the lower, chthonic element be lacking, Mercurialis added sexuality, together with the red slave moved by passion, symbolized by the red lily, and the addition of blood threw in the whole soul. All this was united with the azure quintessence, the *anima mundi* extracted from inert matter, or the God-image imprinted on the world—a mandala produced by rotation; that is to say the whole of the conscious man is surrendered to the self, to the new centre of personality which replaces the former ego.

I'll end with Dorn's description of the product of this second coniunctio, quoted by Jung in paragraph 685:

> At length the body is compelled to resign itself to, and obey, the union of the two that are united [soul and spirit]. That is the wondrous transformation of the Philosophers, of body into spirit, and of the latter into body, of which there has been left to us by the sages the saying, Make the fixed volatile and the volatile fixed.

Thus the Philosophers' Stone is created and brings with it knowledge:

> Learn from within thyself to know all that is in heaven and on earth, and especially that all was created for thy sake. Knowest thou not that heaven and the elements were formerly one, and were separated from one another by divine artifice, that they might bring forth thee and all things? . . . Thou wilt never make from others the One which thou seekest, except first there be made one thing of thyself.

I would especially underscore the phrase "Learn from within thyself to know . . . that all was created for thy sake." That's a hint of moving on to the third stage of the coniunctio, you see: the second stage is now joined with the world, and the individual, who has been reconnected to the body, is now connected to the world. Born initially into a state of oneness with the cosmos, now, at the third stage of the coniunctio, the individual returns on a conscious level to that realization of oneness with the cosmos.

---

[267] See Edinger, *Ego and Archetype,* pp. 227ff.

1. The Conjunction (cont.)

Let me remind you briefly of the three stages of the coniunctio Jung discusses throughout this final chapter.

Stage one of the coniunctio involves a process whereby the original condition—the *unio naturalis*—is split as the *unio mentalis* is being created. This latter, the *unio mentalis,* unites the soul and the spirit, and at the same time separates them from the body. This amounts to a mortificatio and a death of the body at the same time as it brings about a sublimatio of the combined soul and spirit. It also corresponds to the symbolism of the *albedo,* the whitening process.

In stage two the *unio mentalis,* created in the first stage, is united again with the body. This is brought about, in Dorn's recipe, by combining the *caelum* with other ingredients, of which probably the most important is blood. This stage involves bringing the consciousness of wholeness, which in the first stage is a kind of abstract realization, into full-blooded reality, so that one lives it out fully in everyday life. And this phase corresponds to the alchemical *rubedo,* also called reddening.

The third stage involves a union of the previously united substances with the world—at least that's the simplified version. More strictly speaking, the third phase—the creation or realization of the *unus mundus*—is a transcendent, symbolic condition that defies any comprehensive or adequate description. It refers to a superlative experience of unity in which subject and object, inner and outer, are transcended in the experience of a unitary reality really beyond our grasp.

In tonight's material Jung continues his discussion of these three stages and begins by quoting the Quicksilver text of Albertus Magnus, which concerns the transformation of quicksilver from its original state to its ultimate, perfect state. I'm going to read this text and then make a few remarks about Mercurius (which is what quicksilver symbolizes) because this major alchemical symbol is not discussed in depth in *Mysterium.* Jung had already dealt with it extensively in his essay "The Spirit Mercurius,"[268] a companion text to *Mysterium.*

The symbolism of the spirit Mercurius is so important to all our encounters with the autonomous psyche, both in ourselves and in our patients, that it should be uppermost in our consciousness. With that in mind, let me read the Quicksilver text, quoted in paragraph 712. Jung cites it as a parallel to Dorn's *caelum* text in

---

268 See *Alchemical Studies,* CW 13.

our previous assignment. The idea is that the extraction of Mercurius from the prima materia is symbolically equivalent to the extraction of the blue *caelum* from the grape-pips; they correspond to the same psychological fact.

> Quicksilver is cold and moist, and God created all minerals with it, and it itself is aerial, and volatile in the fire. But since it withstands the fire for some time, it will do great and wonderful works, and it alone is a living spirit, and in all the world there is nothing like it that can do such things as it can . . . It is the perennial water, the water of life, the virgin's milk, the fount, the alumen, and [whoever] drinks of it shall not perish. When it is alive it does certain works, and when it is dead it does other and the greatest works. It is the serpent that rejoices in itself, impregnates itself, and gives birth in a single day, and slays all metals with its venom. It flees from the fire, but the sages by their art have caused it to withstand the fire, by nourishing it with its own earth until it endured the fire, and then it performs works and transmutations. As it is transmuted, so it transmutes. . . . It is found in all minerals and has a "symbolum" [tie] with them all. But it arises midway between the earthly and the watery, or midway between . . . a subtle living oil and a very subtle spirit. From the watery part of the earth it has its weight and motion from above downwards, its brightness, fluidity, and silver hue. . . . But quicksilver is clearly seen to have a gross substance, like the Monocalus, which excels even gold in the heaviness of its immense weight. When it is in its nature it is of the strongest composition . . . and of uniform nature, since it is not divided [or: is indivisible]. It can in no way be separated into parts, because it either escapes from the fire with its whole substance or endures with it in the fire. For this reason the cause of perfection is necessarily seen in it.

This is a description of the autonomous psyche that manifests in this kind of miraculous way from the darkness of the unconscious. I want to draw your attention to two of its attributes referred to in the text.

First, it is said to have "immense weight." Keep in mind that we're dealing with the phenomenology of the Self—the source of the autonomous spirit of the psyche—so this notion of immense weight is an aspect of the Self.

It reminds me of a recent concept of astronomy that is quite helpful in understanding certain psychic phenomena. I'm talking about the concept of the black hole.

The idea is that a dwarf star, in the last stage of its evolution, implodes, so to speak, and falls in on itself with great power, creating a black hole. It is very interesting that this idea should appear in modern times because I think it corresponds to a psychological fact. I don't doubt that someday all our present cosmological notions will be recognized as myths, just as Ptolemy's notions are now recognized as myth. What we now think is science will, in the future, very likely be seen as myth—in other words as a psychological projection.

Anyway, listen to this description of a black hole. This comes from the *Micropedia of the Encyclopedia Britannica*:

The black hole in space is a postulated object whose mass is so intensely concentrated that normal properties of space in its vicinity are altered drastically and even light cannot escape the gravitational attraction with a certain distance from the center. . . .

The black hole is one of three postulated final stages of stellar evolution. . . . Most properties of the black hole are not observable. Space-time around the object is so sharply curved that no light escapes, no matter can be ejected and all details of infalling matter are obliterated. No stationary external observer can see anything of phenomena occurring within a radius at which the escape velocity is close to the speed of light. This radius is called the event-horizon, or the Schwartzchild radius. This event-horizon is a certain distance from the black hole and within that horizon no events can take place or are visible.

The idea is that they all fall into the hole, you see.

As the center is approached, the curvature of the space-time whirlpool continues to increase, becoming infinite at the central singularity. At such extreme conditions an outside observer cannot associate meaningful times with interior events and hence no communication is possible with an observer inside the Schwartzchild radius. All matter collapsing into the black hole is soon compressed to a mere infinite density, losing in the process virtually every property of its separate identity.[269]

I consider this to be the description of a certain aspect of the phenomenology of the Self. When this aspect of the Self is activated—and it's an imploding aspect rather than an exploding aspect—then all libido falls inward and none of it can escape the pull of that gravity. An example of this phenomenon is catatonic schizophrenia. I don't know that anybody sees catatonic schizophrenia in its original form anymore because people are medicated so quickly. But it is a very striking phenomenon in which the individual, so far as an observer can perceive, has no visible connection with the external environment. In other words, the "event-horizon" is of such size that there's nothing escaping there.

We get lesser versions of the same black hole phenomenon in certain patients, in certain kinds of psychology. A term that Eleanor Bertine, one of the original New York Jungian analysts, used for this is particularly apt: she called people with such a psychology "sucking mouths of emptiness." Smaller versions of black holes. And people of that kind walk into our offices every now and then. One of the ways you can recognize that psychology is how depleted you feel after you've been within the event-horizon of such a person. If you've been within that space, then part of you has been sucked into that empty mouth. I think it's a phenomenon of the negatively constellated Self that, in Dorn's text, is said to have immense weight—in other words a gravitational pull, a psychic gravity that pulls stuff into it.

---

[269] *Micropedia,* vol. 2, p. 61 (condensed).

Question: How about autism?

That's the early version of catatonic schizophrenia, the same condition. The other attribute I want to draw to your attention is that of indivisibility. The whole notion of an indivisible atom, something of such a nature that it cannot be separated into anything smaller, is, I think, a projection of the Self. Indivisibility is at the root of analysis. One of the major procedures of analysis is a cutting operation, the process of greater and greater discrimination: this is separate from that. And we continue that process of cutting until we get to something that won't be cut anymore; it is indivisible. It is the core of individual identity and will not be divided.[270]

To illustrate that phenomenon, I think of an East Indian anecdote that goes this way: a disciple visits his guru and with great excitement tells him, "Master, I have had the experience of enlightenment." The guru says, "Oh, have you? Tell me about it." So the disciple tells him about it, with all the details. The guru says, "Well, that's only a little enlightenment." The disciple says, "Oh no, Master, I can tell by the way it feels; this is a *big* enlightenment!" And the guru says, "Oh, is that so? Very well then, it's a big one."

This is exactly how the analyst operates—at least it's how I operate. I'll keep cutting just as long as I can until I get something that won't divide anymore, and then I'll acknowledge the fact that that's it. But you have to have the living experience; you can't know whether it's divisible or not until you've pushed it the full length. If you soft-heartedly relent too soon in applying your knife you won't get the real thing—you'll have divisible stuff and you'll be under the illusion that it's indivisible— and the patient will be deprived of the genuine experience. But when you reach that indivisibility, then you know it because the core announces itself as being individual.

As we talk about this text and the spirit Mercurius, I want to urge you at the earliest opportunity to read, or reread, Jung's essay "The Spirit Mercurius." It's particularly fine and particularly relevant. With the symbolism of the spirit Mercurius we're dealing with the autonomous psyche in all its manifestations. The more conscious we are of this entity, the more we'll see it operating everywhere within and around us. To whet your appetite, here's how Jung summarizes the nature of Mercurius in that essay:

> (1) Mercurius consists of all conceivable opposites. He is thus quite obviously a duality, but is named a unity in spite of the fact that his innumerable inner contradictions can dramatically fly apart into an equal number of disparate and apparently independent figures.
>
> (2) He is both material and spiritual.
>
> (3) He is the process by which the lower and material is transformed into the higher

---

[270] See Edinger, *Ego and Archetype,* chap. 6, "Being an Individual."

and spiritual, and vice versa.

(4) He is the devil, a redeeming psychopomp, an evasive trickster, and God's reflection in physical nature.

(5) He is also the reflection of a mystical experience of the artifex that coincides with the *opus alchymicum.*

(6) As such, he represents on the one hand the self and on the other the individuation process and, because of the limitless number of his names, also the collective unconscious.[271]

The final paragraph of that same essay gives us a feel of how Jung perceives the way in which the spirit Mercurius lives itself out in the world:

> Mercurius, that two-faced god, comes as the *lumen naturae,* the Servator and Salvator [the Servant and the Redeemer], only to those whose reason strives towards the highest light ever received by man, and who do not trust exclusively to the *cognitio vespertina* [evening knowledge, i.e., the light of rationality.][272] For those who are unmindful of this light, the *lumen naturae* turns into a perilous *ignis fatuus* [fools' fire], and the psychopomp into a diabolical seducer. Lucifer, who could have brought light, becomes the father of lies whose voice in our time, supported by press and radio, revels in orgies of propaganda and leads untold millions to ruin.

Another term Dorn uses in his text is "Monocalus" (or "monocolus" which, as Jung points out, is "probably the right reading"). In paragraph 720, Jung says this term is unique to this text—it shows up no place else. In other words, it's a "hapax legomenon," a once-only saying. I'm making an issue of this because I think it is a part of the phenomenology of the Self. A hapax legomenon is a word or expression that occurs only once—it is unique.

One of the features of the word "unique" is that, if one is going to be grammatically correct, it may not take any qualifying adjectives. It's not correct to say more unique or most unique or a little unique. This corresponds to the nature of the Self. It cannot be qualified, relativized or compared. Things that are unique are single examples of a whole species, you see; there are no other members of that species to compare them to. This corresponds to the psychological fact— potentially at least—that the individual psyche, if it follows its course of development, becomes a unique entity. In all of space and time there's only one you. Of course that's only a potential condition because as long as an individual lives totally immersed in a collective state then the uniqueness is not realized; it is only a potentiality until it is developed.

In the stage of the *unio mentalis* you could entertain the idea of uniqueness, but only theoretically. But then, to *live* the state of uniqueness, to bring the

---

271 *Alchemical Studies,* CW 13, par. 284
272 See ibid., pars. 301f., for Jung's discussion of *cognitio matutina* (morning knowlege) and *cognitio vespertina.*

uniqueness into flesh-and-blood reality, you would have to achieve the second stage of the coniunctio.

To amplify the term "monocolus" Jung, starting in paragraph 720, talks about the uniped pictures which are reproduced in the middle of *Mysterium*.[273] Let's look at them. They are part of a series of five pictures of which only four are reproduced. The third one, which Jung describes briefly, is left out.

The first picture (figure 25-1) is entitled "The Two Unipeds," and the textual material indicates that they refer to the two sulphurs—yellow and white. The king on the left is in a yellow robe, and the king on the right is in a white robe. I think they have to be considered as Siamese twins—they're united, not separated. And notice that the king on the left side has a temporal crown, while the king on the right has an ecclesiastical or spiritual crown.

In the second picture (figure 25-2), "The 'Revelation of the Hidden,' " those two crowns have been united: they each have a composite crown—a spiritual-temporal crown. And there's been a darkening and a mixing of the two kings: one of them is in a black robe and the other is in a blue robe. This indicates, as Jung remarks in paragraph 721, that the *nigredo* is about to ensue.

In the third picture, the one not reproduced, the two figures have been separated and each has two feet. Jung says in paragraph 722 that this picture refers to the completion of the *nigredo* and the total separation of the two sulphurs, which corresponds to the *unio mentalis.*

Figure 25-1.
The Two Unipeds.

Figure 25-2.
The "Revelation of the Hidden."

---

[273] Plates 4 through 7, following page 330.

Figure 25-3.
The Worldly and the Spiritual Power.

Figure 25-4.
The Royal Pair.

In the fourth picture (figure 25-3) the two figures are united again. This would be a representation of the *unio mentalis* that has first undergone a separation and then a reunion of its components.

In the fifth picture (figure 25-4) we have an entirely new figure. A feminine figure arrives on the scene. This can be thought of as the union of the previously united sulphurs with the earth or the body. In paragraph 736 Jung summarizes the meaning of this fifth picture:

> [It] represents the union of the spirit with material reality. . . . Accordingly, the coniunctio appears here as the union of a consciousness (spirit), differentiated by self-knowledge, with a spirit abstracted from previously unconscious contents. One could also regard the latter as a quintessence of fantasy-images that enter consciousness either spontaneously or through active imagination and, in their totality, represent a moral or intellectual viewpoint contrasting with, or compensating, that of consciousness.

So here's where active imagination starts to come into the picture.

As Jung discusses this picture series it leads him into mortificatio symbolism and to the image of the *caput corvi,* the raven's head, and from there into decapitation symbolism. For instance, concerning beheading—and I would remind you that this is one of the symbolic images describing the *unio mentalis*—in paragraph 730 Jung says:

Beheading is significant symbolically as the separation of the "understanding" from the "great suffering and grief" which nature inflicts on the soul. It is an emancipation of the "cogitatio" which is situated in the head, a freeing of the soul from the "trammels of nature." Its purpose is to bring about, as in Dorn, a *unio mentalis* "in the overcoming of the body."

Another way of seeing beheading symbolism is that it represents the extraction of the rotundum—the round element—from the empirical man. The head is the round element and the beheading, then, extracts that round element. The term *caput corvi* (the head of the raven) and the term *caput mortuum* (death's head) were used in alchemy to refer to the residue left behind after the distillation or sublimation of a substance.

The whole idea of the death's head, the *caput mortuum,* refers to the symbolic image of a skull, which comes up in various ways. It comes up for instance in the lore of the oracular head. There is a human sacrifice; the skull is separated, installed in some kind of ritual or oracular way, and then consulted as an oracle.

The archetypal pattern of consulting an oracular head, the *caput mortuum,* is a well-known dramatic device. There is a good example of it in *Hamlet.* As Hamlet is at Yorick's grave, he comes across Yorick's skull and here's what he says:

To what base uses we may return, Horatio! Why may not imagination trace the noble dust of Alexander till 'a find it stopping a bunghole?
. . . (as thus:) Alexander died, Alexander was buried, Alexander returneth into dust; the dust is earth. Of earth we make loam, and why of that loam, whereto he was converted, might they not stop a beer-barrel?

> Imperious Caesar, dead and turn'd to clay,
> Might stop a hole to keep the wind away.
> O that that earth, which kept the world in awe,
> Should patch a wall t' expel the winter's flaw![274]

This is an image of the mortificatio of the ego, you see: all the power-strivings of the ego are reduced to naught and the contemplation of the skull is what leads Hamlet then into the beginnings of a larger non-ego perspective.

In Goethe's *Faust*, near the beginning of the story, there is also a brief soliloquy to a skull:

> You hollow skull, what has your grin to say,
> But that a mortal brain, with trouble tossed,
> Sought once, like mine, the sweetness of the day,
> And strove for truth, and in the gloam was lost.[275]

The *unio mentalis* is explicitly connected with death. We saw this two weeks ago in the passage, quoted from paragraph 671, where Jung says: "The mind . . .

---

[274] Act 5, scene 1.
[275] Goethe, *Faust*, p. 53.

must be separated from the body—which is equivalent to 'voluntary death.' "[276] Decapitation results in death, and the separation of the soul from the body is accompanied by death. It is highly significant that the earliest forms of religious expression that we know, and what I consider to be the earliest manifestations of man's encounter with the autonomous psyche, involve funeral symbolism. Specifically, I think of Egyptian mortuary symbolism which was the origin of alchemy. It was an attempt to create an immortal body by embalming.

According to Plato, familiarity with death was a basic feature of philosophy. He makes the startling statement that "true philosophers make dying their profession."[277] That's what Socrates says when he's ready to take the hemlock and his friends say, "No, we can sneak you out of here." Socrates says, "Why should I be concerned about death when I've been spending my whole life preoccupied with that anyway?" And this is part of the *unio mentalis.*[278]

Here's what Jung says about it, starting with paragraph 670; I've read it before, but it's worth quoting again:

> The *unio mentalis,* the interior oneness which today we call individuation, he [Dorn] conceived as a psychic equilibrium of opposites "in the overcoming of the body," a state of equanimity transcending the body's affectivity and instinctuality. The spirit . . . which is to unite with the soul, he called a "spiracle . . . of eternal life," a sort of "window into eternity". . . .
>
> But, in order to bring about their subsequent reunion, the mind . . . must be separated from the body—which is equivalent to "voluntary death"—for only separated things can unite. By this separation . . . Dorn obviously meant a discrimination and dissolution of the "composite," the composite state being one in which the affectivity of the body has a disturbing influence on the rationality of the mind.

That's what I had in mind when I spoke about cutting as far as I could—a "discrimination and dissolution of the 'composite.' "

> The aim of this separation was to free the mind from the influence of the "bodily appetites and the heart's affections," and to establish a spiritual position which is supraordinate to the turbulent sphere of the body. This leads at first to a dissociation of the personality and a violation of the merely natural man.
>
> This preliminary step, in itself a clear blend of Stoic philosophy and Christian psychology, is indispensable for the differentiation of consciousness. Modern psychotherapy makes use of the same procedure when it objectifies the affects and instincts and confronts consciousness with them.

I think that's a very important passage which makes the nature of the *unio mentalis* crystal clear.

---

[276] See above, lecture 23, p. 280.

[277] "Phaedo," 67e, in *The Collected Dialogues.*

[278] For further commentary see Edinger, *Anatomy,* pp. 167ff.

Beheading symbolism represents the extraction of the *caelum*—that heavenly stuff—from the body, because the head is the heaven of the body so to speak. It is the round thing. And whenever decapitation symbolism comes up in dreams you can know this process is going on. That immediately orients you because it's alarming at first when you naively encounter this kind of symbolism. You think, "What terrible dissociation process is going on?" and you want to sew them back together again right away.

The Orpheus myth is a good example of beheading symbolism, and reminds us that the imagery of decapitation belongs to the larger symbolism of dismemberment. This links it to a transformation mystery, which is what the symbolism of dismemberment is all about. Let me remind you of the relevant aspects of the Orpheus myth.

Orpheus was the inventor of music who could tame wild beasts by playing his lyre. His wife, Eurydice, is bitten by a serpent, dies and goes to the Underworld, and Orpheus travels to the Underworld to rescue her. He almost succeeds but he looks back at the last minute, which he had been forbidden to do, and thus he loses her. Then, in his grief, he comes across a band of raving maenads who dismember him. His head is cast into the river and goes floating down, singing. It crosses the sea and, still singing, lands on the island of Lesbos where a shrine is built for it. The head is installed as an oracle and continues to prophesy.[279] The conclusion is that he's turned into an eternal prophetic oracle and thus we can think of Orpheus as an early symbolic representation of the *unio mentalis.*

A major Greek religion was called Orphism—largely because one of the features of Orpheus's life was his descent to the Underworld. That amounted to an initiation into the mysteries and thus the mysteries were given his name—the Orphic Mysteries.[280]

Let me give you a couple of examples of this decapitation symbolism. Many years ago I had this dream:

> There was a beautiful crystal head which was to be attached to a little girl. An operation was to be performed to remove her head and replace it with a crystal head. A famous surgeon by the name of Dr. Knight was to do the operation.

Well, if you take that dream just from the personalistic standpoint, it indicates a very dubious relation to the little anima figure. The little girl is going to be decapitated and have her head replaced with a crystal head. But if you interpret it in archetypal terms, this little girl is going to go through something of the same experience that the black Shulamite went through in our earlier text; her head was turned to gold, you remember.[281]

---

[279] For full discussion, see Harrison, *Prolegomena,* chap. 9, "Orpheus."

[280] See ibid., chap. 10, "Orphic Mysteries."

[281] See above, lecture 22, p. 270.

Here's another dream of my own:

A patient brings me a dream in which there is an image of a crystal sphere that is joining with a piece of wood—they're coming together—a piece of wood that had a certain receptacle in it to lodge the crystal sphere. As they come together, great heat is produced. In the dream, the patient who had this dream was quite indifferent to it and I found myself expounding vigorously on the meaning of "his" dream.

"You should consider this dream as very important," I say.

"Wood is matter, flesh, vulnerable organic material, it's a product of the life process. And the crystal sphere is eternal, immortal perfection. The sphere comes from heaven and joins the wood from earth, and this is a picture of man who must carry this intolerable burden of opposites within himself."

This is what I say in the dream, you see.

One should pay attention to such things; what you say in your dream is not something you already know in full consciousness. If you did, you would not have to dream it. So, as with all occasions when one finds oneself giving advice or counsel to others, one should listen to that advice and take it oneself.

Some of my associations to this image were Atlas carrying the world on his shoulders, and St. Christopher carrying Christ as a sphere (figure 25-5). I also thought of the process of making fire by rubbing sticks—the opposites—together. And I must say I also thought of stage two of the coniunctio.

Figure 25-5. St. Christopher carrying Christ as a sphere.

26
Paragraphs 738-758

Now we come to the two last assignments. Jung is finished with his presentation of the heavy, complex symbolism of alchemy that calls for so much elaboration and explanation and now gives us a running commentary on the psychological meaning of all the symbolism of the coniunctio. Some of his very finest descriptive writing is to be found in these last pages; they are the prize, the treasure one arrives at after having plowed through everything that has gone before.

Since there is no point in my saying what Jung himself says so well, I will take a little more freedom and give examples of some of the themes he discusses. In tonight's assignment I will address two particular themes: active imagination and the transference.

1. Active Imagination

As Jung tells us, the process of active imagination is the psychological equivalent of the second stage of the coniunctio. It is one major way to reconnect the *unio mentalis* with the body—to bring about the concrete experiences of living wholeness as opposed to just an abstract concept of it.

No matter how adept one considers oneself in this process of active imagination, each time that it takes place and one has a living experience of it, it is a unique, creative occasion. It is as though it happens for the first time. Back in paragraph 706, Jung gives a good account of active imagination so let's listen together to what he says:

> This process can, as I have said, take place spontaneously or be artificially induced. In the latter case you choose a dream, or some other fantasy-image, and concentrate on it by simply catching hold of it and looking at it. You can also use a bad mood as a starting-point, and then try to find out what sort of fantasy-image it will produce, or what image expresses this mood. You then fix this image in the mind by concentrating your attention. Usually it will alter, as the mere fact of contemplating it animates it. The alterations must be carefully noted down all the time, for they reflect the psychic processes in the unconscious background, which appear in the form of images consisting of conscious memory material. In this way conscious and unconscious are united, just as a waterfall connects above and below.

In other words, the *unio mentalis* is reunited with the body.

> A chain of fantasy ideas develops and gradually takes on a dramatic character: the passive process becomes an action. At first it consists of projected figures, and these images are observed like scenes in the theatre. In other words, you dream with open eyes. As a rule there is a marked tendency simply to enjoy this interior entertainment

and to leave it at that. Then, of course, there is no real progress but only endless variations on the same theme, which is not the point of the exercise at all. What is enacted on the stage still remains a background process; it does not move the observer in any way, and the less it moves him the smaller will be the cathartic effect of this private theatre. The piece that is being played does not want merely to be watched impartially, it wants to compel his participation. If the observer understands that his own drama is being performed on this inner stage, he cannot remain indifferent to the plot and its dénouement. He will notice, as the actors appear one by one and the plot thickens, that they all have some purposeful relationship to his conscious situation, that he is being addressed by the unconscious and that *it* causes these fantasy-images to appear before him. He therefore feels compelled, or is encouraged by his analyst, to take part in the play and, instead of just sitting in a theatre, really have it out with his alter ego. For nothing in us ever remains quite uncontradicted, and consciousness can take up no position which will not call up, somewhere in the dark corners of the psyche, a negation or a compensatory effect, approval or resentment. This process of coming to terms with the Other in us is well worth while, because in this way we get to know aspects of our nature which we would not allow anybody else to show us and which we ourselves would never have admitted. It is very important to fix this whole procedure in writing at the time of its occurrence, for you then have ocular evidence that will effectively counteract the ever-ready tendency to self-deception. A running commentary is absolutely necessary in dealing with the shadow, because otherwise its actuality cannot be fixed. Only in this painful way is it possible to gain a positive insight into the complex nature of one's own personality.

Further important remarks about active imagination come up in tonight's assignment. The latter part of paragraph 749 reads as follows:

Take the unconscious in one of its handiest forms, say a spontaneous fantasy, a dream, an irrational mood, an affect, or something of the kind, and operate with it. Give it your special attention, concentrate on it, and observe its alterations objectively. Spare no effort to devote yourself to this task, follow the subsequent transformations of the spontaneous fantasy attentively and carefully. Above all, don't let anything from outside, that does not belong, get into it, for the fantasy-image has "everything it needs." In this way one is certain of not interfering by conscious caprice and of giving the unconscious a free hand. In short, the alchemical operation seems to us the equivalent of the psychological process of active imagination.

Then he continues in paragraphs 752, 753 and 754. I'm going to read sections of the last two.

The light that gradually dawns on him consists in his understanding that his fantasy is a real psychic process which is happening to him personally. Although, to a certain extent, he looks on from outside, impartially, he is also an acting and suffering figure in the drama of the psyche. This recognition is absolutely necessary and marks an important advance. So long as he simply looks at the pictures he is like the foolish Parsifal, who forgot to ask the vital question because he was not aware of his own participation in the action. Then, if the flow of images ceases, next to nothing has happened even though the process is repeated a thousand times. But if you recognize your own involvement you yourself must enter into the process with your personal reactions, just as if you were one of the fantasy figures, or rather, as if the drama being enacted before your eyes were real. It is a psychic fact that this fantasy is happening, and it is as real as you—as a psychic entity—are real. . . . If you place you yourself in the drama as you really are, not only does it gain in actuality but you also create, by your criticism of the fantasy, an effective counterbalance to its tendency to get out of hand. For what is now happening is the decisive rapprochement with the unconscious. This is where insight, the *unio mentalis,* begins to become real. What you are now creating is the beginning of individuation, whose immediate goal is the experience and production of the symbol of totality.

It not infrequently happens that the patient simply continues to observe his images without considering what they mean to him. He can and he should understand their meaning, but this is of practical value only so long as he is not sufficiently convinced that the unconscious can give him valuable insights. But once he has recognized this fact, he should also know that he then has in his hands an opportunity to win, by his knowledge, independence of the analyst. This conclusion is one which he does not like to draw, with the result that he frequently stops short at the mere observation of his images. . . . Patients . . . . often come to a standstill at this point. As this experience is not uncommon I can only conclude that the transition from a merely perceptive, i.e., *aesthetic,* attitude to one of *judgment* is far from easy.

Let's talk about the importance of having an attitude of judgment toward the active imagination as opposed to a merely aesthetic attitude. This means that one must observe, must notice, how one feels about what one is perceiving and then give expression to what one feels. Once a certain level is reached it becomes urgent that the attitude be active rather than passive .

I want to give you a couple of examples to bring this home. We pay a great deal of attention to the unconscious, to its creative and helpful aspects, and to the profound treasures that contact with it can give us. But we must not relate to the unconscious out of a state of innocence because it can equally be a trickster and expose us to the gravest dangers. We have to be really smart in our dealings with the unconscious. I am going to give you an example of my own. I'll read a page from my journal, written sometime in 1964.

> Tonight I gave a seminar on Greek myths. I did very well. It was a brilliant talk about the son-lover, the *Pharmakos,* Hippolytus and Christ, but in the course of it I got inflated. At the end of the discussion I gave a rather clever but flippant answer to a man's question and cut him off abruptly, unfeelingly. Afterward, I spoke to him and apologized, but it was evident that he felt he'd been treated harshly.
>
> After I left the hall I felt very ashamed of myself. I'd been carried away by my material, had been possessed by it, and had been inflated. I was humiliated. Then I had this active imagination on the way home in the car.

I wouldn't recommend active imagination while one is driving but sometimes things impose themselves on you and you have to take them when they come.

I see an image of Christ on the cross, and at the foot of the cross is a bucket into which his blood is flowing. Then this bucket of blood is taken and put before me and a voice says: "Wash your feet in this." I'm on the verge of unthinkingly doing this, but then I think, "What might happen if I do this?"

Then it is as though I have a secondary imagination inside of my active imagination. I imagine what might happen if I were to put my feet in this blood. I imagine putting my feet in the blood and having my legs consumed by the fiery power of the blood, leaving me only stumps to the knees. And at this thought I say to the one who told me to do this: "But, what if the blood consumes my feet and legs?" Then I'm told: "That's exactly what it would have done," if I'd washed my feet in the blood of Christ. And then he said: "These are real mysteries and are not to be played around with."

The chapter on "The Blood of Christ" in my book *Ego and Archetype* came out of this particular experience. It gives you an example of how the unconscious can act as a trickster to a stupid innocent ego, you see.

There is another example that comes from Jung. In *Memories, Dreams, Reflections,* he describes his initial active imagination in December 1913:

In order to seize hold of the fantasies, I frequently imagined a steep descent. I even made several attempts to get to very bottom. The first time I reached, as it were, a depth of about a thousand feet; the next time I found myself at the edge of a cosmic abyss. It was like a voyage to the moon, or a descent into empty space. First came the image of a crater, and I had the feeling that I was in the land of the dead. The atmosphere was that of the other world. Near the steep slope of a rock I caught sight of two figures, an old man with a white beard and a beautiful young girl. I summoned up my courage and approached them as though they were real people, and listened attentively to what they told me. The old man explained that he was Elijah, and that gave me a shock. But the girl staggered me even more, for she called herself Salome! She was blind. What a strange couple: Salome and Elijah. But Elijah assured me that he and Salome had belonged together from all eternity, which completely astounded me. . . . They had a black serpent living with them which displayed an unmistakable fondness for me. I stuck close to Elijah because he seemed to be the most reasonable of the three, and to have a clear intelligence. Of Salome I was distinctly suspicious. Elijah and I had a long conversation which, however, I did not understand.[282]

In a 1925 seminar he goes into more detail. I'm going to read you some of it:

Then a most disagreeable thing happened. Salome became very interested in me, and she assumed that I could cure her blindness. She began to worship me. I said, "Why do you worship me?" She replied, "You are Christ." In spite of my objections she maintained this. I said, "This is madness," and became filled with skeptical

---

282 *Memories, Dreams, Reflections,* p. 181.

resistance. Then I saw the snake approach me. She came close and began to encircle me and press me in her coils. The coils reached up to my heart. I realized as I struggled, that I had assumed the attitude of the Crucifixion. In the agony and the struggle, I sweated so profusely that the water flowed down on all sides of me. Then Salome rose, and she could see. While the snake was pressing me, I felt that my face had taken on the face of an animal of prey, a lion or a tiger. . . .

Salome's approach and her worshipping of me is obviously that side of the inferior function which is surrounded by an aura of evil. I felt her insinuations as a most evil spell. One is assailed by the fear that perhaps this is madness. This is how madness begins, this *is* madness. For example, in a certain Russian book there is a story of a man who fears he will go mad. Lying in bed at night, he sees a bright square of moonlight in the middle of the room. He says to himself, "If I should sit there and howl like a dog, then I would be mad, but I am not doing it so I am not mad." Then he tries to dismiss this thought, but after a while he says to himself, "I might sit there and howl like a dog, knowing it and choosing it, and still I would not be mad." Again he tries to put the thought away, but finally he can resist it no longer—he gets up and sits in the moonlight and howls like a dog, and then he *is* mad.

You cannot get conscious of these unconscious facts without giving yourself to them. If you can overcome your fear of the unconscious and can let yourself down, then these facts take on a life of their own. You can be gripped by these ideas so that you really go mad, or nearly so. These images have so much reality that they recommend themselves, and such extraordinary meaning that one is caught. They form part of the ancient mysteries; in fact, it is such figures that made the mysteries. Compare the mysteries of Isis as told in Apuleius, with the initiation and deification of the initiate.

Awe surrounds the mysteries, particularly the mystery of deification. This was one of the most important of the mysteries; it gave the immortal value to the individual—. . . One gets a peculiar feeling from being put through such an initiation. The important part that led up to the deification was the snake's encoiling of me. Salome's performance was deification. The animal face which I felt mine transformed into was the famous [Deus] Leontocephalus of the Mithraic mysteries, the figure which is represented with a snake coiled around the man, the snake's head resting on the man's head, and the face of the man that of a lion.

That picture is used as the frontispiece of *Aion,* you may remember (figure 26-1), and this is the experience the image came from. Jung continues:

> In this deification mystery you make yourself into the vessel, and are a vessel of creation in which the opposites reconcile. The more these images are realized, the more you will be gripped by them. When the images come to you and are not understood, you are in the society of the gods or, if you will, the lunatic society; you are no longer in human society, for you cannot express yourself. Only when you can say, "This image is so and so," only then do you remain in human society. Anybody could be caught by these things and lost in them—some throw the expe-

Figure 26-1.
The Mithraic god
Aion.

rience away saying it is all nonsense, and thereby losing their best value, for these are the creative images. Another may identify himself with the images and become a crank or a fool.[283]

You can see from this example that encounter with the collective unconscious in serious active imagination exposes one to the same contents that appear in psychosis. Jung comments on this in paragraphs 755 and 756:

> One naturally asks oneself what fear—if fear it is—prevents him from taking the next step, the transition to an attitude of judgment. [That is, taking the fantasies really seriously.] . . . There are sufficient reasons for fear and uncertainty because voluntary participation in the fantasy is alarming to a naive mind and amounts to an anticipated psychosis.
>
> Naturally there is an enormous difference between an anticipated psychosis and a real one, but the difference is not always clearly perceived and this gives rise to uncertainty or even a fit of panic. Unlike a real psychosis, which comes on you and inundates you with uncontrollable fantasies irrupting from the unconscious, the judging attitude implies a voluntary involvement in those fantasy-processes which compensate the individual and—in particular—the collective situation of consciousness. The avowed purpose of this involvement is to integrate the statements of the unconscious, to assimilate their compensatory content, and thereby produce a whole meaning which alone makes life worth living and, for not a few people, possible at all. The reason why the involvement looks very like a psychosis is that

---

283 *Analytical Psychology: Notes of the Seminar Given in 1925,* pp. 96ff.

the patient is integrating the same fantasy-material to which the insane person falls victim because he cannot integrate it but is swallowed up by it. In myths the hero is the one who conquers the dragon, not the one who is devoured by it. And yet both have to deal with the same dragon. Also, he is no hero who never met the dragon, or who, if he once saw it, declared afterwards that he saw nothing. Equally, only one who has risked the fight with the dragon and is not overcome by it wins the hoard, the "treasure hard to attain." He alone has a genuine claim to self-confidence, for he has faced the dark ground of his self and thereby has gained himself. This experience gives him faith and trust, the *pistis* [the faith] in the ability of the self to sustain him, for everything that menaced him from inside he has made his own. He has acquired the right to believe that he will be able to overcome all future threats by the same means. He has arrived at an inner certainty which makes him capable of self-reliance, and attained what the alchemists called the *unio mentalis.*

Actually, I think it would be more accurate to say that what he has attained is the concretization of the *unio mentalis* by its reunion with the body.

2. Transference and Countertransference

You may remember that Jung states briefly in the foreword to *Mysterium,* and at greater length in the foreword to "The Psychology of the Transference,"[284] that the latter, which was published before the *Mysterium,* is a companion volume and belongs to the same material. Now, in paragraphs 750 and 751, he again brings up the transference:

The analyst has a right to shut his door when a neurosis no longer produces any clinical symptoms and has debouched into the sphere of general human problems. The less he knows about these the greater his chances are of coming across comparatively reasonable patients who can be weaned from the transference that regularly sets in. But if the patient has even the remotest suspicion that the analyst thinks rather more about these problems than he says [in other words, if the analyst has some connection to the archetypal dimension], then he will not give up the transference all that quickly but will cling to it in defiance of all reason—which is not so unreasonable after all, indeed quite understandable. Even adult persons often have no idea how to cope with the problem of living, and on top of that are so unconscious in this regard that they succumb in the most uncritical way to the slightest possibility of finding some kind of answer or certainty. Were this not so, the numerous sects and -isms would long since have died out. But, thanks to unconscious, infantile attachments, boundless uncertainty and lack of self-reliance, they all flourish like weeds.

The analyst who is himself struggling for all those things which he seeks to inculcate into his patients will not get round the problem of the transference so easily. The more he knows how difficult it is for him to solve the problems of his own life, the less he can overlook the fear and uncertainty or the frivolity and dangerously

---

[284] *The Practice of Psychotherapy,* CW 16, p. 166.

uncritical attitude of his patients. Even Freud regarded the transference as a neurosis at second hand and treated it as such. He could not simply shut the door, but honestly tried to analyze the transference away. This is not so simple as it sounds when technically formulated. Practice often turns out to be rather different from theory. You want, of course, to put a whole man on his feet and not just a part of him. You soon discover that there is nothing for him to stand on and nothing for him to hold on to. Return to the parents has become impossible, so he hangs on to the analyst.

And the hanging on to the analyst is the transference.

The transference is probably the arena and the context where all the rich symbolism of the coniunctio can best be observed and encountered and worked with. The basis of the transference is the unconscious connection, the coniunctio archetype constellated unconsciously. In fact, we can put the issue even more broadly and say that the coniunctio archetype is probably the basis of the phenomenology of all human relationships.

Think of those crucial relationships we have to deal with all the time, the terrible power they demonstrate in our patients: the mother-son relationship, father-daughter, brother-sister. These all owe their power to the coniunctio archetype living itself out unconsciously. And this same phenomenon comes up very commonly in the analytic situation when a strong transference develops.

It is evident from "The Psychology of the Transference," and the way Jung elaborates its phenomenology, that he considers the best way of understanding and dealing with the transference is to recognize that its basis is the numinosity of the coniunctio—the archetype of wholeness. It's an image of the constellated Self which is conceived in the analyst-patient relationship. When that happens, it means the relationship takes on a charge of import for either good or ill; it can have very creative and releasing consequences if it evolves consciously, or dangerous, destructive consequences if it lives itself out in an unconscious way.

I think I can best serve the practical application of this profound and difficult material we've been working with all year if I allow myself to speak at a little greater length about the transference-countertransference phenomenon as a manifestation of the coniunctio archetype—how we actually encounter it.

An image that I think is very helpful in understanding what goes on in the transference and countertransference is the notion of induction. This idea derives from electromagnetic phenomena—it's a term used in physics. If, for instance, I take a ring made of conducting material—let's say an iron ring—then run an electric current through a coil wound around that ring, and then I put a second coil around the ring, when current runs through the first coil it will induce a current in the other coil. That's induction.

This image very aptly describes what happens in the analytic process which involves an encounter between two people in a setting that has a containing aspect to it analogous to the ring. The analytic setting is the ring, and each of the participants brings his or her own coil and electric circuit into that setting. So the particular electrical currents flowing through the psyche of the analyst are going to have an inductive effect on the patient. We see that all the time, of course. Another way of putting it is that there is a contagion effect.

Of course, the reverse also takes place: the electrical currents running through the psyche of the patient have an inductive effect on the analyst. Sometimes that inductive effect is of greater power and import than the former one, in which case the analyst can fall under the spell of the patient's psyche.

The contents that are apt to appear in the transference all have to do with the coniunctio, but at different levels of maturity or immaturity, and at different levels of depth. For instance, two major distinctions can be made between different kinds of transferential contents: there is the personal level of the transference and the archetypal level.

In the personal transference will lie the relation to the parent of the opposite sex that will be constellated and projected—induced—into the relationship with the analyst. If, for instance, the patient is a woman working with a man, she's apt to project certain contents of her experience with her father. That can be positive, negative or neutral. But it will be a whole style or pattern of expectations and the transference will be a kind of new edition of the old pattern. This is the familiar Freudian aspect of the transference and of course it will have a definite incestuous quality to it. In fact, the theme of incest runs through all levels of the transference, but the personal level is very obviously incestuous. In such circumstances then, the inductive effect is that the analyst is subtly drawn into the family of the patient and subtly treated as a familiar. After all, "familiar" means belonging to the family. It might manifest itself in certain inappropriate actions or expectations— the atmosphere gets sticky—and if the analyst is not very astute in realizing what's going on, he or she can fall into the induced condition and function out of it.

If there is unconsciousness on both sides, then one doesn't get any farther; one remains stuck. The crucial point of course is for the analyst to be aware of it and then, with that awareness, apply a reductive component of interpretation while at the same time not throwing out the baby with the bath water. We must remember that the transference does not come in neatly compartmentalized levels with one piece labeled "personal" and another labeled "archetypal." It comes all as one hunk. While we're interpreting the personal level of the transference we have to keep in mind that the archetypal, creative level is also there. That is the baby, and it is most important not to throw it out with the bath water.

Not long ago I had a patient tell me explicitly that she had the irrational fear I was going to discharge her after just a brief period. The fantasy was, as she said, "You are carrying my baby and I'm afraid you're going to insist on an abortion." Well, I didn't know that I looked all that maternal, but you see the fantasy thought so. The fantasy was speaking of the ring that had been created—the analytic container—and already within that container the potential Self had been conceived and was growing.

That supreme life value, then, is residing in the transference, and that indeed is typically the case when a sizable transference develops. Therefore, though it often has immature and disagreeable outer trappings, the core of it is the coniunctio, the Self, the highest goal of psychic development. That's the baby we mustn't throw out with the bath water.

What frequently happens as one proceeds is that the personal level of the transference is assimilated and then the archetypal level is opened up. That feature is utterly unique to Jungian psychology—no other school of psychotherapy knows beans about the archetypal transference. It's unknown. That's a treasure we carry, the awareness of that archetypal dimension of the transference. What it then opens us up to is that very often the analyst becomes the target of archetypal projections, not just personal projections, not just the projections of one's experience of one's parents.

So the Self is born out of the transference, potentially; the whole promise of individuation is carried temporarily in projection onto the analyst.

In certain cases this issue is of such extreme importance that it takes on the urgency of a life or death situation. That means the ultimate archetypal projections are often activated: God and the devil, two sides of the same phenomenon. Another way of seeing it is that an extreme transference is a psychological version of the clutchings of a drowning person.

One has to be very careful when one is the recipient of such extreme projections. Usually the transference is positive at first; if it is initially a negative projection of any size, then the patient will go to somebody else or the whole process will break down. But usually the archetypal transference appears in positive form and the analyst is then granted some of the attributes and prerogatives of deity—not consciously and overtly, but subtly and unconsciously. And it is exceedingly important that the analyst not fall into a passive acceptance of that state of affairs which is easy to do since it's so flattering. It's very gratifying to be so perceived, you know; it's a great balm to one's vanity. But it is exceedingly dangerous to accept the projection of God, because if you accept it, you then take on divine responsibility which you are not able to fulfill; and sooner or later the projection will reverse and you'll be seen as the devil. With your divine power you fail to make things right for the patient and then you become the devil.

Well, I'm going to stop there, but I have some more remarks to make about countertransference which I'll go into next time.

Last time we spoke about two psychological manifestations of the coniunctio, namely active imagination and transference. I want to make a few more remarks tonight about transference—specifically about countertransference, which, as I described last week, is an induction phenomenon.

1. Transference and Countertransference (cont.)

An archetypal image can manifest in human psychology consciously or unconsciously, or, as is so often the case, some mixture of the two. Problems are always a consequence of the unconscious manifestation of an archetype. That's what countertransference is—an *unconscious* manifestation of the coniunctio, the most profound and highly charged archetype in the whole pantheon. The coniunctio is the symbolic expression of the goal of the opus and that's why Jung titled his book *The Mystery of the Coniunctio.*

The whole transference and countertransference phenomenon, with its powerful inductive aspect, illustrates the fact that analysis is a risky enterprise and involves a very sizable occupational hazard. It is not an innocuous procedure, especially if the depths are touched or constellated. As long as one scoots along the surface and has no connection to the depths, as long as they're not constellated, then usually one can skip around pretty safely. But when they've been opened within the analyst's personality, or within that of the patient, then the whole induction phenomenon can take on quite serious proportions.

I want to talk about some of the aspects of the countertransference since it can show up in many different ways and often eludes our observation; it slips in unconsciously and then neither patient nor therapist knows what's going on. It's a kind of infallible truth that the countertransference will hit one wherever one is weakest, in one's personal complexes and vulnerabilities. Let me mention just a few of the modes in which the countertransference coniunctio can appear.

A common one is the constellation of the parent-child pattern. It happens almost regularly that when one seeks some sort of therapeutic help, the child role is activated on the part of the patient, and the parent role tends to be projected onto the therapist. Now the countertransference danger is that the therapist will identify with the projected role of parent. There's a certain gratification to be gained by being the parent to a child—the gratification of being needed, of being the mature one, the knowledgeable one in comparison to the immature, helpless one. If the therapist identifies to some extent with that role, then he or she lives out the need to be attached to a dependent child. Any efforts the child might make to become independent are apt to be subtly, and of course quite unconsciously, sabotaged.

That's not as uncommon as it seems, you know. We think we're above such things, but we aren't, not at all. And many is the time that the new-born efforts to achieve autonomy and independence on the part of the patient are belittled or disparaged, one way or another, by the analyst's critical or negative interpretation. Another way to say the same thing is that the Cronus archetype is activated. Cronus was the Greek god who devoured his own children (figure 27-1).[285] In order to keep the child a child, and relatively impotent, the child is devoured or consumed, incorporated into the psychology of the therapist, and not permitted to have his or her own separate psychology.

Figure 27-1
Cronus devouring
his children.

---

[285] For a summary of the myth see *Funk and Wagnalls Standard Dictionary,* p. 263.

A similar situation can occur if the patient is particularly talented psychologically. The countertransference can take the form of a projection of the divine child onto the patient and then, in a subtle way, the therapist expects to be redeemed by the psychological work of the patient. That's not as far-fetched as it sounds. It is not at all uncommon to have a need to cure the patient, especially with young therapists, because they're not too sure of their therapeutic capacity. They're insecure and therefore, in order to preserve their own self-esteem, they need to have the patient do well. The patient's doing well redeems them and proves their own worth as therapists.

Another variant is the pattern of the wounded patient on the one hand, and the healer, on the other. If one is identified with the role of healer, one then has a need to have somebody wounded to work on. No healer has anything to do, you see, unless he or she has a wounded one to take care of. This constellation can have the subtle effect of keeping the patient a patient in order for the healer to retain the function of healing.

One more pattern is the power countertransference. (You notice that what we're dealing with here are the opposites, the constellation of the opposites—which is what the coniunctio consists of.) In this pattern, the opposites at work are domination as opposed to submission. Although it is probably much more frequent that the therapist falls into the role of being the dominant one and the patient the submissive one, that's not universally the case. I see a certain number of cases where the reverse takes place, where the therapist fancies a therapeutic function is being performed by being submissive. But it turns out, when a crisis comes up, that actually the power countertransference has been constellated and the therapist has been caught in an unconscious pattern of submission to the patient. That's the less common version, but it does come up.

Then (and these are all variations of the same theme), there is what I would call the inflation countertransference. In this pattern the analyst is the recipient of a projection of the savior or Self archetype, and that is such a flattering attitude with which to be treated that one subtly succumbs to it. As I said last week, it's especially dangerous because, if one accepts the projection of savior, sooner or later it will turn into its opposite. One is then saddled with a devil projection. That's very hard to get out from under if one has previously accepted the savior projection, so it's much better to catch this early.

Now comes the big one: the erotic countertransference. There are different degrees of this of course, but when it's activated in a major way it means that the two people concerned—analyst and patient—have been gripped by the coniunctio archetype in a particularly powerful way, so that the conviction emerges on each side (though we're talking particularly about the analyst and the countertransference) that "If I can just unite, concretely, physically, personally and humanly with this other person I'll be fulfilled and made whole; the conjunction will be established." That's the conviction, with all the highly charged libido that accompanies it.[286] If this state of affairs develops in a full-blown form it is a crisis personally, professionally and legally.

As far as its personal meaning is concerned, it means that the individuation process has gripped the analyst in an unconscious way and manifested itself in projection onto the patient. What that calls for immediately is more personal analysis for the analyst.

On the professional level, it means that one's function as a psychotherapist is profoundly jeopardized. If the analyst's personal needs are so urgent and so insistent that they require the projection to be lived out, then the minimum responsibility one must take in the situation is to disqualify oneself as an analyst for that patient. Then what you do subsequently you at least do on an equal basis. Of course, it's not strictly equal because you've already been the recipient of projections that make it highly unequal. I don't feel able to make any prescriptions for what each individual ought to do in such a situation, except that the absolute minimum is to withdraw as a therapist or analyst and see that the patient gets suitably settled with someone else.

Then of course there's a legal meaning. That's the collective meaning, the meaning that society applies to the situation. Health care givers and clergy often face the basic problem of being the targets of transferences, and therefore of being caught, by the inductive effect, in their own corresponding countertransferences. It becomes a legal issue because it is collectively recognized that taking erotic advantage of the patient or client is grounds for malpractice. That collective determination is absolutely valid; such exploitation does take unfair advantage of the professional situation.

Fortunately, that sort of full-blown event doesn't happen very often in one's professional life, but lesser versions certainly do happen all the time. It then brings up questions as to just what kind of social or personal relations are proper or permissible while in the analytic relationship. In my opinion, there should be no social contacts when one is in the midst of an analytic process because transference aspects and reality aspects almost invariably get confused and mixed up. It's hard enough to bring unconscious complexes into consciousness under the best of circumstances, and if the analytic process is contaminated with social contacts it almost always makes for an unholy mess.

And certainly there should be no physical intimacy. In addition, I think one should not accept or request any sizable gift or favor or service because the danger of taking advantage of the transference projection is so very great. You must always remember that you are carrying an unconscious value for the patient, and

---

[286] For further discussion see Mario Jacoby, *The Analytic Encounter: Transference and Human Relationship,* chap. 7, "Erotic Love in Analysis."

very often that is the supreme value, the Self.

That's all I'm going to say about the countertransference—an unconscious manifestation of the coniunctio archetype. Now some final, more general remarks about the coniunctio.

2. The Coniunctio

The coniunctio is made up of the opposites. If there is one thing you can't help but understand from the *Mysterium,* it's that. The factors that come together in the coniunctio are the opposites and they constitute the most elemental structure of the psyche. The flow of libido is generated by the polarization of opposites in the same way that electricity flows between the positive and negative poles of an electrical circuit. This means that the opposites, and the coniunctio they allude to, are everywhere—everywhere in one's own life-functioning and everywhere in the evidence of the psyche all about us. Whenever one is attracted toward a desired object, or repelled away from a hated object, one is caught up in the drama of the opposites because these are the dynamo of the psyche.

Now this happens all the time of course—it is how, by and large, we govern our lives. We go toward what's pleasing to us and away from what's displeasing. So there's no growth of consciousness or promotion of the coniunctio just by that kind of natural functioning. But the more conscious we become of these operations of attraction and repulsion in ourselves, the closer we come to the goal of the coniunctio.

In the early stages of ego development the opposites must be separated, and you might say that it is the task of the ego to get out of them. The young ego is obliged to separate from its environment and to define itself in terms of being different; it must establish itself as something definite and that involves saying, "I am this and not that." It involves a great deal of no-saying, and the result of this operation is the creation of the shadow, the unconscious figure that stands over and against the ego.

Sooner or later, if psychic development is to proceed, that split-off shadow figure must be encountered as an inner reality; then one is confronted with the problem of bringing the opposites together as opposed to separating them. Separating the opposites is a task for the early part of life, and the union of the opposites is a task for the later part of life.

Of course one can speak quite glibly about the opposites, but when one encounters them in living reality it's a momentous occasion. Perhaps the most crucial and terrifying pair of opposites is good and evil. The very survival of the ego depends on how it relates to this matter because in order to survive it is essential that the ego experience itself as more good than bad. If it experiences itself as more bad than good, it has no grounds for survival. It will have to commit suicide, or annihilate itself some way or other. This fact explains the creation of the shadow in the first place: that which is carrying the notion of badness or evil has to be banished in order that the self-esteem of the ego can grow sufficiently for the ego itself to develop.

The young ego can tolerate very little experience of its own badness without succumbing to demoralization. And since there are a lot more young egos around than there are old egos, this accounts for the universal phenomenon that we see all about us: the obligatory process of locating the source of evil. Whenever something evil happens, the need to locate the blame or the source of it is immediately activated because free-floating evil is not tolerable. So, whenever something bad happens, if it is at all possible, blame or responsibility must be established and then suitable punishment administered. It is an apotropaic procedure that mitigates our terror of evil. Someone or something must carry the burden of evil if society as a whole is going to go its happy-go-lucky way.[287]

With maturation of the ego in the process of individuation, this need to locate the source of evil changes, and of course that's one of the features of the coniunctio. As that comes into consciousness, it's no longer possible to identify oneself with the good and project the evil; the coniunctio requires that those two be carried in the same place by the same person. An individual who has had some contact with the coniunctio then takes on the task of being the carrier of evil as well as of good—in other words, he or she becomes a carrier of the opposites.

In the early period of this recognition of the opposites we have what might be called the pendulum phase. That is when the individual is cast back and forth between moods of guilty inferiority about being evil on the one hand, and optimistic hope about being pretty good after all, on the other. There's the pendulum swing between darkness and light. Jung makes a remarkable statement about this stage in paragraph 206:

> The one-after-another [that's the pendulum] is a bearable prelude to the deeper knowledge of the side-by-side, for this is an incomparably more difficult problem. Again, the view that good and evil are spiritual forces outside us, and that man is caught in the conflict between them, is more bearable by far than the insight that the opposites are the ineradicable and indispensable preconditions of all psychic life, so much so that life itself is guilt.

Guilt—that's one of the things the coniunctio brings to consciousness.

I think it is fair to say that an understanding of the opposites is the key to understanding the psyche. And once you become familiar with the phenomenon of the opposites, once you've really got it, then you'll see them operating everywhere, because they're the very core of the psyche. Every war, every contest, every dispute, every game, is an expression of coniunctio energies concerning the

---

287 See Sylvia Brinton Perera, *The Scapegoat Complex: Toward a Mythology of Shadow and Guilt.*

opposites. Whenever you fall into an identification with one of a pair of warring groups or factions of any kind, then you have momentarily—so far as you are identified, anyway—lost the possibility of being a carrier of the opposites. Instead, you identify with one side and project the other. You locate the enemy on the outside and, in the process, become a "mass man."[288]

Here's what Emerson said about it:

Is it not the chief disgrace in the world, not to be a unit; not to be reckoned one character; not to yield that peculiar fruit which each man was created to bear, but to be reckoned in the gross, in the hundred, or the thousand, of the party, the section, to which we belong; and our opinion predicted geographically, as the north or south?[289]

And Jung puts it this way in his essay, "On the Nature of the Psyche":

If the subjective consciousness prefers the ideas and opinions of collective consciousness and identifies with them, then the contents of the collective unconscious are repressed. . . . And the more highly charged the collective consciousness, the more the ego forfeits its practical importance. It is, as it were, absorbed by the opinions and tendencies of collective consciousness, and the result of that is the mass man, the ever-ready victim of some wretched "ism." The ego keeps its integrity only if it does not identify with one of the opposites, and if it understands how to hold the balance between them. This is possible only if it remains conscious of both at once.[290]

Now that's a pretty hard thing to do—to hold on to a consciousness of the opposites. But let me try to give you a hint or two about how it can be done. First of all, locate the opposites in your own experience. This is not an abstract idea, but an absolutely personal, empirical matter: you find the opposites in your own experience by scrutinizing whatever you love or hate. This is not so easy because the inclination to scrutinize does not usually accompany the passions of love and hate—yet it is in our loves and our hates that the opposites reside.

I would remind you of the very first sentence of *Mysterium,* where Jung says: "The factors which come together in the coniunctio are conceived as opposites, either confronting one another in enmity or attracting one another in love." So the phenomenology of love or hate—either one—leads us to the opposites. And there's even good psychological reason to believe that hate does a better job of leading us than love does—it's more painful and we're more apt to be driven to scrutinize it.

Whenever we take too concretely an urge to love or to hate, the coniunctio is exteriorized and the possibility of its conscious realization, at least for the mo-

---

[288] See *Mysterium,* pars. 470 and 510f.
[289] "The American Scholar," in *Complete Essays,* p. 63.
[290] *The Structure and Dynamics of the Psyche,* CW 8, par. 425.

ment, is destroyed. So, whenever we're gripped by a strong attraction or repulsion to a person or a thing, we should reflect. As Jung puts it in "The Psychology of the Transference":

> Unless we prefer to be made fools of by our illusions, we shall, by carefully analysing every fascination, extract from it a portion of our own personality, like a quintessence, and slowly come to recognize that we meet ourselves time and again in a thousand disguises on the path of life.[291]

Similarly, our passionate antipathies need to be subjected to analytic scrutiny. What persons do I hate? What groups or factions do I fight against? Whatever they are, they are a part of me because I am bound to that which I hate as surely as I am bound to that which I love, and psychologically the important thing is where one's libido is lodged, not whether one is for or against a given thing. So if one pursues such reflections diligently, one will gradually collect one's scattered psyche from the outer world, like the dismembered body of Osiris, and such work promotes the coniunctio.

I think one can say there's a certain psychological or symbolic equation between the effects of the coniunctio and consciousness. The coniunctio might be defined as consciousness of wholeness, for instance, but it is exceedingly difficult to define precisely. I might feel like calling coniunctio-consciousness a kind of higher or larger consciousness, but that wouldn't be strictly true to the opposites because if it's higher consciousness, it's also lower consciousness; if it's larger consciousness, it's also smaller consciousness. Maybe we could call it eternal or transpersonal consciousness, if these terms do not call to mind a contrary but are considered to include the opposites of temporal and nontemporal, personal and nonpersonal.

These thoughts just go to show how impossible it is to articulate a paradoxical experience and a paradoxical entity that is beyond logical categories, categories of rational discourse which are based on the separation of opposites.

I am convinced that coniunctio means consciousness, and as I think of it, consciousness is both the cause and the effect of the coniunctio. We have to state it in this paradoxical way because, as I see it, the coniunctio is a product of both centers of the psyche—it's the product of both the ego and the Self. On the one hand we have the efforts of the ego to create the coniunctio; on the other hand, fate decides what's going to happen in these crucial matters, and then, as Jung puts it, "You have become the victim of a decision made over your head or in defiance of the heart." That comes from a profound passage in *Mysterium,* in paragraph 778:

> The self, in its efforts at self-realization, reaches out beyond the ego-personality on

---

[291] *The Practice of Psychotherapy,* CW 16, par. 534.

all sides; because of its all-encompassing nature it is brighter and darker than the ego, and accordingly confronts it with problems which it would like to avoid. Either one's moral courage fails, or one's insight, or both, until in the end fate decides. The ego never lacks moral and rational counter-arguments, which one cannot and should not set aside so long as it is possible to hold on to them. For you only feel yourself on the right road when the conflicts of duty seem to have resolved themselves, and you have become the victim of a decision made over your head or in defiance of the heart. From this we can see the numinous power of the self, which can hardly be experienced in any other way. For this reason *the experience of the self is always a defeat for the ego.*

So to finish up my remarks for tonight, and for the whole year, allow me to enlarge my field of vision and look at the world as a whole in the light of con-iunctio symbolism. With that perspective, we see it utterly torn apart in multi-tudinous conflicts between the opposites, different manifestations of the oppo-sites, going to make up what Jung calls the "wretched isms"—innumerable na-tionalisms and factionalisms. As Emerson put it so well, "All men plume them-selves on the improvement of society, and no man improves."[292] Or, as Jung writes in "The Undiscovered Self":

> If the individual is not truly regenerated in spirit, society cannot be either, for society is the sum total of individuals in need of redemption.[293]

Later in that same essay he says:

> If only a world-wide consciousness could arise that all division and all fission are due to the splitting of the opposites in the psyche, then we should know where to begin.[294]

> What does lie within our reach . . . is the change in individuals who have, or create for themselves, an opportunity to influence others of like mind. I do not mean by persuading or preaching—I am thinking, rather, of the well-known fact that anyone who has insight into his own actions, and has thus found access to the unconscious, involuntarily exercises an influence on his environment.[295]

An inductive influence, we might say.[296]

You see, these individuals with insight into their own actions, who are aware of the operation of the opposites within themselves, have, to a greater or lesser extent, experienced the coniunctio—the subject matter of the *Mysterium.* Such people, then, are conscious carriers of the opposites. And, to the extent that such

---

[292] "Self-Reliance," in *Complete Essays,* p. 166.
[293] *Civilization in Transition,* CW 10, par. 536.
[294] Ibid., par. 575.
[295] Ibid., par. 583.
[296] A good example of this is the Rainmaker story, which Jung recounts in *Mysterium,* par. 604, note 211.

individuals exist and carry the opposites within themselves, they do not feed the exteriorization of the terrible strife between the opposites. There is reason to believe that if society is to be redeemed, it will be done through the cumulative effect of such individuals. And when a sufficient number of people carry the consciousness of wholeness, the world itself has a chance to become whole.

You know in the Old Testament, in Genesis, when God is about to destroy Sodom and Gomorrah for its sins, Abraham remonstrates with God and says "What if we've got some righteous people in those cities, what if there are fifty?" And Yahweh says, "Well, then I'll save the city if there are fifty." And Abraham works him all the way down to ten—"What if there are ten?" And Yahweh says, "I'll save the city if there are ten." Abraham doesn't want to push his luck too far, so he stops there.[297] But it's not beyond the realm of possibility that just *one* person might be enough to preserve the world.

I would suggest that you entertain such an idea, and furthermore, consider that perhaps *you* are the one.

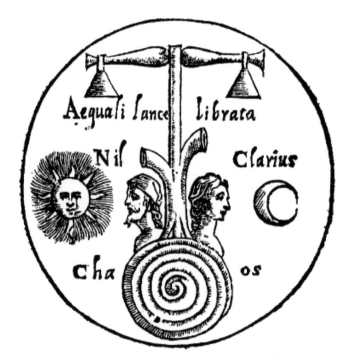

Figure 27-2. Coniunctio as Sol and Luna in balance.

---

[297] Gen. 18: 23-32; see discussion in Edinger, *Creation of Consciousness,* pp. 94ff.

Bibliography

For details of alchemical texts, see the bibliography in *Mysterium Coniunctionis*

Adler, Gerhard. *The Living Symbol: A Case Study in the Process of Individuation* (Bollingen Series LXIII). New York: Pantheon, 1961.

Atwood, M.A. *Hermetic Philosophy and Alchemy*. Reprint. New York: Johnson Reprint Corp., 1967.

Augustine, Saint. *City of God*. Trans. Marcus Dodds. The Modern Library. New York: Random House, 1950.

Barlett's Familiar Quotations. 13th ed. Boston: Little, Brown & Co., 1956.

Bevan, Edwyn. *Stoics and Sceptics*. Oxford: Clarendon Press, 1913.

Boehme, Jacob. *The Signature of All Things*. New York: Dutton, n.d.

Burkert, Walter. *Lore and Science in Ancient Pythagoreanism*. Trans. Edwin L. Minar, Jr. Cambridge: Harvard University Press, 1972.

Campbell, Joseph. *The Masks of God: Occidental Mythology*. New York: Penguin Books, 1976.

Cook, Roger. *The Tree of Life: Image for the Cosmos*. London: Thames and Hudson, 1974.

Coughlan, Robert. *The World of Michelangelo, 1475-1564*. Alexandria, VA: Time-Life Books, 1966.

Daniélou, Alain. *The Myths and Gods of India*. Rochester, VT: Inner Traditions International, Ltd., 1991.

Edinger, Edward F. *Anatomy of the Psyche: Alchemical Symbolism in Psychotherapy*. La Salle, IL: Open Court, 1985.

_____. *The Bible and the Psyche: Individuation Symbolism in the Old Testament*. Toronto: Inner City Books, 1986.

_____. *The Christian Archetype: A Jungian Commentary on the Life of Christ*. Toronto: Inner City Books, 1987.

_____. *The Creation of Consciousness: Jung's Myth for Modern Man*. Toronto: Inner City Books, 1984.

_____. *Ego and Archetype: Individuation and the Religious Function of the Psyche*. Boston: Shambhala Publications, 1992.

_____. *Encounter with the Self: A Jungian Commentary on William Blake's* Illustrations of the Book of Job. Toronto: Inner City Books, 1986.

_____. *Goethe's Faust: Notes for a Jungian Commentary*. Toronto: Inner City Books, 1990.

_____. *Lectures on Jung's* Aion. Audio tapes. C.G. Jung Institute of Los Angeles, 1988. Edited transcript in preparation.

_____. *Lectures on Jung's* Mysterium Coniunctionis. Audio tapes. C.G. Jung Institute of Los Angeles, 1987.

_____. *The Living Psyche: A Jungian Analysis in Pictures*. Wilmette, IL: Chiron Publications, 1990.

_____. *The Mystery of the Coniunctio: Alchemical Image of Individuation*. Toronto: Inner City Books, 1994.

_____. *Transformation of the God-Image: An Elucidation of Jung's* Answer to Job. Toronto: Inner City Books, 1992.

Emerson, Ralph Waldo. *The Complete Essays and Other Writings of Ralph Waldo Emerson*. Ed. Brooks Atkinson. New York: Modern Library, 1940.

Fabricius, Johannes. *Alchemy: The Medieval Alchemists and Their Royal Art*. Copenhagen: Rosenkilde and Bagger, 1976.

Frazer, James George. *The Golden Bough*. Abridged Ed. New York: Macmillan, 1957.

Freud, Sigmund. *Collected Papers*. Trans. Joan Rivière. New York: Basic Books, 1959.

Funk and Wagnalls Standard Dictionary of Folklore, Mythology and Legend. New York: Harper and Row, 1984.

Gaer, Joseph. *Lore of the Old Testament*. New York: Grosset and Dunlop, 1966.

Ginzberg, Louis. *Legends of the Bible*. New York: Simon and Schuster, 1956.

Goethe. *Faust*. Trans. Philip Wayne. 2 vols. Baltimore: Penguin Books, 1969.

Grant, Robert M. *The Secret Sayings of Jesus*. London: Collins, 1960.

Grimm. *The Complete Grimm's Fairy Tales*. New York: Pantheon Books, 1972.

Hannah, Barbara. *Jung: His Life and Work. A Biographical Memoir*. New York: G.P. Putnam's Sons, 1976.

Harding, M. Esther. *Woman's Mysteries: Ancient and Modern*. New York: Harper, 1971.

Harrison, Jane. *Prolegomena to the Study of Greek Religion*. London: Merlin Press, 1980.

Hawthorne, Nathaniel. *The Complete Novels and Selected Tales*. Ed. Norman Holmes Pearson. Modern Library. New York: Random House, 1965.

Hoffmann, Edward. *The Way of Splendor: Jewish Mysticism and Modern Psychology*. Boulder: Shambhala, 1981.

Hyppolytus, "Elenchos." In *The Anti-Nicene Fathers*. Vol. 5. Reprint. Grand Rapids, MI: Eerdmans Publishing Co., 1986.

The I Ching or Book of Changes. Trans. Richard Wilhelm. Rendered into English by Cary F. Baynes. Princeton: Princeton University Press, 1971.

Jacoby, Mario. *The Analytic Encounter: Transference and Human Relationship*. Toronto: Inner City Books, 1984.

Jaffé, Aniela, ed. *C.G. Jung: Word and Image* (Bollingen Series XCVII:2). Princeton: Princeton University Press, 1979.

James, William. *The Varieties of Religious Experience: A Study in Human Nature*. The Modern Library. New York: Random House, n.d.

Janson, H.W. *History of Art*. New York: Harry N. Abrams, Inc., 1963.

Jerusalem Bible. Garden City, NY: Doubleday and Co., 1966.

Jonas, Hans. *The Gnostic Religion: The Message of the Alien God and the Beginnings of Christianity*. 2nd ed., revised. Boston: Beacon Press, 1963.

Jung, C.G. *Analytical Psychology, Notes of the Seminar Given in 1925* (Bollingen Series XCIX). Ed. William McGuire. Princeton: Princeton University Press, 1989.

_____. *The Collected Works* (Bollingen Series XX). 20 vols. Trans. R.F.C. Hull. Ed. H. Read, M. Fordham, G. Adler, Wm. McGuire. Princeton: Princeton University Press, 1953-1979.

_____. *Letters* (Bollingen Series XCV). 2 vols. Trans. R.F.C. Hull. Ed. G. Adler, A. Jaffé. Princeton: Princeton University Press, 1973.

_____. *Man and His Symbols.* London: Aldus Books, 1964.

_____. *Memories, Dreams, Reflections.* Ed. Aniela Jaffé. New York: Random House, 1963.

_____. *The Visions Seminars.* Vol. 1. Zürich: Spring Publications, 1976.

Klossowski de Rola, Stanislas. *The Secret Art of Alchemy.* London: Thames and Hudson, 1973.

Kluger, Rivkah Sharf. *Psyche and Bible.* Zurich: Spring Publications, 1974.

Lake, Kirsopp, trans. *The Shepherd of Hermas.* In *The Apostolic Fathers.* Vol. 2. Loeb Classical Library. Cambridge, MA: Harvard University Press, 1976.

Lattimore, Richmond, trans. *The Odyssey of Homer.* New York: Harper and Row, 1965.

Mathers, S.L. MacGregor. *The Kabbalah Unveiled.* London: Routledge and Kegan Paul, 1962.

Micropedia of the Encyclopedia Britannica. 15th ed. 1974.

Neumann, Erich. *Amor and Psyche: The Psychic Development of the Feminine* (Bollin-gen Series LIV). Princeton: Princeton University Press, 1971.

_____. "On the Moon and Matriarchal Consciousness." In *Spring 1954.* New York: Spring Publications, 1954.

_____. *The Origins and History of Conciousness* (Bollingen Series XLII). Princeton: Princeton University Press, 1969.

New Larousse Encyclopedia of Mythology. Trans. Richard Aldington and Delano Ames. New York: Prometheus Press, 1968.

Nietzsche, Friedrich. *The Portable Nietzsche.* Ed. and trans. Walter Kaufmann. New York: Viking Press, 1954.

Oxford Dictionary of Saints. Ed. David Hugh Farmer. 2nd ed. New York: Oxford University Press, 1987.

Ovid. *Metamorphoses.* Trans. Frank Justus Miller. 2nd ed. Loeb Classical Library. Cambridge, MA: Harvard University Press, 1984.

Patai, Raphael. *The Messiah Texts.* New York: Avon Books, 1979.

Perera, Sylvia Brinton. *The Scapegoat Complex: Toward a Mythology of Shadow and Guilt.* Toronto: Inner City Books, 1986.

Perry, John Weir. *The Far Side of Madness.* Englewood Cliffs, NJ: Prentice-Hall, 1974.

_____. *The Heart of History: Individuality in Evolution.* Albany, NY: State University of New York Press, 1987.

Plato. *The Collected Dialogues* (Bollingen Series LXXI). Ed. Edith Hamilton and Huntington Cairns. Princeton: Princeton University Press, 1961.

_____. *Symposium.* Trans. W.R.M. Lamb. Loeb Classical Library. Cambridge, MA: Harvard University Press, 1961.

Plutarch. *Plutarch's Moralia.* Vol. 5. Trans. F.C. Babbitt. Loeb Classical Library. Cambridge, MA: Harvard Univerity Press, 1969.

Pope, Marvin H., trans. and ed. "Job." *Anchor Bible,* vol. 15. Garden City, NY: Doubleday and Co., 1977.

Porter, Eliot. *The Greek World.* New York: E.P. Dutton, 1980.

Rahner, Hugo. *Greek Myths and Christian Mystery.* New York: Harper and Row, 1963.

Richardson, Joanna, trans. *Baudelaire: Selected Poems.* New York: Penguin, 1980.

Rundle Clark, R.T. *Myth and Symbol in Ancient Egypt.* London: Thames and Hudson, 1978.

Schickel, Richard. *The World of Goya, 1746-1828.* Alexandria, VA: Time-Life Books, 1968.

Scholem, Gershom. *Major Trends in Jewish Mysticism.* New York: Schocken Books, 1954.

_____, ed. *Zohar, The Book of Splendor: Basic Readings from the Kabbalah.* New York: Schocken Books, 1977.

Shakespeare, William. *The Complete Works of William Shakespeare.* London: Oxford University Press, 1965.

Sharp, Daryl. *Personality Types: Jung's Model of Typology.* Toronto: Inner City Books, 1987.

Snyder, James. *Medieval Art: Painting, Sculpture, Architecture, 4th-14th Century.* New York: Harry N. Abrams, Inc., 1989.

Vaughan, Henry. *The Complete Poetry of Henry Vaughan.* Ed. French Fogle. Garden City, NY: Anchor Books, Doubleday & Company, 1964.

von Franz, Marie-Louise, ed. *Aurora Consurgens.* New York: Pantheon, 1966.

_____. *C.G. Jung: His Myth in Our Time.* Trans. William F. Kennedy. New York: G.P. Putnam's Sons for the C.G. Jung Foundation, 1975.

_____. *On Divination and Synchronicity: The Psychology of Meaningful Chance.* Toronto, Inner City Books, 1980.

Waite, Arthur Edward, Trans. *The Hermetic Museum.* Restored and Enlarged. York Beach, ME: Samuel Weiser, Inc., 1991.

_____. *The Holy Kabbalah.* Reprint. New Hyde Park, NY: University Books, n.d.

_____. *Pictorial Key to the Tarot.* New York: Causeway Books, n.d.

_____. *The Secret Doctrine in Israel.* Reprint. New York: Occult Research Press, n.d.

Warren, Henry Clarke. *Buddhism in Translation.* New York: Atheneum, 1963.

Whitmont, Edward C. "The Magical Dimension in Transference and Countertransference." In *Current Trends in Analytical Psychology.* Ed. G. Adler. London: Tavistock, 1961.

Wickes, Frances. *The Inner World of Choice.* New York: Harper and Row, 1963.

_____. *The Inner World of Man.* 2nd ed. Boston: Sigo Press, 1988.

Index

331

Scholem, Gershom, 46, 251n
scintillae (sparks), 58-64
sea, 123, 138-145
Sebastian, St., 193, *194*
Secret Sayings of Jesus, The, 96
seduction, 294
Sefirotic Tree, *39,* 40, 41n, 74, *243,* 250,
  251, 272, 282n
Self: in analytic relationship, 314, 316
  as Anthropos, 233
  as *caelum,* 287-288
  collective, 246-247
  as coniunctio, 316
  as divine water, 162
  dog as, 120-121
  and ego, 28-29, 34, 40, 46, 58, 60, 65-67,
    78, 86, 93-94, 119, 136-137, 158, 172-
    176, 190, 204-205, 211, 215, *229,* 231-
    232, 246-248, 271, 281, 295, 324-325
  emergence from lump, 136-137
  Eye of the, 66
  as fate, 231
  formulation of the, 146, *147,* 148
  fountain as, 125-126
  glassy body as, 139
  as golden bough, 176, *177*
  identification with, 28-29, 40,
    46, 90, 93, 179-180, 190
  and indivisibility, 299
  mandrake root as image of, 117
  memory as function of, 291-292
  Mercurius as, 56
  negatively constellated, 297-298
  numinous power of, 325
  as orphan, 33
  as pairs of opposites, 25
  and paradox, 55
  as peacock, 190
  as point, 58
  in primitive psychology, 172
  projection of, 299, 316, 319-321
  and sulphur, 97, 99-100, 103
  uniqueness of, 300
  united with ego and world, see *unus
    mundus*

  weight as aspect of, 297-298
self-knowledge/-reflection, 182, 280, 286,
  288-289, 295, 302
"Self-Reliance," 288n, 325n
Senior text, 79-80
sensation function, 151-152, 190, 255
separatio/separation *(see also* beheading *and
  unio mentalis),* 159, 177-178, 279-280,
  286, 295, 299, 302-305, 321
Septenary, magical, *30,* 31
serpent: 36-38, 44, 65, *66,* 74, 76-77, 79-80,
  81, 83, *131, 133,* 134, 147-148, 153,
  213, 231, 249-255, 297, 305, 310-311
  Agathodaimon, *28*
  brazen, 262-267
  buried with woman, *37*
  -chariot text, 144-145, 154
  crowned, *28,* 213
  Mercurius as, 130, *131*
seven: 28, 30, 40, 54, 60, 150, 154-155, 193,
  195, 206-207, 216, 269
  and eight, 242
sexuality, 37, 292, 295
shadow: 87-88, 100, 143, 147-148, 176,
  207-208, 221-224, 255, 274, 280, 305,
  313, 321-323
  assimilation of, 46-47, 140, 190
  creation of, 321-322
  Quaternio, 147
  of sun *(Sol niger),* 87, *88, 94*
Shakespeare, William, 130, 135, 176, 198
Sharp, Daryl, 190n
Shaw, George Bernard, 237
Sheba, Queen of, 69
sheep, 89, 120, 294
Shekinah, 254, 258
Shepherd of Hermas, 149, 155-158
shrinks/shrinking, 180
Shulamite: black, 208, 250, 252-275, 305
  white, 256-257
Signature of All Things, The, 42n
silver, 54, 97, 99, 195, 206
sirens, 118, 277-278
Sirius (Dog Star), 121
sister: 81, *110*

INNER CITY BOOKS
Studies in Jungian Psychology by Jungian Analysts
21 Milroy Cres. Toronto, ON M1C 4B6, Canada 416-927-0355